Storage of potatoes

Post-harvest behaviour, store design, storage practice, handling

List of authors

N. Buitelaar
A. van Es
P.H. de Haan
Ms K.J. Hartmans
C.P. Meijers
A. Rastovski
J.H.W. van der Schild
P.H. Sijbring
H. Sparenberg
B.H. van Zwol
(Institute for Storage and Processing of Agricultural Produce (IBVL),
Wageningen
D.E. van der Zaag
(Directorate of Agricultural Research (DLO), Wageningen

The authors thank everyone who has helped in the preparation of this
book. In particular, C.D. van Loon for checking most of the draft and
J.D. Howells for checking the English.

Storage of potatoes

Post-harvest behaviour, store design, storage practice, handling

A. Rastovski, A. van Es et al.

Centre for Agricultural Publishing and Documentation

Wageningen, 1981

Drawings:
E.E. van de Born (IBVL), Wageningen,
W. Scheepmaker, Doorwerth,
J. Welgraven (IBVL), Wageningen.
Photographs:
Office of Joint Services (BGD), Wageningen
Electron Micrographs: Technical and Physical Engineering Research
Service (TFDL), Wageningen

ISBN 90-220-0780-4
© Centre for Agricultural Publishing and Documentation, Wageningen, 1981

Printed in the Netherlands

Contents

Foreword

While the potato still remains an important crop in the temperate zone, its significance as a staple food is increasing in a number of tropical and subtropical regions. The potato has valuable characteristics such as high productive capacity and high nutritional value. On the other hand these are to some extent offset by, for example, the greater care and attention which must be devoted to the storage of potatoes than to that of grain. The potato is a swollen stem composed of about 80 % water. This makes it a bulky product which reacts strongly to prevailing temperature and the atmospheric humidity; it is also extremely susceptible to attack by a variety of harmful organisms.

Research on potatoes began with the study of diseases such as late blight (*Phytophthora infestans*) and virus diseases. Attention was also devoted early on to the processing of potatoes and to all kinds of cultivation problems. It is interesting to note that research on the behaviour of the tuber after harvest and on potato storage only really got under way in the middle of this century. Pioneering work in this field was mainly done in the United States, perhaps partly as a result of the influence of the potato processing industry which developed there at an early date.

At the beginning of the 1950s, Dr W.H. de Jong, together with some enthusiastic colleagues, commenced experimental research on potato storage in the Netherlands, partly as a result of trends in the USA. The results of this research were readily accepted in the field, and it was not long before clamps had been largely superseded by storage buildings with outside air cooling facilities. This success was partially responsible for the establishment of the Netherlands Institute for the Storage and Processing of Agricultural Produce (IBVL). The fact that the Netherlands has played an important part in work on potato storage in Europe is due in no small measure to this Institute.

Fortunately, the research was not confined to the technical aspects of storage; a great deal of attention was also devoted to the tuber and, in particular, to a wide range of storage diseases. The prevention of storage diseases by the use of modern methods of storage was quickly found to be one of the principal advantages achieved. The behaviour of the potato

1

after harvesting has been the subject of innumerable studies. More research has justifiably been devoted to this topic by the IBVL in the last few years and the results may well have an important bearing on future research in the fields of storage and processing.

There has for a long time been a need in the Netherlands for a publication in which all relevant information on potato storage can be found. This need was spelt out a few years ago by the Netherlands Potato Association. It was an excellent idea of the governing body of the IBVL to celebrate the Silver Jubilee of the Institute by the publication of a manual of this kind. During compilation it has become a comprehensive work in which a number of IBVL research workers have presented in a logical sequence all the available information on the principal aspects of potato storage. Some readers may find certain parts difficult to follow; others might perhaps have preferred a more comprehensive treatment of particular aspects. Unfortunately a publication of this kind must always be a compromise between conflicting requirements. I nevertheless believe that this book will satisfy an important demand not only in the Netherlands but also elsewhere in the world. For this latter reason I am pleased to see that the work includes a section on potato storage in warm climates.

I hope and expect that this book will enable many, both in the Netherlands and in other countries, to improve their knowledge and understanding of potato storage, so that the produce, which is usually of good quality when grown, will also reach its final destination in good condition.

Wageningen, February 1981   D.E. van der Zaag

History of potato storage

J.H.W. van der Schild

Perhaps 2000 years ago, the Quechas in the Andes, living in an area
which is now called Peru, already knew that the potato was a perishable
product which could not be stored indefinitely. The Quechas therefore
made chuno, a kind of flour, out of their potatoes, as follows: The potatoes were placed on mats and exposed to the night frost which occurs in
the valleys of the high equatorial mountains. Next morning, the potatoes,
now soft and wrinkled, were trodden with the bare feet to a pulp. The
pulp was dried in the sun and then processed into a white flour which
kept for years and was stored in barns (Smith, 1968).

The problems associated with the storage of potatoes as perishable
produce soon led, in Europe too, to a search for some form of preservation. Burton (1966) noted that Parmentier had written a treatise on dried
potatoes in 1781. He described potato biscuits, made from a dough of
boiled potatoes, and included in ship's supplies. According to
Parmentier, the aim was to provide the crew with the scurvy-preventing
characteristics of fresh potatoes.

How the potato came to Europe

Völksen (1975) states that there are many ineradicable stories and·
anecdotes concerning the first appearance of the potato in Europe. All
these traditions involve the names of Drake, Raleigh and Hawkins, the
English maritime heroes of the time. Indeed, statues have been erected
and paintings made in honour of Drake and Raleigh as the discoverers of
the potato. Later, Safford (1925) and Salaman (1937) irrefutably demonstrated that these great sailors were certainly not the first to bring
the potato to Europe (Völksen, 1975). According to Harris (1978), the
potato was brought from South America to Europe on two occasions, viz.,
to Spain about 1570 and to England between 1588 and 1593. Burton (1966)
mentions a description of the potato by the Spaniard Cieza de León published in 1550.

Harris (1978) describes the subsequent history of the potato both inside and outside Europe. Carmelite monks brought the potato from Spain to
Italy. In 1601, the Italian Clusius wrote that potatoes had already been

grown in Italy before 1587. The potato made its début in Portugal even earlier.

Clusius sent samples of potatoes to botanists in many parts of Germany and Austria. The Swiss botanist Baudin, who named our potato *Solanum tuberosum*, evidently also came into the possession of tubers from Clusius. Baudin was also responsible for introducing the potato to France, where it was being grown on a large scale by the mid-seventeenth century. The potato was known in France at that time by the name cartoufle, a word derived from the Italian name tartuffolo. Tartuffolo became Kartoffel in the German-speaking parts of Europe. The potato came to be known in the Netherlands as aardappel (earth apple), and this was in turn translated into French as pomme de terre; the latter is still the official French name for the potato (Smith, 1968). The Slav peoples seem to have made the acquaintance of the potato through the Germans, and this is borne out by the fact that their names for the potato closely resemble the German Kartoffel and Grundbirne. Tsar Peter the Great, who learned naval architecture in the Netherlands, is said to have brought the potato from the Netherlands to Russia at the end of the seventeenth century. The potato has been kwown in the Netherlands since the time of Clusius.

As in other European countries, the potato in England was originally regarded as a botanical curiosity or as a delicacy for which there was a ready demand at the royal courts. It was only in the mid-eighteenth century that the potato (the English name derives from the Spanish patata) was grown on a large scale in England. The same is true of most other European countries. Incidentally, there seems to have been considerable potato cultivation in the south-west of Ireland as early as the beginning of the seventeenth century.

From Scotland, the potato spread to Norway and hence probably to Sweden and Denmark.

The North American continent obtained its first potatoes in 1621 from England via Bermuda.

The European colonial powers were responsible for the further spread of the potato to Asia, Australia and Africa.

Harris (1978) also states that it is a matter of record that the potato reached the Canary Islands from Peru in 1622. Apart from western Europe, this is the only historically confirmed case in which the potato was introduced directly to another region from its South American cradle.

It took a very long time before the potato acquired the status of a staple food for the people in Europe. One factor which greatly promoted the spread of potato cultivation was the Industrial Revolution in the first half of the nineteenth century (Burton, 1966). Supplemented with milk and/or bacon, the potato provided our artisan forefathers with an adequate menu.

Potato storage

Owing to the climatological conditions prevailing in the growing a-
reas, potatoes have to be planted and harvested at particular times of
the year. The colder and temperate climate zones (including Europe) have
only one potato growing season. This means that most of the crop has to
be stored if demand is to be satisfied throughout the year. For centuries, this storage problem was solved in Europe by placing the potatoes
after the harvest in clamps. The potatoes were lifted and collected in
baskets and hampers, from which they were tipped out at the edge of the
field. The resulting heap of potatoes was covered with wheat or rye
straw, followed later by a layer of earth before the onset of cold winter
weather. Where the water table was low, holes were also dug at the edge
of the potato field. These holes were filled with potatoes to above
ground level, after which the resulting heap was covered with straw and
earth. The shape and size of the clamps and heaps varied from region to
region and from place to place, and so did the names given to them. In
England, for example, the following names were used: 'clamp', 'pie',
'pit', 'grave', 'hog', 'cave' and 'bury' (Burton, 1966). Nash (1978) mentions a Scottish publication of 1814 which states that the winter store
of potatoes was kept in dry, cool outhouses and cellars, covered with
straw and protected from frost, or in so-called pits, pies or clamps.

Unventilated clamps

The oldest clamps had no special provision for the elimination of respiration products and the supply of fresh air (oxygen). With unventilated
clamp storage, some 20 to 25 % of the potatoes were often lost as a result of disease, frost damage, rot due to accumulation of moisture, etc.
There was absolutely no temperature control in the unventilated clamp, so
that the temperature in the centre of the clamp corresponded to the mean
maximum temperature of the ambient air (Nash, 1978). In some western European countries, however, the mean maximum temperature in autumn and
winter is seldom below 4 °C, and so the potatoes - especially early varieties - obviously sprouted before the spring, to the inevitable detriment of consumption quality. On the other hand, if there was a severe
frost, the temperature in the clamp could readily fall far below 4 °C
for a longer or shorter period.
Unventilated clamps are obsolete in many countries (Nash, 1978).

Ventilated clamps

The ventilated clamp, which is still widely used even in western Europe for short-term storage, constituted an important improvement compa-

red with the unventilated clamp. The ventilated clamp makes use of triangular air ducts on the bottom of the clamp and some means of top ventilation - ranging from a grille to a kind of chimney. These clamps can also be equipped with fans, but obviously only if electricity is available.
A telling example of the effect of ventilation is given by Plissey
(1976). Quoting from the book *The Potato* (Grubb, 1912), he describes a
lot of twelve sacks of potatoes which were stored for two years in a rock
tunnel in Colorado (USA) at a depth of 60 m at a temperature of about
4 °C. The potatoes looked as if they had only just been harvested. They
were not wrinkled or shrivelled and had not sprouted. When cooked, they
were just as tasty as freshly lifted potatoes. There was an air shaft at
the end of the tunnel, in which there was a natural draught, so that the
potatoes were exposed to a current of dry, cool air.

In the course of time, improvements were made to the covering of the
clamps, in particular, by interposing plastic sheeting between the layers
of straw. With the spread of combine harvesters since the 1960s, the form
of straw produced is no longer suitable for covering clamps, so that
plastic sheeting must be used to prevent the straw from getting wet. The
ventilation facilities allow the potatoes in a ventilated clamp to be
piled higher and wider than in an unventilated clamp.

Owing to the limited capacity per storage unit, clamp storage is always at a disadvantage compared with storage in buildings. Bad weather
when the clamps are emptied or partially emptied, and open-air grading

Fig. 1. Unventilated clamp.

Fig. 2. Ventilated clamp (natural draught).

and bagging of the potatoes, are not conducive to tuber quality. Again, the storage conditions in a building can be controlled much more readily.

Potato huts

The potato hut probably arose before 1900 in the Netherlands, in the south-east of the country (Gelderland Province). The shape and dimensions of the potato huts varied. The most common form of construction was roughly as follows. A site of the required area was excavated to a depth of about 30 cm. Robust walls of, for example, turves of heather were then erected to a height of some 1.5 or 2 m. The walls absorbed the pressure exerted by the potatoes against the inside. The roof of the hut was made of coppice wood or used wood. The entire structure was covered with straw or flax awns. A small opening was made in the south side of the hut, a door sometimes being fitted in it. In very cold weather, the opening was sealed with manure as a protection against frost. The hut was a small permanent store for the potatoes for the farmer's family table, and was therefore of limited size (Hensums, 1981). The potato hut was much more accessible than a clamp. Being a permanent structure, the hut was also cheaper and less time-consuming than a clamp, which had to be rebuilt every year. This type of potato hut was certainly also used in Germany. There is a fine picture of one by the German painter F. Witte (Völker, 1975).

Potato huts became much larger around 1920. They were found in the Netherlands in the vicinity of large towns. They were frost-free huts which served for relatively long-term storage of somewhat larger lots of potatoes (Hofstra, 1959).

Fig. 3. Potato hut in the Netherlands and Germany; 19th century (free after Witte).

Fig. 4. Dutch potato hut built in 1910.

In 1953, Van Bruggen designed a new type of potato hut. It was cooled with outside air and had a concrete floor with air supply ducts incorporated in it. The wooden internal lining was capable of fully absorbing the lateral thrust exerted by the potato heap, while the outer wall was of brick. The cavity between the outer brick wall and the wooden internal lining was completely filled with dry flax awns. The lath ceiling was covered over its entire area with flax awns. The roof covering consisted of corrugated asbestos panels. The hut had a wide central passage for grading operations, etc.

The storage bins, in which potatoes could be heaped to a height of 3 m, were situated on either side of the central passage. The potato huts were equipped with fans and had a capacity of from 45 to about 300 tonnes

Fig. 5. Dutch potato hut in the forties.

Fig. 6. The potato hut designed in 1953.

Fig. 7. Glass store for seed potatoes.

of potatoes (Van Bruggen, 1953). Within the space of a few years, hundreds of potato huts of this type were built in the Netherlands; their development dates from the same time as that of the modern potato store. The construction costs could be kept relatively low by using secondhand timber or wood from demolished structures and by do-it-yourself construction.

Glass stores for seed potatoes

The objections to large-scale potato storage in clamps quickly led in the Netherlands, at the beginning of the twentieth century, to a search for better storage methods. The potato hut is an example. Another striking example is the development of the glass store for seed potatoes. This method of storage, which was developed in the Netherlands about 1920, served its purpose well. The various lots of potatoes could be stored separately in small crates. The potatoes could be prepared for planting quickly and excellent green sprouts were obtained in spring (Hofstra, 1959).

Research on potato storage in the Netherlands

Both the potato clamp and the potato hut had shortcomings. These were exacerbated in the Netherlands by a number of factors in potato cultivation which took a turn unfavourable to storage. Hofstra (1959) mentions three factors. Firstly, seed potatoes are lifted early. Secondly, there was the trend away from the Rode Star towards the cv. Bintje in terms of relative growing areas. In 1930, 20 % of the area under potato cultivation in the Netherlands was accounted for by Rode Star, but this proportion had fallen to 0.5 % by the end of the 1950s. Rode Star is a late-maturing variety, which also sprouts relatively late and therefore readily lent itself to clamp storage. This was not the case with Bintje. The third factor mentioned by Hofstra is the great expansion of potato growing in the second world war and the immediate postwar period. This expansion was greatest in the sandy soil regions and in the south of the Netherlands - precisely the areas where the keeping quality of the cv. Bintje, then grown on a large scale, left much to be desired or where weather conditions were most unfavourable (the south-western Netherlands). For this reason, an urgent demand for soundly based research on potato storage arose in the Netherlands after the second world war.

Storage in air-cooled buildings

A store with outside air cooling was built by the "De Bommelerwaard" cooperative seed potato growers' association in Kerkwijk, Netherlands, in 1948. It was the first of its kind in Europe. Storage tests were carried out here by research workers from the Commissie voor de Aardappelbewaring (Potato Storage Commission) which had been set up in 1947 [in 1952, Stichting voor de Aardappelbewaring (Potato Storage Foundation); since 1956, IBVL]. On the basis of the resulting research results, the first potato stores equipped with outside air cooling systems were built in the Netherlands in 1950. There were already 1160 of these by 1955, with a to-

Fig. 8. One of the first Dutch potato stores with an outside air cooling system.

tal storage capacity of 244 000 tonnes (Ophuis, 1956). De Jong (1954) mentions two reasons for the great enthusiasm for storing potatoes in buildings with outside air cooling. Firstly, it was desired for many reasons to store potatoes under a solid roof and no longer in clamps - mainly because of the ever increasing cost of labour. Clamp storage was extremely labour-intensive, while storage in buildings offered more opportunities for mechanization. Secondly, it was generally considered that storage in buildings with outside air cooling gave much better results, the risks being much smaller.

The modern method of storage was originally used in the Netherlands only for seed and ware potatoes. Since the beginning of the 1960s, potatoes have increasingly been stored for the ware potato product industry (chips, crisps, etc.). One of the factors in the development of this industry has been modern potato storage, allowing potatoes to be supplied virtually throughout the year.

Fig. 9. Modern potato storehouse for storage in bins.

Fig. 10. Modern potato storehouse for storage in bulk.

According to the Produktschap voor Aardappelen (Produce Board for Potatoes), the storage capacity for potatoes in ventilated buildings in the Netherlands has increased from 27 000 tonnes in 1950 to over 2 million tonnes today. Some of the potatoes are sold immediately after harvesting, so that this capacity is sufficient to store the entire balance of the Dutch potato harvest.

One further point. In 1960 a bin containing 100 tonnes of potatoes was a very large storage unit. Now, twenty years later, 6000-tonne storage units are by no means the exception.

References

Bruggen, O. van, 1953. Luchtgekoelde aardappelhut. Landbouwmechanisatie 4: 405-409.

Burton, W.G., 1966. The potato. A survey of its history and factors influencing its yield, nutritive value, quality and storage. H. Veenman & Zonen N.V., Wageningen. Second edition.

Harris, P.M., 1978. The potato crop. The scientific basis for improvement. Halsted Press, New York. First edition.

Hensums, H., 1981. Personal communication.

Hofstra, D., 1959. Problemen rond de bewaring van aardappelen in gebouwen. Lezing voor L.C.C. Zuid-West Nederland. IBVL Wageningen.

Jong, W.H. de, 1954. De ontwikkeling van de aardappelbewaring in Nederland in de laatste jaren. Landbouwkundig Tijdschrift 66: 8 (August).

Nash, M.J., 1978. Crop conservation and storage. Pergamon Press Ltd., Oxford. First edition.

Ophuis, B.G., 1956. Moderne luchtgekoelde aardappelbewaarplaatsen. Stichting voor Aardappelbewaring Publicatie No. 113 Serie A.

Plissey, E.S., 1976. Philosophy of potato storage. The potato storage. Design, construction, handling and environmental control. Editor: B.F. Cargill. Michigan State University.

Smith, O., 1968. Potatoes: production, storage, processing. AVI Publishing Co. Inc. Westport.

Völksen, W., 1975. Auf den Spuren der Kartoffel in Kunst und Literatur. Gieseking Verlag, Bielefeld. 2. Auflage.

THE POTATO

1 Structure and chemical composition of the potato

A. van Es and K.J. Hartmans

1.1 Introduction

The potato was introduced to Europe from South America at the end of the
sixteenth century and spread from Europe throughout the world within a
few centuries (Burton, 1966; Hawkes, 1978). The potato of Europe belongs
to the species *Solanum tuberosum* and, together with cereals and sugar
beet, is her most important crop. Potato tubers are used both for consumption and for vegetative reproduction. The intended use of the tubers
has consequences not only for cultivation but also for storage of the potatoes.

1.2 Structure of the potato tuber

1.2.1 Formation of the tuber

During growth of a potato plant, a number of lateral shoots are formed
below soil level at the base of the main stem. These stems usually remain
below soil level and, unlike the above-ground stems, grow mainly horizontally (diageotropic) (Fig. 1.1). These stolons, as they are known, have
elongated internodes, spirally arranged lateral buds, small leaves and a

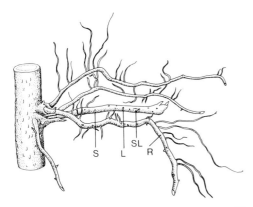

Fig. 1.1. Part of a stem below soil level with roots and developing stolon.
S = stolon; L = lenticel; Sl = scale leaf; R = root
(redrawn from Danert, 1961).

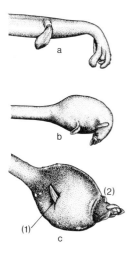

Fig. 1.2. Schematic drawing of young developing tubers (redrawn from Krijthe, 1946). a. Stolon with hooked tip and scale leaf; b. a swelling has developed subapically, just proximal to the stolon hook; c. young tuber with second internode becoming incorporated. Tuber has two eyes (1) and (2). The stolon hook has almost straightened out.

hooked tip with a terminal bud. At a certain stage during growth, the part just behind the hook of the stolon begins to swell and longitudinal growth of the stolons ceases.

A potato tuber is in fact a modified stem with a shortened (and broadened) axis (Artschwager, 1924). Fig. 1.2 shows the initial development of a tuber on a stolon. A tuber may form at the end of each stolon.

According to Krijthe (1955), the largest tubers are not formed on the most basal stolons - those formed close to the mother tuber - but on the stolons in third, fourth or fifth position from the base of the stem. Plaisted (1957), however, found that the first and largest tubers were formed on the most basal stolons.

1.2.2 Morphology of the tuber

1.2.2.1 The shape of the tuber

Each variety has a relatively characteristic tuber shape, as described for Dutch and other varieties in the List of Varieties (Nederlandse rassenlijst, 1980). However, growing conditions and disease may cause variations from this genetically determined tuber shape.

The uniformity of tuber shape of a lot of potatoes is determined not only by varietal characteristics but also by plant spacing. Closer plant spacing would give more uniform tubers (Gray and Hughes, 1978).

18

1.2.2.1.1 *Influence of second growth on tuber shape*

Due to 'stress' during tuber growth the developing tuber may become malformed. A stress situation may occur, for example, as a result of a period of drought followed by heavy rain causing rapid new growth (Bodlaender et al., 1964). Bodlaender et al. (1964) found that second growth was also induced by exposure of the plants to high temperatures. These workers also showed that liability to second growth depends on variety.

The malformations may, for example, take the form of large cracks, prolongation of the bud end or protrusions of knob-like growth. Sometimes varieties exhibit 'chain tuberization' (Fig. 1.3).

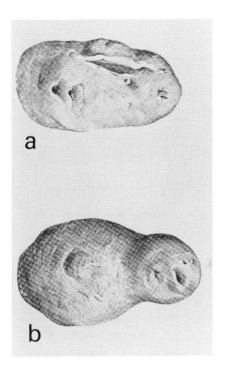

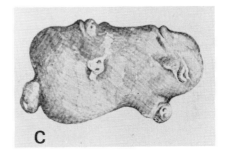

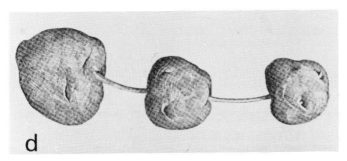

Fig. 1.3. Types of second growth. a. cracking; b. prolongation of bud end; c. gemmation and d. chain tuberisation (from Whitehead et al., 1953).

The type of malformation occurring depends to some extent on variety. Apart from the reduction in market value due to malformation of the tubers, the quality of a lot in which second growth occurs is adversely affected. The secondary parts or tubers often grow at the expense of the first-formed, so that the tubers formed first may have a very low dry matter content. It is possible for the latter to be almost completely denuded of starch. These 'glassy' tubers or tuber parts cannot easily be detected. By virtue of their poor quality, they cause problems when the potatoes are processed (crisps, chips, etc.) and in batches of edible potatoes and seed material (Krijthe, 1959; Lugt, 1960).

1.2.2.2   Eyes

The apex and the eyes can be distinguished on the tuber (Fig. 1.4) and, at the other end, the scar where the tuber was attached to the stolon - the stem end (sometimes still with a residual part of the stolon). Small buds are visible at the apex and in the eyes. The bud at the apex is called the apical bud of the tuber.

The eyes often contain not only a main bud but also a few small lateral buds (Fig. 1.4). As many as 20 or more buds may be present on a tuber (Krijthe, 1962). Each eye lies in the axil of an originally existing scale leaf which has attained little height and which, because of the growth in diameter of the tuber, has a base which is greatly extended tangentially (Fig. 1.2, c 1 and 2). This scale leaf, known as the 'eyebrow', may be distinct, slight or indistinct. The eyes are arranged spirally on the tuber. The eyes at the stem end are the first to be formed during tuber development (Fig. 1.4). The apical eye is the last to be formed and contains the physiologically youngest bud.

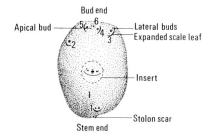

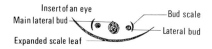

Fig. 1.4. A potato tuber showing morphological details. Eyes numbered in order of formation (redrawn from Allen, 1978).

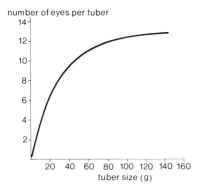

number of eyes per tuber

tuber size (g)

Fig. 1.5. Relationship between number of eyes per tuber and tuber size (from Allen, 1978).

The number of eyes per tuber increases with tuber size, but the increase is not linear, as Fig. 1.5 shows. Eye depth is a varietal characteristic. Determination of the exact number of eyes is often problematic in varieties with deep eyes. It is then difficult to decide whether buds close to the apical bud are to be regarded as lateral buds of the apical bud or as the main bud of a different eye.

1.2.3 Anatomy of the tuber

Tuberization first becomes visible as a thickening of the youngest elongating internode of the stolon tip. This thickening is mainly due to enlargement of the pith cells of the stolon (Artschwager, 1924; Cutter, 1978) and to cell division in all parts of the stolon (Artschwager, 1924; Plaisted, 1957).

Cell size increases with tuber size. Most of the increase in tuber size in tubers larger than 30 to 40 g is attributed to the increase in cell size (Lehman, 1926; Reeve, 1973b). In the preceding stage, the main growth

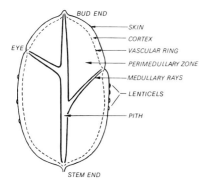

Fig. 1.6. Longitudinal diagram of a potato tuber (redrawn from Reeve et al., 1969a).

factor would be the increase in the number of cells. This view is not shared by Plaisted (1957), who observed that cell division still occurred in tubers weighing up to 200 g (cv. Cobbler).

The anatomy of the tuber is shown diagrammatically in Fig. 1.6. The parts which can be distinguished are the skin or periderm with the lenticels, the eyes, the bud and stem ends, the cortex, the ring of vascular bundles, the perimedullary zone and the pith with medullary rays which are homologous with the medulla of the stolon.

1.2.3.1 Skin or periderm

During development of a stolon tip into a tuber, a suberized layer of cells constituting the skin or periderm is formed on the outside of the tuber. If the tuber tissue is wounded, the tuber is able to form a new layer of suberized cells, known as wound periderm. This process is called wound healing (Chapter 20).

1.2.3.1.1 Skin (periderm) formation and structure

As soon as the tips of the stolon swell, formation of the periderm starts. Periderm formation usually begins at the stem end of the young tuber (Reeve et al., 1969a). The outer cell layer (epidermis) divides from the outside inwards, while the layer below the epidermis (the hypodermis) divides from the inside outwards (Artschwager, 1924; Reeve et al., 1969a; Cutter, 1978). This dividing cell layer is called phellogen. The newly formed cells (phellem) constitute the periderm and become suberized (see Fig. 1.7, Reeve, 1969a). The cells of the hypodermis may deposit parenchyma cells (phelloderm) towards the inside of the tuber (Fig. 1.7c).

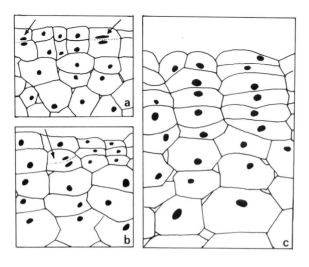

Fig. 1.7. Periderm development in bud end regions of a young tuber. a. Cell divisions in epidermal cells; b. cell divisions in subepidermal cells; c. periderm files; (redrawn from Reeve et al., 1969a).

In young tubers the layer of repeatedly dividing cells is extremely active and the skin can easily be removed from the tuber. This is no longer the case once this layer becomes inactive. This phenomenon is used to determine the maturity of the tuber (v.d. Zaag, 1970). The phellogen is active throughout the growth of the tuber. The skin of the potato usually consists of six to ten suberized cell layers (Cutter, 1978) and is usually thicker at the stem end than at the bud end. However, this number of suberized cell layers, and the total skin thickness, may vary substantially; being partly dependent on variety (Artschwager, 1924) and also on growing conditions. The effect of different temperatures during growth on the number of cell layers and on skin thickness has been investigated for the Russet Burbank variety. The number of cell layers was found to increase at higher temperatures (Table 1.1).

Table 1.1 Effect of temperature on number of cell layers in the periderm of Russet Burbank (from Cutter, 1978).

Temperature (°C)	Number of cell layers	Periderm thickness (µm)
7.2 - 10	7 - 12	100 - 140
18.3 - 21.1	9 - 25	120 - 250
23.8 - 26.6	10 - 28	125 - 270

The number of cell layers tended to be smaller in extremely dry conditions than in wet conditions (v.d. Zaag, 1970). Application of potassium and nitrogen fertilizers tended to produce a thinner skin, while phosphate fertilizers produce a comparatively thick skin (Artschwager, 1924). Other workers have, however, been unable to confirm these results.

The suberized cells remain in position in smooth-skinned potatoes. In rough-skinned tubers, the outer layers of these cells have become partly detached, giving rise to a rough surface (v.d. Zaag, 1970).

The skin colour is an inheritable varietal characteristic, and is caused by the presence of anthocyanin compounds dissolved in the cell sap of both the periderm and cells of the peripheral cortex (Burton, 1966).

1.2.3.1.2 Formation and structure of wound periderm
Wounding of the tuber tissue initially gives rise to suberizing of the cells on the surface of the cut. This is called primary suberization (Rosenstock, 1963). Suberization of cells involves the deposition of suberin along the cell walls (Bareckhausen and Rosenstock, 1973). Suberin (cork) formation in an important process, as suberin protects the tissue from moisture loss and microbial attack. Suberin is a polymer, mainly composed of lipids (Kolattukudy and Dean, 1974), comparable with the waxy layer (cutin) of, for example, leaves.

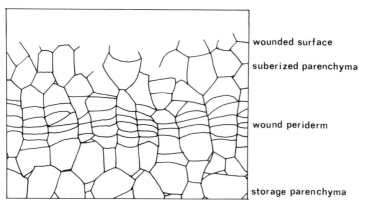

wounded surface

suberized parenchyma

wound periderm

storage parenchyma

Fig. 1.8. Wound periderm formation (redrawn from Lange and Rosenstock, 1963).

The wound periderm is formed after the onset of primary suberization. A few cell layers away from the wound surface, new cell walls are formed parallel to the wound surface (Fig. 1.8). This gives rise to a phellogen (cork cambium), which serves as the basis for wound periderm formation: the phellogen cells form a number of phellem cells parallel to the wound surface. These phellem cells subsequently become suberized, this process being known as secondary suberization (Rosenstock, 1963).

The process of wound healing is affected by several factors, such as variety, temperature, moisture, etc. (Chapter 20).

1.2.3.2 Lenticels

Lenticels are formed in the periderm (skin) on the sides of the young tuber where a stoma had originally been (Artschwager, 1924). These stomata are formed on the stolons, which are in fact underground stems.

Lenticels are composed of a circular group of suberized cells with a central opening communicating with the intercellular spaces between the cells of the tuber tissue (Fig. 1.9). Lenticels are essential for the respiration of the tuber since hardly any CO_2 or O_2 can pass through the skin itself (see also Chapter 4).

The number of lenticels per unit of tuber area may be influenced by tuber size, soil type and weather conditions during growth. The moisture content of the soil at the time of tuberization is particularly important (Meinl, 1966).

In the English variety King Edward, the number of lenticels larger than 0.5 mm in diameter in tubers ranging between 95 and 230 g was found to be 75 to 140 per tuber (Wigginton, 1973).

Our own observations with the cv. Doré grown on sandy soil, have shown the average number of lenticels per tuber to be 250, for an average tuber weight of about 115 g.

The size of the opening in the lenticels (proliferation) is also af-

24

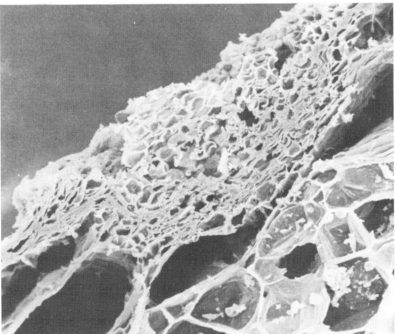

Fig. 1.9. Lenticels from cv. Spunta. a. Outside of the skin with a crater formed by a lenticel (magnification x 735); b. transverse section of a lenticel with suberized filling cells (magnification x 122). (Micrographs obtained with a Scanning Electron Microscope).

fected by the moisture content of the soil or by relative humidity of storage atmosphere. The lenticels swell in wet conditions and the opening increases in size. This reaction is more evident in newly lifted tubers than during storage. When the tubers begin to sprout, the swelling reaction of the lenticels increases again owing to the high ambient humidity (Adams, 1975).

1.2.3.3 Structure of an eye

The anatomical structure of a potato eye (Fig. 1.10) corresponds to that of a bud on a stem, with which it is homologous.

The 'eyebrow' is formed by a scale leaf inside which is an axillary bud, or main bud. This axillary bud is surrounded by two leaf primordia, which separate as the tuber grows (Fig. 1.10). Second order axillary buds are formed in the axilla of these first leaf primordia of the main bud (Cutter, 1978). In this way, therefore, a number of buds may be formed in each eye, all of them originally axillary buds. It is these buds which develop if the main sprout of an eye is removed by desprouting, damage or disease.

1.2.3.4 Anatomy of the parenchyma tissue

The major part of the tuber tissue consists of parenchyma cells - those of the cortex and of the perimedullary zone (Fig. 1.6). The parenchyma cells contain starch grains as reserve material (storage parenchyma). The potato tuber parenchyma cells are generally of a uniform shape in more or

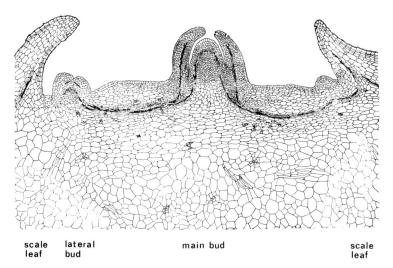

scale   lateral   main bud   scale
leaf   bud   leaf

Fig. 1.10. Drawing illustrating structure of potato buds and surrounding tissue (from Artschwager, 1924).

less all directions (isodiametric). The cortex lies between the periderm and the vascular ring. The parenchyma of the perimedullary zone is located between the vascular ring and the medulla (pith) and the medullary rays. The parenchyma cells of the perimedullary zone are formed by dividing cells on the inside of the vascular ring (Lehman, 1926; Reeve et al., 1969a) and are thus not medullary cells in origin. Tuber growth is caused primarily by the increase of this perimedullary zone (Reeve et al., 1969a).

1.2.3.4.1 Cell wall
The cell walls consist mainly of microfibrillae of cellulose and pectic substances. Cellulose is a polymer of β-glucose. Cell wall thickness increases during tuber growth (Fig. 1.11). Reeve et al. (1973 c) observed a doubling of cell wall thickness when tuber weight increased from 100 to 250 g in the Russet Burbank variety. The thickness of the cell wall was then about 1μ. Any influence of manuring (nitrogen) and moisture supply during growth on cell wall thickness could not be observed.

Varietal differences in the thickness of the cell walls in mature tubers were found to be relatively small, except in the cv. Doré, which was found to have relatively thick cell walls (1.36 μ) (Reeve et al., 1973c). The measured cell wall thickness in the cv. Bintje was 0.64 μ.

1.2.3.4.2 Middle lamella
The cell walls are linked together by means of a middle lamella, which consists mainly of pectin, a polymer of galacturonic acid. The middle lamella is responsible for the cohesion between the cell walls (Fig. 1.11). Upon impact damage, the cell walls sometimes become detached from each other along the middle lamella, without any eventual discoloration (black spot) (Hartmans and Van Es, 1974). In this case the cells themselves remain intact. The suitability of potatoes for processing into certain products (boiled or fried products, potato salads, etc.) largely depends on the degree of disintegration of the potato tissue on heating. This disintegration is a consequence of the separation of the cells. Apart from factors such as swelling of the starch grains, this is attributed to other factors such as the solubility of pectins in the middle lamella during cooking (Gray and Hughes, 1978).

1.2.3.4.3 Intercellular spaces
The middle lamellae are often interrupted in some cell positions, thus forming intercellular spaces (Fig. 1.12). The intercellular spaces are interconnected and allow gas exchange with the environment for respiration (see Chapter 3). The total volume of the intercellular space of a potato tuber depends on variety, as Kushman and Hayenes (1971) showed for a number of American varieties.

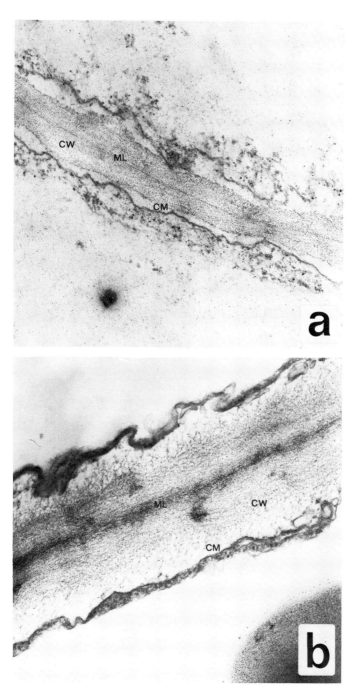

Fig. 1.11. Cell wall with middle lamella and membranes of the plasma lemma of cortex cells, cv. Bintje. a. Young immature tuber (tuber size ± 4 cm); b. mature tuber. (Micrographs obtained with a Transmission Electron Microscope) (magnification x 39,900).
cw = cell wall; ml = middle lamella; cm = cell membrane.

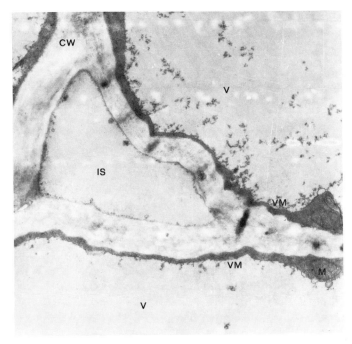

Fig. 1.12. Intercellular space with surrounding cell walls of cortex cells from immature tuber of cv. Jaerla. (Micrographs obtained with a Transmission Electron Microscope) (magnification x 10,830). is = intercellular space; cw = cell wall; v = vacuole; vm = vacuole membrane; m = mitochondria.

Different varieties may differ in intercellular space volume by a factor of three, the range being from a minimum of 0.33 ml per 100 ml tuber volume to a maximum of 0.92 ml per 100 ml tuber volume.

Storage for two months at 4.5 °C reduced this volume, by an average of 0.28 ml per 100 ml tuber volume for small-volume varieties and by an average of 0.43 ml per 100 ml tuber volume for large-volume varieties. Substantial difference in the intercellular space volume may have consequences for calculation of the dry matter content from the underwater weight (Kushman and Hayenes, 1971).

Hudson (1975) showed that variations in manuring, soil moisture conditions and temperature during growth have little effect on the volume of the intercellular space.

1.2.3.4.4 Cell size

Cell size increases with increasing tuber size (Table 1.2).

The eventual cell size of the mature tuber depends on variety (Lehman, 1926; Linehan et al., 1968) and on growing conditions. For instance, Lehman (1926) and Reeve et al. (1971) showed that the application of nitro-

gen fertilizer reduces the cell size of both cortex and perimedullary zone. Lehman (1926) was unable to show any effect of phospate and potassium
fertilizer application.

Table 1.2   Increase in cell size during tuber growth (from Plaisted, 1957)

Tuber weight	Cortex cell volume	Perimedullary zone parenchyma cell volume
(g)	($mm^3 \cdot 10^{-4}$)	($mm^3 \cdot 10^{-4}$)
1	1.1	1.7
10	1.5	3.2
50	2.4	4.1
100	3.3	6.4
200	6.3	9.8

The average cell size of the perimedullary zone is 1.5 to 2.5 times
that of the cortex (Reeve et al., 1971 and 1973 a). These workers also
observed a decreasing cell size gradient from the stem end to the bud
end, particularly for the cortex but also, although to a lesser extent,
for the perimedullary zone. Van Es et al. (1975) showed that there may be
considerable differences in cortex cell size in one and the same tuber.
Unlike Reeve et al. (1971 and 1973 a), they found that where these differences occurred, the largest cell volume was on the apical side of the
middle of the tuber and not on the stem side (Fig. 1.13).

1.2.3.4.5 Starch grains
   Most (60 to 80 %) of the dry matter of a potato tuber consists of
starch grains. Starch is a polymer of glucose (Chapter 2) and forms the
reserve material in the tuber, for use in respiration and sprouting.
Starch grains are formed from the very earliest stages of tuberization,
as soon as the stolon tip begins to swell. The starch content increases
during tuber growth. This increase is caused both by an increase in the
number of grains and by increasing grain size. Fig. 1.14 shows starch
grains in very young tissue, when the tuber size is 1 to 2 cm. The grains
in this case are small, homogeneous in size and small in number. Fig.
1.13 a and b show cortex tissue of a mature tuber. The number and size of
the grains in each cell are seen to be appreciably larger. In this case
the grains are not homogeneous in size.
   The starch grains are located in the cytoplasm of the cell (Fig. 1.15),
surrounded by a membrane (Chapter 2). The size of starch grains in a mature tuber may range from 1 to about 120 µ (Burton, 1966). The largest
grains are often present in the large cells of the perimedullary zone
(Reeve, 1967). The small grains largely occur in the tissue around the

30

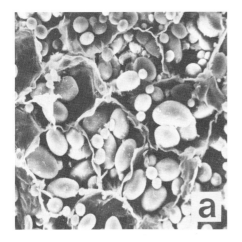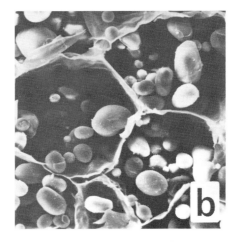

Fig. 1.13. Cortex parenchyma cells (cv. Bintje). a. Tissue with small cells; average cell volume $0.9 \times 10^{-3} mm^3$; b. tissue with larger cells; average cell volume $3.5 \times 10^{-3} mm^3$. (Micrographs obtained with a Scanning Electron Microscope) (magnification x 204).

vascular ring (Table 1.3). The cells of the cortex contain the largest number of grains per cell, and those of the pith and medullary rays the smallest (Reeve, 1967).

Table 1.3 Starch grain size in different tissues of Russet Burbank (from Reeve, 1967)

Tissue zone	Average starch grain length (μ)
Cortex	24
Vascular ring	7.3
Perimedullary zone	32
Medullary rays and pith	27

Reeve (1967) found that average starch grain size increased during storage owing to the fall in the number of smaller starch grains. He assumed that the smaller grains might be more readily broken down than the larger ones. Chung and Hadziyeve (1980) showed that average grain size is not influenced by tuber size and origin. Putz et al. (1978), on the other hand, observed some influence of origin and tuber size, with larger tubers containing larger starch grains. These workers also found that the principal parameter affecting starch grain size variation was the season. Varietal influences were also observed.

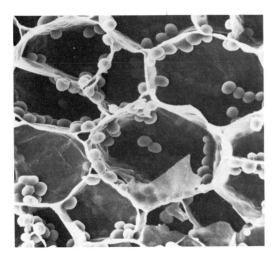

Fig. 1.14. Cortex parenchyma cells from a young tuber (tuber size 1 to 2 cm) with small starch grains of uniform size. (Micrographs obtained with a Scanning Electron microscope) (magnification x 231).

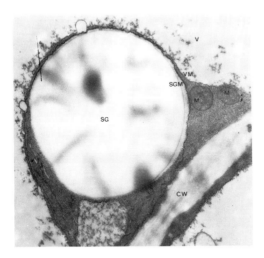

Fig. 1.15. Small starch grain located in the cytoplasm of the cell and surrounded by a membrane. Part of cortex cell from immature tuber of cv. Jaerla. (Micrographs obtained with a Transmission Electron Microscope) (magnification x 13,125). cw = cell wall; v = vacuole; m = mitochondria; sg = starch grain; vm = vacuole membrane; sgm = starch grain membrane.

1.2.3.5 Vascular ring

If a tuber is cut lengthwise, part of the vascular tissue, the xylem, is visible as a ring (Fig. 1.6). The xylem connects the stem end with the eyes. The xylem tissue (xylem vessels) is shown in detail in Fig. 1.16. The parenchyma cells near the xylem tissue are small. The phloem strands (sieve tubes) are spread out on the outside and inside of the xylem tissue in the form of countless bundles of small cells (Fig. 1.17) in the cortex and perimedullary zone respectively. This is called the external and internal phloem. Reeve (1967) found that the zone containing the internal phloem comprises about three quarters of the total tuber tissue. The phloem strands themselves contain about 5 % of the total tissue of the mature tuber (Reeve et al., 1973 b).

1.2.3.6 Medulla and medullary rays

The medullary rays and medulla (pith) are homologous with the medulla of the stolons. The medullary rays run from the stem end to the eyes (Fig. 1.6). The medullary parenchyma contains cells whose sizes lie between those of the cortex and the perimedullary zone (Reeve et al., 1971, 1973 a and b). The cells contain relatively few starch grains and for this reason the tissue looks wet and translucent.

1.2.4 Morphology of the sprout

One or more sprouts develop on a tuber at the end of the dormancy period. The structure of the sprouts formed depends on the conditions during growth - mainly temperature and light.
The factors affecting dormancy, sprout inhibition and sprouting are described in Chapter 3.

1.2.4.1 Morphology of sprouts formed in the dark

In principle, all the buds present on the tuber can sprout if conditions are favourable. The rate of growth depends on the storage period and on temperature.
Sprouts with elongated internodes are formed in the dark (Fig. 1.18). The apex of the sprout, with young leaflets, is often curved. The root primordia are visible at the base and around the lateral buds (Fig. 1.19). If the relative humidity of the storage atmosphere is high, roots may form from these while the tubers are still in store. The stolons later form from the lowest lateral buds. Since chlorophyll does not form in the dark, the sprouts are light in colour, except often at the base of the sprouts, which may be red to purple owing to formation of anthocyanin.

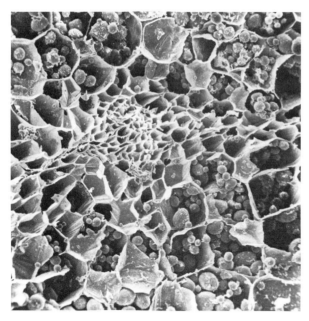

Fig. 1.16. Transverse section of vascular tissue with xylem surrounded by
small parenchyma cells. (Micrograph obtained with a Scanning Electron
Microscope) (magnification x 79).

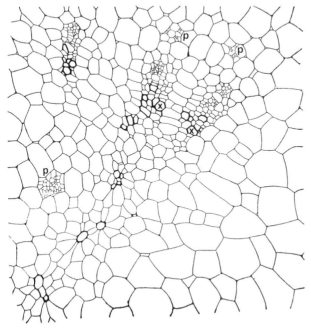

Fig. 1.17. Part of transverse section of a mature tuber showing the vascular tissue (x = xylem; p = phloem) (from Artschwager, 1924).

34

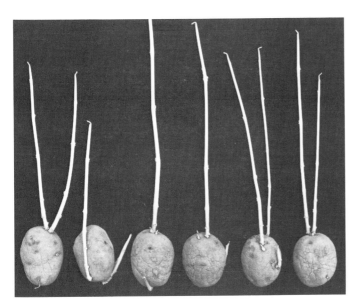

Fig. 1.18. Regrowth of sprouts during four weeks' storage at 18 °C in the dark, after desprouting. Storage conditions: ± 3 months at 12 °C; cv. Jaerle.

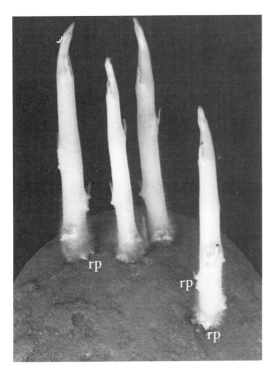

Fig. 1.19. Sprouts (cv. Désirée) grown in the dark, showing root primordia (rp) visible at the base and around the lower lateral buds.

This, like the formation of hairs on the sprout, is a variety characteristic. If temperature and humidity are favourable, the sprouts may continue to grow almost without limitation in the dark, reaching a length sometime of as much as 1 to 1.5 m. If the apex of the sprout is damaged, the lateral buds sprout and branching occurs. Branching also occurs due to prolonged storage of the seed tubers. The tubers become physiologically old.

If tubers are stored at relatively high temperatures (13 to 15 °C), internal sprouts may form if the sprout apex is damaged or dead (Davis, 1961). Sprouts then form from the lateral buds at the base and may grow into the tuber or a neighbouring tuber.

1.2.4.2   Morphology of sprouts formed with exposure to light

The elongation of the internodes is greatly inhibited in the light; only a small amount of light is sufficient to produce this effect. A short, thickened sprout is formed, with leaflets around the apex developing lateral buds and root primordia at the base (Fig. 1.20). In special carefully chosen conditions of light, temperature and humidity, the developing light-exposed sprout eventually acquires such a characteristic

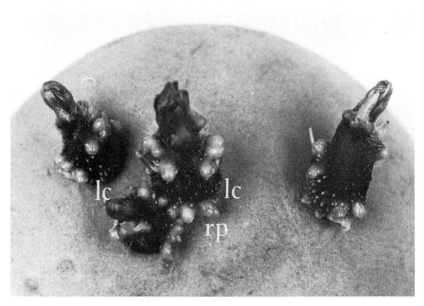

Fig. 1.20. Sprouts (cv. Désirée) grown in the light, showing coloration of the sprouts and development of small leafs and root primordia (rp). The lenticels (lc) are clearly visible as white dots at the base.

36

shape, colour and hairiness that the variety can be reliably determined. For this reason, sprouting in the light is used not only as a method of presprouting (Chapter 25) but also for varietal identification.

1.3 Chemical composition of the potato

The chemical composition of the potato is very important not only for storage but also for processing and consumption. Storability and the system of storage to be used are, for example, very much associated with the problem of carbohydrate metabolism and the substances affecting the latter. The potato-processing industry must take account of such factors as dry matter content, sugars, proteins and other nitrogen compounds. The lipids are also relevant here in connection with the keeping properties of the processed product. For the consumer, it is important what he consumes and in what quantities. The potato still occupies an important position in the daily diet of large sections of the population of many countries. Particularly in our time, it is very important to obtain an idea of the composition of this diet in terms of nutritional value.

1.3.1 Dry matter content

The dry matter content is a very important factor in potatoes. It is mainly determined genetically and thus depends on variety. Since 60 to 80 % of the dry matter consists of starch, there is a major correlation between dry matter content and the starch content of the tuber.

The dry matter content is important for the quality of both boiled and fried potato products such as chips and crisps. It is of direct importance in chips and crisps, as the weight of the processed product depends directly on the amount of dry matter present per quantitative unit of fresh potatoes. The same applies to dried potato products. The dry matter content is also important with boiled potatoes, as it may be a measure of the mealiness of the boiled product (Warren and Woodman, 1974) and of mushiness on cooking (Talburt and Smith, 1967). (The canning industry demands potatoes with a low dry matter content.)

There is also a relation between the dry matter content and susceptibility to black spot caused by impact (Jacob, 1959).

The dry matter content is influenced by a large number of factors (Fig. 1.21), chief among which are:

Variety

Maturity

Growth pattern as influenced by nitrogen fertilizer application

Climate, soil and potassium fertilizer application.

These factors are reviewed by Beukema and Van der Zaag (1979).

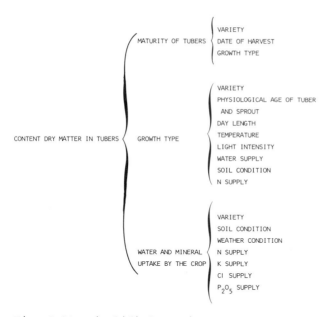

Fig. 1.21. Simplified version of a survey of factors influencing the percentage of dry matter in tubers (from Beukema and Van der Zaag, 1979 after Bernelot Moens, 1973).

1.3.1.1 Variety

The main factor is perhaps the choice of variety. Varieties which mature early usually have lower dry matter contents than later varieties (Burton, 1966). However, the effects of the differences are virtually all expressed by way of the first three factors in Fig. 1.21. The dry matter contents of a few Dutch varieties are set out in Table 1.4 (Beukema and Van der Zaag, 1979).

Table 1.4 Average dry matter content of 4 varieties grown on different soils (from Beukema and Van der Zaag, 1979).

Variety	Soil type		
	silt	sand	peat
Bintje	21.3	19.6	-
Woudster	25.4	23.3	23.5
Saturna	25.0	23.1	23.1
Maritta	24.7	23.1	22.7

1.3.1.2 Maturity

The dry matter content of the tubers increases with the progress of the growing season (Appleman and Miller, 1926). Fig. 1.22 shows the average increase in underwater weight at the end of the potato growing season, determined from random samples of 60,000 ha of potatoes in the north-east of the Netherlands (Beukema and Van der Zaag, 1979). The degree of maturity is a means of controlling the dry matter content. Note the difference between the years 1970 and 1971.

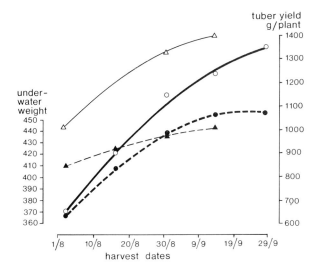

Fig. 1.22. Increasing tuber yield and under-water weight (5 kg tubers) of potatoes grown for starch (average of more than 100 samples per data) in 1970 and 1971; Δ —— Δ = g/plant 1971; 0 —— 0 = g/plant 1970; ▲ —— ▲ = uww 1971; ● —— ● = uww 1970 (from Beukema and Van der Zaag, 1979).

1.3.1.3 Growing season

The growing season greatly influences the degree of maturity obtained. The growing pattern is affected by a variety of deficiencies (stress factors). The effect of nitrogen on the growing pattern is important because this element delays maturity during growth. It is generally assumed that nitrogen reduces the dry matter content. This effect is sometimes unclear or even contrary to the general assumption (Schippers, 1968). The variation of the dry matter content at different rates of nitrogen and potassium fertilizer application is set out in Fig. 1.23 (Temme, 1979; Beukema and Van der Zaag, 1979).

Haulm weight during growth is relevant to the effect of nitrogen on

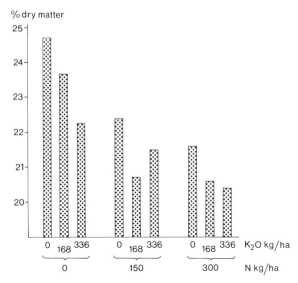

Fig. 1.23. Effect of N and K (K_2SO_4) on dry matter content of tubers (cv. Bintje, silt soils, 1963) (from Temme, 1970).

dry matter content, as nitrogen increases the haulm weight. If high N fertilizer application causes the haulm weight to become greater than necessary for optimum photosynthesis, the dry matter content of the tubers may fall (Beukema and Van der Zaag, 1979).

1.3.1.4 Climate, soil and potassium fertilizer application

These factors may have an effect by way of growth pattern, or they may directly affect the dry matter content.

In Dutch conditions, potatoes with the highest dry matter content are obtained from silt soil, while sandy soil gives the lowest content. This is related to the availability of water for the plant. The availability of potassium may also be relevant here, as well as the weather (Burton, 1966). Warm, dry weather is favourable to high dry matter content, while cold, wet weather tends to reduce it (Fig. 1.24).

Phosphorus has no effect under normal conditions; a higher dry matter content may be observed if very large quantities of phosphate fertilizer are applied.

Potassium has a very important effect on dry matter content, which is normally inversely proportional to the potassium content of the soil (Fig. 1.25) (Beukema and Van der Zaag, 1979; White et al., 1974).

40

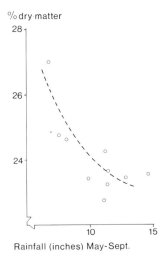

Rainfall (inches) May-Sept.

Fig. 1.24. Effect of rainfall on dry matter content (from Burton, 1966).

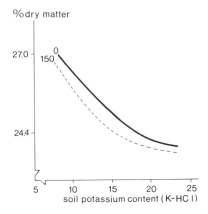

soil potassium content (K-HC l)

Fig. 1.25. Dry matter content of tubers as influenced by potassium content (K-HC1) of silt soil on which no fertilizer and 150 kg K_2O has been
applied (from Van der Paauw and Ris, 1955).

*1.3.2 Relationship between underwater weight, dry matter content, starch
content and specific gravity*

It may be necessary to determine the dry matter content of batches of
potatoes not only for the marketing and processing of potatoes but also
when they are stored. Within limits this can be done very simply by
weighing under water. The underwater weight (UWW) is the weight under water in grams of 5000 g of potatoes. The specific gravity can be obtained
directly from this:

$$\text{Specific gravity (SG)} = \frac{5000}{5000 - \text{UWW}}$$

41

The relation between specific gravity (SG) and percentage dry matter (% DM) is less simple; it has been determined empirically by a number of workers, and varies to some extent as between different batches of potatoes. A very well known relationship is that established by von Scheele et al. (1935):

% DM = 24.182 + (211.04 x SG) - (211.04 x 1.0988)

If the dry matter content is expressed in UWW then:

% DM = 0.0493 x UWW + 1.95

Other authors have given somewhat different regression lines (Porter et el., 1964; Houghland, 1966; Carlsson, 1967; Verma et al., 1971; Ludwig, 1972; Schippers, 1976). One of the reasons is the differences in intercellular space in the tuber tissue (Burton, 1966; Kushman and Haynes jr., 1971). The temperatures of the potatoes and of the water in which they are weighed are also relevant (Adler, 1971; Basker, 1975).

Table 1.5 shows the relationship between underwater weight, dry matter content and starch content for a large number of batches of potatoes from sandy and peat soils in the north of the Netherlands;

% DM = 0.05 x UWW + 1.0. The potatoes were used for the starch industry.

1.3.3 Dry matter distribution in the potato

There are differences in dry matter content both between potato tubers and within a single tuber (Burton, 1966; Ifenkwe, 1974; Cole, 1975).

Differences between tubers

Differences are found not only between varieties and batches of different origins (differences in climate, soil and fertilizer application) but also between tubers of a single plant. Tubers initiated early may have an advantage in dry matter accumulation. Again, dry matter formed in the last tubers to be initiated may sometimes be resorbed on maturing, thus benefiting the larger tubers.

Meijers and Van Veldhuisen (1972) investigated the UWW of a large number of samples of the cv. Bintje and the specific gravity distribution of the tubers in these samples. Both the UWW and the specific gravity distribution varied substantially from year to year and from area to area. When the UWW was roughly equal, the specific gravity distribution was also found to be more or less identical. Large differences were observed from year to year.

The dry matter content of large tubers is usually lower than that of small tubers, as the latter contain relatively less of the water-rich inner medullary tissue. Possible departures from this rule may be due to immaturity of the tubers (Burton, 1966).

Ifenkwe et al. (1974) found that the relation between tuber size and dry matter content is not linear (Fig. 1.26). There is a clear optimum

Table 1.5 Conversion table for dry matter content, starch content and specific gravity from the under water weight (uww) of 5 kg of potatoes (data from Proefstation voor Aardappelverwerking TNO, Groningen, the Netherlands). These data count for potatoes from peat and sandy soils.

uww	% dm	% starch	spec. gravity	uww	% dm	% starch	spec. gravity	uww	% dm	% starch	spec. gravity	uww	% dm	% starch	spec. gravity
350	18.5	13.4	1.075	389	20.4	15.3	1.084	427	22.3	17.1	1.093	465	24.2	18.9	1.102
351	18.6	13.4	1.075	390	20.5	15.3	1.084	428	22.4	17.1	1.093	466	24.2	19.0	1.102
352	18.6	13.5	1.075	391	20.5	15.4	1.084	429	22.4	17.2	1.093	467	24.3	19.0	1.103
353	18.7	13.5	1.075	392	20.6	15.4	1.085	430	22.4	17.2	1.094	468	24.3	19.1	1.103
354	18.7	13.6	1.076	393	20.6	15.5	1.085	431	22.5	17.3	1.094	469	24.4	19.1	1.103
355	18.8	13.6	1.076	394	20.7	15.5	1.085	432	22.5	17.3	1.094	470	24.4	19.2	1.103
356	18.8	13.7	1.076	395	20.7	15.6	1.085	433	22.6	17.4	1.094	471	24.5	19.2	1.103
357	18.9	13.7	1.076	396	20.8	15.6	1.086	434	22.6	17.4	1.095	472	24.5	19.3	1.104
358	18.9	13.8	1.077	397	20.8	15.7	1.086	435	22.7	17.5	1.095	473	24.6	19.3	1.104
359	18.9	13.8	1.077	398	20.9	15.7	1.086	436	22.7	17.5	1.095	474	24.6	19.4	1.104
360	19.0	13.9	1.077	399	20.9	15.8	1.086	437	22.8	17.6	1.095	475	24.7	19.4	1.104
361	19.0	13.9	1.077	400	21.0	15.8	1.086	438	22.8	17.6	1.096	476	24.7	19.4	1.105
362	19.1	14.0	1.078	401	21.0	15.8	1.087	439	22.9	17.7	1.096	477	24.8	19.5	1.105
363	19.1	14.0	1.078	402	21.1	15.9	1.087	440	22.9	17.7	1.096	478	24.8	19.5	1.105
364	19.2	14.1	1.078	403	21.1	15.9	1.087	441	23.0	17.8	1.096	479	24.9	19.6	1.105
365	19.2	14.1	1.078	404	21.2	16.0	1.087	442	23.0	17.8	1.096	480	24.9	19.6	1.106
366	19.3	14.2	1.078	405	21.2	16.0	1.088	443	23.1	17.9	1.097	481	25.0	19.7	1.106
367	19.3	14.2	1.079	406	21.3	16.1	1.088	444	23.1	17.9	1.097	482	25.0	19.7	1.106
368	19.4	14.3	1.079	407	21.3	16.1	1.088	445	23.2	18.0	1.097	483	25.1	19.8	1.106
369	19.4	14.3	1.079	408	21.4	16.2	1.088	446	23.2	18.0	1.097	484	25.1	19.8	1.107
370	19.5	14.4	1.079	409	21.4	16.2	1.089	447	23.3	18.1	1.098	485	25.2	19.9	1.107
371	19.5	14.4	1.080	410	21.5	16.3	1.089	448	23.3	18.1	1.098	486	25.2	19.9	1.107
372	19.6	14.5	1.080	411	21.5	16.3	1.089	449	23.4	18.2	1.098	487	25.3	20.0	1.107
373	19.6	14.5	1.080	412	21.6	16.4	1.089	450	23.4	18.2	1.098	488	25.3	20.0	1.108
374	19.7	14.6	1.080	413	21.6	16.4	1.089	451	23.5	18.2	1.099	489	25.4	20.1	1.108
375	19.7	14.6	1.081	414	21.7	16.5	1.090	452	23.5	18.3	1.099	490	25.4	20.1	1.108
376	19.8	14.6	1.081	415	21.7	16.5	1.090	453	23.6	18.3	1.099	491	25.5	20.2	1.108
377	19.8	14.7	1.081	416	21.8	16.6	1.090	454	23.6	18.4	1.099	492	25.5	20.2	1.109
378	19.9	14.7	1.081	417	21.8	16.6	1.090	455	23.7	18.4	1.100	493	25.6	20.3	1.109
379	19.9	14.8	1.082	418	21.9	16.7	1.091	456	23.7	18.5	1.100	494	25.6	20.3	1.109
380	20.0	14.8	1.082	419	21.9	16.7	1.091	457	23.8	18.5	1.100	495	25.7	20.4	1.109
381	20.0	14.9	1.082	420	22.0	16.8	1.091	458	23.8	18.6	1.100	496	25.7	20.4	1.110
382	20.1	14.9	1.082	421	22.0	16.8	1.091	459	23.9	18.6	1.101	497	25.8	20.5	1.110
383	20.1	15.0	1.082	422	22.1	16.9	1.092	460	23.9	18.7	1.101	498	25.8	20.5	1.110
384	20.2	15.0	1.083	423	22.1	16.9	1.092	461	24.0	18.7	1.101	499	25.9	20.6	1.110
385	20.2	15.1	1.083	424	22.2	17.0	1.092	462	24.0	28.8	1.101				
386	20.3	15.1	1.083	425	22.2	17.0	1.092	463	24.1	18.8	1.102				
387	20.3	15.2	1.083	426	22.3	17.0	1.093	464	24.1	18.9	1.102				
388	20.4	15.2	1.084												

tuber size within a batch of given origin. The dry matter content declines again in larger tubers. This is thought to be due to the conversion of starch into sugars caused by moisture stress in certain parts of the tuber. Wurr et al. (1978) observed a non-linear relation in certain circumstances.

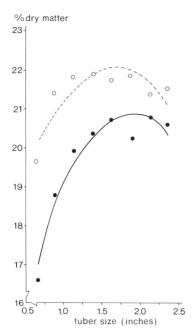

Fig. 1.26. Relationship between tuber size and dry matter content
(O———O Majestic; ●———● King Edward) (from Ifenkwe et al., 1974).

Differences within a tuber

There are differences in dry matter content within a tuber, both from
the outside to the inside in different tissues and from the bud to the
stem end.

The bud and stem ends are of different physiological ages. The pattern
of dry matter distribution is disturbed in second growth tubers, in which
the originally normal dry matter structure has been redistributed. A lower
dry matter content can also be observed near the eyes than in the surrounding tissue. Table 1.6 illustrates the dry matter distribution from
outside to inside for different tuber sizes (Burton, 1966).

Dry matter content increases from the outside towards the inside as
far as the innermost part of the cortical tissue and the outermost tissue
of the perimedullary zone, only to fall again further towards the heart
of the tuber. The tissue with the highest dry matter content (storage
parenchyma) comprises the innermost part of the cortex (inner cortex) and
the outermost part of the perimedullary zone (outer medulla).

In most potato literature, the cortex proper is considered together
with the outermost part of the phloem parenchyma, both being described by
the term 'cortex' for the sake of convenience, while the parenchyma of
the perimedullary zone together with the innermost part of the phloem parenchyma is called 'medulla' (Burton, 1966).

44

Table 1.6 Distribution of dry matter and the proportion of different zones in the potato tuber (after Glynne and Jackson, 1919; from Burton, 1966).

Zone	Number and size of tubers						
	6 small (54-84.5 g)		6 medium (139.5-169.2 g)		6 large (184.9-259.9 g)		Average of 18 tubers
	% of whole	% of dry matter	% of whole	% of dry matter	% of whole	% of dry matter	% of dry matter
Skin	2.78	14.29	1.85	15.08	2.83	13.44	14.01
Cortical, outer 2.5 mm	27.54	24.86	20.29	23.43	18.11	23.36	23.71
Cortical, inner	24.68	29.25	20.11	28.72	18.92	27.57	28.30
Medullary, outer 2.5 mm	31.32	25.76	36.43	25.49	39.95	25.05	25.28
Medullary, inner	13.67	20.16	21.32	18.46	20.19	17.48	18.15
Whole tuber	–	25.29	–	24.04	–	23.35	–

Table 1.7 Distribution of dry matter in the potato tuber (based on samples of 20 tubers of the variety King Edward VII) (after Glynne and Jackson, 1919; from Burton, 1966).

Zone	Section (bud to stem)			
	bud end ———————— stem end			
	1	2	3	4
	Percentage of dry matter			
Skin	14.69	15.38	15.20	16.73
Outer 2.5 mm of cortex	21.06	23.20	24.73	24.34
Inner cortex	25.99	28.03	29.52	30.04
Peripheral 2.5 mm of outer pith (outer medulla)	25.96	27.04	28.08	28.65
Rest of outer pith ⎫ (inner medulla)	22.05	22.94	23.14	24.97
Inner pith ⎭	17.52	16.37	17.43	19.81

The potato tuber is thus found to be extremely inhomogeneous as regards dry matter distribution. This inhomogenity is even more evident in terms of chemical composition. Table 1.7 sets out the dry matter content distribution between different tissues proceeding from the bud to the stem ends. The increase in dry matter from the bud to the stem end in all tissues is clearly shown.

1.3.4 Chemical composition of the dry matter

The composition of the dry matter in potatoes can vary substantially according to variety, conditions during growth - e.g., type of soil, fertilizer application, temperature, moisture supply and light - and degree of maturity.

Changes may occur during storage, as Fig. 1.28 shows for sugars and Fig. 1.31 for organic acids (Rumpf, 1972).

Levels and ranges for a number of components are given in Table 1.8.

Table 1.8   Approximate composition of the dry matter of the potato tuber.

Chemical composition	From Painter & Augustin, 1976	From Burton, 1966	
		range (approx.)	normal value (approx.)
Dry matter %	22.48		
Alcohol insoluble Solids %	92.65		
Crude Fiber %	1.08	1 - 10	2 - 4
Starch %	74.24	60 - 80	70
Reducing Sugars %	0.55	0.25 - 3 *	0.5 - 2 *
Total Sugars %	1.28		
Total Nitrogen %	1.16	1 - 2	1 - 2
Amino Nitrogen %	4.09		
Ascorbic Acid mg/100 g	92.08		
Thiamin mg/100 g	0.73		
Niacin mg/100 g	10.08		
Riboflavin mg/100 g	0.118		
Ash %	4.20	4 - 6	4 - 6
Calcium %	0.019		
Magnesium %	0.084		
Potassium %	1.47		
Sodium %	0.022		
Iron ppm	15.70		
Copper ppm	1.30		
Citric acid %		0.5 - 7	2
Protein-N %		0.5 - 1	0.5 - 1
Fat %		0.1 - 1	0.3 - 0.5
Sucrose %		0.25 - 1.5 *	0.5 - 1.0 *

All data except for dry matter are recorded on a dry weight basis.
The dry matter normally comprises about 18 to 28 % of the fresh weight, dependent upon factors discussed in the text. Average value about 23 %.
* These figures are representative of mature unstored tubers. The content of sugar is very markedly affected by the stage of maturity and by temperature of storage.

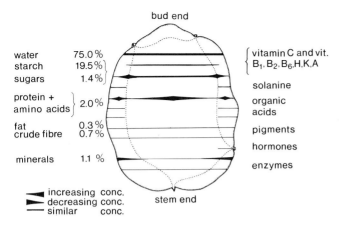

bud end

water 75.0%
starch 19.5%}
sugars 1.4%

protein +
amino acids } 2.0%

fat 0.3%
crude fibre 0.7%

minerals 1.1 %

{ vitamin C and vit.
B₁, B₂, B₆, H, K, A

solanine

organic
acids

pigments

hormones

enzymes

◄ increasing conc.
► decreasing conc.
── similar conc.

stem end

Fig. 1.27. Chemical composition and distribution within the tuber (from
Fischnick and Heilinger, 1959).

Table 1.9 Comparative summary of relative concentrations of several minor
components within specific tuber tissues [1] (Reeve et al., 1969b).

Tissue	Chlorogenic acid	Tyrosine	Phenolase	Peroxidase	Iron	Solanin-solanidine
Skin						
Periderm			+	++		
Phellogen	+		++	++	+	
Phellem			++	+	+	++
Cortex						
Parenchyma	++	+	++	+	+	++
Outer phloem	++	+	++	++	+	+
Phloem Parenchyma	++	+	++	++	+	+
Vascular 'ring'						
Xylem			+	++	++	
Xylem parenchyma	+	++	++	++	++	+
Perimedullary zone						
Storage parenchyma	+	++	+	+	+	
Internal phloem	++	++	++	++	++	
Phloem parenchyma	++	++	++	++	++	
Pith branches	+	++	+	+	+	
Pith						
Pith parenchyma	+	+	+	+	+	

[1] Based on a general evaluation of analytical reports and histochemical evidence;
+ = present, ++ = greater concentration. Lack of symbol does not indicate absence.

47

See also Tables 1.27 (True et al., 1978) and 1.13 (Augustin, 1975) for the ranges of minerals and vitamins.

As with the dry matter content, the chemical compounds are not distributed homogeneously over the tuber. Here again, there are clear differences in concentration for a number of components. For instance, chlorogenic acid is found in the outermost part of the tuber, and so is solanine. Solanine is concentrated mainly around the eyes, while, for instance, the enzyme phenolase is distributed throughout the tuber.

Fig. 1.27 shows the distribution of the components over the tuber in the radial direction relative to the apex - stem axis.

Table 1.9 distinguishes between the types of tissue within the tuber, while Table 1.10 shows the gradient in the direction from the apex to the stem end. The area around the eyes is also included in the distribution.

Table 1.10 Summary of bud end to stem end gradients of minor components within the tuber (Reeve et al., 1969b).

Component	Tuber zone [1]			
	'eye' areas	bud end	middle	stem end
Chlorogenic acid	+	+	++	++
Tyrosine		+	++	+++
Phenolase	+	++	+	+++
Peroxidase	+	+	+++	++
Catalase		+	+++	++
Ascorbic acid	+	+	++	+++
Citric acid		+++	++	+
Acidity		+	++	+++
Iron	++	+	++	+++
Phosphorus		+++	++	+
Potassium		+++	++	+
Solanin-solanidine	+++	++	+	+

[1] + = present, ++ = concentrated, +++ = more concentrated.
Lack of symbol does not indicate absence.

1.3.5 Starch

Apart from water, potatoes consist mainly of starch. This is present in the cells in the form of starch grains or amyloplasts and consists of the two polymers amylose (21 to 25 %) and amylopectin (75 to 79 %) (McCready and Hassid, 1947; Effmert, 1967; Weaver et al., 1978; Chung and Hadziyev, 1980).
Both polymers consist of α-D glucose. Amylose, however, is unbranched, while amylopectin has a branched chain (see also Chapter 2).

48

Samotus (1958) states that 55 to 75 % of the dry matter of potatoes consists of starch. Burton (1966) mentions a normal value of 70 % with a range from 60 to 80 %.

The distribution of the quantity of starch over the tuber parallels that of dry matter. Hence the starch content increases from the outside to the area of the vascular bundles, decreasing again further towards the inside. There is also more starch at the stem end than at the bud end.

As the tuber develops on the plant and become larger, the percentage of starch in the dry matter composition increases (Burton, 1966). Potato starch contains small quantities of phosphorus, present mainly in the amylopectin fraction (0.079 %). The amylose fraction is said to contain 0.0103 % phosphorus (Burton, 1966).

Posternak (1951) found that there was one phosphate group for every 300 glucose units in the amylopectin.

Burton (1966) gives values for the phosphorus content of starch in 24 varieties, ranging from 0.063 to 0.124 %. An increase in phosphorus content is found to be accompanied by an increase in viscosity in water.

Starch from large tubers is found to be more viscous than that from small tubers. The viscosity of starch from the stem end of small tubers is lower than that from the bud end; it is the other way round in large tubers.

The amylose content of starch from small tubers is lower than that from large ones. Starch from the bud end of small tubers mainly contained less amylose than starch from the stem end; the situation was again reversed in large tubers. This is probably because large tubers are more mature and contain more of the larger granules.

The mineral composition of the starch relative to that of the tuber was determined (Table 1.11) in an investigation into the composition of the ash content of potatoes grown in Alberta, varying from south to north

Table 1.11 The range of average mineral composition of potato tubers and of starch from potato tubers grown in Alberta (from Chung and Hadziyev, 1980).

	potato tubers [a] mg/100 g	starch [b] mg/100 g
P	146 - 217	67.8 - 80.4
Ca	32.8 - 46.9	14.4 - 23.6
Mg	119 - 130	17.3 - 22.3
Na	27.9 - 35.3	7.7 - 24.8
K	1844 - 1897	13.1 - 20.3

a = on dry matter basis of peeled tubers
b = expressed on dry matter basis

(Chung and Hadziyev, 1980). The ash content of the potatoes ranged from 2.7 to 5.7 % of the dry matter.

Tegge et al. (1976) showed that the phosphate and ash content of starches is substantially influenced by the year of cultivation and by locality and, to a lesser degree, by variety.

Mica (1976) determined the levels of the minerals potassium, calcium and phosphorus in starch after harvesting and in storage at 2 and 10 °C. Only slight differences were found. Since starch is the main component of the dry matter content, it is understandable that there is a good correlation between it and the starch content (Table 1.5, which applies to Dutch conditions).

Von Scheele et al. (1937) found the following relationship between starch content and dry matter content:

% starch = 17.55 + 0.891 (% dry matter - 24.18)

Correlation coefficient r = + 0.956

1.3.6 Sugars

The principal sugars occurring in potatoes are the reducing sugars glucose and fructose and the non-reducing disaccharide sucrose.

Table 1.12 shows the quantities of sugars occurring in potatoes.

Considerable variations in sugar content may occur during storage, as Fig. 1.28 shows (Chapter 2 for more quantitative information).

Table 1.12 Contents of sugar of potato varieties grown at Sutton Bonnington and analysed (11.10.56) one week after harvest and transport to Ditton Laboratory. Stored at 10 °C (from Burton, 1965).

Variety	Content of sugar, g/100 g fresh weight		
	total	reducing	non-reducing
Kind Edward	0.14	0.06	0.08
Arran Consul	0.36	0.23	0.13
Majestic	0.38	0.23	0.15
Golden Wonder	0.39	0.13	0.26
Craig's Defiance	0.50	0.34	0.16
Home Guard	0.51	0.33	0.18
Ulster Prince	0.71	0.45	0.26

1.3.7 Nitrogen, protein nitrogen and non-protein nitrogen

Nitrogen occurs primarily in the form of inorganic nitrogen, proteins, free amino acids, and a large number of different organic chemical compounds. Neuberger and Sanger (1942) used a classification which distin-

Sugar content (% fresh wt)

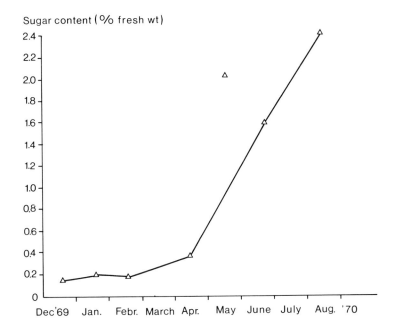

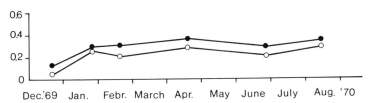

Fig. 1.28. Changes in sugar content during storage. Storage conditions, 10 °C and 85 to 90 % relative humidity. Δ ── Δ = sucrose; ● ── ● = glucose and 0 ── 0 = fructose content in % of fresh weight (from Rumpf, 1972).

guished between insoluble protein N, soluble protein N, soluble non-protein N (amino acids, amides) and 'basic N'.

The term 'crude protein' is frequently used in the literature. To determine this, the total nitrogen is measured by the Kjeldahl method and multiplied by a factor of 6.25. Desborough and Weiser (1974) showed that this factor should be 7.5 for potato protein owing to the amino acid composition. Pol and Labib (1963) determined the relationship between protein and non-protein nitrogen for four Dutch varieties (Fig. 1.29). The part of the crude protein which can be regarded as true protein was originally called tuberin. A second fraction was later distinguished within the tuberin and was called tuberinin. This created the impression that the proteins concerned were very special ones.

It is of course much better to distinguish albumin, globulin, prolamin and glutelin.

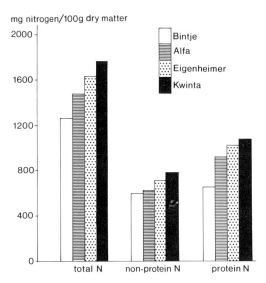

mg nitrogen/100g dry matter

Bintje
Alfa
Eigenheimer
Kwinta

Fig. 1.29. Total, non-protein and protein nitrogen content of four potato varieties (from Pol and Labib, 1963).

Using the extraction method of Nagy et al. (1941), Kapoor et al. (1975) determined the levels of these protein components (Table 1.13).

Seibles (1979) investigated the protein patterns of four varieties. Fractionation of the variety Katahdin gave 25 % globulin and 75 % albumin. This analysis can also give an impression of the quality of potato protein in terms of nutritional value (Table 1.14).

Between 10 and 40 proteins can now be observed by electrophoresis (Stegemann, 1975). Much of the protein is made up of 'storage proteins', whose functions are largely unknown; these storage proteins are highly amidated.

During senescence the molecular weight of some proteins falls substantially, owing mainly to dissociation of the larger protein complexes.

Table 1.13 Protein fractions as percentages of total protein nitrogen expressed on a freeze-dry basis (from Kapoor et al., 1975)

Protein fraction	mg of protein-N/g powder	% of total protein-N
albumin	412	48.9
globulin	218	25.9
prolamin	36	4.3
glutelin	74	8.8
residue	75	8.9

Table 1.14 Chemical Score, Essential Amino Acid Index (EAA) and
Biological Value determined in protein fractions
(from Kapoor et al., 1975).

Protein fraction	Chemical Score [1]	EEA [2]	Biological Value [3]
Albumin	61	82	77
Globulin	57	83	79
Prolamine	40	53	46
Glutelin	60	83	79
Residue	69	82	77

1. Chemical Score is the content of each essential amino acid in a
   protein fraction expressed as a percentage of the content of the
   same amino acid in the same quantity of egg (Anon., 1970).
2. Essential Amino Acid Index (EAA) is defined as the geometrical
   means of the ratios of amino acids from potato and egg protein
   (Oser, 1959).
3. Biological Value was determined by an equation of Oser (1959).

The main group of proteins in mature potatoes consists of subunits
with a molecular weight of 16,800 to 18,000 and 19,500.

The protein contains a component whose mobility during electrophoresis
is identical at pH 8.9 and 7.9. This protein band is only fully developed
when the potato is mature.

Another component disappears when sprouting begins. The electrophore-
tic protein patterns are characteristic and have already been used for
many years for identification of varieties.

The following groups (Tables 1.15 and 1.16) can be distinguished by
fractionation of the nitrogenous compounds:

Insoluble protein N
   Some 8 to 10 % of the total N content of the tuber is insoluble. This
   is almost certainly an insoluble part of the protein N fraction (Neuberger and Sanger, 1942; Slack, 1948; Burton, 1966).

Soluble protein N
   This fraction may contain more than half the total amount of nitrogen
   and consists of two different components in the proportions 7:3. The
   first component (70 %) has the character of a globulin (insoluble in
   water after dialysis) and was previously known as tuberin. The second
   component (30 %) has the character of an albumin (soluble in water
   after dialysis) and used to be known as tuberinin (Mulder and Bakema,
   1956). The latter fraction was more hydrophilic and had a lower iso-
   electric point (IEP) (De Groot et al., 1947).

The amino acid composition of the two fractions was found to be very similar (Kiesel et al., 1934).

Table 1.18 sets out the amino acid composition of hydrolysed potato material of 20 to 33 varieties grown with different doses of nitrogen (Rexen, 1976).

Soluble non-protein N

This fraction contains 'free amino acids' and the amides glutamine and asparagine. The inorganic nitrate also belongs to this fraction. The compounds glutamine and asparagine account for an important part of the total fraction, averaging 15.9 and 36.5 % respectively. The composition of this fraction is shown in Table 1.17 (Davies, 1977). Synge (1977) compares the results of 13 varieties in seven different countries.

Basic N

The compounds in this group include the amino acids arginine, lysine and histidine; nitrogenous glycol derivatives such as choline; the purine derivatives adenine, guanine, xanthine and hypoxanthine; the pyridine alkaloids such as trigonelline and also the steroid alkaloids. The last group contains the well-known glycoalkaloids α-solanine and α-chaconine (Burton, 1966).

Table 1.15 shows the distribution of some fractions within the potato tuber (taken from Burton, 1966). Table 1.16 shows the distribution of the nitrogenous components among the fractions (taken from Burton, 1966).

Table 1.15 Distribution of dry matter and nitrogen in the potato tuber and the loss of them caused by peeling. (Analysis from Neuberger and Sanger, 1942). (Peel, 5.88 per cent of tuber; cortex, 33.01 per cent; outer medulla, 35.39 per cent; inner medulla, 25.67 per cent. Loss of peel and half the cortex assumed to be caused by preparation) (taken over from Burton, 1966).

Constituent	Amount and distribution of the fraction					
	Grammes per 100 g whole tuber	Percentage in peel	Percentage in cortex	Percentage in outer medulla	Percentage in inner medulla	Grammes per 100 g raw prepared potato
Dry matter	20.3	4.3	35.3	38.7	21.7	20.4
Total N	0.370	8.4	29.5	35.7	26.4	0.366
Soluble N	0.3408	7.0	28.8	36.4	27.9	0.345
Total protein-N	0.1235	9.0	32.6	36.1	22.2	0.119
Soluble protein-N	0.0935	3.9	33.9	39.4	22.8	0.095

54

Table 1.16 Nitrogen content of several varieties of potato grown
at Sutton Bonington (from Neuberger and Sanger, 1942; taken over
from Burton, 1966).

Total N as percentage of fresh weight	0.236 - 0.359
Total N as percentage of dry weight	1.159 - 1.949
Protein-N as percentage of total N	37.5 - 63.7
Protein (protein-N x 6.25) as percentage of fresh weight	0.657 - 1.20
Soluble protein-N as percentage of total N	28.0 - 51.2
Asparagine-N as percentage of total N	11.8 - 25.5
Glutamine-N as percentage of total N	7.6 - 19.7
Glutamine/asparagine ratio	0.51 - 0.86
α-amino-acid-N as percentage of total N	6.4 - 12.8
Basic-N as percentage of total N	$20.4^1 - 27.7^1$

1 = Probably high due to simultaneous precipitation of amino acids
    with phosphotungstic acid.

Table 1.17 Free amino acids of potato tubers (mg amino acid/100 g tuber
dry matter). Glutamine results for the 1969 and 1970 samples, including
glutamic acid (from Davies, 1977).

Amino acid [1]	Record 1969(2), 1970		Désirée 1969, 1970, 1973		Alpha 1969, 1970	Bintje 1969, 1970
Aspartic acid	259	(199-376)	183	(162-212)	247, 233	197, 249
Asparagine	1937	(1200-2594)	2183	(1518-2756)	1159, 1947	1230, 2554
Threonine	69	(40-103)	62	(48-74)	39, 34	45, 63
Serine	63	(43-83)	66	(52-86)	47, 53	44, 47
Glutamine	1479	(973-2050)	1630	(822-2450)	871, 1260	984, 1861
Glutamic acid	-	(-)	-	(345-)	-, -	-, -
Proline	130	(42-303)	79	(48-137)	62, 201	49, 297
Glycine	11	(7-18)	13	(8-17)	9, -	9, 20
Alanine	24	(23-25)	29	(19-45)	24, 30	36, 118
Valine	152	(74-281)	251	(179-312)	60, 182	110, 220
Methionine	48	(32-64)	95	(76-108)	55, 56	51, 72
Isoleucine	58	(42-88)	131	(109-165)	45, 52	59, 67
Leucine	33	(25-38)	58	(43-71)	16, -	31, 44
Tyrosine	66	(51-93)	229	(174-316)	36, 27	59, 33
Phenylalanine	81	(49-102)	149	(91-204)	56, 50	55, 27
Tryptophan	-	(42-)	79	(67-91)	-, -	145, -
Lysine	52	(33-64)	112	(84-144)	39, 75	32, 45
Histidine	163	(85-247)	161	(71-239)	62, 107	91, 183
Arginine	434	(258-670)	326	(196-419)	181, 298	143, 280
4-Aminobutyric acid	171	(49-326)	206	(50-398)	66, 310	146, 442
Ornithine	-	(26-)	75	(5-148)	-, -	-, -

1 = Where there were three or more samples of the same variety, the average and
    range are reported; otherwise the actual results are given.

1.3.7.1 Amino acid composition

The free amino acid content may vary from variety to variety and from
year to year, as Table 1.17 shows for four varieties and several different years (taken from Davies, 1977).

The free amino acid content of potatoes is affected not only by variety and year of cultivation but also, and just as significantly, by such
factors as soil type, fertilizer application, climate and origin (Talley
et al., 1970; Davies, 1977).

An example of the effect of nitrogen fertilizer application on total
amino acid content (free and bound amino acids) is given in Table 1.18.

Table 1.18 Average amino acid content (total after hydrolysis) for different years and fertilizer
levels (from Rexen, 1976).

Amino acid	1971						1972					
	110 kg N/ha - 20 varieties			180 kg N/ha - 20 varieties			114 kg N/ha - 33 varieties			186 kg N/ha - 33 varieties		
	g/16 g N	% of dry mat- ter	% of fresh tubers	g/16 g N	% of dry mat- ter	% of fresh tubers	g/16 g N	% of dry mat- ter	% of fresh tubers	g/16 g N	% of dry mat- ter	% of fresh tubers
Aspartic acid	18.59	1.52	0.41	18.82	1.73	0.47	20.46	1.57	0.44	21.71	2.03	0.55
Threonine	4.16	0.34	0.09	4.01	0.37	0.10	4.06	0.31	0.09	4.25	0.40	0.11
Serine	3.54	0.29	0.08	3.30	0.30	0.08	4.25	0.33	0.09	4.16	0.39	0.11
Glutamic acid	13.47	1.10	0.30	14.25	1.31	0.35	13.36	1.03	0.29	13.42	1.26	0.34
Proline	3.43	0.28	0.08	3.25	0.30	0.08	3.82	0.29	0.08	3.77	0.35	0.09
Glycine	3.23	0.26	0.07	3.03	0.28	0.08	3.28	0.25	0.07	3.18	0.30	0.08
Alanine	3.37	0.28	0.08	3.18	0.29	0.08	3.68	0.28	0.08	3.12	0.29	0.08
Valine	4.81	0.39	0.11	4.65	0.43	0.12	4.70	0.36	0.10	4.54	0.43	0.12
Isoleucine	3.49	0.29	0.08	3.33	0.31	0.08	3.49	0.27	0.08	3.34	0.31	0.08
Leucine	5.57	0.46	0.12	5.35	0.49	0.13	5.59	0.43	0.12	5.51	0.52	0.14
Tyrosine	3.54	0.29	0.08	3.13	0.29	0.08	3.35	0.26	0.07	3.22	0.30	0.08
Phenylalanine	4.03	0.33	0.09	4.01	0.37	0.10	3.94	0.30	0.08	3.77	0.35	0.09
Lysine	5.55	0.45	0.12	5.30	0.49	0.13	5.49	0.42	0.12	5.27	0.49	0.13
Histidine	1.92	0.16	0.04	1.86	0.17	0.05	1.93	0.15	0.04	1.79	0.17	0.05
Arginine	4.37	0.36	0.10	4.30	0.39	0.10	4.20	0.32	0.09	4.19	0.39	0.11
Methionine	1.65	0.14	0.04	1.67	0.15	0.04	1.85	0.14	0.04	1.68	0.16	0.04
Nitrogen (% of dry matter)		1.31			1.47			1.23			1.50	
Dry matter (% of fresh tubers)		26.97			26.89			28.10			26.99	

1.3.7.2 Glycoalkaloids

When potato tubers are exposed to light during harvesting, handling
and marketing, a green colour develops in the periderm and in the outer
parenchyma cells of the cortex. Also a bitter-tasting substance is
formed.

The green coloration is a consequence of chlorophyll synthesis, while
the bitter taste is attributable to the formation of glycoalkaloids. The
formation of chlorophyll and glycoalkaloids on exposure to light are independent processes (Gull, 1960).

Although chlorophyll development in itself has no bearing on the quality of the tuber, green potatoes are undesirable, as the glycoalkaloids
which also form in the light are bitter-tasting and toxic. Potato glycoalkaloids comprise mainly two substances: α-solanine (solanidine-galac-
tose-glucose-rhamnose) and α-chaconine (solanidine-glucose-rhamnose-
rhamnose). In addition to the glycoalkaloids, the alkaloid solanidine
occurs in the tuber.

The consumption of potatoes with high glycoalkaloid contents may cause
serious illness, sometimes leading to death (Jadhav and Salunkhe, 1975),
whether in humans or in animals. The disease symptoms are those of acute
food poisoning. It has been found that α-solanine has an inhibiting effect on cholinesterase (Jadhav and Salunkhe, 1975). Bergers and Alink
(1980) demonstrated the toxic effect of α-solanine on rat heart cells.

Some authors associate teratogenic abnormalities such as spina bifida
and anencephaly with the consumption of excessively high levels of alkaloids (Jadhav and Salunkhe, 1975; Keeler et al., 1976). However, other
authors deny this (Ruddick et al., 1974).

The glycoalkaloid formation is affected by the following factors.

Variety

The glycoalkaloid content depends on the potato variety and averages
2 to 10 mg/100 g fresh weight for the entire tuber. Glycoalkaloids are
not distributed uniformly over the tuber. The highest levels are found
in the outermost cell layers (periderm and outside of the cortex). Hence
about 60 % is eliminated on peeling.

Sinden and Webb (1972) investigated five American varieties, in which
the whole-tuber content ranged from a minimum of 4.3 mg/100 g fresh
weight for the cv. Red Pontiac to a maximum of 9.7 mg/100 g fresh weight
for Kennebec. However, breeding may give rise to varieties with high glycoalkaloid levels. For example, cultivation of the American variety
Lenape was halted because the glycoalkaloid content was too high - viz.,
an average of 29 mg/100 g fresh weight (Sinden and Webb, 1972). It is
assumed that a level in excess of 20 mg/100 g fresh weight constitutes

a potential health hazard (Jadhav and Salunkhe, 1975). A glycoalkaloid content exceeding 30 mg/100 g fresh weight, corresponding to a level of 11 to 14 mg/100 g fresh weight in the peeled tuber, causes a bitter taste (Sinden et al., 1976).

Location and growing conditions

The glycoalkaloid content of potatoes of a single variety may vary substantially as between different origins. Sinden and Webb (1972), however, in a study of five varieties from 39 different locations, found levels in excess of 20 mg/100 g fresh weight in a few cases only. The property of forming high levels of glycoalkaloids is therefore primarily determined genetically. But it was shown that a short, cool growing season may lead to the production of immature tubers, which have higher levels (Sinden and Webb, 1972). The effects of soil and manuring are unclear (Jadhav and Salunkhe, 1975).

Wounding

Damaging and bruising increase the glycoalkaloid content. Sinden (1972) observed higher levels in immature tubers which had been graded mechanically and then stored for two days in the dark than in tubers exposed to sunlight in the field for two days. Fitzpatrick et al. (1978) and Ahmed and Müller (1978) observed an approximately 50 % increase in glycoalkaloid content due to mechanical damage.

When potatoes are cut into chips for processing, the raw products exhibit an increase in glycoalkaloid content when stored in the dark (Ahmed and Müller, 1978). This increase is extremely temperature-dependent, being slight at low temperature (Salunkhe et al., 1972). The process of chipping was found to be non-destructive to total glycoalkaloids (Sizer et al., 1980). When the sprout suppressant CIPC is used, the increase due to wounding is found to be inhibited (Wu and Salunkhe, 1977 a).

Storage

The glycoalkaloid content of potatoes increases during storage (Cronk et al., 1974; Jadhav and Salunkhe, 1975); the storage temperature is relevant here (Zitnak, 1953).

Storage at low temperature (4 to 8 °C) and high relative humidity doubled the glycoalkaloid content of the cv. Netted Gem in six weeks, while storage for an equal period in dry, warm conditions (12 to 15 °C) had nearly no effect on this content (Zitnak, 1953). Sprouting during storage increases the glycoalkaloid content in the tissue surrounding the eyes.

The sprouts themselves have a high alkaloid content, which depends on variety and may amount to as much as 400 mg of total glycoalkaloids and solanidine per 100 g fresh weight (Burton, 1966).

Exposure to light

The main factor which increases the glycoalkaloid content is the effect of light during storage. Jadhav and Salunkhe (1975) review the results of a number of workers concerning the effect of light on greening and glycoalkaloid formation.

The increase in glycoalkaloid and alkaloid levels depends on the duration of exposure to light, the light intensity and the wavelength of the light. Zitnak (1953) observed a rapid increase in glycoalkaloids when newly lifted tubers were exposed to sunlight (Table 1.19).

Liljemark and Widoff (1960) investigated the influence of the light intensity on the glycoalkaloid formation. They examined Arran Consul containing 40 mg/100 g dry matter and found an approximately 50 % increase in solanine + solanidine after storage for nine days in light of 14 ft-c. The increase was about 100 % in light of 56 ft-c.

This is contradicted by the results of Patil et al. (1971) and Gull and Isenberg (1958), who did not observe any increase in glycoalkaloid content dependent on light intensity.

Jeppsen et al. (1974) showed that coloured light increases the solanine content less than white light (Table 1.20).

Table 1.19 Increase in glycoalkaloid content in mg/100 g fresh weight of newly lifted tubers of two potato varieties when exposed to sunlight (after Zitnak, 1953, from Jadhav and Salunkhe, 1975).

Hours' light	Netted Gem	Katahdin
0	1.7	1.5
6	12.0	5.0
12	13.2	7.1
36	20.4	16.3

Table 1.20 Mean volumes of total solanine determined in potato tubers illuminated through coloured cellophane filters; light intensity 50 ft-c; tubers exposed to each colour light for 10 days at 15.5 °C and 60 % RH (from Jeppsen et al., 1974).

Colour of cellophane filter	Solanine (mg/100 g fresh peel)
Clear	49.5
Red	42.5*
Orange	52.0
Yellow	47.0
Green	35.8*
Blue	45.5
Violet	42.5*

* Significant at 0.05 level.

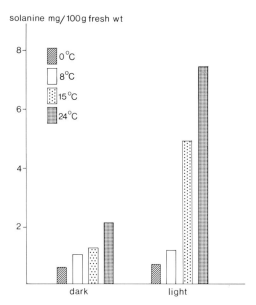

solanine mg/100g fresh wt

0°C
8°C
15°C
24°C

dark   light

Fig. 1.30. Effect of temperature on solanine formation in Russet Burbank potato slices stored 48 hours in dark or light (200 ft-c). Original concentration 0.3 mg/100 g fresh wt. (from Salunkhe et al., 1972).

Green light is thus found to increase the solanine content least. The highest value was observed with orange light. In 1937 Connor exposed tubers to different wave-lengths of light. The blue end of the spectrum encouraged glycoalkaloid formation the most.

The storage temperature is important in solanine formation - both in light and due to wounding, as shown by Salunkhe et al. (1972) in potato discs (Fig. 1.30). At higher temperatures, there is an appreciably greater increase in glycoalkaloids in these cases. Zitnak (1953), on the other hand, observed a smaller increase when whole tubers (Netted Gem) were exposed to light in warm, dry storage conditions (12 to 15 °C) than in cold, wet storage (4 to 8 °C). The initial level was 5.9 mg/100 g fresh weight; the level in warm storage, averaged over six weeks, was 5.9 mg, rising to 19.0 mg in cold storage.

A number of workers have tried to reduce light-dependent glycoalkaloid synthesis with chemicals. The sprout inhibitor CIPC is found to have no effect on this synthesis, although it had an inhibitory effect on wound induced glycoalkaloid formation (Wu and Salunkhe, 1977). A substantial reduction is observed on treatment with mineral oil (Jadhav and Salunkhe, 1974) and spray lecithin (Wu and Salunkhe, 1977 b).

1.3.7.3 Nitrate (NO_3-N)

Increasing interest is being focused on the nitrate content of various types of agricultural produce for human consumption (McDole and McMaster, 1978; Augustin et al., 1977).

Heisler et al. (1973) also give values for nitrite levels.

It has been found that high levels of nitrogen fertilizer application combined with periods of moisture stress may give rise to very high nitrate levels in potato tubers.

McDole and McMaster (1978) found that with low nitrogen fertilization and optimum, high irrigation, tubers contained 70 to 80 ppm NO_3-N. If there was a moisture deficiency during growth, the level rose to 144 ppm. With excessive nitrogen fertilizer application, these nitrate contents were 151 to 154 ppm and 370 ppm respectively.

Carter and Bosma (1974) determined the nitrate content over three years, finding levels of 36 to 131, 34 to 75 and 25 to 50 ppm respectively. A limit of 67 ppm NO_3-N based on fresh weight has been set for spinach for baby food.

1.3.8 Lipids; fatty acids

The lipid fraction of potato tubers accounts for only a very small proportion of their composition. A study of 23 varieties showed that the lipid content was about 0.1 % of fresh weight and was substantially the same for all varieties. No significant varietal differences were observed for the individual lipid components either (Galliard, 1973).

Table 1.21 sets out the total lipid content of a number of varieties (figures from Galliard, 1973).

Fricker (1969) found a total lipid content ranging between 0.60 and 0.84 g/100 g in freeze-dried material of nine varieties. The results were as follows for Bintje (percentages referred to dry weight):
Skin 2.00 to 3.36 %; flesh 0.58 to 0.61 %; tuber total 0.70 to 0.77%.

Table 1.21 Total lipid content of tubers from different varieties of potato (from Galliard, 1973).

Variety	Average tuber weight	Dry weight (% of fresh wt.)	Total lipid content (mg/100 g fresh wt.)
Bintje	106	20.0	107
Désirée	92	20.0	113
King Edward	93	20.6	93
Pentland Crown	119	18.9	91
Pentland Marble	96	20.8	126
Record	117	24.0	77
Sientje	79	21.0	75
Sirtema	95	21.2	84

Table 1.22 Composition of the lipid fraction of potatoes in percentages of total lipid on weight basis (from Galliard, 1968)

neutral lipids	21.0
phosphatidylcholine	25.8
digalactosyldiglyceride	14.2
phosphatidylethanolamine	12.6
phosphatidylinositol	6.3
esterified steryl glucoside	6.4
monogalactosyldiglyceride	5.7
glucocerebroside	2.4
steryl glucoside	2.0
sulfolipid	1.3

The total lipid content of the potato (in terms of weight) is composed as shown in Table 1.22.

It was found that more than 80 to 90 % of the total fatty acid content of these lipids in potatoes was composed of the saturated fatty acid, palmitic acid and two polyunsaturated fatty acids, linoleic acid and lino-lenic acid. In addition to these fatty acids, stearic acid, oleic acid and palmitoleic acid are present only in small quantities. This is shown by Cherif (1973), Galliard (1973) and other workers.

Cherif (1973) investigated the fatty acid composition of the total lipid fraction of skin, tuber tissue, newly formed tubers and potato sprouts (Table 1.23). Only traces of the other fatty acids $C_{10:0}$, $C_{12:0}$, $C_{14:0}$, $C_{14:1}$, $C_{15:0}$, $C_{16:1}$ and $C_{20:0}$ were found. Corresponding values are given by Cherif and Ben Abdelkader (1970) for the main fatty acids palmi-tic acid, linoleic acid and linolenic acid.

The fatty acid composition of a number of varieties is given in Table 1.24. Comprehensive analyses, in which the fatty acids occurring in small

Table 1.23 Fatty acid content (µg/g fr.wt. and in % of total lipids) of potato tubers and sprouts (from Cherif, 1973).

Fatty acids		Dormant tubers				Newly formed tubers		Sprouts	
		skin		flesh					
		µg/g fr.wt.	%	µg/g fr.wt.	%	µg/g fr.wt.	%	µg/g fr.wt.	%
Palmitic acid	$C_{16:0}$	95	21	68	20	252	21	204	22
Stearic acid	$C_{18:0}$	40	9	24	7	48	4	37	4
Oleic acid	$C_{18:1}$	14	3	10	3	36	3	19	2
Linoleic acid	$C_{18:2}$	166	37	168	49	624	52	492	53
Linolenic acid	$C_{18:3}$	135	30	70	21	240	20	176	19
Total		450		340		1200		928	

62

Table 1.24 Total fatty acid content and composition in lipids of tubers from different varieties of potato (from Galliard, 1973).

Variety	Total fatty acid content (mg/100 g fr. wt.)	Fatty acid composition (% of total fatty acids)					
		palmitic acid	linoleic acid	linolenic acid	palmitoleic acid	stearine acid	oleic acid
Bintje	57.1	15.6	58.4	16.9	0.7	5.9	2.0
Désirée	54.6	18.2	59.6	14.5	0.7	4.9	2.0
King Edward	53.9	17.8	59.9	13.4	1.3	5.9	1.9
Pentland Crown	46.3	18.5	54.8	18.2	1.2	5.3	2.2
Pentland Marble	61.6	17.2	59.4	16.5	1.0	4.3	2.0
Record	54.5	16.3	52.7	24.0	0.8	5.3	1.1
Sientje	57.8	18.5	51.3	18.6	2.1	6.6	2.9
Sirtema	46.2	17.4	60.7	13.7	1.0	5.7	1.7

quantities were also determined, were carried out by Fricker et al. (1972).

Cherif (1973) also states that 60 to 80 % of the fatty acids in potatoes are unsaturated, the main representative being linoleic acid. The total content of fatty acids increases substantially during the first few months of storage at 10 and 18 °C. Most of the increase takes place after the end of the dormancy period and during growth of the sprouts. This increase was also observed by Cherif and Ben Abdelkader (1970).

The crude lipid and phospholipid contents fall when tubers are bruised and cut. The composition of the fatty acids is unchanged on bruising, but in the case of cut wounds to the cortical tissue, an increase in saturated fatty acids and a decrease in unsaturated fatty acids were observed in the phospholipid fraction (Mondy and Koch, 1978a).

Tubers infected with potato X-virus also show a fall in both the crude lipid fraction and the phospholipid fraction (Mondy and Koch, 1978b). The crude lipid and phospholipid contents are higher at the bud end of the tuber than at the stem end, this being correlated with more intense enzymatic discoloration of the stem end (Mondy and Mueller, 1977). The principal lipids in potato tubers are the ones associated with the lipoprotein membrane structures and their maintenance in vivo. The osmotic characteristics of these membranes - ion transport - are very important for the life functions. They are also important for the stability of processed potato products.

Levels of lipids and their breakdown by the enzymes lipolytic acyl hydrolase and lipoxygenase, present in the potato tuber, are important in connection with off-flavours and rancidity problems when potatoes are cut during processing, the fatty acids linoleic acid and linolenic acid quickly being broken down. A low polyunsaturated fatty acid content may be favourable to the stability of the processed products.

Mondy and Koch (1978c) found a negative correlation (r = - 0.95) between the degree of enzymatic browning and lipid content. Enzymatic
browning is stated to be more intense, and the crude lipid and phospholipid content lower, when potatoes are treated with the sprout suppressant maleic hydrazide (MH) (Mueller and Mondy, 1977).

Berkeley and Galliard (1974) found that early-maturing varieties
sprouted after six months' storage, accumulation of both the total lipid
fraction and fatty acids being observed. When the dormancy of the potato
came to an end, the triglyceride fraction was regenerated, the sterol and
carotenoid contents at the same time increasing.

Cheng and Muneta (1978) observed a large increase in phosphatidic acid
and a fall in phosphatidyl choline in experiments with Russet Burbank
stored at 5 to 6 °C.

Liljenberg et al. (1978) observed that storage in the dark had little
effect. Storage exposed to light resulted in an increase in the absolute
quantity and relative content of linolenic acid in the galactolipid fraction, with at the same time an equivalent decrease in the percentage of
linoleic acid. The percentages of the other fatty acids remained unchanged.

1.3.9 Cellulose, hemicelluloses, lignin and glycoproteins

In addition to pectins, cellulose, hemicellulose and lignin are the
main components of the cell walls, and are as such important for the
boiling and frying properties and the texture of the potato. Little information is available on the amounts of these components present in the
potato in general and in the cell wall fractions in particular.

Cellulose is formed by a linear polymer of glucose with β (1-4) links.

Hemicelluloses are formed by polymers of pentoses - in particular,
D-xylan polymers of D-xylose with β (1-4) links and side chains of arabinose and other carbohydrates. Potato hemicellulose is made up of 57 %
glucose, 23 % xylose, 12 % galactose and 6 % mannose (Hoff and Castro,
1969).

Lignin is a polymer of aromatic alcohols.

In many chemical analyses of potato tubers, the above substances are

Table 1.25 Potato cell wall composition (% of dry matter) (after Keijbets, 1974).

	From Le Tourneau, 1956	From Emiliani-Retamar, 1968	From Hoff-Castro, 1969
Pectic substances	60	64 - 66	55
Hemicellulose	10	8 - 10	7
Cellulose	15	24 - 26	28
Glycoprotein	15	1	10

consolidated under the terms 'fibre' and 'crude fibre', whose levels
range from 1.14 to 10 % of the dry matter (Burton, 1966).

Carpenter (1940) quotes values for cellulose of 2.74 to 3.82 % of the
dry matter. Table 1.25 sets out the cellulose contents of cell wall fractions of potatoes (Keijbets, 1974).

1.3.10 Pectins

The structure of pectins consists mainly of partially esterified
straight chains of polygalacturonic acid, the galacturonic acid groups
being joined by α (1-4)-glycosidic links. The carboxyl groups are partially esterified with methanol. They also contain neutral sugar chains
such as arabinose, galactose and rhamnose, and sometimes also xylose and
glucose. The sugar rhamnose is thought to be incorporated in the chain
at specific intervals, forming a 'rhamnogalacturonane' which holds the
cellulose fibrils in the cell walls together (Neukom et al., 1980). The
non-water-soluble pectins contain more calcium than those which are soluble in water; they have a higher degree of polymerization and are less
methylated (Bettelheim and Sterling, 1955).

The total pectin content of potatoes, expressed as calcium pectate is:
0.21 to 0.41 % referred to fresh tuber weight (Burton, 1966; Adler, 1971).
It is present mainly in the middle lamellae of the cell walls and plays a
role in the texture of cooked potato products. Values ranging from 55 to
66 % of their weight of dry matter are reported for cell walls (Table
1.25) (Le Tourneau, 1956; Emiliani and Retamar, 1968; Hoff and Castro,
1969). The influence of pectins in the cell wall on intercellular cohesion of potato tissue when potatoes are cooked was examined by Keijbets
(1974) and Linehan and Hughes (1969).

1.3.11 Ash content; minerals

On incineration, 4 to 6 % of the dry matter is found to consist of
minerals. Most of the elements concerned occur in a number of organic
chemical compounds, while some are present as ions dissolved in the cell
sap. The ash content depends on the type of soil in which the potato was
grown. There are also varietal differences. Table 1.26 sets out the composition of the ash fraction (taken from Burton, 1966).

Table 1.27 gives the mineral composition referred to fresh weight. The
mineral composition is very important in terms of nutrition. Since potatoes are consumed by a high proportion of the population in many countries, it is necessary to know how much of the mineral requirement they
satisfy. Research has therefore recently been conducted on the mineral
composition of potatoes (True et al., 1978; Toma et al., 1978).

Certain elements also play an important part in determining the keep-

Table 1.26 Composition of the ash of the potato tuber. All values given as
mg/100 g of dry matter. (Data from Lampitt and Goldenberg, 1940 except where
stated to the contrary; taken over from Burton, 1966).

Element	Maximum variations reported	Average variations
Aluminium	0.2-35.4	2.94-8.85
Arsenic	0.035	0.035
Boron	0.45-0.86	0.45-0.86
Bromine	0.48-0.85	0.48-0.85
Calcium	10.0-130	31.8-88.3
Chlorine	44.7-805	112-530
Cobalt	0.0065	0.0065
Copper	0.06-2.83	0.38-1.00
Fluorine	0.0277-0.038[1]	0.0277-0.038[1]
Iodine	0.001-0.387	0.0022-0.0565
Iron	2.61-71.5	2.61-10.46
Lithium	Trace	Trace
Magnesium	45.9-216.5	65.2-136.5
Manganese	0.0-51.1	0.56-8.5
Molybdenum	0.026	0.026
Nickel	0.008-0.037[2]	0.008-0.037[2]
Phosphorus	119-605	166.5-314
Potassium	1394-2825	1811-2530
Silicon	5.1-17.3	5.1-17.3
Sodium	0.0-332	26.1-332
Sulphur	42.7-423	109-213
Zinc	1.74-2.17	1.74-2.17

[1] Pisareva (1955)   [2] Bambergs (1953)

ing ability, dry matter content, strength of tuber tissue and sprouting
vigour of seed potatoes.

Some major elements - phosphorus, potassium and calcium - are discussed briefly below, as they are relevant to the storage and sprouting of
potatoes.

1.3.11.1 Phosphorus

The element phosphorus, which occurs in a number of phosphate compounds, is very important in the tuber. Many energy-rich phosphate compounds play an essential part in metabolism. Phosphorus accelerates the
maturing process. There is no agreement on its effect on dry matter content (Beukema and Van der Zaag, 1979). Apart from a large number of compounds occurring in small concentrations only, the phosphate in the tuber
is present mainly in the form of phosphate bound to amylopectin (see also

Table 1.27   Mineral content of raw unpeeled potatoes (from True et al., 1978)

	mg/100 g fresh weight	
	mean [1]	range [1]
Aluminium	0.609	0.301 - 1.484
Boron	0.136	0.081 - 0.168
Calcium	5.30	2.67 - 16.67
Copper	0.193	0.087 - 0.327
Iodine	0.019	0.010 - 0.035
Iron	0.741	0.276 - 2.311
Magnesium	20.9	16.7 - 27.3
Manganese	0.253	0.143 - 0.699
Molybdenum	0.091	0.008 - 0.186
Phosphorus	47.9	31.3 - 65.3
Potassium	564	205 - 901
Selenium	0.006	0.002 - 0.029
Sodium	7.71	2.0 - 17.3
Zinc	0.409	0.297 - 0.543

1. The means and ranges represent the mean and range of three replicated
   values of nine varieties and of five locations of growth.

Section 1.3.5 and Chapter 2), as inorganic phosphate and as phytate (phytate consists of mesoinositol esterified with phosphate groups).

Samotus and Schwimmer (1963) examined the concentrations of these components and their variation during storage (Table 1.28).

Table 1.28   Changes in distribution of P in various fractions during a
six weeks storage period. Storage temperature 0 to 2 °C (average values
adapted from Samotus and Schwimmer, 1963).

Phosphate fraction	mg/g fresh weight	
	before storage	after storage
starch - P	0.181	0.133
inorganic - P	17.6	21.4
phytate - P	16.0	13.5
*T.C.A. insoluble non starch-P	13.2	14.9
*T.C.A. soluble organic-P	19.6	17.4

*T.C.A. = trichloro acetic acid.

1.3.11.2 Potassium

Under normal conditions the potassium concentration of the dry matter in the tubers is inversely proportional to the dry matter content (see also Section 1.3.1.3). Where large quantities of nitrogen fertilizer have been applied, the effect of potassium is not always equally clear. Potassium plays an important part in the water balance of the tuber, influencing the permeability of the cell membranes to water. In general it can be stated that potassium tends to keep the level of reducing sugars down and is not conducive to a high dry matter content (or a lower water content). The latter point is directly related to susceptibility to black spot caused by impact. It has been shown that tubers with less than 2 % potassium in the dry matter are usually highly susceptible to impact discoloration. A too low potassium fertilization increases susceptibility to black spot (Hughes, 1975). Tubers with a dry matter potassium content above 2 % are less susceptible, if at all, to black spot caused by impact (Beukema and Van der Zaag, 1979).

1.3.11.3 Calcium

Although only present in the potato in low concentrations, calcium performs an important function, especially in seed potatoes, in which it is closely connected with the process of sprouting (Dyson and Digby, 1975).

It is also found that high calcium levels in the fertilizer improve keeping ability (Combrink et al., 1975). Schaller and Amberger (1974) found that the calcium content of tubers influences susceptibility to black spot. If the calcium content is low, the tuber tissue is less firm.

The calcium content of potatoes can be modified to a reasonable extent (Krausz and Marschner, 1975) and does not affect the concentration of magnesium and potassium (Table 1.29).

Table 1.29 Influence of calcium nutrition on calcium content of the tubers and interaction with potassium and magnesium content (from Krausz and Marschner, 1973).

Ca fertilization	Mineral composition (mg/g dry matter)		
	Ca	K	Mg
Ca high (15 mM Ca/l)	0.82	23.65	1.32
Ca low (0.02 mM Ca/l)	0.37	25.02	1.28
without Ca	0.14	25.50	1.26

68

De Kock et al. (1979) observed in a series of experiments that the calcium content of potatoes is connected with the pH of the soil. Increasing pH is found to cause an increase in the calcium content of the tubers. Concentrations at the stem end of tubers at various soil pH values are set out in Table 1.30; differences were also observed at the bud end.

Table 1.30 Influence of soil pH on the calcium content of the tubers measured at the stem end (adapted from De Kock et al., 1979).

Soil pH	Calcium content m.equiv. kg^{-1} fr. wt.
5.5	1.21
6.0	2.48
6.5	2.77
7.0	3.58
7.5	3.14

1.3.12 Vitamins

The vitamins are an important group of compounds for nutrition. The main vitamins in potatoes are vitamin C, which is present in substantial quantities, and the vitamins of the B group. The latter comprise B_1 (thiamine), B_2 (riboflavine), B_5 (probably nicotinic acid = niacin) and B_6 (pyridoxine) (Pol and Labib, 1963; Burton, 1966; Adler, 1971; Müller, 1975). Niacin and folacin also belong to this group (Augustin, 1975). The levels are set out in Table 1.31.

Table 1.31 Contents of vitamins in the potato tuber.

	from Augustin, 1975	from Adler, 1971	Average values
	mg/100 g fresh weight		
Vit. C - ascorbic acid	8 - 30	1 - 54	15
Vit. B - thiamine	0.034 - 0.146	0.024 - 0.180	0.110
riboflavine	0.010 - 0.052	0.007 - 0.200	0.051
niacin (nicotinic acid)	0.54 - 0.310	0.63 - 2.0	1.22*
folacin (folic acid)	0.005 - 0.01		
pyridoxin	0.130 - 0.42		0.190

* nicotinamid.

Augustin (1975) investigated the effect of nitrogen fertilizer application on the levels of some important vitamins in two different types of soil. The results are summarized in Table 1.32. It was found that the thiamine content increased sharply with increasing N fertilizer application. There was also a difference between soils. Niacin, however, was affected by N fertilizer application but not by the type of soil.

The thiamine content fluctuates during storage (Table 1.33), while the riboflavine and niacin contents vary little (Augustin, 1975).

Table 1.32 Effect of nitrogen fertilization on the contents of some water soluble vitamins in Russet Burbank potatoes (in mg/100 g dry matter) (from Augustin, 1975).

	Nitrogen (lb/acre)	Ascorbic acid mean	CV, %	Thiamine mean	CV, %	Riboflavin mean	CV, %	Niacin mean	CV, %
Loamy soil	0	125.50	1.32	0.299	25.91	0.080	10.45	8.09	3.2
	300	106.50	6.06	0.579	15.45	0.090	6.08	8.22	6.9
	600	100.29	4.73	0.572	13.54	0.097	12.20	9.10	6.6
Sandy soil	0	150.50	1.25	0.252	30.70	0.102	9.80	8.22	7.9
	300	137.82	5.76	0.360	24.84	0.103	13.73	8.48	6.4
	600	127.81	4.70	0.457	6.91	0.097	6.52	9.19	6.3

The vitamin C content, on the other hand, falls appreciably as the N dose increases; it is also affected by the type of soil. The vitamin C content of potatoes falls during storage (Table 1.33). Augustin (1975) demonstrated a linear relationship between ascorbic acid content and the logarithm of time.

Table 1.33 Effect of storage time (storage conditions 7.2 °C and 95 % RH) on the contents of some water soluble vitamins in Russet Burbank potatoes (in mg/100 g dry matter) (from Augustin, 1975).

	Storage time (days)	Ascorbic acid mean	CV, %	Thiamine mean	CV, %	Riboflavin mean	CV, %	Niacin mean	CV, %
Loamy soil	10	108.10	5.24	0.498	19.04	0.089	9.38	8.52	7.85
	90	63.88	4.74	0.561	15.65	0.084	7.95	8.27	6.30
	170	51.86	3.59	0.481	9.71	0.089	12.55	8.48	5.70
	240	47.10	3.39	0.522	7.23	0.092	7.95	7.67	5.71
Sandy soil	5	136.49	5.13	0.379	21.14	0.100	8.20	8.70	9.43
	90	68.13	6.37	0.510	7.34	0.089	8.17	9.58	5.56
	170	54.65	5.93	0.448	10.23	0.095	7.68	9.86	6.25
	240	46.58	5.54	0.522	12.58	0.093	14.75	9.15	7.94

1.3.13 Pigments

The tissue of potatoes is coloured light yellow to a greater or lesser extent. The degree of coloration is a varietal characteristic (Salaman, 1926; Burton, 1966). Caldwell et al. (1945) showed that potatoes with white flesh contain
0.014 to 0.054 mg of carotenoids per 100 g fresh material,
while yellower tubers contain
0.110 to 0.187 mg of carotenoids per 100 g fresh weight.
Respective average values are
0.021 and 0.138 mg/100 g fresh weight. Adler (1971) mentions values of
0.199 to 0.560 mg/100 g fresh weight. The carotenoids are highly fat-soluble, are modified by light and contain a large number of different compounds, such as α-carotene; auroxanthine; violaxanthine; ξ-carotene; β-carotene; lutein; isolutein; a flavoxanthine and neo-β-carotene-u. Smaller quantities of flavonols, flavones and flavin are also found in the tuber (Lampitt and Goldenberg, 1940; Harborne, 1962).

Red-skinned potatoes contain anthocyanin dissolved in the cell sap of the periderm cells and the outer cell layers of the cortical parenchyma.

1.3.14 Organic acids; phenols

A number of organic acids occur in the potatoes in varying quantities. An important one is the amino acid *tyrosine*, which is converted via dopa, dopaquinone and dopachrome into the brown-black pigment melanin. This is a well-known oxidation process which occurs when potato tissue is cut and homogenized (Adler, 1971). The average tyrosine content found in 10 Dutch potato varieties, grown on clay and sandy soil, was 220 µg/g fresh weight, with a range of 70 to 490 µg/g fresh weight (unpublished, Van Es and Hartmans).

Chlorogenic acid and caffeic acid may also be mentioned. Chlorogenic acid is involved in discoloration after cooking (Gray and Hughes, 1978).

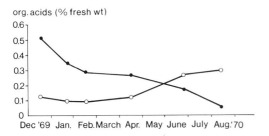

Fig. 1.31. Citric acid (● —— ●) and malic acid (0 —— 0) content during storage. Storage conditions: 10 °C and 85 to 90 % relative humidity (from Rumpf, 1972).

Investigations with tubers of 10 Dutch varieties, grown on clay and sandy soil, showed an average chlorogenic acid content of 66 µg/g fresh weight, with a range of 34 to 144 µg/g fresh weight (unpublished, Van Es and Hartmans). Korableva et al. (1973) found caffeic acid contents of 18.7 µg/g fresh weight in the growing points and of 2.3 µg/g fresh weight in the pulp of dormant tubers. At the end of the dormancy period there is a decline in these caffeic acid contents.

Finally, there are *citric acid* and malic acid. The concentration of citric acid increases during storage, while that of malic acid declines proportionately (Fig. 1.31) (Adler, 1971; Rumpf, 1972). Citric acid can bind iron in the tuber so that it cannot be bound to chlorogenic acid. It is the binding of iron with chlorogenic acid which causes discoloration on cooking (Gray and Hughes, 1978).

References

Adams, M.J., 1975. Potato tuber lenticels: Development and structure. Ann. Appl. Biol., 79: 265-273.

Adler, G., 1971. Kartoffeln und Kartoffelerzeugnisse. Grundlagen und Fortschritte der Lebensmitteluntersuchung 13. Parey, Berlin, Hamburg.

Ahmed, S.S. & K. Müller, 1978. Effect of wound-damages on the glyco-alkaloid content in potato tubers and chips. Lebensm.-Wiss. u. Technol., 11: 144-146.

Allen, E.J., 1978. Plant density. The potato crop: 278-326. Editor: P.M. Harris. Chapman and Hall, London.

Anonymous, 1970. Amino acid content of foods and biological data on proteins. FAO Nutr. Stud., 24, FAO, Rome.

Appleman, C.O. & E.V. Miller, 1926. A chemical and physiological study of maturity in potatoes. J. Agric. Res., 33: 569-577.

Artschwager, E., 1924. Studies on the potato tuber. J. Agric. Res., 27: 809-935.

Augustin, J., 1975. Variations in the nutritional composition of fresh potatoes. J. Fd. Science, 40: 1295-1299.

Augustin, J., R.E. McDole & C.G. Painter, 1977. Influence of fertilizers, irrigation and storage treatments on nitrate-N content of potato tubers. Am. Potato J., 54: 125-136.

Bambergs, K., 1953. Nickel content in some plants and plant products. Latv. PSR Zinät. Akad. Vest., 4: 5-8.

Barckhausen, R. & G. Rosenstock, 1973. Feinstrukturelle Beobachtungen zur traumatogenen Suberinisierung beim Knollenparenchym von Solanum tuberosum L. Z. Pflanzenphysiol., 69: 193-203.

Basker, D., 1975. Centigrade scale temperature corrections to the specific gravity of potatoes. Potato Res., 18: 123-125.

Bernelot Moens, H.L., 1973. Handboek voor de Akkerbouw. Deel I. Algemeen en Gewassen. Publikatie no. 9, PAGV, Lelystad.

Bettelheim, F.A. & C. Sterling, 1955. Factors associated with potato texture. II. Pectic substances. Fd. Res., 20: 118-129.

Bergers, W.W.A. & G.M. Alink, 1980. Toxic effect of the glycoalkaloids solanine and tomatine on cultured neonatal rat heart cells. Toxicology Letters, 6: 29-32.

Berkeley, H.D. & T. Galliard, 1974. Lipids of potato tubers. III. Effect of growth and storage on lipid content of the potato tuber. J. Sci. Fd. Agric., 25: 861-867.

Beukema, H.P. & D.E. van der Zaag, 1979. Potato improvement: Some factors and facts. International Agricultural Centre, (IAC), Wageningen.

Bodlaender, K.B.A., C. Lugt & J. Marinus, 1964. The induction of second growth in potato tubers. Eur. Potato J., 7: 57-71.

Burton, W.G., 1965. The sugar balance in some British potato varieties during storage. I. Preliminary observations. Eur. Potato J., 8: 80-91.

Burton, G.W., 1966. The potato. H. Veenman & Zonen, Wageningen.

Caldwell, J.S., B.C. Brunstetter, C.W. Culpepper & B.D. Ezell, 1945. Causes and control of discoloration in dehydration of white potatoes. Canner, 100 (13), 35; 100 (14), 15; 100 (15), 14.

Carlsson, H., 1967. The relationship between specific gravity, dry matter and starch in potatoes. Lantbr. Högsk. Ann., 33: 695-702.

Carpenter, T.M., 1940. Composition of some common foods with respect to the carbohydrate content. J. Nutr., 19: 415-422.

Carter, J.N. & S.M. Bosma, 1974. Effect of fertilizer and irrigation on nitrate-nitrogen and total nitrogen in potato tubers. Agron. J., 66: 263-266.

Cheng, F.C. & P. Muneta, 1978. Lipid composition of potatoes as affected by storage and potassium fertilization. Am. Potato J., 55: 441-448.

Cherif, A., 1973. Metabolisme des lipides dans le tubercule de pomme de terre (Solanum tuberosum L.) I. Evolution des lipides au cours de la conservation des tubercules. Potato Res., 16: 126-147.

Cherif, A. & A.B. Abdelkader, 1970. Analyse quantitative des acides gras présents dans différentes régions du tubercule de pomme de terre; variation au cours de la conservation à 10 °C. Potato Res., 13: 284-295.

Chung, I. & D. Hadziyev, 1980. Tuber and starch characteristics of Alberta grown potatoes. Can. Inst. Fd. Sci. Technol. J., 13: 143-153.

Cole, C.S., 1975. Variation in dry matter between and within potato tubers. Potato Res., 18: 28-37.

Combrink, N.J.J., K.P. Prinsloo & A.C. Jandrell, 1975. The effect of calcium, phosphate and boron on the keeping quality and quality-determining tuber characteristics of potatoes. Agroplantae, 7: 81-84.

Conner, H.W., 1937. Effect of light on solanine synthesis in the potato tuber. Plant Physiol, 12: 79-98.

Cronk, T.C., G.D. Kuhn & F.J. McArdle, 1974. The influence of stage of maturity, level of nitrogen fertilization and storage on the concentration of solanine in tubers of three potato cultivars. Bull. of Environm. Contam. and Toxicology, 11 (2): 163.

Cutter, E.G., 1978. Structure and development of the potato plant. The potato crop: 70-152. Editor: P.M. Harris. Chapman and Hall, London.

Danert, S., 1961. Morphologie und Anatomie. Die Kartoffel: 19-45. R. Schick & M. Klinkowski. VEB Deutscher Landwirtschaftsverlag.

Davies, A.C.M., 1977. The free aminoacids of tubers of potato varieties grown in England and Ireland. Potato Res., 20: 9-21.

Davis, R.M. Jr., 1961. Ingrown sprouts in potato tubers: Factors accompanying their origin in Ohio. Am. Potato J., 38: 411-413.

De Kock, P.C., A. Hall & R.H.E. Inkson, 1979. Nutrient distribution in the potato tuber in relation to soil pH. Ann. Bot., 43: 299-304.

Desborough, S. & C.J. Weiser, 1974. Improving potato protein. I. Evaluation of selection techniques. Am. Potato J., 51: 185-196.

Dyson, P.W. & J. Digby, 1975. Effects of calcium on sprout growth and sub-apical necrosis in majestic potatoes. Potato Res., 18: 290-305.

Effmert, B., 1967. Über den Einfluss der Düngung auf das Amylose Amylopektin-Verhältnis der Kartoffelstärke. Albrecht-Thaer- Archiv, 11 (8).

Emiliani, E. & J.C. Retamar, 1968. Las paredes celulares del parenquima de reserva de las papas (Sol. tub.). Rev. Fac. Ing. quim., Univ. Nac. Litoral, 37: 7-23.

Es, A. van, K.J. Hartmans & M.H. van Calker, 1975. Onderzoek naar de diepergelegen oorzaken van de blauwgevoeligheid van aardappelen. III. De invloed van de celgrootte. IBVL-Publikatie 288, IBVL, Wageningen.

Fischnich, O. & F. Heilinger, 1959. Die Inhaltsstoffe der Kartoffel: Bildung, Verwertung, Erhaltung. Mitteilungsblatt der Forschungsanstalt für Landwirtschaft Braunschweig-Völkenrode, 9 (1).

Fitzpatrick, T.J., J.A. McDermott & S.F. Osman, 1978. Evaluation of injured commercial potato samples for total glycoalkaloid contents. J. Fd. Sci., 43: 1617.

Fricker, A., 1970. Untersuchungen über die Fettsäurezusammensetzung von Lipiden aus Kartoffeln. Z. Lebensmittelunters. u.- Forsch., 142: 24-30.

Fricker, A., R. Duden & W.D. Koller, 1972. Über die Zusammensetzung einiger Lipidfraktionen von Kartoffeln. Potato Res., 15: 365-373.

Galliard, T., 1968. Aspects of lipid metabolism in higher plants. I. Identification and quantitative determination of the lipids in potato tubers. Phytochemistry, 7: 1907-1914.

Galliard, T., 1973. Lipids of potato tubers. I. Lipid and fatty acid composition of tubers from different varieties of potato. J. Sci. Fd. Agric., 24: 617-622.

Gray, D. & J.K.A. Bleasdale, 1972. The production of potatoes for canning. Bull. Potato Marketing Board, London.

Gray, D. & J.C. Hughes, 1978. Tuber quality. The potato crop: 504-544. Editor: P.M. Harris. Chapman and Hall, London.

Groot, E.H., L.W. Jansen, A. Kentie, H.K. Oosterhuis & H.L.J. Trap, 1947. A new protein in potatoes. Bioch. Biophys. Acta, 1: 410-414.

Gull, D.D., 1960. Chlorophyll and solanine changes in tubers of Solanun tuberosum induced by fluorescent light and a study of solanine toxico-logy by bioassay technique. Ph.D. thesis, Cornell University.

Gull, D.D. & F.M. Isenberg, 1958. Lightburn and off-flavour development in potato tubers exposed to fluorescent lights. Proc. Amer. Soc. Hort. Sci., 71: 446-454.

Harborne, J.B., 1962. The plant polyphenols. VI. The flavonol glycosides of wild and cultivated potatoes. Bioch. J., 84: 100-106.

Hartmans, K.J. & A. van Es, 1974. Onderzoek naar de diepergelegen oorza-ken van de blauwgevoeligheid van aardappelen, I. IBVL-Publikatie 272, IBVL, Wageningen.

Hawkes, J.G., 1978. History of the potato. The potato crop: 1-14. Editor: P.M. Harris. Chapman and Hall, London.

Heisler, E.G., J. Siciliano, S. Krulick, W.L. Porter & J.W. White Jr., 1973. Nitrate and nitrite content of market potatoes. J. Agric. Fd. Chem., 21: 970-973.

Hoff, J.E. & M.D. Castro, 1969. Chemical composition of potato cell wall. J. Agric. Fd. Chem., 17: 1328-1331.

Houghlund, G.V.C., 1966. New conversion table for specific gravity dry matter and starch in potatoes. Am. Potato J., 43: 138.

Hudson, D.E., 1975. The relationship of cell size, intercellular space and specific gravity to bruise depth in potatoes. Am. Potato J., 52: 9-14.

Hughes, J.C., 1975. Factors influencing the quality of ware potatoes. II. Environmental factors. Potato Res., 17: 512-547.

Ifenkwe, O.P., E.J. Allen & D.C.E. Wurr, 1974. Factors affecting the re-lationship between tuber size and dry matter content. Am. Potato J., 51: 233-241.

Jacob, W.C., 1959. Studies on internal black spot of potatoes. Cornell Univ. Agric. Expt. Sta. Mem., 368: 1-86.

Jadhav, S.J. & D.K. Salunkhe, 1974. Effects of certain chemicals on pho-toinduction of chlorophyll and glycoalkaloid synthesis and on sprouting of potato tubers. J. Inst. Can. Sci. Technol. Aliment., 7: 178-182.

Jadhav, S.J. & D.K. Salunkhe, 1975. Formation and control of chlorophyll and glycoalkaloids in tubers of Solanum tuberosum L. and evaluation of glycoalkaloid toxicity. Contribution no. 1777 from Utah Agric. Expt. Sta., published in Adv. in Fd. Res., 21: 308-354.

Jeppsen, R.B., M.T. Wu & D.K. Salunkhe, 1974. Some observations on the
  occurence of chlorophyll and solanine in potato tubers and their control by N[6] Benzyladenine, ethephon and filtered lights. J. Fd. Sci.,
  39: 1059-1061.

Kapoor, A.C., S.L. Desborough & P.H. Li, 1975. Potato tuber proteins and
  their nutritional quality. Potato Res., 18: 469-478.

Keeler, R.F., D. Brown, D.R. Douglas, G.F. Stallknecht & S. Young, 1976.
  Teratogenicity of the Solanum alkaloid Solasodine and of Kennebec potato sprouts in hamsters. Bull. Environm. Contam. Toxicol., 15:
  522-524.

Keijbets, M.J.H., 1974. Pectic substances in the cell wall and the intercellular cohesion of potato tuber tissue during cooking. IBVL-Publikatie 275, IBVL, Wageningen.

Kiesel, A., A. Belozersky, P. Agatow, N. Biwschich & M. Pawlowa, 1934.
  Vergleichende Untersuchungen über Organeiweis von Pflanzen. Hoppe
  Seiler's Z. Physiol. Chem., 226: 73-86.

Kolattukudy, P.E. & B.B. Dean, 1974. Structure, gas chromatographic
  measurement and function of suberin synthesized by potato tuber tissue
  slices. Plant Physiol., 5: 116-121.

Korableva, N.P., E.V. Morozova & L.V. Metlitskii, 1973. Participation of
  phenolic growth inhibitors in the regulation of the dormancy of potato
  tubers and their resistance to Phytophthora infestans. Dokl. Bioch.,
  212: 472-474.

Krauss, A. & H. Marschner, 1975. Einfluss des Calcium-Angebotes auf
  Wachstumsrate und Calcium-Gehalt von Kartoffelknollen. Z. Pflanzenern.
  Bodenk., 3: 317-326.

Krijthe, N., 1955. Observations on the formation and growth of tubers on
  the potato plant. Neth. J. Agric. Sci., 3: 291-304.

Krijthe, N. & G. Hulstein, 1959. Onderzoek aan pootgoedpartijen waarin
  'glas' voorkomt. IBVL-Publikatie Serie A no. 30, IBVL, Wageningen.

Krijthe, N., 1962. Ontwikkeling en groei van aardappelknol en aardappelplant. IBVL-Publikatie 84, IBVL, Wageningen.

Kushman, L.J. & F.L. Haynes Jr., 1971. Influence of intercellular space
  differences due to variety and storage upon tuber specific gravity -
  dry matter relationship. Am. Potato J., 48: 173-181.

Lampitt, L.H. & N. Goldenberg, 1940. The composition of the potato.
  Chem. Ind.: 748-761.

Lange, H. & G. Rosenstock, 1963. Physiologisch-anatomische Studien zum
  Problem der Wundheilung. II. Kansalanalytische Untersuchungen zur
  Theorie des Wundreizes. Beitr. Biol. Pfl., 39: 383-488.

Lehman, R., 1926. Untersuchungen über die Anatomie der Kartoffelknolle,
  unter besonderer Berücksichtigung des Dickenwachstums und der Zell-
  grösse. Planta, 2: 87-131.

Liljemark, A. & E. Widoff, 1960. Greening and solanine development of white potato in fluorescent light. Am. Potato J., 37: 379-389.

Liljenberg, C., A.S. Sandelius & E. Selstam, 1978. Effect of storage in darkness and in light on the content of membrane lipids of potato tubers. Physiol. Plant, 43: 154-159.

Linehau, D.J. & J.C. Hughes, 1969. Texture of cooked potatoes. Relationship between intercellular adhesion and chemical composition of the tuber. J. Sci. Fd. Agric., 20: 113-119.

Ludwig, J.W., 1972. Bepaling van het droge-stofgehalte van aardappelen via onderwaterweging. IBVL-Publikatie 247, IBVL, Wageningen.

Lugt, C., 1960. Second-growth phenomena. Eur. Potato J., 7: 219-227.

McCready, R.M. & W.Z. Hassed, 1947. Separation and quantitative estimation of amylose and amylopectin in potato starch. J. Am. Chem. Soc., 65: 1154-1157.

McDole, R.E. & G.M. McMaster, 1978. Effects of moisture stress and nitrogen fertilization on tuber nitrate-nitrogen content. Am. Potato J., 55: 611-619.

Meinl, G., 1966. Untersuchungen zur Sorten- und Umweltbedingten Variation der Lentizellenanzahl von Kartoffelknollen. Flora B., 156: 419-426.

Meijers, C.P. & G. van Veldhuisen, 1972. De spreiding van onderwater- en soortelijke gewichten van aardappelen. Intern Rapport 376, IBVL, Wageningen.

Mica, B., 1976. Charakteristik der Stärke ausgewählter Kartoffelsorten. II. Gehalt an Phosphor, Kalium und Calcium in der Stärke. Die Stärke, 28: 410-413.

Mondy, N.I. & R.L. Koch, 1978a. Effect of mechanical injury on the lipid content and quality of potatoes. J. Fd. Sci., 43: 1622-1623.

Mondy, N.I. & R.L. Koch, 1978b. Effect of potato virus x on enzymatic darkening and lipid content of potatoes. J. Fd. Sci., 43: 703-705.

Mondy, N.I. & R.L. Koch, 1978c. Influence of nitrogen fertilization on potato discoloration in relation to chemical composition. I. Lipid, potassium and dry matter content. J. Agric. Fd. Chem., 26: 666-669.

Mondy, N.I. & T.O. Mueller, 1977. Potato discoloration in relation to anatomy and lipid composition. J. Fd. Sci., 42: 14-18.

Mueller, T.O. & N.I. Mondy, 1977. Effect of sprout inhibition on the lipid composition of potatoes. J. Fd. Sci., 42: 618-621.

Mulder, E.G., 1956. Effect of mineral nutrition of potato plants on the biochemistry and the physiology of the tuber. Neth. J. Agric. Sci., 4: 333-356.

Mulder, E.G. & K. Bakema, 1956. Effect of the nitrogen, phosphorus, potassium and magnesium nutrition of potato plants on the content of free amino acids and on the amino acid composition of the protein of tubers. Pl. Soil, 7: 135-166.

Müller, K., 1975. Veränderungen wertgebender Inhaltsstoffe in der Kartoffelpflanze und -Knolle. Hefte für den Kartoffelbau no. 17, Hamburg.

Nagy, D., W. Weidlein & R.H. Hixon, 1941. Factors affecting the solubility of corn protein. Cereal Chem., 18: 514-522.

Neuberger, A. & F. Sanger, 1942. The nitrogen of the potato. Bioch. J., 36: 662-671.

Neukom, H., R. Amadò & M. Pfister, 1980. Neuere Erkentnisse auf dem Gebiete der Pektinstoffe. Lebensm.-Wiss. u. - Technol., 13: 1-6.

Oser, B.L., 1959. An integrated essential amino acid index for predicting the biological value of proteins. In: Protein and amino acid nutrition: 281-295. Editor: A.A. Albanese. Academic Press, New York.

Paauw, F. van der & J. Ris, 1955. De betekenis van de kalitoestand van aardappelen op de kleigrond in Noord-Holland. Versl. Landbouwk. Onderz., 61.6, 's-Gravenhage.

Painter, C.G. & J. Augustin, 1976. The effect of soil moisture and nitrogen on yield and quality of the Russet Burbank potato. Am. Potato J., 53: 275.

Patil, B.C., D.K. Salunkhe & B. Singh, 1971. Metabolism of solanine and chlorophyll in potato tubers as affected by light and specific chemicals. J. Fd. Sci., 36: 474-476.

Pisareva, M.F., 1955. Content of fluroine in some food products of Kazakhstan. Vest. Akad. Nauk. Kazakh. SSR, 11 (10): 86-89.

Plaisted, P.H., 1957. Growth of the potato tuber. Plant Physiol., 32: 445-453.

Pol, G. & A.I. Labib, 1963. De voedingswaarde van aardappelen van verschillende rassen en de invloed daarop van bemesting en bewaring. Voeding, 83: 479-499.

Porter, W.L., T.J. Fitzpatrick & E.A. Talley, 1964. Studies on the relationship of specific gravity to total solids of potatoes. Am. Potato J., 41: 329-336.

Posternak, T., 1951. On the phosphorus of potato starch. J. Biol. Chem., 188: 317-325.

Putz, B., G. Tegge & W. Kempf, 1978. Untersuchungen über den Einfluss von Umwelt, Sorte und Düngung auf die Korngrösse der Kartoffelstärke. Die Stärke, 30: 52-56.

Reeve, R.M., 1967. A review of cellular structure, starch and texture qualities of processed potatoes. Econ. Bot., 21: 294-308.

Reeve, R.M., E. Hautala & M.L. Weaver, 1969a. Anatomy and compositional variation within potatoes. I. Developmental histology of the tuber. Am. Potato J., 46: 361-373.

Reeve, R.M., E. Hautala & M.L. Weaver, 1969b. Anatomy and compositional variation within potatoes. II. Phenolics, enzymes and other minor components. Am. Potato J., 46: 347-386.

Reeve, R.M., E. Hautala & M.L. Weaver, 1970. Anatomy and compositional variation within potatoes. III. Gross compositional gradients. Am. Potato J., 47: 148-162.

Reeve, R.M., H. Timm & M.L. Weaver, 1971. Cell size in Russet Burbank potato tubers with various levels of nitrogen and soil moisture tensions. Am. Potato J., 48: 450-456.

Reeve, R.M., H. Timm & M.L. Weaver, 1973a. Parenchyma cell growth in potato tubers. I. Different tuber regions. Am. Potato J., 50: 49-57.

Reeve, R.M., H. Timm & M.L. Weaver, 1973b. Parenchyma cell growth in potato tubers. II. Cell division vs. cell enlargement. Am. Potato J., 50: 71-78.

Reeve, R.M., H. Timm & M.L. Weaver, 1973c. Cell wall thickness during growth of domestic and foreign potato cultivars. Am. Potato J., 50: 204-211.

Rexen, B., 1976. Studies of protein of potatoes. Potato Res., 19: 189-202.

Rosenstock, G., 1963. Physiologische und anatomische Studien zum Problem der Wundheilung. I. Untersuchungen über Zusammenhänge zwischen dem Wassergehalt verletzten Kartoffelparenchyms und dessen Vernarbungsreaktionen nebst Bemerkungen zur Theorie des Wundreizes. Beitr. Biol. Pfl., 38: 275-319.

Ruddick, J.A., J. Harwig & P.M. Scott, 1974. Nonteratogenicity in rats of blighted potatoes and compounds contained in them. Teratology, 9: 165-168.

Rumpf, G., 1972. Gaschromatographische Bestimmung löslicher Inhaltsstoffe in bestrahlten und mit chemischen Keimhemmungsmitteln behandelten Kartoffeln. Potato Res., 15: 236-245.

Salaman, R.N., 1926. Potato varieties. Cambr. Univ. Press: 378.

Salunkhe, D.K., M.T. Wu & S.J. Jadhav, 1972. Effects of light and temperature on the formation of solanine in potato slices. J. Fd. Sci., 37: 969-970.

Samotus, B., 1958. Studies on variations in the level of starch, sugars and phosphorus in potato tubers in the vegetation period. Zesz. Nank. Wyzsz. Szk. voln. Krakow, 5: 117-149.

Samotus, B. & S. Schwimmer, 1963. Changes in carbohydrate and phosphorus content of potato tubers during storage in nitrogen. J. Fd. Sci., 28: 163-167.

Schaller, K. & A. Amberger, 1974. Zusammenhänge zwischen den für die Blaufleckigkeit der Kartoffelknolle verantwortlichen Inhaltsstoffen. Qual. Plant. - Pl. Fds. Hum. Nutr., XXIV: 191-198.

Scheele, C. von, G. Svensson & J. Rasmussen, 1935. Om bestämming an potatisens. Stärkelse och torrsubstanshalt med tilhjälp av dess specifika vikt. Nord. Jordbr. Forsk.: 17-37.

Scheele, C. von, G. Svensson & J. Rasmussen, 1937. Die Bestimmung des Stärkegehaltes und der Trockensubstanz der Kartoffel mit Hilfe des spezifischen Gewichts. Landw. Vers. Sta., 127: 67-96.

Schippers, P.A., 1968. The influence of rates of nitrogen and potassium application on the yield and specific gravity of four potato varieties. Potato Res., 11: 23-33.

Schippers, P.A., 1976. The relationship between specific gravity and percentage dry matter in potato tubers. Am. Potato J., 53: 111-122.

Seibler, T.S., 1979. Studies on potato proteins. Am. Potato J., 56: 415-425.

Sinden, S.L., 1972. Effect of light and mechanical injury on the glycoalkaloid content of greening resistant potato tubers. Am. Potato J., 49: 368.

Sinden, S.L., K.L. Deahl & B.B. Aulenbach, 1976. Effect of glycoalkaloids and phenolics on potato flavour. J. Fd. Sci., 41: 520-523.

Sinden, S.L. & R.E. Webb, 1972. Effect of variety and location on the glycoalkaloid content of potatoes. Am. Potato J., 49: 334-338.

Sizer, C.E., J.A. Maga & C.J. Craven, 1980. Total glycoalkaloids in potatoes and potato chips. J. Agric. Fd. Chem., 28: 578-579.

Slack, E.B., 1948. Nitrogenous constituents of the potato. Nature, Lond., 161: 211-212.

Sneep, J., D.E. van der Zaag & W. Scheijgrond, 1980. 55^e Beschrijvende Rassenlijst voor Landbouwgewassen 1980. RIVRO, Wageningen.

Stegemann, H., 1975. Properties of and physiological changes in storage proteins. Chemistry and biochemistry of plant proteins. Editors: J.B. Harborne and C.F. van Sumere. Phytochemic. Soc. Symposia II. Acad. Press.

Synge, R.L.M., 1977. Free amino acids of potato tubers: A survey of published results set out according to potato variety. Potato Res., 20: 1-7.

Talburt, W.F. & O. Smith, 1967. Potato processing. Avi Publishing Company, Westport, Connecticut.

Talley, E.A., T.J. Fitzpatrick & W.L. Porter, 1970. Chemical composition of potatoes. VIII. Effect of variety, location and year of growth on the content of nitrogen compounds. Am. Potato J., 47: 231-244.

Tegge, G., B. Putz & H.D. Keitmann, 1976. Einfluss von Sorte und Standort auf die Viskositätseigenschaften von Kartoffelstärke. Die Stärke, 28: 130-135.

Temme, J., 1970. Kaliumvoorziening van de aardappel. Landb. Techn. Ber. NKIM, no. 4: 1-76. Amsterdam.

Toma, R.B., J. Augustin, J. Shaw, R.H. True & J.M. Hogan, 1978. Proximate composition of freshly harvested and stored potatoes (Solanum tuberosum L.). J. Fd. Sci., 43: 1702-1704.

Tourneau, D.J. le, 1956. Carbohydrate compounds of the potato tuber. J. Agric. Fd. Chem., 4: 543-545.

True, R.H., J.M. Hogan, J. Augustin, S.J. Johnson, C. Teitzel, R.B. Toma & R.L. Shaw, 1978. Mineral composition of freshly harvested potatoes. Am. Potato J., 55: 511-519.

Verma, S.C., V.P. Malhotra, K.C. Joshi & T.R. Sharma, 1971. Specific gravity and dry matter content of potato. Potato Res., 14: 94-95.

Warren, D.S. & J.S. Woodman, 1974. The texture of cooked potatoes: A review. J. Sci. Fd. Agric., 25: 129-138.

Weaver, M.L., H. Timm, M. Nonaka, R.N. Sayre, R.M. Reeve, R.M. McCready & L.C. Whitehand, 1978. Potato composition. I. Tissue selection and its effect on solids content and amylose/amylopectin ratios. Am. Potato J., 55 (2): 73-82.

White, R.P., D.C. Munro & J.B. Anderson, 1974. Nitrogen, potassium and plant spacing effects on yield, tuber size, specific gravity and tissue N., P and K of Netted Gem potatoes. Can. J. Plant Sci.: 535.

Whitehead, T., T.P. McIntosh & W.M. Findlay, 1953. The potato in health and disease. Oliver and Boyd, Edinburg.

Wigginton, M.J., 1973. Diffusion of oxygen through lenticells in potato tuber. Potato Res., 16: 85-87.

Wu, M.T. & D.K. Salunkhe, 1977a. Inhibition of wound induced glyco-alkaloid formation in potato tubers (Solanum tuberosum L.) by isopropyl-N-(3-chlorophenyl)-carbamate. J. Fd. Sci., 42: 622-624.

Wu, M.T. & D.K. Salunkhe, 1977b. Use of spray lecithin for control of greening and glycoalkaloid formation of potato tubers. J. Fd. Sci., 42: 1413-1415.

Wurr, D.C.E., J.N. Bean & E.J. Allen, 1978. Effect of variety and date of harvest on the tuber dry matter percentage of potatoes. J. Agric. Sci. Camb., 90: 597-604.

Zaag, D.E. van der, 1970. Groei, morfologie en anatomie van de aardappel-knol (vervolg). De Pootaardappelwereld, 1-5.

Zitnak, A., 1953. The influence of certain treatments upon solanine synthesis in potatoes. M.S. Thesis Univ. of Alberta, Edmonton, Alberta, Canada.

2 Sugars and starch during tuberization, storage and sprouting

A. van Es and K.J. Hartmans

2.1 Introduction

Sugars (carbohydrates) are produced in plants in large quantities by photosynthesis and constitute the principal source of energy for respiration and the initial substratum for the formation of many carbohydrate and non-carbohydrate cell components. The reserve material (starch) in the potato cells consists mainly of carbohydrate polymers.

The reducing sugar content is very important where potatoes are processed into fried products. On frying, the potatoes darken owing to the reaction between the reducing groups (the aldehyde groups) of the sugars and the amino groups of the amino acids; this is known as the Maillard reaction (Van der Schaaf, 1974). This darkening may be so intense as to greatly reduce the value of the end product. During this darkening process, many intermediate products, which subsequently polymerize, are formed. Apart from the intense darkening and associated bitter taste, proteins and amino acids, including the essential ones, are removed from the product, thus decreasing its nutritional value.

Research has shown that 2.5 to 3 mg per gram fresh weight must be regarded as the maximum permissible level of reducing sugars for crisping. The limit is about 5 mg per gram fresh weight for chipping.

The main carbohydrates involved here are as follows:

Sugars: Glucose: ⓖ
     Fructose: [F]
     Sucrose: ⓖ - [F]

The starch is formed from these sugars, and accounts for 60 to 80 % (average 70 %) of the dry matter content of the potato. The starch in turn is composed of 21 to 25 % amylose and 75 to 79 % amylopectin, polymers of glucose which can be represented diagrammatically as follows:

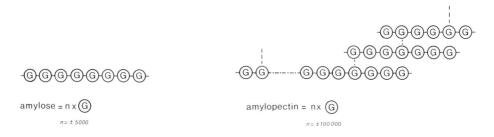

amylose = n x ⓖ

n = ± 5000

amylopectin = n x ⓖ

n = ± 100 000

82

Both glucose and fructose have a free reducing group, and this is why they are known as reducing sugars. These groups are not free in sucrose, owing to the bonding of glucose and fructose to each other, and sucrose is therefore not reducing.

Amylose is a straight chain of glucose units, while amylopectin includes many branches of about 20 glucose units. The relative proportions of amylose and amylopectin are rather constant, and this is a characteristic feature of potato starch.

2.2 Tuberization; second growth

Tuberization

To understand the formation of sugars in potatoes during storage, it is useful to have a diagrammatic representation of the formation of the sugars and the associated starch level during tuberization. It is known that dry matter is synthesized during plant growth by means of photosynthesis (Fig. 2.1). When leaves are exposed to light, carbon dioxide from the atmosphere accumulates in the leaves. Water and minerals are taken up

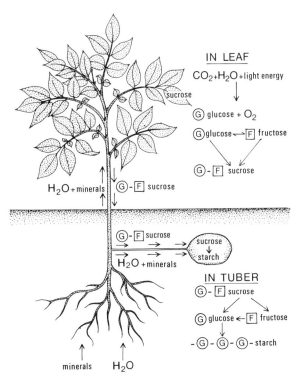

Fig. 2.1. Starch production in potato tubers due to photosynthesis and sucrose transport.

from the soil by the roots and transported to the leaves. The reducing sugar (glucose) is then formed in the leaf by the reaction:

Carbon dioxide (CO_2) + water (H_2O) + light energy → glucose ($C_6H_{12}O_6$) + oxygen (O_2).

During tuberization, the glucose has to be transported through the stem to the tuber, where starch is formed from n x glucose. Since the plant is virtually unable to transport glucose, sucrose is formed enzymatically by partial conversion of glucose into fructose, also a reducing sugar, and the coupling of the two sugars. The non-reducing sugar, sucrose, is transported to the tuber. Hence the sucrose from the sucrose 'store' in the cytoplasm or cell sap on the boundary of the membrane surrounding the incipient starch grain is split up again into the original glucose and fructose by means of the enzyme sucrose synthetase (the enzyme here has the opposite splitting effect). The fructose is again transformed into glucose inside the starch grain, and is then polymerized to starch.

During tuberization, the splitting of sucrose in the cytoplasm into glucose and fructose by the enzyme invertase is blocked because this en-

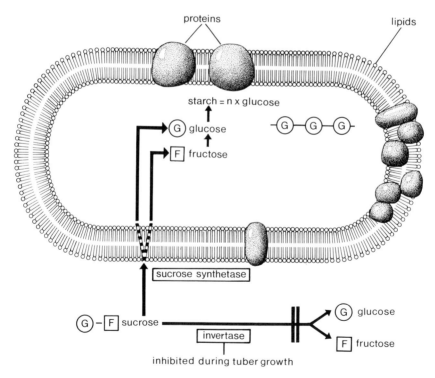

Fig. 2.2. Schematic drawing of the starch synthesizing mechanism during tuber growth. The starch grain is surrounded by a membrane, composed of lipids and proteins.

zyme is then strongly inhibited (Fig. 2.2). Conversion of sucrose into glucose and fructose by means of sucrose synthetase, followed by the formation of starch, can take place uninhibited. Sweetening due to splitting into glucose and fructose in the cytoplasm, one of the factors causing darkening during processing, does not occur.

Hence the entire process of sugar formation in the leaves, conveyance to the tuber and transport through the membrane (which consists of a lipid bilayer surrounding the starch grain) is utilized to make starch or to produce dry matter in general. From the stage of formation in the leaf to that of incorporation in the tuber, the process is based upon equilibria, the permeability of the membrane being an important parameter here. The equilibria of the concentrations of carbohydrates over the membranes are subject to variation during the formation and subsequent storage of the tuber. The amount of sugars in the cell sap in equilibrium with the amount of starch formed in the starch grains is largely a matter of variety, although the conditions of tuber formation - e.g., light, temperature, moisture availability, minerals and the type of soil - are also relevant. Sucrose is thus always supplied during tuberization. For this reason the sucrose level during tuber formation is higher than in the final phase at full maturity. During tuber initiation, the sucrose content is about 15 mg per gram or more of the fresh weight. It decreases constantly with increasing maturity to about 2 mg (Burton, 1978b).

Glucose and fructose levels are also higher in immature tubers than in mature ones. However, in this case the minimum is apparently already reached about half way through the period of tuber formation. A concen-

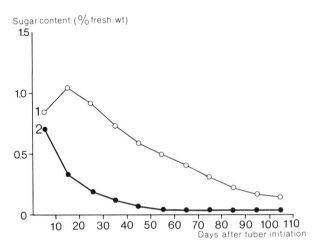

Fig. 2.3. Sucrose and reducing sugar content of potato tubers related to the time elapsed after tuber initiation; 1: average for sucrose content; 2: for reducing sugar content (from Burton and Wilson, 1970).

85

tration of 1 mg per gram fresh weight was measured at this minimum point; see Fig. 2.3 (Burton and Wilson, 1970).

Second growth

Second growth may be induced when after a period of growth inhibition of the tubers due to 'stress' (see also Chapter 1), there is renewal of growth of these tubers at the top. New stolon growth at the apex may also occur, followed by tuberization of these stolons (see also Fig. 1.3, Chapter 1). The dry matter for this process may be supplied by renewed synthesis of carbohydrates in the leaves, but may in part also be with-drawn from the already existing tubers. The level of reducing sugars, and usually also of sucrose, increases in the remaining glassy structure at the stem end, where the dry matter content may decline to about 6 % (Iritani and Weller, 1973).

2.3 Effect of previous history of the potato on sugar content during storage

Burton (1969) states that the variation of the sugar content during storage at high temperatures depends on variety, location and environ-mental factors during growth, age of the tuber, maturity and the storage conditions preceding actual cold storage. He also reports that the reaction of the tubers to cold storage depends on the metabolic equili-brium at the moment of starting the low temperature storage. In parti-cular, the effects of soil, manuring, light and water supply are extre-mely difficult to predict. A kind of stress theory has recently evolved. According to this theory, all factors disturbing the metabolic equili-brium in the plant (stress factors) give rise to an increase in the sugar content. The main factors involved, however, are probably variety, and to a lesser extent maturity, as reflected in the sucrose content at the time of lifting (Sowokinos, 1973).

2.3.1 Influence of variety

Van Vliet and Schriemer (1960), using 12 different varieties grown under identical conditions, showed that there were differences in maximum reducing sugar levels, ranging from 5.9 mg to 26.5 mg per gram fresh weight when the potatoes were stored at 2 °C. The sucrose content varied from 4.3 mg to 14.9 mg per gram fresh weight. Approximately the same values were measured in a different year. The order of the varieties as regards sugar content was in good agreement in the two years. Samotus et al. (1974) also reported that sugar formation in a number of Polish va-rieties stored at 1, 2 and 6 °C for 18 to 22 weeks was correlated with variety. Sowokinos (1973) states that the sugar content of potatoes during tuberization and at the time of lifting is largely dependent on variety

86

even under virtually identical growing conditions from year to year at
specific locations in the USA. He also found that the response of potatoes to storage at low temperatures is a typical varietal characteristic
and is connected with the sugar content at the beginning of storage. It
was found that for a given degree of maturity, at the time when 97 % of
maximum tuber size and maximum starch content were attained, there were
differences in the sucrose content ranging from 1.9 to 4.5 mg per gram of
tuber fresh weight. The main differences between varieties in terms of
suitability for processing as potato products at full maturity were found
in the final concentrations of sucrose.

2.3.2 *Maturity; sugar content on lifting*

Tuber maturity is very imporant for the sugar content at the beginning
of the storage period and its variation during storage. It is one of the
most important parameters, determining the potato quality for processing.
However, one problem is the precise definition of maturity and its
determination in a batch of tubers. In other words, the term 'maturity'
is only vaguely defined and can give rise to a great deal of confusion.
It is often related to the degree of suberization or cork formation of
the skin. The problem is that suberization is also affected by such factors as destruction of the haulm prior to lifting, soil temperature and
soil moisture content.
Sowokinos (1973) relates the concept of physiological maturity to the
moment when 97 % of the final tuber size and starch content is reached.
Wiese et al. (1975) observed a fall in the reducing sugar content at the
end of flowering. This decline continues until the haulm wilts. The reducing sugar content is than at a minimum, while the starch content is at a
maximum. Here again, the concept of physiological maturity is related to
carbohydrate levels. Burton (1966) also states that, apart from varietal
differences affecting sugar content, maturity may be one of the principal
factors. He describes maturity as a condition preceding destruction of
the haulm when the tuber is no longer growing and when the total sugar
content is no longer declining (Burton, 1978b). However, he also states
that this definition is of little use for practical purposes, as 'growth'
then has to be measured and sugars always have to be determined. In the
absence of laboratory facilities, he recommends the old practical test of
maturity by using the thumb to apply a tangential force to 'scrape off'
the skin of the tuber prior to destruction of the haulm. If this is no
longer possible, the skin is set and the tuber is assumed to be mature.
The foliage also gives an indication of maturity: if many leaves have
wilted naturally, the tuber is probably mature. However, the question is
whether maturity determined in these ways is sufficiently correlated with
physiological maturity at the time of minimum sugar content.

Sowokinos (1977), dealing with the quality of potatoes to be stored for crisping and chipping, indirectly related the reducing sugar content to the sucrose content at the time of lifting. The basis here is the fact that the sucrose content at the time of 'maturity for processing' is minimum and can be used as a quality criterion in the relevant year, apart from the effects of variety. Potatoes with a low sucrose content would then be more suitable for storage and processing. The higher the sucrose content at the time of lifting, the faster reducing sugars are formed during storage. The sucrose content should not exceed 2.8 mg per gram of fresh tuber weight for crisping potatoes and 3.5 mg for chipping potatoes. Tests with this system under Dutch conditions have hitherto not been very successful.

Recent research into the 'quality' of the membranes which surround the starch grains and separate the starch from the sugars in the cytoplasm may provide a better understanding of the notion of maturity in relation to sugar formation. It has already been found that sugar formation in senescence is associated with the reduction in 'quality' of these membranes (Isherwood, 1976).

Workman et al. (1976) observed that storage of potatoes at temperatures of 0 to 5 °C causes an increase in membrane permeability. The work of Isherwood (1973) and Ohad et al. (1971) also indicates that the 'quality'

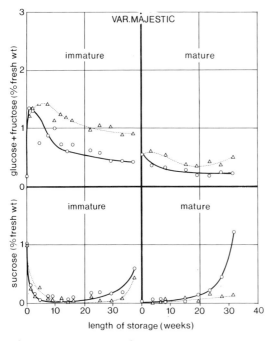

Fig. 2.4. Changes in the content of sugar of immature and mature tubers of the variety Majestic stored over 30 weeks. Δ —— Δ = storage at 10 °C; O———O = storage at 20 °C (from Burton, 1965).

of the membranes is associated with the maturity and 'behaviour' of the potato in terms of sugar formation during cold storage. The importance of maturity is clearly demonstrated by Fig. 2.4 (Burton, 1965). The immature potatoes were harvested on 16th June and the mature ones on 2nd October. Sometimes the reducing sugar content of immature potatoes at the time of lifting is sufficiently low (about 3 mg per gram fresh weight) but increases sharply a few days later (about 13 mg per gram fresh weight).

2.3.3 Other environmental factors - 'stress'

Apart from the temperature prior to storage, little can be said about the other factors affecting cold storage - soil, manuring, environment, water supply and age of the tuber, as the results differ.

As stated, it seems that any factor disturbing the overall metabolic balance under certain conditions may have a negative effect. Factors resulting in such a 'physiological stress situation' include high temperatures during certain growth periods, lack of moisture, the heat sum of days when the temperature remains below 10 °C (Findlen, 1964) and early dying off due to lack of minerals.

2.3.4 Temperatures prior to cold storage

The temperatures to which the potatoes are exposed before cold storage may affect the eventual variation of the sugar content. Burton (1969)

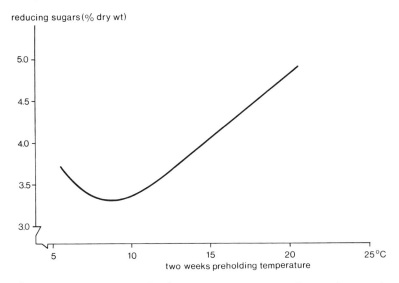

Fig. 2.5. Average reducing sugar content after six months in storage at 5.6 °C (from Iritani et al., 1976).

found that with newly harvested potatoes, if the temperature in the store was gradually reduced, the amount of sugars formed was much less. Findlen (1964) found that it was inadvisable to leave the potatoes in the ground for too long before lifting after destruction of the haulm. If the soil temperature is low, the crisps will have a very dark colour.

Iritani and Weller (1976) showed that a great deal can go wrong in a 14-day period preceding the commencement of final storage at low temperature. If the temperature during this period is higher or lower than 9 to 10 °C, the level of reducing sugars will be much higher later on - in this case, after six months' cold storage at 5.6 °C; (Fig. 2.5).

According to Burton (1969), however, a gradual reduction from 10 to 2 °C, leads to a permanent reduction in the sugar content.

2.4 VARIATIONS IN SUGAR CONTENT DURING STORAGE

The foregoing shows that the potatoe itself (in particular, the variety, maturity and previous history) already has a very significant effect on storage behaviour. Besides this, several clearly distinguishable mechanisms of sugar formation may operate during storage. These concern differences in 'behaviour' associated with the effects of storage at high and low temperatures, senescence and sprouting and possible sprout inhibition. These effects are discussed separately below. In reality, however, two or more of these effects will nearly always occur more or less simultaneously, thus making the overall picture very complex.

2.4.1 Storage at high temperatures

Lately, more emphasis has been placed on storage at high temperatures. This is often necessary in the warmer developing countries, where mechanically cooled stores and sufficient trained staff are not usually available.

Verma et al. (1974a, 1974b) found that potatoes can be stored just as well, as regards sugar content, at temperatures ranging from 24.7 to 36.2 °C. Total sugar content increases at these temperatures just as in the case of cold storage, but the increase is smaller. On transfer to higher temperatures, the total sugar content initially increased sharply, but then fell back to virtually the original level. Just as with cold storage, the reducing sugar content also increased, although only slightly at first, compared with cold storage. Towards the end of the period of cold storage, however, the reducing sugar content increased to 1.2 %. Loss of dry matter and also rotting increased sharply at high storage temperatures. Hak and Vermeer (1979) found that even a product which was not fully mature and sufficiently hardened could be stored at up to 20 °C for about four months if CIPC was applied in combination with the fungicide thiabendazole at the right time - i.e., after suberization and wound healing. The quantitative and qualitative losses could then be limited.

2.4.2 Storage at low temperatures

Sugar formation at low temperatures differs from that due to senescence in that the resulting sugar content can be decreased again by reconditioning - i.e., treatment at higher temperatures - although the original level is no longer attained (Burton, 1975). Reversible changes in composition of the membranes surrounding the starch grains may also be involved in this process. The mechanism of sugar formation at low temperatures is illustrated in Fig. 2.6. Sugar formation is plotted against temperature in Fig. 2.7 (Burton, 1965). This figure clearly shows that below 10 °C both reducing sugars (glucose and fructose) and non-reducing sugars (sucrose) are formed to an increasing degree.

In mature potatoes, the sucrose content and the glucose and fructose levels are found to respond differently to an increase in temperature from 2 to 10 °C (Isherwood, 1976). Sucrose responds with a fairly sharp decline in level, whereas the decline is gradual with glucose and fructose.

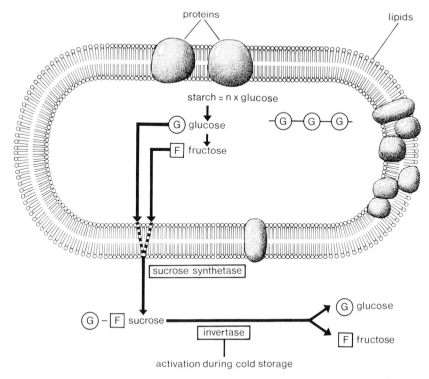

Fig. 2.6. Schematic drawing of the breakdown of starch into sugars during storage.

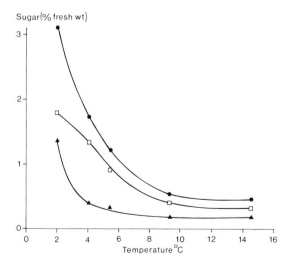

Fig. 2.7. Low temperature sweetening: sugar contents of potato tubers (cv. Majestic) after storage for 4 weeks (17th Dec.-14th Jan.) at different temperatures. ● ── ● = total sugar; □ ── □ = glucose + fructose; ▲──── ▲ = sucrose (from Burton, 1965).

In immature potatoes, the sucrose level is much lower and the glucose and fructose (reducing sugars) levels are much higher. However, in this case the sugars respond virtually identically to an increase in temperature to 10 °C. This suggests that sucrose on the one hand and glucose and fructose on the other occur in better separated compartments in the cell in mature potatoes than in immature potatoes.

2.4.3 Increase in sugar content due to senescence

The increase in sugar content due to senescence is a separate phenomenon. In conditions of constant temperature, the sugar content remains relatively constant for a certain time, and then increases, at first slowly and finally very sharply. This is clearly illustrated in Fig. 2.8 (Barker, 1938).

It is characteristic of this sugar formation that it is not reversible. Reconditioning measures are ineffective (Isherwood, 1976). This sugar formation, called 'senescent sweetening' by Burton (1966), is characterized by changes in the membranes surrounding the starch grains (Isherwood and Burton, 1975). In popular terms, the membranes may be said to have become 'leaky' (Fig. 2.9). Glucose and fructose originating from the breakdown of starch enter the cell sap to an increasing degree. The rate and extent of this sweetening depends on variety. The history of the potato during growth and at the time of lifting is also relevant (Dwelle and Stallknecht, 1978). There seems to be some connection with the sprout-

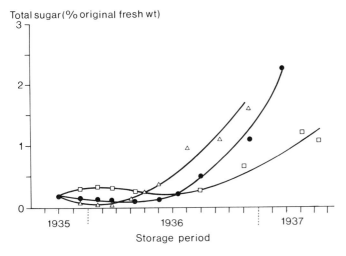

Total sugar (% original fresh wt)

Storage period

Fig. 2.8. Senescent sweetening of potato tubers (cv. King Edward) after prolonged storage at 7.5 °C (□ —— □) and less prolonged storage at 10 °C (● —— ●) and 15 °C (Δ —— Δ) (from Burton, 1966; adapted from Barker, 1938).

ing potential: sugar formation is stated to be higher the greater this potential (Burton, 1965). The only effect of sprouting control in this case is to increase the 'accumulation' of the sugars (Burton, 1965). The same applies to potato irradiation.

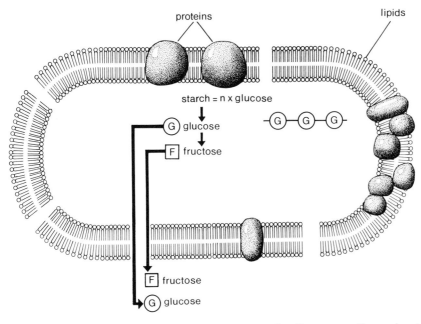

proteins   lipids

starch = n x glucose

Ⓖ glucose
F fructose

F fructose
Ⓖ glucose

Fig. 2.9. Schematic drawing of 'leakage' of sugars through starch grain membranes due to senescence.

How then can this senescent sweetening be counteracted? It has been found that the process can be delayed by storing the potatoes at progressively lower temperatures. This is, however, of no practical help, as low-temperature sugar formation will then occur, which, while in principle reversible, will at least partially also be affected by senescence.

2.4.4 Changes due to sprouting and sprout suppression

Sprouting is usually associated with the mobilization and transport of carbohydrates to the sprout. The transporting sugar is once again sucrose. Desprouting, IPC/CIPC treatment and inhibition by gamma irradiation thus greatly increase the sucrose content, as this sugar can no longer be translocated (Burton et al., 1959; Van Vliet and Schriemer; 1963; Isherwood and Burton, 1975); Fig. 2.10.

Fig. 2.10 also shows an increase in the glucose and fructose contents from less than 1 mg to 5 mg and 3 mg respectively in the untreated group during the course of sprouting over a 17-week period.

The increase in glucose and fructose levels is found to be somewhat smaller in the group treated with CIPC.

Sugar content (mg/g fresh wt)

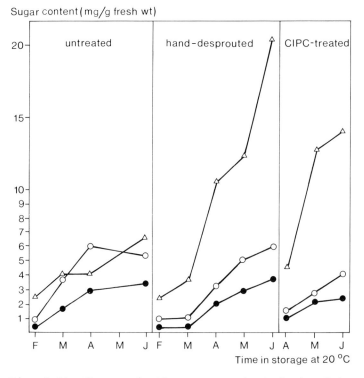

Fig. 2.10. Changes in the sugar content during late storage; Δ —— Δ = sucrose; 0 —— 0 = glucose; ● —— ● = fructose. Type of treatment indicated appropriately on graphs (from Isherwood and Burton, 1975).

The sucrose content also increases substantially in the case of irradiation. Where, however, the increase due, for example, to storage is already considerable, irradiation has little effect. The later in the season the potatoes are irradiated, the more the reducing sugars are also likely to increase (Burton, 1975).

2.4.5 Reconditioning

In potato reconditioning, the temperature is increased to 10 to 20 °C in an attempt to decrease the reducing sugar content, which has become too high as a result of cold storage. During this process, a high proportion of the reducing sugar content is for 80 % converted into starch, the remaining 20 % is lost in respiration. The sugars present, however, are for several reasons found to be incompletely eliminated by reconditioning. Burton found in 1975 that potatoes which had first been stored cold for four weeks and then kept for 90 days at 10 °C had a higher sugar content than potatoes stored constantly at 10 °C. The work of Isherwood (1976) and Iritani and Weller (1978) showed that in general only those sugars formed by cold storage could be reconditioned. Sugars arising from senescence of the potato - i.e., later in the storage season - could not be reconditioned. It was found that the factors involved in the development of a high sugar content are also partly responsible for difficulties with reconditioning. On the one hand, reconditioning is easier the later in the storage season it is carried out, probably by virtue of sprouting and the associated increase in respiration. On the other hand, Burton and Wilson (1978) point out that the required decrease may not then occur, because of senescence. The problem is to find the exact time at which sprouting, respiration and senescence are in optimum balance for good reconditioning.

The foregoing applies to potatoes lifted when mature. Yamaguchi (1959) found that relatively immature potatoes were harder to recondition.

2.4.6 Controlled atmosphere storage

Prevention is better than cure. Rather than resorting to reconditioning, with variable results, it would be better, if possible, to store the potatoes under conditions which would as far as possible limit the formation of sugars, and in particular of reducing sugars. This means storage in an atmosphere made up of gases other than air - 'controlled atmosphere' (CA) storage. This system has, however, had little practical use so far. Burton (1978a) comes to the following conclusions in a review of the literature: Investigation of the effect of low O_2 concentrations shows that the system of sucrose synthesis no longer operates under anaerobic conditions, such as storage in a nitrogen atmosphere. Sugar

formation at low temperatures (0 °C) declines sharply or ceases altogether. An oxygen content of 1.2 % is just as effective as anaerobic
storage and also decreases the reducing sugar content. An O_2 level of
5 %, however, is much less effective (Workman and Twoney, 1970). Experiments with higher than normal atmospheric O_2 concentrations (Harkett,
1971) resulted in more sugar formation than with storage in air. CO_2
concentrations of 5 to 20 % initially reduce sugar formation at low
temperatures, but it increases after a few months to such an extent that
the content is higher than with storage in normal air. The effect is thus
highly complex. Moreover, concentrations exceeding 10 % may cause partial
tissue necrosis.

Burton (1969) found that sugar formation could be limited by storage
at temperatures varied daily from 2 to 10 °C. The cost of repeated cooling and the moisture loss due to cooling from 10 to 2 °C were so high as
to rule out any practical application.

References

Barker, J., 1938. Changes in sugar content and respiration in potatoes
    stored at different temperatures. Rep. Fd. Invest. Bd., Londen,
    1937: 175-177.
Burton, W.G., T. Horne & D.B. Powess, 1959. The effect of γ-irradiation
    upon the sugar content of potatoes. Eur. Potato J., 2: 105-116.
Burton, W.G., 1965. The sugar balance in some British potato varieties
    during storage. I Preliminairy observations. Eur. Potato J. 8: 80-91.
Burton, W.G., 1966. The potato, Veenman, Wageningen.
Burton, W.G., 1969. The sugar balance in some British potato varieties
    during storage. II The effect of tuber age, previous storage tempe-
    rature and intermittent refrigeration upon low-temperature sweetening.
    Eur. Potato J., 12: 81-95.
Burton, W.G. & A.R. Wilson, 1970. The apparent effect of the latitude
    of the place of cultivation upon the sugar content of potatoes grown
    in Great Britain. Potato Res., 13: 269-283.
Burton, W.G., 1975. The immediate effect of gamma irradiation upon
    the sugar content of potatoes previously stored at 2, 4, 5, 6, 10
    and 15.5 °C. Potato Res., 18: 109-115.
Burton, W.G., 1978 (a). The physics and physiology of storage. The
    potato crop; Editor P.M. Harris; Chapman and Hall, London.
Burton, W.G., 1978 (b). Post-harvest behaviour and storage of potatoes.
    Applied Biology, vol. III. Editor T.H. Coaker, Academic Press, London,
    New York, San Francisco.
Burton, W.G. & A.R. Wilson, 1978. The sugar content and sprout growth
    of tubers of potato Cultivar Record, grown in different localities,
    when stored at 10, 2 and 20 °C. Potato Res., 21: 145-162.

Dwelle, R.B. & G.F. Stallknecht, 1978. Respiration and sugar content
    of potato tubers as influenced by storage temperature. Am. Potato
    J., 561-571.
Findlen, H., 1964. Effect of maturity on the chipping quality of Irish
    Cobbler and Kennebec potatoes. U.S. Dept. of Agric., Market Res.
    Rep. no. 644.
Hak, P.S. & H. Vermeer, 1979. Bewaring van aardappelen bij hoge tempe-
    raturen. IBVL-Rapport 236, IBVL, Wageningen.
Harkett, P.J., 1971. The effect of oxygen concentration on the sugar
    content of potato tubers stored at low temperature. Potato Res.,
    14: 305-311.
Iritani, W.M. & L. Weller, 1973. The development of translucent end
    tubers. Am. Potato J., 50: 223-233.
Iritani, W.M. & L. Weller, 1976. The influence of early storage (pre-
    holding) temperatures on sugar accumulation in Russet Burbank pota-
    toes. Am. Potato J., 53.
Iritani, W.M. & L. Weller, 1978. Factors influencing reconditioning of
    Russet Burbank potatoes. Am. Potato J., 55: 425-430.
Isherwood, F.A., 1973. Effects of changes in storage temperature on the
    metabolism of the potato tuber. Proc. 5th Triennial Conf. Eur. Ass.
    Potato Res., Norwich, 1972: 156-157.
Isherwood, F.A., 1976. Mechanism of starch-sugar interconversion in
    Solanum tuberosum. Phytochemistry, 15: 33-41.
Isherwood, F.A. & W.G. Burton, 1975. The effect of senescence, handling,
    sprouting and chemical sprout suppression upon the respiratory
    quotient of stored potato tubers. Potato Res. 18: 98-104.
Ohad, I., I. Friedberg, Z. Ne'eman & M. Schramm, 1971. Biogenesis and
    degradation of starch. I The fate of the amyloplast membranes during
    maturation and storage of potato tubers. Plant Physiology, 47: 465-477.
Samotus, B., M. Niedźwiedź, Z. Kolodziej, M. Leja & B. Czajkowska, 1974.
    Storage and reconditioning of tubers of Polish potato varieties and
    strains. I Influence of storage temperature on sugar level in potato
    tubers of different varieties and strains. Potato Res., 17: 64-81.
Schaaf, D. van der, 1974. De Maillard reaktie bij het drogen van land-
    bouwprodukten in het algemeen en bij het verwerken van aardappelen
    in het bijzonder (Een literatuurstudie). IBVL-Rapport 38. IBVL,
    Wageningen.
Sowokinos, J.R., 1973. Maturation of Solanum tuberosum. I Comparative
    sucrose and sucrose synthetase levels between several good and poor
    processing varieties. Am. Potato J., 50: 234-247.
Sowokinos, J.R., 1977. Sucrose rating as an index of processing potato
    maturity. Valley Potato Grower, Ann. Rep., 43, no. 101, p.31.

Verma, S.C., T.R. Sharma & S.M. Varma, 1974 (a). Sucrose accumulation during high-temperature storage of potato tubers. Potato Res., 17: 224-226.

Verma, S.C., T.R. Sharma & S.M. Varma, 1974 (b). Effects of extended high temperature storage on weight losses and sugar content of potato tubers. Indian J. Agric. Sci., 44 (11): 702-706.

Vliet, W.F. van & W.H. Schriemer, 1963. High temperature storage of potatoes with the aid of sprout inhibitors. Eur. Potato J., 6 (3). IBVL-Publication no. 92. IBVL, Wageningen.

Wiese W., D. Bommer & C. Patzold, 1975. Einfluss differenzierter Wasserversorgung auf Ertragebildung und Knollenqualität der Kartoffelpflanze (Solanum tuberosum L.). Potato Res., 18: 618-631.

Workman, M. & J. Twoney, 1970. The influence of storage on the physiology and productivity of Kennebec seed potatoes. Am. Potato J., 47: 372-378.

Workman, M., E. Kerschner & M. Harrison, 1976. The effect of storage factors on membrane permeability and sugar content of potatoes and decay by Erwinia Carotovora var. atroseptica and Fursarium Roseum var. sambucinum. Am. Potato J., 53: 191-204.

Yamaguchi, M., 1959. Effect of certain areas of production and storage on chipping quality, chemical composition and specific gravity of California potatoes. Proc. Am. Soc. Hort. Sci., 74: 649-660.

3 Dormancy period, sprouting and sprout inhibition

A. van Es and K.J. Hartmans

In general potatoes remain dormant for a period after harvesting, and can only be made to sprout in this period by specific measures. When the dormancy period is over, sprouting occurs spontaneously and can only be suppressed artificially. This phenomenon is very important for storage, which is largely directed towards both maintaining the 'natural dormancy period' and delaying sprouting for as long as possible after dormancy. Of course, the storage conditions - temperature, moisture and atmospheric composition - substantially influence this process. Sprout suppressants have also been developed for this purpose and can be applied dry, as either a mist or in the form of vapour. Two of the best known compounds are IPC (isopropyl N-phenylcarbamate) and chloro-IPC, a chlorine-containing variant.

Sprouting can also be controlled by radioactive irradiation, but this has hitherto been carried out only on a very limited scale, in Japan and elsewhere.

In the seed potato sector, stimulation of sprouting may be important. Some of the agents used for this purpose are carbon disulphide (CS_2), thiourea, rindite, potassium thiocyanate and gibberellic acid (GA).

3.1 Dormancy period

Owing to its great importance from the point of view of keepability and storage, the dormancy period in potatoes constitutes an important field of research. During the last decennia there have been different opinions about the definition of dormancy in potatoes. Emilsson (1949) distinguishes two separate states of dormancy:
a. The time after harvesting when tubers will not sprout under favourable conditions. He defines this as the 'rest period'.
b. The time after harvesting when the buds are not growing, for whatever reason.

Burton (1963) refers to a bud as dormant if it is not growing for any reason, including an adverse environment, provided the bud has retained the potential for future growth.

This definition is the same, as far as the period after harvesting is concerned (see above b), distinguished by Emilsson (1949).

In his review (Burton, 1978b), a bud is referred to as 'dormant' if it does not grow at a favourable temperature; the period over which this holds true is referred to as the 'dormant' period. The latter definition is the same as that used by Goodwin (1966) and also that used for 'rest period' by Emilsson (1949), (see above a).

Burton (1978b) concludes that his definition (Burton, 1963) may be too broad and states that it serves no useful purpose to restrict the term 'dormancy' to a condition of no change, nor to contrast a 'dormant' bud with a 'resting' bud (Emilsson, 1949). A condition in which no changes at all take place does not in fact exist - such a bud would be dead, not dormant.

Another important point is the precise moment at which the dormancy period commences. For convenience, many publications equate this with the moment of harvesting the tubers. Burton (1978a), however, states that the date of harvesting has no physiological significance and that it is much more logical both biochemically and physiologically to equate the beginning of the dormancy period with the moment of tuber initiation. This implies that dormancy as well as tuber initiation, via the above-ground parts of the plant, are affected by environmental factors during growth. The resulting suppression of sprouting of the tubers would then be at a maximum at the moment of tuber initiation, after which it would decline. Depending on weather conditions, dormancy may sometimes ens in a warm summer before harvesting. This makes it clear that the date of harvesting, although used as a practical tool, has no physiological significance. For research purposes, the moment of tuber initiation is a valuable criterion for the beginning of the dormancy period.

Many authors will agree with the concept of 'dormancy' as described in the foregoing (see also Burton, 1978b). It will, however, be necessary to indicate clearly the definition of dormancy and the precise conditions under which experimental data are collected. This is to avoid confusion, because most of the experimental data obtained so far in the past decennia deal with the old concept (Burton, 1963; Emilsson, 1949; Schippers, 1956).

The length of the dormancy period depends on variety, maturity of the tuber and soil and weather conditions during growth. Even in the period just before harvesting if the foliage is still intact.

Extreme weather conditions affect the length of the dormancy period of the tubers (Krijthe, 1962; Burton, 1963). Extremely cold, wet weather increased the dormancy period by about four weeks. Extremely dry, warm weather reduced it by some nine weeks. Under more normal conditions, however, this effect is relatively slight (Burton, 1966).

Krijthe (1962) considered the tubers no longer dormant as soon as 90% of the tubers in a sample put at 20 °C for a period of three weeks showed sprouts of at least 3 mm.

She used 20 tubers per sample. This procedure was shown to be useful in practice.

Besides variety, maturity and weather conditions and whether or not the tuber is injured, the storage regime is an important factor influencing the length of the dormant period.

Research has often been directed towards the chemical processes in the tuber - i.e., the substances keeping the potato in a biochemical equilibrium resulting in dormancy (Rappaport & Wolf, 1969). Any additional understanding of these processes is, of course, valuable. Much more important, however, is the hope that more knowledge about the nature of these substances will make it possible for them to be used as 'natural' sprout inhibitors, the idea being that anything that is 'natural' cannot be harmful to health. But this is by no means necessarily the case. Even so, much research has been, and is still being done on this point.

The work of Hemberg (1949, 1952 and 1954) was very important in this connection. Using the Avena coleoptile test, he showed that the 'acid ether fraction' of potato tissue contains substances which inhibit cell extension. He also showed that the levels of these substances remain high during the dormancy period, decreasing prior to sprouting. Bennet-Clark & Kefford (1953) purified the extracts to some extent by paper chromatography. The residual fraction, which they called the 'inhibitor-β complex' had a strongly inhibitory effect in the test mentioned. Over the years, various compounds have been isolated from this complex. However, the nature of the compounds has not hitherto provided a full explanation of the phenomenon of dormancy. The most important component so far is certainly ABA (abscisic acid), which was discovered almost simultaneously by Cornforth et al. (1965) in sycamore leaves and Ohkuma et al. (1965) in cotton bolls. This substance has also been detected in potatoes (Cornforth et al., 1965). Many authors - e.g., Blumenthal-Goldschmidt & Rappaport, 1965; El Antably et al., 1967; Van Es & Hartmans, 1969; Hartmans & Van Es, 1979 - found that ABA inhibits sprout growth. However, ABA was not found to have any effect on the duration of the dormancy period. Apart from ABA, which thus has an inhibitory effect as a plant hormone, it is known that gibberellins - in particular GA_3 - break the dormancy period in potatoes (Rappaport et al., 1957; Bruinsma, 1967; Bruinsma et al., 1967).
It is, however, assumed that the balance of the two hormones ABA and GA may determine dormancy.

3.2 Sprouting

During the development of the tubers on the plant, the buds in the eyes on the tuber successively become dormant, starting at the stem end. The apical eye is the last to become dormant. At the end of the dormancy period, the eyes again sprout. If the tubers are placed under appropriate temperature conditions, one or more sprouts form on each tuber.

The number of sprouts per tuber is greatly affected by the physiological age of the tuber - which in turn is related to the duration of storage coupled with the storage conditions. Tubers placed at a suitable temperature immediately after the end of the dormancy period produce only one sprout. The apical eye sprouts first. This phenomenon is known as 'apical dominance'. A number of sprouts are formed later in the storage season. In addition, the sprouts may branch, but usually only in January or February. Finally, after a long period of storage, very thin branches (filamentous sprouts) and even small tubers, called 'little potatoes', form on the sprouts (Fig. 3.1). This is an indication of important changes in the tuber. The increase in the number of sprouts can be attributed to a decline in the dominance of the apical sprout of the tuber during storage. This apical dominance and its loss are ascribed to changes in the tuber itself. There is a direct relation between the vigour of sprout growth after planting and the condition of the tuber itself. The tuber condition is referred to as the physiological age of the tuber.

The rate of growth of the sprout after the seed potato has been plan-

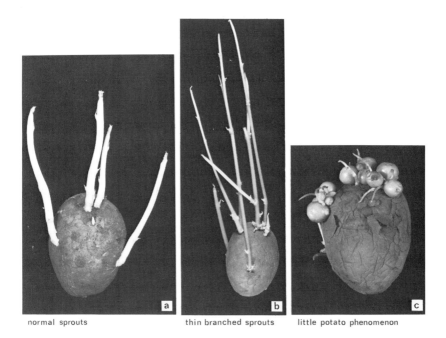

normal sprouts   thin branched sprouts   little potato phenomenon

Fig. 3.1. Influence of physiological age of seed potatoes on the sprouting behaviour. Tubers stored at ± 4 °C. Sprouting experiments carried out at 18 °C in dark during 2 to 4 weeks. a. cv. Bintje, stored at 4 °C during 6 months; b. cv. Désirée, stored at 4 °C during 13 months; c. cv. Jearla, stored at 4 °C during 13 months.

ted is directly correlated with the length and nature of the sprout at the time of planting; Also the conditions during growth - the time of harvesting of the seed potato, tuber size, storage temperature and other storage conditions - influence the growth rate and are thus very important.

The phenomenon of apical necrosis may occur during sprouting. The branches which then occur are often due to loss of apical dominance of the sprout caused by damage. The apex of the sprout then becomes darker in colour and dies. Dyson & Digby (1975) showed that this is due to calcium deficiency. The growth rate of the sprouts of a tuber and the possible occurrence of apical necrosis is affected by the calcium content of the tuber and the pH of the soil in which the tubers were grown. A high soil pH (pH 7) and a high tuber calcium level are associated with faster sprout growth and a reduction in apical necroses.

3.2.1   Sprout growth during storage

The nature of the tubers, disease and storage conditions greatly affect sprout growth during storage.

The length of the dormancy period and sprouting behaviour depend on the variety and on the previous history of the tubers. Storage conditions such as temperature, humidity of the storage atmosphere, light, oxygen concentration, carbon dioxide concentration and the possible presence of volatile substances from the potato also affect the length of the dormancy period and sprouting.

3.2.1.1   Effect of tuber size on the number of sprouts and sprout growth rate

The number of sprouts per tuber increases with the size of the tuber, as shown in Fig. 3.2 (Allen, 1978). Similarly, the number of stems per plant increases with the size of the seed potato, but to a lesser extent. Although Krijthe (1962) found no difference in dormancy between two different seed potato sizes, a difference in the growth of rate of the sprouts was observed (Fig. 3.3). Sprouts of smaller tubers are found to grow more slowly than those of larger ones, this difference being greater the lower the storage temperature (Fig. 3.3, Krijthe, 1962).

3.2.1.2   Effect of the physiological age of the tuber on 'sprouting potential'

To characterize the physiological age, Krijthe (1962) determined the 'sprouting potential' at intervals during the storage season. For this purpose, the tubers of a batch of sprout-free potatoes were stored at

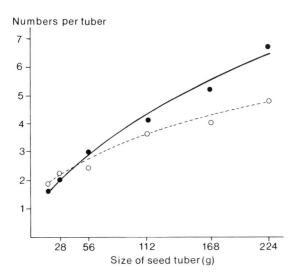

Numbers per tuber

Size of seed tuber(g)

Fig. 3.2. Relationship between number of sprouts and stems per seed tuber
and tuber size (after Scott and Younger, 1972, from Allen, 1978).
● —— ● = sprouts; 0 —— 0 = stems.

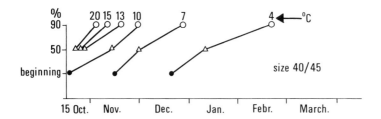

size 40/45

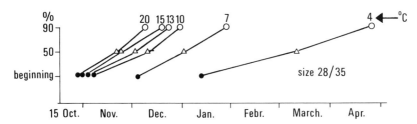

size 28/35

Fig. 3.3. Dates on which samples of 20 tubers graded to different sizes
begin to sprout, and on which 50 % and 90 % have sprouted, after storage
at different temperatures (4 to 20 °C) (from Krijthe, 1962).

2 °C after harvesting. A sample was taken regularly and placed for four
weeks at 20 °C and 80 % relative humidity. The resulting sprout weight,
expressed as a percentage of the initial weight of the tubers, was called
the 'sprouting potential'. There is a clear optimum in the shape of the

Sprout wt (% of tuber wt)

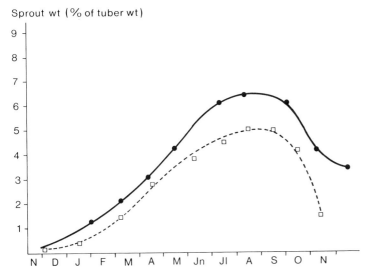

Fig. 3.4. Influence of the variety on the sprouting capacity. Sprouting capacity is measured as the weight of sprouts as percentage of tuber weight, which grew during a 4-week period at 20 °C, prior storage temperature having been 2 °C (from Krijthe, 1962). ● —— ● = Bintje; □ —— □ = Alpha.

sprouting potential curve during the storage season (Fig. 3.4). The shape of this curve depends on the variety (Fig. 3.4), harvesting year (Fig. 3.5) and lot. Krijthe (1962) points out that the maximum in nearly all cases falls in July or August if the tubers are stored at

Sprout wt (% of tuber wt)

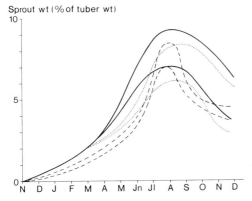

Fig. 3.5. Seasonal trend in sprouting capacity of various lots of Bintje in different years. Sprouting capacity is here given as the weight of sprouts, expressed as a percentage of the tuber weight, which grew during a 4-week period at 20 °C, prior sprout-free storage having been at 2 °C (from Krijthe, 1962). ---- = 1956; .... = 1957; —— = 1958.

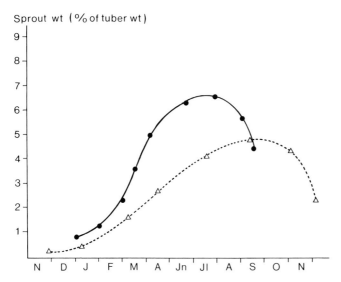

Sprout wt (% of tuber wt)

Fig 3.6. Influence of prior storage temperature on the sprouting capacity of cv. Libertas. Sprouting capacity is measured after desprouting as the weight of sprouts as percentage of tuber weight, which grew during a 4-week period at 20 °C (from Krijthe, 1962). Δ —— Δ = storage temperature 2 °C; ● —— ● = storage temperature 7 °C.

2 °C. If they are stored at higher temperatures, the optimum occurs sooner (Fig. 3.6). This process of senescence is also accelerated by desprouting.

Physiologically old seed potatoes develop faster into plants than physiologically young ones. Tuber initiation takes place early and the foliage is poorly developed.

Since tuber growth depends on photosynthesis by the foliage, this means that although old seed potatoes give rapid tuber growth initially,

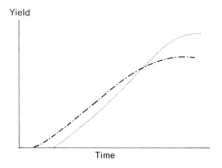

Yield

Time

Fig. 3.7. Typical patterns of tuber development of crops grown from physiologically old and younger seed (after Wurr, 1978). .... = younger seed; −·−·−·− = old seed.

106

their yield is ultimately lower than that of younger stock (Fig. 3.7, Wurr, 1978).

If seed potatoes already have small tubers growing on the sprouts, this means that a plant will no longer develop after planting. The seed potato is then 'worn out'. This abnormality is called the 'little potato phenomenon' (Fig. 3.1). Apart from the length of the storage period and temperature, growth conditions also affect physiological age, as differences in origin and year show.

Tubers grown in relatively warm conditions lose their dormancy earlier and age faster (Iritani, 1968).

Late planting of seed potatoes produces tubers whose dormancy is broken at a later stage and which (Wurr, 1978) also become 'physiologically old' later. This may be important in the growing of early varieties.

Gray (1974) also found that fertilization with high nitrogen doses gave physiologically younger tubers.

3.2.1.3 Effect of variety

The effect of variety on the length of the dormancy period was comprehensively investigated by Emilsson (1949), Schippers (1956) and Burton (1963). Table 3.1 shows the variation from year to year, for four Dutch varieties at various temperatures, of the dormant period (called by Schippers 'rest period') (Beukema & v.d. Zaag, 1979).

Table 3.1 Dormant period (called by Schippers rest period) expressed in weeks after harvest of some varieties at various temperatures in two seasons (from Beukema & v.d. Zaag, 1979: adapted from Schippers, 1956)

Variety	Earliness *	2 °C		5 °C		10 °C		20 °C	
		1953[+]	1954[+]	1953	1954	1953	1954	1953	1954
Bintje	6.5	14	17	12	16	12	15	10	11.5
Eigenheimer	7	9.5	11	9.5	11	9.5	11	6.5	8
IJsselster	6.5	9.5	19	10	19	9.5	16	9	12
Libertas	4.5	12	23	12	19	14	19	10	15

* low figure late maturity   [+] 1953 normal temperature, 1954 low temperature

Schippers (1956) found that the average period of dormancy was 19.5 weeks in 41 varieties harvested in mid-July and stored at 10 °C. The dormancy period measured from the time of harvesting ranged from 17 to 27 weeks. Burton (1963) found at 10 °C an average dormancy, measured from the time of harvesting, of 8 weeks in 11 varieties harvested in September, the range being 5 to 14 weeks.
Measured after tuber initiation, the average dormancy period was 24.5 weeks, the range being 20 to 33 weeks.

107

3.2.1.4 Effect of disease on tubers

The example of infection with *Phytophtora infestans*, which reduces the dormancy period, is well known; this was observed for the first time by Dostal (1942).

3.2.1.5 Effect of storage temperature

Temperature strongly influences the duration of the dormancy period and subsequent sprouting. Temperature can easily be controlled and is thus of practical relevance (Table 3.1 and Fig. 3.8).

As long ago as 1956, Schippers found that reducing the storage temperature of potatoes from 10 to 3 °C increased the dormancy period by 150 %. The increase was 67 % at 5 °C, while a change in the temperature from 10 to 20 °C reduced the period by 18 %. It is also important for the temperature not to vary too much, as this generally reduces the dormancy period (Schippers, 1956; Burton, 1973).

Wurr & Allen (1976) found that a storage period of 14 days at 2 to 3 °C, followed by storage at 15.6 °C, was favourable for sprouting. The sprouts developed earlier and sprout length increased. Allen et al. (1978) discovered this effect for a number of varieties (including Desiree). In other varieties, however, this low-temperature treatment increased the number of sprouts developing per tuber. Some of the varieties (British and American) examined by these authors exhibited no reaction to the low-temperature treatment.

3.2.1.6 Effect of moisture content of storage atmosphere

There has been hardly any good systematic research on this point. Experiments have, however, been conducted with 'moistening' of the potatoes, the tubers being covered with a film of water. Tests of this kind

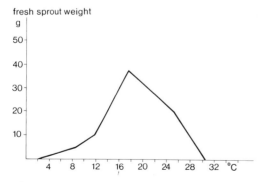

Fig. 3.8. Influence of temperature on sprout growth (from Beukema and Van der Zaag, 1979; adapted from Hogetop, 1930).

108

indicate that 'moistening' reduces the period of dormancy - i.e., that dormancy is broken.
But this could just as well be caused by a reduction in the oxygen pressure due to the water film (Burton & Wigginton, 1970).

3.2.1.7 Effect of oxygen content of storage atmosphere

The O_2 content affects not only termination of dormancy but also the rate of sprout growth. The O_2 concentration required for optimum sprout growth depends on the physiological age of the potatoes. For example, 4 to 5 % O_2 is optimum at a storage temperature of 10 to 20 °C at the beginning of the season, while 17 to 20 % O_2 is best around June (Burton, 1968). The low O_2 concentration which has a stimulating effect at the beginning of storage clearly inhibits sprout growth later in the season.

To induce sprouting, an O_2 content of 2 % is sufficient at the beginning of storage. However, the sprouts then either fail to grow, or grow only slightly.

Burton (1971) attributes this to the inability to mobilize the reserve carbohydrates for sprout growth.

3.2.1.8 Effect of carbon dioxide content of storage atmosphere

As long ago as 1931, Braun showed that a storage atmosphere with a CO_2 content of 2.2 to 9.1 % clearly stimulated sprout growth in potatoes irrespective of the stage of dormancy. This was confirmed in a later investigation (Burton, 1958).
This author found that the optimum CO_2 content was 2 to 4 %, corresponding to a CO_2 concentration dissolved in the cell sap of about 2×10^{-3}M. The stimulatory effect declined again at higher concentrations, the result at 7 to 10 % being the same as with normal air storage.

3.2.1.9 Effect of volatile substances in the storage atmosphere

Volatile substances are released during the storage of potatoes and, if not eliminated by ventilation, may totally inhibit sprouting even at normal oxygen and carbon dioxide concentrations (Burton, 1952 and 1965; Burton & Meigh, 1971). The latter authors initially assumed that the substances concerned were olefin-like ethereal molecular structures, possibly containing sulphur.

3.2.2 Effect of sprouting on respiration and moisture loss

The weight losses occurring during storage due to sprouting are considerable. The total weight loss of dry matter is made up of the sum of the factors sprouting + respiration + evaporation.

3.2.2.1 Respiration

The effect of sprouting on respiration was investigated by Burton et al. (1955). These authors found that normal respiration increased by 50 % at about 10 mg sprouts per gram (1 %) tuber fresh weight. This respiration increases to 400 to 500 % with tubers showing considerable sprouting (50 mg per gram) in June (Isherwood & Burton, 1975). The increase in respiration is due not only to the sprouts but also to the tuber. The increase in tuber respiration after removal of the sprouts, however, was no more than 30 % of the normal basal value.

Assuming that the presence of sprouts on the tuber in itself has little effect on the respiration of the tuber, it can be assumed that most of the increase is due to the respiration of the sprouts.

3.2.2.2 Moisture loss

The effect of sprouting on moisture loss is clearly demonstrated for the cv. Dr. McIntosh in Fig. 3.9, taken from the work of Burton & Hannan (1957). The water evaporation measured here took place by direct evaporation to the air, which had a relative humidity corresponding to a vapour pressure deficit of 2.7×10^2 Pa and a temperature of 10 °C.

An impression of the magnitude of the losses represented by the sum of respiration and moisture losses is given in Fig. 3.10, derived from figures presented by Krijthe (1962), relating to the cv. Bintje. This diagram shows that the weight losses due to the sum of respiration and evaporation are greater than the sprout weight. Since the material concerned

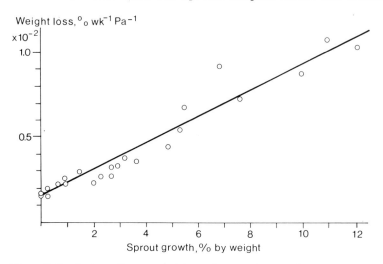

Fig. 3.9. Rate of evaporation from tubers of cv. Dr. McIntosh in relation to sprout growth. Temperature: 10 °C; water vapour pressure deficit of store air: 2.7×10^2 Pa (from Burton & Hannan, 1957).

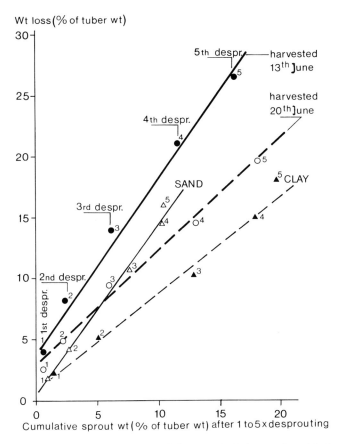

Fig. 3.10. Influence of harvest date and soil type on the relation between sprout weight and weight loss due to respiration and evaporation (drawn from data of Krijthe, 1962).

consists of seed potatoes, the total losses are greatly increased because the potatoes were desprouted up to five times. However, more important than the quantitative data is the fact that these tests show that lifting one week before full maturity, eventually has a permanent effect on respiration and moisture losses during sprouting.

Since moisture loss is much greater in potatoes which have sprouted than in ones which have not, the effect of immature lifting thus extends to the sprouting of the tubers. Burton (1955) calculated that the epidermis of the sprouts is about 100 times as permeable to water as the surface of the tuber. Hence sprout growth corresponding to a 1 % increase in the tuber area causes a doubling of the moisture loss. The sprout thus has a relatively substantial effect on evaporation.

Fig. 3.10 also shows that potatoes from clay soils lose much more weight by moisture loss and respiration for a given total sprout weight.

In addition to the direct consequences for respiration and evapora-

111

tion, intense sprouting can in practice clog the space between the tubers. This may result in a microclimate with different conditions in
terms of CO_2 and O_2 concentrations temperature, humidity and volatile
compounds, which may have indirect effects on sprouting.

3.3 Sprouting control

For many years a large number of chemical compounds have been shown to
have sprout-inhibiting effects - e.g., ethylene, nonanol, abscisic acid,
indolacetic acid and dichlobenil. Most of these substances have either
never, or only for a short time, been used in practice.

The compounds IPC, chloro-IPC and maleic hydrazide (MH) have proved to
be of more or less permanent practical value. The dimethylnaphthalenes
are new and their value and practical applicability still have to be proved. In addition to the chemical agents, considerable experimentation has
been carried out with the irradiation of potatoes.

The following general point must be made about sprouting control
treatments. Substances or treatments, such as irradiation, having sprout-
inhibiting effects - i.e., which inhibit 'growth' - will also suppress
suberization and the formation of wound periderm, thus favouring infection from outside and consequent rotting. High moisture losses may also
occur as a result of insufficient suberization. The potatoes must therefore be treated with sprout inhibitors only after the wounds have healed
and   wound periderm has formed.

3.3.1 IPC and chloro-IPC

The principal sprout inhibitors used today are isopropyl N-phenylcarbamate (abbreviation: IPC) (Rhodes et al., 1950) and isopropyl N-(3-chlo-
rophenyl) carbamate (abbreviation: chloro-IPC) (Marth & Schultz, 1952).
Since then, many authors have experimented with these substances and published papers on them, and the compounds have been widely used in practice. Chloro-IPC and IPC are often mixed in specific proportions. The
compound can be applied in a number of ways (see Chapter 21).

3.3.2 Maleic hydrazide (MH)

Apart from chloro-IPC and IPC, maleic hydrazide (MH) is the only agent
to have been used on a relatively large scale. Application with potatoes
is at present very limited and is prohibited in the Netherlands. In the
United States, on the other hand, the use of MH is increasing again. It
is applied to the crop three to five weeks before foliage death. If the
treatment is carried out too early, the yield will be reduced, while late
treatment will have an insufficient effect on sprouting. Where the com-

pound is administered at the correct time, good control of sprout growth is achieved.

3.3.3 Dimethylnaphthalene

Although not (or at least not yet) available for practical use, the compounds 1.4- and 1.6-dimethylnaphthalene have also shown noticable sprout-inhibiting effects. Initial tests have shown that these substances, which occur naturally in the storage atmosphere, have a sprout-suppressant effect (Meigh et al., 1973).

3.3.4 Irradiation

3.3.4.1 Light

Light is known to reduce the length to which potato sprouts will grow. Even a low light intensity can almost completely (about 95 %) inhibit sprout length. Exposure to light of wavelengths 350 to 450 nm and 650 to 950 nm - i.e., at the lower and upper limits of the visible spectrum - is found to be the most effective (Wassink et al., 1950). This inhibitory effect is utilized for seed potatoes. The sprouts are coloured by chlorophyll development, differentiation occurs in stems and leaflets and root primordia are initiated (Krijthe, 1946; Fig. 3.11). Branching and direct

Fig. 3.11. Influence of different storage temperatures on sprouting behaviour of tubers (cv. Eersteling) stored in light. Storage period 3.5 months (from Krijthe, 1946).

113

tuber formation on the sprouts are thereby counteracted, and the process of senescence is delayed.

3.3.4.2 Radioactive irradiation

Irradiation with beta, gamma or X-rays completely inhibits sprouting, and is from this point of view the best solution. It has been found that virtually total inhibition is achieved with doses of 50 to 100 Gy or even lower (Burton & Hannan, 1957). Gamma irradiation with a cobalt source (Co^{60}) has been found to be particularly effective. A number of commercial-scale installations have been in operation in various countries, including Japan and Canada. In the Netherlands, the former Food Irradiation Test Centre of ITAL-Wageningen carried out extensive pilot plant investigations together with the Institute for the Storage and Processing of Agricultural Produce (IBVL) (Sparenberg & Ulmann, 1973).

It is assumed that irradiated potatoes do not constitute a health hazard. However, it has not been established that irradiation does not give rise to the formation in the tuber of compounds which may be harmful to health. One objection is a grey discoloration occurring when the potatoes are cooked, but this has not been observed everywhere to the same extent. The biggest disadvantage, however, is the high cost of irradiation. A further disadvantage to the potato-processing industry is that both reversible reducing sugar formation and senescent sweetening are accelerated (Burton et al., 1959).

3.3.5 Internal sprout formation

This type of malformed sprouting, in which sprouts grow inwards into the tuber occurs occasionally. It is caused by the ingrowing of a lateral sprout from an axillary bud at the base of a normal sprout whose growing point has been damaged (Davis, 1961). This damage can be caused by insufficient sprout suppressant concentrations or too late application of sprout suppressants. This defect occurs chiefly in ware potatoes.

3.4 Sprout stimulation

Sprouting can be stimulated by chemicals, by damaging the tuber, by increasing the humidity of the storage atmosphere and by temperature variation. Although this subject is not directly relevant to potato storage, it seems appropriate in the context of potato physiology to refer briefly to sprout stimulation by means of chemical compounds and wounding of the tuber tissue.
The main chemical agents used in practice are rindite, carbon disulphide and gibberellic acid.

114

3.4.1 Rindite

The substance known by this brand name is a mixture of ethylene chlorohydrin, ethylene dichloride and carbon tetrachloride in the proportions 7:3:1 (Denny, 1945; Keller & Berces, 1966). The substances act in the vapour phase. The concentration is about 1 litre per m³ of air and the treatment lasts about 48 hours. One objection is the toxicity of the substance, which necessitates strict safety precautions.

3.4.2 Carbon disulphide (CS₂)

The use of sulphur compounds such as mercaptoethanol, thiourea and CS_2 for dormancy breaking has long been familiar (Denny, 1926) and is common, for example, in India and Brazil. Under Dutch conditions, CS_2 was tested by Meijers (1972). Treatment for about three days at 20 °C using 12.5 to 25 ml CS_2 per m³ containing an average of 500 kg of potatoes is sufficient to obtain optimum sprouting. CS_2, however, also has the disadvantage of being toxic.

3.4.3 Gibberellic acid (GA)

Immersion of tubers in a solution of GA (Van Hiele, 1961) or spraying them with this solution (Holmes et al., 1970; Marinus & Bodlaender, 1978) stimulates sprout growth and increases the number of stems per plant and the number of smaller tubers (seed potatoes). The total yield is unaffected by treatment of the tubers with GA (Holmes et al., 1970).

Excessive concentrations of GA (over 25 ppm) can cause defects in the plant, such as thin stems and small, rapidly yellowing leaves (Timm et al., 1962).

GA is usually absorbed more efficiently by the tubers after wounding. For this reason, application directly after harvesting or cutting of seed potatoes is the most effective.

3.4.4 Effect of damage to the tuber tissue

The 'wound effect' caused by damage and cutting of the tissue is well known. This gives rise, for example, to the synthesis of gibberellins (Rappaport & Sachs, 1967), thus stimulating sprout growth.

References

Allen, E.J., 1978. Plant density. The potato crop: 278-362. Editor
    P.M. Harris, Chapman and Hall, London.
Allen, E.J., J.N. Bean & R.L. Griffith, 1978. Effects of low temperature

on sprout growth of several potato varieties. Potato Res. 21: 249-255.

Bennet-Clark, T.A. & N.P. Kefford, 1953. Chromatography of the growth substances in plant extracts. Nature, 171: 645-647.

Beukema, H.P. & D.E. van der Zaag, 1979. Potato improvement - some factors and facts. IAC, Wageningen.

Blumenthal-Goldschmidt, S. & L. Rappaport, 1965. Regulation of bud rest in tubers of potato (Solanum tuberosum L.). II. Inhibition of sprouting by inhibitor β-complex and reversal by gibberellin A_3. Plant Cell Physiol., 6: 601-608.

Braun, H., 1931. Untersuchungen über den Einfluss von Kohlensäure und Sauerstoff auf Keimung und Pflanzgutwert der Kartoffelknolle. Arb. biol. Bund. Anst. Land- und Forstw., 19: 17.

Bruinsma, J. 1967. Termination of dormancy with gibberellic acid. Mededel. Rijksfakulteit Landbouwwetensch., Gent, 32: 1013-1020.

Bruinsma J., A. Sinnema, D. Bakker & J. Swart, 1967. The use of gibberellic acid (G.A.) and N-dimethylaminosuccinamic acid (B_9) in the testing of seed potatoes for virus infection. Eur. Potato J., 10: 136-152.

Burton, W.G., 1952. Studies on the dormancy and sprouting of potatoes. III The effect upon sprouting of volatile metabolic products other than carbon dioxide. New Phytol., 51: 154-161.

Burton, W.G., 1955. Biological and economic aspects of the refrigerated storage of potatoes. Proc. Institute Refrigeration, 51: 168-172.

Burton, W.G., G. Mann & H.G. Wagner, 1955. The storage of ware potatoes in permanent buildings. II The temperature of unventilated stacks of potatoes. J. Agric. Sci., 46: 150-163.

Burton, W.G. & R.S. Hannan, 1957. Use of γ-radiation for preventing the sprouting of potatoes. J. Sci. Fd. Agric., 12: 707-715.

Burton, W.G., 1958. The effect of the concentrations of carbon dioxide and oxygen in the storage atmosphere upon the sprouting of potatoes at 10 °C. Eur. Potato J., 1 (2): 47-57.

Burton, W.G., T. Horne & D.B. Powell, 1959. The effect of γ-irradiation upon the sugar content of potatoes. Eur. Potato J., 2: 105-116.

Burton, W.G., 1963. Concepts and mechanism of dormancy. The growth of potato: 17-41. Eds. J.D. Ivins and F.L. Milthorpe, Butterworths, London.

Burton, W.G., 1965. The effect of oxygen and the volatile products of metabolism upon the sprout growth of potatoes. Eur. Potato J., 8: 245.

Burton, W.G., 1966. The potato. Veenman, Wageningen.

Burton, W.G., 1968. The effect of oxygen concentration upon sprout growth on the potato tuber. Eur. Potato J., 11: 249-265.

Burton, W.G. & M.J. Wigginton, 1970. The effect of a film of water upon the oxygen status of a potato tuber. Potato Res., 13: 180-186.

Burton, W.G., 1971. Postscript to Harkett (1971) q.v. Potato Res., 14: 311.

Burton, W.G. & D.F. Meigh, 1971. The production of growth-suppressing volatile substances by stored potato tubers. Potato Res., 14: 96-101.

Burton, W.G. 1973. Physiological and biochemical changes in the tuber as affected by storage conditions. Proc. 5th Triennial Conf. Eur. Ass. Potato Res., Norwich, 1972: 63-81.

Burton, W.G., 1978 (a). The physics and physiology of storage. The potato crop. Editor P.M. Harris, Chapman and Hall, London.

Burton, W.G., 1978 (b). Post-harvest behaviour and storage of potatoes. Applied Biology, vol. III. Editor T.H. Coaker, Academic Press, London, New York, San Francisco.

Cornforth, J.W., B.V. Milborrow, G. Ryback & P.F. Wareing, 1965. Identity of sycamore 'dormin' with abscisin II. Nature, 205: 1269-1270.

Cornforth, J.W., B.V. Milborrow & G. Ryback, 1966. Identification and estimation of (+)-abscisin II ('dormin') in plant extracts by spectro-polarimetry. Nature, 210: 627-628.

Davis, R.M., 1961. Ingrown sprouts in potato tubers: factors accompanying their origin in Ohio. Am. Potato J., 38: 411-413.

Denny, F.E., 1926. Hastening the sprouting of dormant potato tubers. Am. J. Bot., 13: 118-125.

Denny, F.E., 1945. Synergistic effects of three chemicals in the treatment of dormant potato tubers to hasten germination. Contributions from the Boyce Thompson Institute for Plant Research, 14: 1-14.

Dóstal, R., 1942. Ueber das Fruhtreiben der Fliederzweige (Syringa vulgaris) und Kartoffelknollen (Solanum tuberosum) durch Verletzung und die hormonale Deutung dafür. Gartenbauwissenschaft, 16: 195.

Dyson, P.W. & J. Digby, 1975. Effects of calcium on sprout growth and subapical necrosis in Majestic potatoes. Potato Res., 18: 290-305.

El Antably, H.M.M., P.F. Wareing & J. Hillman, 1967. Some physiological responses to D.L. Abscisin ('dormin'). Planta, 73: 74-90.

Emilsson, B., 1949. Studies on the rest period and dormant period in the potato tuber. Acta Agricultarae Suecana, 3: 189-284.

Es, A. van & K.J. Hartmans, 1969. The influence of abscisin II and gibberellic acid on the sprouting of excised potato buds. Eur. Potato J., 12: 59-63.

Gray, D., 1974. Effect of nitrogen fertilizer applied to the seed crop on the subsequent growth of early potatoes. J. Agric. Sci. Camb., 82: 363-369.

Goodwin, P.B., 1966. The effect of water on dormancy in the potato. Eur. Potato J., 9: 53-64.

Hartmans, K.J. & A. van Es, 1979. The influence of growth regulators GA_3, ABA, Kinetin and IAA on sprout and root growth and plant development using excised potato buds. Potato Res., 22: 319-332.

Hemberg, T., 1949. Significance of growth-inhibiting substances and auxins for the rest period of the potato tuber. Physiologia Pl., 2: 24-36.

117

Hemberg, T., 1952. The significance of the acid growth inhibiting substances for the rest period of the potato tuber. Physiologia Pl., 5: 115-129.

Hemberg, T., 1954. Studies on the occurrence of free and bound auxins and of growth inhibiting substances in the potato tuber. Physiologia Pl., 7: 312-322.

Hiele, F.J.H. van, 1961. Unsprouted tubers with gibberellic acid. Eur. Potato J., 4: 26-39.

Hogetop, K., 1930. Untersuchungen über den Einfluss der Temperatur auf Keimung und Lebensdauer der Kartoffelknollen. Bot. Arch., 30: 350-413.

Holmes, J.C., R.W. Lang & A.K. Sing, 1970. The effect of five growth regulators on apical dominance in potato seed tubers and on subsequent tuber production. Potato Res., 13: 342-352.

Iritani, W.M., 1968. The effect of storage temperature and source on productivity of Russet Burbank seed. Am. Potato J., 45: 322-326.

Isherwood, F.A. & W.G. Burton, 1975. The effect of senescence, handling, sprouting and chemical sprout suppression upon the respiratory quotient of stored potato tubers. Potato Res., 18: 98-104.

Keller, E.R. & S. Berces, 1966. Check-testing for virus Y and leaf-roll in seed potatoes with particular reference to methods of increasing precision with the A6-leaf test for virus Y. Eur. Potato J., 9: 1-14.

Krijthe, N., 1946. De invloed van de bewaring van aardappelknollen op den bouw van de knoppen en op de ontwikkeling tot volwassen plant. Meded. Landbouwhogeschool, 47: 3-36.

Krijthe, N., 1962. Ontwikkeling en groei van aardappelknol en aardappelplant. IBVL-Publikatie 84. IBVL, Wageningen.

Marinus, J. & K.B.A. Bodlaender, 1978. Growth and yield of seed potatoes after application of gibberellic acid to the tubers before planting. Neth. J. Agric. Sci., 26: 354-365.

Marth, P.C. & E.S. Schultz, 1952. A new sprout inhibitor for potato tubers. Am. Potato J., 29: 268-278.

Meigh, D.F., A.A.E. Filmer & R. Self, 1973. Growth-inhibitory volatile aromatic compounds produces by Solanum tuberosum tubers. Phytochemistry, 12: 987-993.

Meijers, C.P., 1972. Effect of carbon di-sulphide on the dormancy and sprouting of seed potatoes. Potatoes Res., 15: 160-165.

Ohkuma, K., F.T. Addicott, O.E. Smith & W.E. Thiessen, 1965. The structure of abscisin II. Tetrahedron Lett., 29: 2529-2535.

Rappaport, L., L.F. Lippert & H. Timm, 1957. Sprouting, plant growth and tuber production as affected by chemical treatment of white potato seed pieces. I. Breaking the rest period with gibberellic acid. Am. Potato J., 34: 254-260.

Rappaport, L. & M. Sachs, 1967. Wound-induced gibberellins. Nature, 214: 1149-1150.

Rappaport, L. & N. Wolf, 1969. The problem of dormancy in potato tubers
    and related structures. Dormancy and survival. Symp. of the Soc. for
    Experimental Biology (no. XXIII), Cambridge, University Press.
Rhodes, A., W.A. Sexton, L.G. Spencer & W.G. Tempelman, 1950. Use of
    isopropylphenylcarbamate to reduce sprouting of potato tubers during
    storage. Research Lond., 3: 189-190.
Schippers, P.A., 1956. De duur van de rustperiode van een veertigtal
    aardappelrassen, bewaard bij verschillende constante temperaturen.
    Stichting Aardappelbewaring, Wageningen, Publ. 112, serie A.
Sparenberg, H. & R. Ulmann, 1973. Inhibition of sprouting in potatoes by
    irradiation in the Netherlands. Economic and commercial aspects. Comm.
    Eur. Communities. Eurisotop Office Information, booklet 58.
Timm, H., L. Rappaport, J.C. Bishop & J.B. Hoyle, 1962. Sprouting, plant
    growth and tuber production as affected by chemical treatment of white
    potato seed pieces. IV Responses of dormant and sprouted seed potatoes
    to gibberellic acid. Am. Potato J., 39: 107-115.
Wassink, E.C., N. Krijthe & C. v.d. Scheer, 1950. On the effect of light
    of various spectral regions on the sprouting of potato tubers. Proc.
    K. Ned. Akad. Wet., 53: 1228-1239.
Wurr, D.C.E. & E.J. Allen, 1976. Effects of cold treatment on the sprout
    growth of three potatoes varieties. J. Agric. Sci. Camb., 86: 221-224.
Wurr, D.C.E., 1978. 'Seed' tuber production and management. The potato
    crop: 327-354. Editor P.M. Harris, Chapman and Hall, London.

4 Respiration

A. van Es and K.J. Hartmans

4.1 General

In respiration or dissimilation the required energy is obtained from conversion of the reserve substances in the tuber. The main reserve compound is starch, a polymer of glucose units. In this process oxygen (O_2) is taken up and carbon dioxide (CO_2) and water (H_2O) plus energy in the form of heat are released. This reaction can be represented as follows:

starch → n x glucose

$$C_6H_{12}O_6 \quad + \quad 6\ O_2 \quad \rightarrow \quad 6\ CO_2 \quad + \quad 6\ H_2O + \text{energy}$$
glucose   oxygen   carbon   dioxide   water   (heat)

The complete combustion of 1 g of glucose gives 1.47 CO_2 + 16 kJ.

In practice, about 32 % of this energy is fixed in ATP (metabolic energy); 68 % is 'lost' as heat (about 10.9 kJ.).

With a good oxygen supply, the volumes of the amount of oxygen taken up and the amount of carbon dioxide released per unit time are virtually the same.

The respiration quotient

$$RQ = \frac{\text{volume absorbed } O_2 \cdot h^{-1}}{\text{volume formed } CO_2 \cdot h^{-1}} = 1$$

Burton (1974), however, found values of RQ = 0.8 to 0.9 early in the storage period, during dormancy, while RQ later rose to 1.3 during sprouting.

In senescent potatoes, CO_2 production is permanently greater than oxygen consumption (RQ less than 1) (Isherwood & Burton, 1975). Isherwood (1973) gives for basal respiration at 10 °C a formation value of 2 ml $CO_2 \cdot$ $kg^{-1} \cdot h^{-1}$, which is equivalent to the formation of 1.4 mmol ATP·100 $g^{-1} \cdot 24\ h^{-1}$.

This also entails the breakdown of starch and the formation of anhydro glucose units of 0.5×10^{-2} mmol·$g^{-1} \cdot 24^{-1}$, or dry matter conversion of 0.855 mg $\cdot g^{-1} \cdot 24\ h^{-1}$. This corresponds to a loss of dry matter of about 0.85 mg/g fresh weight per 24-hour period. Part of this loss is compensated by the water released.

The above mentioned values for the respiration rate during storage are influenced by a number of factors.

Firstly, they are influenced by factors associated with the potato itself
as presented for storage - e.g., morphological characteristics. The skin
and lenticels are very important for the oxygen permeability. Other determinants are also important - e.g., maturity, dormancy, physiological
age, variety, inhibitory or stimulatory chemical compounds present and
handling followed by healing of wounds.

Secondly, of course, the conditions prevailing in the store are very important - e.g., the storage temperature and the oxygen and carbon dioxide
concentrations in the storage atmosphere. The usual situation is storage
in an atmosphere of 'normal' composition, which means that the potato is
surrounded by air consisting of:

    20.93 % O_2 (oxygen)
     0.03 % CO_2 (carbon dioxide)
    78.10 % N_2 (nitrogen)
     0.93 % Ar (argon)
     0.01 % H_2 (hydrogen)

Variations in this 'normal' composition have direct consequences for
respiration. The possibilities thereby offered are sometimes utilized in
the storage of, for example, horticultural produce. Controlled-atmosphere
(CA) storage (Section 4.3.4) has not hitherto been applied much to potatoes, partly owing to the high cost.

4.2 Effect of tuber characteristics on respiration

4.2.1 Function of the skin with regard to respiration

    The skin plays a very important part in respiration. Oxygen and carbon
dioxide have to pass through it, the former inwards and the latter outwards. Hence its permeability as a whole is of great importance.
    Burton (1965) found that the overall permeability for oxygen varies
from 10×10^{-3} ml $O_2 \cdot cm^{-2} \cdot h^{-1} \cdot kPa^{-1}$ to 2.5×10^{-3} ml $O_2 \cdot cm^{-2} \cdot$
$h^{-1} \cdot kPa^{-1}$. The former value was measured in young, growing tubers and the
latter in tubers one week after the dying back of the foliage in the cv.
King Edward and Majestic. Hence permeability declines with tuber age during this period. However, the cork layer is not homogeneous in area. The
lenticels, of which there are 0.5 to 3 per cm^2 of tuber area (Burton,
1965; Wigginton, 1973), are the parts which play an important part in gas
exchange.

Lenticels
    The lenticels (see also Chapter 1) in the periderm (skin) of a potato
tuber are the only places where gas exchange (mainly CO_2 and O_2) can take
place with the environment (Burton, 1965; Wigginton, 1973). The cork layer is thus irrelevant in this connection. Lenticels are also the possible

sites of entry into the tuber for pathogenic microorganisms, as has been shown for potato scab (*Streptomyces scabies*), *Phytophthora infestans* and the soft rot bacterium (*Erwinia caratovora*) (Adams, 1975). The diffusion rate of oxygen per lenticel varies from 24×10^{-2} to 302×10^{-2} $\mu l \cdot h^{-1} \cdot kPa^{-1}$ with an average of $113 \times 10^{-2} \pm 13 \times 10^{-2}$ $\mu l \cdot h^{-1} \cdot kPa^{-1}$ (Wigginton, 1973).

4.2.2 Maturity

Differences also exist between mature and immature potatoes with regard to respiration rate and its variation during storage. Burton (1964) measured values at the time of tuberization of 50 ml $\cdot$ $kg^{-1} \cdot h^{-1} O_2$ uptake at 10 °C in the cv. Majestic. From this stage onwards, a decline to a value of 4 to 5 ml $\cdot kg^{-1} \cdot h^{-1}$ was observed, this being attained at maturity. This shows that immature potatoes respire much more intensively than mature ones. Although values are high in immature potatoes after harvesting (about 17 ml $O_2 \cdot kg^{-1} \cdot h^{-1}$), they often decrease in a period of some four weeks to about 4 ml $O_2 \cdot kg^{-1} \cdot h^{-1}$. They then decrease further during the next three months to about 2 ml $O_2 \cdot kg^{-1} \cdot h^{-1}$, increasing again at the time of sprouting (Burton, 1974). A considerable loss of dry matter can therefore occur in immature potatoes immediately at the beginning of storage.

The following values were found in mature potatoes:
After harvesting: 4 to 5 ml $O_2 \cdot kg^{-1} \cdot h^{-1}$; after three months: 2 to 3 ml $O_2 \cdot kg^{-1} \cdot h^{-1}$.

4.2.3 Effect of physiological age and sprouting

It was stated in Section 4.2.2 (Maturity) that very young tubers may have a respiration rate up to ten times as high as mature tubers. A good average is then 4 ml $O_2 \cdot kg^{-1} \cdot h^{-1}$. As the tuber ages during storage, this value falls, reaching 2 ml $O_2 \cdot kg^{-1} \cdot h^{-1}$ prior to sprouting. When the tuber has about 1 % of its own weight of sprouts, respiration has increased by 50 % (Burton et al., 1955). This process continues until the respiration rate in potatoes which have sprouted substantially has increased to about 4 to 5 times that of desprouted tubers (Isherwood & Burton, 1975). This increase is almost entirely attributable to the sprouts, as the respiration of the tuber itself has increased by only about 30 % (Isherwood & Burton, 1975).

4.2.4 Effect of damage and healing of wounds

Damage and wound healing greatly influence respiration. Simply cutting through a potato doubles the respiration rate. Mulder (1955) also

discovered that dropping the potato from a height of about 1 metre increased respiration by 30 to 50 %. The severity of the damage determines
whether the respiration rate returns to its original level; it often does
not. Treatments such as washing and drying also cause an increase in respiration rate (Burton, 1974). In general, it makes a difference whether
the potato has just been harvested or has already softened to some extent. With soft potatoes, washing and drying cause O_2 uptake to double;
the increase in newly-harvested potatoes is about 30 %. Similar differences are observed with regard to handling.

Apart from other aspects, such as moisture loss and microorganism attack, wound healing is also important as regards respiration. Wounds caused by transport and handling damage must heal as completely and as
quickly as possible. This healing process, of course, depends on the type
of damage. Again, the older the tuber, the less well a wound will heal.
However, healing of wounds is also affected by the following factors:

Temperature
Wounds heal faster the higher the temperature. Although they heal somewhat faster at 20 °C than at 10 °C, the latter is a reasonable practical value, at which the cork layer is restored in 9 to 16 days (Wigginton, 1974).

Oxygen and carbon dioxide concentration
Sufficient oxygen (10 to 20 % O_2) has been proved to be a necessity, as
healing is greatly retarded under anaerobic conditions. An increase in
the carbon dioxide content of the storage atmosphere is unfavourable.

Humidity
Low moisture level in the storage atmosphere are detrimental to wound
healing, as the damaged surface dries out. Wiggington (1974) found that
no wound periderm was formed and suberization failed to occur at 20 °C
and a vapour pressure deficit of 1.6 kPa (30 % relative humidity). The
limit was about 0.7 kPa. Lower values resulted in complete suberization
of the surface and formation of a layer of periderm.
Wound healing was found to be optimum at 10 °C and a vapour pressure deficit of 0.02 kPa, corresponding to 98 % relative humidity.

Sprout suppressants
Sprout suppressants in the widest sense (including gamma irradiation) not
only inhibit sprouting but also the 'growth processes' involved in wound
healing. To prevent this, these treatments should only be used after
wounds have already healed. See also Section 3.3 (Sprouting control).

4.2.5 Effect of potato variety

Schander et al. (1931) observed differences in the respiration rates of different potato varieties. In an experiment with 12 different varieties, the minimum respiration rates, reached in December at 15 °C, were found to range from 4.3 to 12.2 mg $O_2 \cdot kg^{-1} \cdot h^{-1}$.

Schippers (1977) also found that the minimum respiration rate is a varietal characteristic and is independent of earliness or lateness and the length of the dormancy period. This is in contradiction with, for example, Schander et al. (1931), who found that 'late' varieties have a somewhat higher respiration rate.

In addition to variety, soil and manuring (Baumeister, 1948; Mulder, 1955) and maturity affect the respiration rate.

Because of these effects, the difference between the varieties is not always apparent (Burton, 1978a).

4.2.6 Stimulatory and inhibitory substances occurring in the tuber

Substances such as malonic acid, ethylene, HCN, azide, antimycin and dinitrophenol are known to affect respiration (Burton, 1978a). The effect of ethylene is now the subject of discussion in connection with controlled-atmosphere (CA) storage, and will therefore be dealt with in some detail here. Experiments by Creech et al. (1973) conducted at 0 °C and 7.2 °C showed that production of the plant hormone ethylene, with air storage at 0 °C, was of the order of 1 to 5 x 10^{-4} $\mu l \cdot kg^{-1} \cdot h^{-1}$. After 20 weeks storage at 7.2 °C, during which time sprouting occurred, an increase in the production of ethylene was observed. A maximum of 30 x 10^{-4} $\mu l \cdot kg^{-1} \cdot h^{-1}$ was reached after 29 weeks. A lower O_2 content than 2 % at 7.2 °C resulted in an increase to 80 x 10^{-4} $\mu l \cdot kg^{-1} \cdot h^{-1}$, while an increase in the CO_2 content to 4 %, at which optimum sprouting was observed, reduced ethylene production to 10 x 10^{-4} $\mu l \cdot kg^{-1} \cdot h^{-1}$.

Very high levels were measured when the O_2 concentration was greatly increased (to 80 %), viz., 3000 x 10^{-4} $\mu g \cdot kg^{-1} \cdot h^{1}$.

Tests with ethylene application showed that 100 μl per liter ethylene gave rise to a maximum increase in respiration. At 1000 μl per liter, an increase of 100 to 150 % was measured after two or three days (rather lower than application of 100 μl per liter). Below 100 μl per liter ethylene, respiration definitely falls but even at 1 μl per liter there was a stimulation of 38 % (Herklots, 1928; Heulin, 1932).

After 20 weeks storage at 7.2 °C, during which time sprouting occurred, an increase in the production of ethylene was observed.

124

4.3 Effect of storage conditions

4.3.1 Effect of temperature

Temperature first of all affects the respiration rate. For biological material in general, Q_{10} = 2 - i.e., the rate is doubled for a 10 °C increase in temperature (Müller-Thurgau, 1882). Considerable variations from this figure are possible in practice, and may be due to the degree of maturity at the time of harvesting, damage, sugar formation at low temperatures (0 to 4 °C), the physiological age of the material, varietal differences, chemical composition, etc. (Burton, 1974).

Fig. 4.1 gives an indication of the variation of the respiration rate with temperature for the British varieties Arran Consul, King Edward and Majestic, about one month after harvesting.
The Q_{10} for 10 to 20 °C is thus found to be only 1.2 to 1.3. Even in the range 0 to 5 °C, there is a decline, probably associated with sugar formation at low temperatures.

4.3.2 O_2 concentration in the storage atmosphere

In freshly harvested mature tubers, a fall in the O_2 concentration of the surrounding atmosphere from 20.9 % to about 3 % only causes a decline in uptake of about 20 to 30 %. The O_2 uptake (respiration), therefore, still remains at about 70 to 80 %. A further decrease in the O_2 content of the atmosphere below 3 %, however, results in a rapid, more or less linear, decline in O_2 uptake from 70 to 80 % to 0 % (Mapson & Burton, 1962) (Fig. 4.2). This is because 20 to 30 % of the uptake occurs with

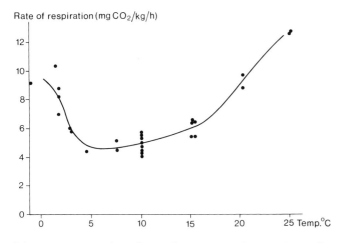

Fig. 4.1. Respiration of potato tubers at various storage temperatures. The points relate to a number of varieties and investigations (redrawn from Burton, 1966).

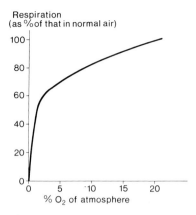

Respiration
(as % of that in normal air)

% O_2 of atmosphere

Fig. 4.2. Relation between the oxygen uptake by potato tubers, cv. King Edward, at 20 °C and different oxygen concentrations (from Mapson and Burton, 1962, redrawn from Burton, 1978).

the aid of an oxidase having a low affinity for O_2 and about 70 to 80 % is possibly taken up by the cytochrome-c-oxidase, which is already sa-turated at low O_2 levels. An increase in the oxygen concentration in the storage atmosphere above the normal level of 20.93 % to 100 % can lead to an increase in O_2 uptake of up to about 15 to 20 % (Burton, 1974).

In older potatoes, the low-O_2-affinity oxidase hardly plays any part, so that a decrease in the O_2 content of the storage air has virtually no effect down to a concentration of 5 %. The low-affinity uptake reappears after the start of sprouting and increased respiration.

4.3.3 CO_2 concentration in the storage atmosphere

If the ventilation in the store is in any way insufficient, the CO_2 concentration may increase by virtue of the gas exchange O_2 uptake and CO_2 release.

What effect does this have on tuber respiration? An investigation by Burton (1952) showed that storage for a period of 11 to 14 weeks in an atmosphere containing 5 to 7 % CO_2 inhibited respiration. Both O_2 uptake and CO_2 release fell by 25 to 30 %. Schippers (1977) also observed this phenomenon.

4.3.4 Controlled - atmosphere storage

CA storage is mainly of interest for fruit and vegetables. As the name implies, the oxygen and carbon dioxide contents of the storage atmosphere are not left to chance but are actively controlled. The main possibili-ties are then reduction in oxygen concentrations and increases in carbon dioxide levels.

126

Low oxygen concentrations greatly stimulate the ending of dormancy in potatoes and promote sprout growth. Optimum break of dormancy occurs at 2 to 5 % O_2; optimum promotion of sprout growth is observed at 5 % O_2. For storage purposes, a reduced oxygen level is virtually useless.

Increased CO_2 levels (2 to 4 %) also stimulate sprout growth at 10 °C. It has been shown that 5 % CO_2 at 5 °C inhibits the formation of reducing sugars. However, the sucrose content is increased at the same time (Burton, 1978b).

References

Adams, M.J., 1975. Potato tuber lenticels. Development and structure. Ann. Appl. Biol., 79: 265-273.

Baumeister, W., 1948. Ueber die Atmung verschiedener Kartoffelsorten in Abhänigkeit von den Klima- und Bodenverhältnissen der Anbaugebiete. Planta, 36: 214-229.

Burton, W.G., 1952. Studies on the dormancy and sprouting of potatoes. II The carbon dioxide content of the potato tuber. New Phyt., 50: 287-296.

Burton, W.G., G. Mann & H.G. Wager, 1955. The storage of ware potatoes in permanent buildings. II The temperature of unventilated stacks of potatoes. J. Agric. Sci., 46: 150-163.

Burton, W.G., 1964. The respiration of developing potato tubers. Eur. Potato J., 7: 90-101.

Burton, W.G., 1965. The permeability to oxygen of the periderm of the potato tuber. J. Exp. Bot., 16: 16-23.

Burton, W.G., 1974. The oxygen uptake, in air and in 5 % O_2, and the carbon dioxide output of stored potato tubers. Potato Res., 17: 113-137.

Burton, W.G., 1978 (a). Post-harvest behaviour and storage of potatoes. Applied Biology, vol. III. Editor T.H. Coaker, Academic Press, London, New York, San Francisco.

Burton, W.G., 1978 (b). Biochemical and physiological effects of modified atmospheres and their role in quality maintenance. Post-harvest Biology and Biotechnology (ch. 4). Editor H.O. Hublin; M. Milner. Fd. and Nutr. Press, inc., Westport, Connecticut, USA.

Creech, D.L., M. Workman & M.D. Harrison, 1973. The influence of storage factors on endogenous ethylene production by potato tubers. Am. Potato J., 50: 145-150.

Herklots, G.A.C., 1928. The effect of ethylene on the respiration of plant organisms. Ph. D. Thesis, University of Cambridge.

Huelin, F.E., 1932, The effect of ethylene on the metabolism of potatoes. Rep. Fd. Invest. Bd. Lond., 1931: 90-92.

Isherwood, F.A., 1973. Effects of changes in storage temperature on the metabolism of the potato tuber. Proc. 5th. Triennial Conf. Eur. Ass.

Potato Res., Norwich, 1972: 156-157.

Isherwood, F.A. & W.G. Burton, 1975. The effect of senescence, handling, sprouting and chemical sprout suppression upon the respiratory quotient of stored potato tubers. Potato Res., 18: 98-104.

Mapson, L.W. & W.G. Burton, 1962. The terminal oxidases of the potato tuber. Biochem. J., 82: 19-25.

Mulder, E.G., 1955. Effect of mineral nutrition of potato plants on respiration of the tubers. Acta Botanica Neerl., 4: 429-451.

Müller-Thurgau, H., 1882. Ueber Zuckeranhäufung in Pflanzenteilen in Folge niederer Temperatur. Landw. Jb., 11: 751-828.

Schander, R., E. Profft & P. Münchberg, 1931. Beiträge zur Atmung der Kartoffelknolle I. Pflanzenbau, 8: 1-6.

Schippers, P.A., 1977. The rate of respiration of potato tubers during storage. II Results of experiments in 1972 and 1973. Potato Res., 20: 189-206.

Wigginton, M.J., 1973. Diffusion of oxygen through lenticels in potato tuber. Potato Res., 16: 85-87.

Wigginton, M.J., 1974. Effects of temperature, oxygen tension and relative humidity on the wound-healing process in the potato tuber. Potato Res., 17: 200-214.

5 Water balance of the potato tuber

A. van Es and K.J. Hartmans

5.1 Introduction

Water loss after harvesting and during subsequent storage is one of
the reasons for quality deterioration and thus an important parameter.
On the one hand the losses are determined by the characteristics of the
potato tuber and on the other hand by the storage regime as designed by
the storage technologists. In this chapter some factors concerning the
water status in the potato tuber will be discussed.

Moisture transport of the kind occurring during potato storage depends
on the following factors:
- The extent to which water inside the tuber is free for transport to the
  outside, is relative to the extent to which the 'outside' - in this case, the storage atmosphere - can absorb this water. This 'difference'
  between 'inside' and 'outside' is expressed by the difference in vapour
  pressure, or water potential difference.
- The second important factor is the permeability of the skin. Owing to
  differences in structure, this layer allows water vapour to diffuse at
  different rates and thus constitutes a resistance to water loss.

These two factors therefore determine the quantitative water loss per
unit time. The magnitude of these factors depends, for example on the
water potential of the soil while the tuber is growing and on the degree
of suberization and periderm formation. The relative humidity of the storage atmosphere and the maturity of the tubers at the moment of lifting
are important.

5.2 Water status in the potato

Water potential Ψ

Before further consideration of the moisture balance in the potato tuber, some biophysical concepts must be briefly defined. Since Slatyer &
Taylor (1960), the energy status of water has been generally represented
by the concept of water potential Ψ. The water potential Ψ represents the
energy content of water bound in a system relative to pure free water. Ψ =
0 (evaporation of pure free water under atmospheric pressure) constitutes
a reference point in the system.

Water potential Ψ and vapour pressure are related by the equation:

$$\Psi = \frac{RT}{V_W} \ln \, {}^{e}\!/e_o$$

in which

R $= 8.3147 \cdot J \cdot K^{-1} \cdot mol^{-1}$ (gas constant)

e $=$ partial vapour pressure of water

e_o $=$ saturation vapour pressure of water

T $:$ K (temperature in kelvins)

$V_W = 18.03 \times 10^{-6}$ m³ $\cdot$ mol^{-1} (molecular volume of H_2O)

Ψ $: J \cdot m^{-3}$ (Pa) $\qquad 10^5$ Pa $= 1$ bar

(In older literature: 10^6 dyne cm^{-2} $= 0.987$ atm $= 1$ bar.)

Ψ is related to the relative humidity of the air as follows:

$$\Psi = \frac{RT}{V_W} \cdot \ln \frac{\% \text{ relative humidity}}{100}$$

The water potential Ψ is the sum of the forces acting on water in a system:

$$\Psi = \Psi_{hydr.} + \Psi_{osm.} + \Psi_{matrix}$$

in which

$\Psi_{hydr.}$ $=$ hydrostatic potential - in plants, the turgor potential Ψ_{turgor}

$\Psi_{osm.}$ $=$ osmotic potential - caused by the chemical compounds dissolved in the water

$\Psi_{matr.}$ $=$ matrix potential - the water bound in the 'system' by biocolloids

The pressure at which water is transported outwards through the semipermeable membrane of the cell and cork layer is thus equal to the pressure difference between 'outside' and 'inside'. 'Outside' here means the water potential of the air at a specific relative humidity and temperature. 'Inside', the water potential is determined by the sum of the turgor, osmotic and matrix potentials.

5.2.1 *Energy status of water 'inside' the tuber*

This refers to the water relation inside the tuber as far as the dead

130

suberized periderm layer. The amount of water inside the tuber, like the
dry matter content, depends firstly on the potato as presented for storage after harvesting. On the one hand, water is added as a result of dry
matter conversion during respiration (see Chapter 4), while on the other,
water is lost by desiccation. The loss due to respiration is accompanied
by the elimination of sugars, whether or not after decomposition of
starch, in accordance with the equation already mentioned (Chapter 4.1):

$$C_6H_{12}O_6 + 6 O_2 \rightarrow 6 CO_2 + 6 H_2O + energy$$

i.e., 1 gmol of glucose, corresponding to 180 g, forms 6 gmol of water,
corresponding to 108 g of water. Thus, for each gram of dry matter lost
in respiration, 0.6 g of water is added.

The amount of water becoming available to the tuber per unit time thus
depends on the respiration rate. The respiration rate may vary substantially. For immature potatoes, for example, O_2 absorption of 50 ml $\cdot$ kg^{-1}
$\cdot$ h^{-1} at 10 °C corresponds to a dry matter loss due to respiration of
67 mg $\cdot$ kg^{-1} $\cdot$ h^{-1}. The equivalent figure for mature potatoes is 4 ml
kg^{-1} $\cdot$ h^{-1}, corresponding to a dry matter loss of 5.4 mg $\cdot$ kg^{-1} $\cdot$ h^{-1}.
Hence 60 % of this is regained in the form of water (Burton, 1964).
In 100 g potatoes, this loss of dry matter per day is thus:

For immature tubers: 67 x 0.1 x 24 = 160.8 mg

For mature tubers: 5.4 x 0.1 x 24 = 12.96 mg

The water gain from dry matter conversion is offset by the water loss
which, as stated earlier, depends partly on the water potential at the
boundary of the living tissue. The calculation of Ψ_i (i = internal) is
not simple. We have done measurements using a thermocouple psychrometer,
often obtaining values between Ψ_i = -15 x 10^5 and -25 x 10^5 Pa. Towards
the interior, these values in the cells of the potato tissue are in equilibrium with the partial potentials mentioned earlier:

$$\Psi_i = \Psi_{turgor} + \Psi_{osm.} + \Psi_{matrix}$$

in which the osmotic potential $\Psi_{osm.}$ and the matrix potential Ψ_{matrix} are
always negative.

During growth of the plant and extension of the cells of the tuber
tissue, the turgor potential Ψ_{turgor} is positive.
Measured values for Ψ_{turgor} of growing potato tubers are in the region of
+4 $\cdot$ 10^5 Pa (Gandar & Tannar, 1976). When water absorption by the tuber
ceases at lifting and storage begins, the value of Ψ_{turgor} falls to 0.
The $\Psi_{osm.}$ in the potato juice ranges from -8 x 10^5 to -12 x 10^5 Pa.
A problem however is that part of the water does not participate in $\Psi_{osm.}$
The matrix potentials, for example in leaves, are very low during growth.

131

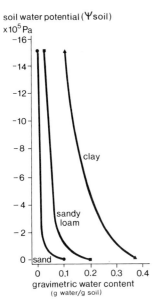

soil water potential (Ψsoil)
$\times 10^5$ Pa

Fig. 5.1. Typical water characteristic curves for sand, sandy-loam and clay soils (from Slatyer and McIlroy, 1961).

As far as is known, only a few direct measurements of this parameter are available for potato tubers during storage, given low values of Ψ_{matrix} = -0.1 x 10^5 to -1 x 10^5 Pa for potatoes, desiccated 50 % dry matter (Wiebe, 1972). The following can be calculated indirectly for a potato during storage at an average value of Ψ_i = -20 x 10^5 Pa.

$$\Psi_{osm.} + \Psi_{turgor} = \Psi_i - \Psi_{matrix} \rightarrow (-20 + 1) \cdot 10^5 = -19 \text{ x } 10^5 \text{ Pa.}$$

If during storage Ψ_{turgor} will become near zero, $\Psi_{osm.}$ will become ± -19 · 10^5 Pa, a rather high value! Further investigations will have to show if Ψ_{turgor} during storage will possibly become negative.
The value Ψ_i of the tuber tissue cannot be regarded independently of the water potential of the soil during tuber formation, as some degree of equilibrium will exist during growth, the difference $\Psi_{soil} - \Psi_i$ possibly playing some part in water absorption in addition to active absorption by the roots.
    Fig. 5.1 gives an impression of the differences in soil water potentials Ψ_{soil} occurring in different types of soil and water contents.

5.2.2 Energy status of water 'outside' the tuber

5.2.2.1 Immediately after lifting

    A critical situation for the potato may arise immediately after lifting. In exactly the same way as upon exposure to the storage atmosphere, the potato here also becomes into contact with the surrounding air, which may in this case have a low relative humidity (RH). The vapour pressure potentials for water Ψ_o (0= outside) at 20 °C may then be low, as follows:

98 % RH: Ψ_o = -27.3 x 10^5 Pa   70 % RH: Ψ_o = -482.2 x 10^5 Pa
95 % RH: Ψ_o = -69.5 x 10^5 Pa   65 % RH: Ψ_o = -582.4 x 10^5 Pa
90 % RH: Ψ_o = -142.5 x 10^5 Pa   60 % RH: Ψ_o = -690.6 x 10^5 Pa
85 % RH: Ψ_o = -219.9 x 10^5 Pa   50 % RH: Ψ_o = -937.1 x 10^5 Pa
80 % RH: Ψ_o = -301.7 x 10^5 Pa

After lifting, depending on the microclimate formed by soil and moisture sticking to the surface of the potato, substantial losses may occur in the absence of sufficient periderm formation, especially with potatoes lifted before maturity.

5.2.2.2 During storage

During storage the tuber is in constant contact with the storage atmosphere, which, in this case means the air (of normal composition with a certain moisture content) surrounding the potato. Depending on the amount of moisture contained in the air, the latter will have a specific relative humidity (% RH). Air with a high RH can take up little more moisture,

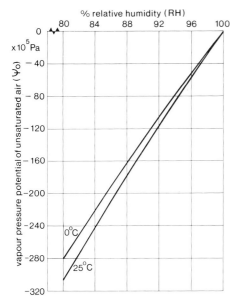

Fig. 5.2. Relation between relative humidity and vapour pressure potential of unsaturated air at 0 °C and 25 °C.

whereas air with a low RH can take up a great deal of moisture per unit weight. This is again expressed by the vapour pressure potential for water, or water potential Ψ_o (see Equation 5.2). Ψ_o has thus the dimension of a pressure, the minus sign indicating the direction. The relationship between the relative humidity and the water potential Ψ_o for the range 90 to 100 % RH, which is important for storage, is given in Fig. 5.2 at 0 °C and 25 °C. At 100 % RH, Ψ_o = 0. If the temperature remains the same no further moisture can be taken up by the air.

The relative humidity and hence also the amount of moisture which air can contain per kg depends on temperature. The same applies to the vapour pressure potential for water. However, the relationship between % RH and Ψ_o is only slightly influenced by temperature (Fig. 5.2).

5.2.3 Potential difference between 'inside' and 'outside'

The vapour pressure potential difference for water $\Psi_i - \Psi_o$ is clearly subject to variations due to desiccation or to the formation of water from the dry matter as a result of respiration. It may also assume different values depending on the environment of the potato. For example, for a potato tuber with a water potential Ψ_i of -10×10^5 Pa:

- After lifting:
  at 25 °C and 85 % RH $\Psi_i - \Psi_o = -(10-223.6) \cdot 10^5 = 213.6 \times 10^5$ Pa

- At the beginning of the storage period:
  at 10 °C and 96 % RH $\Psi_i - \Psi_o = -(10-53.2) \cdot 10^5 = 43.2 \times 10^5$ Pa
  at 10 °C and 98 % RH $\Psi_i - \Psi_o = -(10-26.3) \cdot 10^5 = 16.3 \times 10^5$ Pa

- After six months storage with a water potential of the tuber Ψ_i of for example, $- 50 \times 10^5$ Pa:
  at 10 °C and 96 % RH $\Psi_i - \Psi_o = -(50-53.2) \cdot 10^5 = 3.2 \times 10^5$ Pa

The difference in water potential $\Delta\Psi = \Psi_i - \Psi_o$ gives a clear indication of the difference in water status between the tuber and the surrounding atmosphere.

Although the difference in water potential $\Delta\Psi$ is important, it has become customary when discussing the movement of water vapour to express the driving force over a given pathway as the difference in water vapour concentrations over the pathway or as the corresponding differences in water vapour pressures.

The reason being that the picture of gaseous diffusion leads to a Fick's Law type of equation in which the resistance to flow is more or less constantly independant of the driving force, and the resistance associated with the use of $\Delta\Psi$ will vary with $\Delta\Psi$ (Dainty, 1969).

However, in most cases it has been assumed for calculation purposes that the water potential Ψ at the liquid-air interface is zero ($\Psi \cong 0$); that is that the water vapour concentration at the interface is the saturation vapour concentration at that temperature.

Measurements, however, indicate that the water potentials of the tubers during the storage period can easily increase to values of $\Psi_i = -40 \cdot 10^5$ Pa under normal conditions. It is obvious that figures of this magnitude significantly reduce the effective tuber-air vapour concentration difference, compared with that to be expected if it is assumed that $\Psi_{tuber} \cong 0$.

5.3 Water permeability of the skin

The permeability of water through the periderm, and thus also the degree of suberization, plays a very important part in limiting moisture loss during storage.

The permeability to water can be divided into three parts:

a. The water permeability of the semipermeable membranes of the cells constituting the tuber tissue. This permeability is high.

b. The permeability of the skin or periderm, which is much less than that of the membranes; the diffusion rate of water is low.

c. The permeability of the lenticels. About 98 % of the moisture loss is stated to be attributable to water transport through the periderm. Only 2 % of losses were found to be due to diffusion of water vapour in the gas phase through the lenticels (Burton, 1978a).

In undamaged mature potatoes the evaporative loss at 10 °C may be between 62 and 109 $\mu g \cdot cm^{-2} \cdot h^{-1} \cdot kPa^{-1}$ (Burton, 1973). Burton et al. (1955) found a value of 35 $\mu g \cdot cm^{-2} \cdot h^{-1} \cdot kPa^{-1}$ after removal of the skin, apart from losses due to wound healing - several hundred times as much. This clearly demonstrates the importance of a good periderm formation. The maturity of the tubers is also very important. Immature tubers 24 hours after lifting, produced moisture losses, depending on size, ranging from 1 to 6 $mg \cdot cm^{-2} \cdot h^{-1} \cdot kPa^{-1}$ (15 to 100 times as much) (Burton, 1973).

Damaging and bruising due to lifting and grading are also a significant cause of high moisture loss. Theoretical calculations followed by experiments (Burton & Hannan, 1957) suggest that the resulting moisture loss can easily become 3 to 5 times as great - this emphasizes the importance of preventing damage and of wound healing. The healing of wounds reduced moisture loss to one third of its initial level in two weeks of storage at 10 °C.

The degree of sprouting is also important. About 10 $mg \cdot cm^{-2} \cdot h^{-1} \cdot kPa^{-1}$ moisture loss occurs on the surface of the sprouts - 100 to 150 times as much as through the periderm. Intense sprouting thus substantially increases moisture loss. For every 1 % by weight of sprouts, the free moisture loss to the air increases by 0.075 % of the initial tuber weight per week per millibar of vapour pressure deficit (Burton & Hannan, 1957). The values mentioned above were determined per kPa of vapour pressure deficit of the unsaturated storage atmosphere. So the vapour pressure deficit was considered to be the driving force.

The part played by varietal differences is not clear. Appleman et al. (1928) considered that they had observed clear variations after harvesting, but these may have been due to differences in maturity and wound healing.

Differences were also found later in the storage season, but here again sprouting and the thickness of the periderm may also have played a part.

With regard to the moisture loss by evaporation on the surface of the tuber, it is important to remember that heat is required for this. The amount of heat required for example at a storage temperature of 5 °C is 2.49 kJ · g^{-1}. The spec. heat at 5 °C is ± 3.6 J · °C^{-1} (Burton, 1978b).

References

Appleman, C.O., W.D. Kimbrough & C.L. Smith, 1928. Physiological shrinkage of potatoes in storage. Bull. Maryland Agric. Exp. Stn., 303: 159-175.

Burton, W.G., G. Mann & H.G. Wager, 1955. The storage of ware potatoes in permanent buildings. II The temperature of unventilated stacks of potatoes. J. Agric. Sci., 46: 150-163.

Burton, W.G. & R.S. Hannan, 1957. Use of γ-radiation for preventing the sprouting of potatoes. J. Sci. Fd. Agric., 12: 707-715.

Burton, W.G., 1964. The respiration of developing potato tubers. Eur. Potato J., 7: 90-101.

Burton, W.G., 1973. Physiological and biochemical changes in the tuber as affected by storage conditions. Proc. 5th Triennial Conf. Eur. Ass. Potato Res., Norwich, 1972.

Burton, W.G., 1978 (a). The physics and physiology of storage. The potato crop. Editor P.M. Harris, Chapman and Hall, London.

Burton, W.G., 1978 (b). Post-harvest behaviour and storage of potatoes. Applied Biology, vol. III. Editor T.H. Coaker, Academic Press, London, New York, San Francisco.

Dainty, J., 1969. The water relations of plants. The physiology of plant growth and development. Editor: Malcolm B. Wilkins. McGraw-Hill, London.

Gandar, P.W. & C.B. Tanner, 1975. Comparison of methods for measuring leaf and tuber water potentials in potatoes. Am. Potato J., 52: 387-397.

Slatyer, R.O. & S.A. Taylor, 1960. Terminology in plant and soil-water relations. Nature, 187: 992-924.

Slatyer, R.O. & I.C. McIlroy, 1961. Practical microclimatology. Unesco, Paris.

Wiebe, H.H., 1966. Matric potential of several plant tissyes and biocolloids. Plant Physiol., 41: 1439-1442.

6 Diseases and defects liable to affect potatoes during storage

C.P. Meijers

During storage, potatoes may be affected by fungus or bacterial diseases, which may spread extensively in appropriate conditions. The tubers are almost always initially (or externally) infected with spores in the field. The principal defects may also already be caused in the field or during transport to the store. Some of the defects, such as bruising and black heart, are typical of stored potatoes.

6.1 Fungus diseases

6.1.1 Potato blight (Phytophthora infestans)

This tuber disease used to be very common, but serious outbreaks are now rare, owing to the development of new fungicides which prevent infection of the above-ground part of the plant during the growing season if applied at the correct time. The haulm is generally destroyed in the growing of ware potatoes, and this also tends to control blight because it kills any spores present on the leaves (particularly the lower leaves), thus preventing the tuber from being affected. Affected tubers have irregularly shaped brown patches inside. The fungus may spread throughout the tuber. In some years the condition is barely visible in the tubers ('initially attack'). The disease process evolves rapidly at temperatures of 20 to 25 °C and the condition becomes more readily visible. Hence, if 'initially attack' is observed in an export lot, storage under warm conditions for a few weeks (quarantine) is sufficient to allow the affected tubers to be removed. To control fungus diseases, the prime requirement is for the lot to be dry. The affected patches may eventually shrink inwards somewhat, but the tuber remains hard. If the potatoes are stored under humid, warm conditions, secondary infection by fungi and bacteria often occurs. The affected tubers, and sometimes also adjacent healthy tubers, then turn into a soft, rotten, evil-smelling mass.

If the consignment is quickly dried out with a forced draught and remains dry, the presence of a small percentage of blighted tubers does not constitute any problem for further storage. Affected tubers must be removed from consignments of both seed and ware potatoes. If diseased tubers

138

are planted, they in turn give rise to new diseased plants, each constituting a further source of infection.

6.1.2 Silver scurf (Helminthosporium solani)

Silver scurf is a very common fungus disease of potato tubers. At
first, more or less round, brownish patches appear, increasing if the tuber is severely affected, turning more silvery and coalescing (Fig. 6.1).
The entire tuber may be covered with silver scurf. The mycelium of this
fungus lives exclusively in the outermost cell layers (the periderm) of
the tuber. The cell walls thus locally become detached, giving rise to
openings through which air can penetrate and causing the typical silver
sheen. The condition makes the skin more permeable to water vapour, and
the skin shrivels owing to the resulting moisture loss. The fungus pro-
pagates by conidia, which are formed in large numbers in rings on the
dark conidiophores; the conidiophores can be distinguished with a magni-
fying glass, and resemble lamp brushes.

This fungus disease used to be regarded as a mere superficial blemish,
but it was subsequently found that serious attack not only substantially
increases weight losses (Mooi, 1968; Meijers, 1966), but also susceptibility to blue discoloration (Meijers, 1964). There are also indications
that severe shrivelling of the tubers reduces sprouting vigour (Mooi,
1968). For this reason, some seed potato importing countries lay down

Fig. 6.1. Silver scurf.

stringent standards for the permissible extent of silver scurf. The unattractive appearance of the tubers, which shows up particularly after
washing, is in practice also becoming increasingly relevant for ware potatoes.

The initial infection occurs in the soil, and is usually still relatively insignificant at harvesting, especially with seed potatoes. For this
reason, silver scurf can be regarded as a true disease of storage. Optimum conditions for propagation are storage temperatures of 20 to 24 °C
and high relative atmospheric humidity. Propagation does not occur if the
relative humidity of the atmosphere is below 90 % or the storage temperature falls below 3 °C (Mooi, 1957). This thus indicates the conditions
which should in principle be aimed at to prevent the spread of silver
scurf.

However, low relative atmospheric humidity encourages weight loss,
while a storage temperature of about 3 °C using outside air cooling is
generally not feasible until November. Again, such a low storage temperature directly after harvesting is not recommended as it inhibits wound
healing. Very rapid cooling after the curing period can be achieved by
mechanical means, thus facilitating control of silver scurf (Table 6.1).
Since both temperature and humidity are rather higher at the top of the
potato stack than at the bottom, silver scurf spreads most at the top of
the stack. The table shows that this disease spreads extensively in warm,
humid storage conditions. Conditions of this kind occur principally in
clamp storage, but even with modern storage methods it is difficult to
prevent the spread of this disease where a great deal of soil is present,
especially if in the form of local accumulations in the stack.

To control this disease during storage, an initial requirement is ra-

Table 6.1 Spread of silver scurf during storage with outside
air cooling (A) and mechanical cooling (B). The figures for
silver scurf attack are expressed as average percentages of
affected tuber surface.

Layer height in stack (m)	1962 / 1963		1963 / 1964	
	A 3-4 °C	B 3-4 °C	A 7-10 °C	B 3-5 °C
0.50	6.8	6.3	15.9	3.4
1.50	3.4	6.1	24.9	4.5
2.50	12.0	6.0	32.0	5.0
Affected on harvesting:	1.3		1.8	

pid forced-draught drying of the lot, which must then be kept dry. The spread of silver scurf remains limited if the tubers are and remain dry within seven days after harvesting (Mooi, 1968). This may be the case if they are stored in planting trays from the time of lifting onwards. However, forced-draught drying of the lot in modern stores does not usually take place so quickly, especially if there is a great deal of soil on and between the tubers. For this reason the potatoes should be harvested with as little soil as possible, such as there is not being too moist.

For the last few years a number of chemical agents have been available - the benzimidazoles, which, if properly applied, almost entirely prevent the spread of silver scurf. To control silver scurf in particular, it is important for these substances to be applied immediately after harvesting - i.e., when the tubers are placed in store. If seed potatoes are not treated until they are graded in autumn, silver scurf will have already spread substantially during the preceding period of relatively warm storage.

The effect of these systemic agents in controlling silver scurf is clearly evident even in the progeny (Table 6.2).

Table 6.2   Effect of spraying tubers with thiabendazole in autumn 1975 at the rate of 2 l/tonne to control silver scurf.

Treatment	Thiabendazole (g of active ingredient tonne)	Silver scurf (% affected tuber surface)		
			progeny	
		March 1967	December 1976	June 1977
Spraying	10	11.9	10.0	27.6
Spraying	20	4.0	6.2	16.2
Spraying	40	3.1	1.9	9.0
Untreated	-	33.7	18.9	41.9

The clear limitation of the spread already evident in the tubers sprayed in autumn 1975 after storage can still be detected in the progeny in virtually the same proportions even after many months of storage. See Chapter 22 for the application of these agents.

6.1.3 Black dot (Colletrotrichum coccodes)

This condition affects the tubers much less commonly than silver scurf. However, the signs and symptoms closely resemble those of silver scurf and both fungus diseases in fact often occur on the same tuber.

In black dot the patches have a brownish to grey tinge and are less

Fig. 6.2. Black dot.

clearly defined. The microsclerotia characteristic of this disease are also somewhat further apart than the conidiophores in silver scurf.

Slight attack is sometimes evident on a few tubers on harvesting. The fungus continues to grow in the skin and various microsclerotia later a-rise in the affected patches. The disease does spread somewhat during storage, but usually to a lesser extent than silver scurf.

Where potatoes are stored at low temperatures (not more than 3 °C), the areas badly affected by this fungus may assume a pockmarked appearance due to local necrosis of the skin; these patches become dark brown to black in colour and the surface becomes very superficially sunken (Fig. 6.2). This peel or skin necrosis is thought to be initiated by an attack of black dot (Mooi, 1959). In serious cases of peel necrosis, sprouting is likely to be adversely affected.

As with silver scurf, the primary method of control will be prompt forced-draught drying of the potato lot and maintenance of dry conditions thereafter. Chemical control seems to be possible only by immersion in an organomercury bath, as described for stem canker.

6.1.4 Rhizoctonia or stem canker

In this fungus disease (*Thanatephorus cocumeris*), the tubers are af-fected by brown-black scabs measuring 1 to 20 mm, which can be scratched off with a fingernail (Fig. 6.3). They consist of densely interwoven fi-laments and may be considered as a kind of dormant phase of the fungus (pseudosclerotia).

142

Fig. 6.3. Rhizoctonia.

The brown mycelium filaments may also occur in the eye pits and stem ends of otherwise non-sclerotic tubers.

If the seed material is not disinfected, these sclerotia after planting give rise to a mycelium which attacks and may kill the developing sprouts. Emergence is thereby delayed and becomes irregular. In cold a spring, in particular, this fungus may kill many slow-growing sprouts. For this reason, many seed potato importing countries lay down stringent requirements concerning *Rhizoctonia*-affected tubers.

The tubers are infected in the field. They may already be severely affected on harvesting, particularly if the seed material had not been disinfected and the period between destruction of the haulm and lifting was longer than two weeks. The condition may spread during storage (Labruyère & Meijers, 1965).

Like silver scurf, this spread takes place primarily in local soil accumulations in the stack. *Rhizoctonia* disease is found to be transferable from the surrounding contaminated soil to the tubers. Its spread is stimulated by humid, warm storage (Table 6.3).

As with silver scurf and black dot, this disease must be controlled during storage by, first of all, ensuring that not too much soil clings to the potatoes on harvesting, by avoiding local soil accumulations in stacking the potatoes and by drying the lot as quickly as possible.

Sprout suppressants based on propham and chlorpropham counteract the spread of this disease during storage (Labruyère & Meijers, 1965). This

Table 6.3 Percentage of tubers affected with Rhizoctonia
after 0, 2 and 4 months' storage at 8-12 °C.

		Storage (months)		
Extent of attack		0	2	4
Free		81	-	-
Mycelium only		13	63	27
Very slight		4	31	64
Slight		2	4	9
Moderate	sclerotia	-	1	-
Severe		-	1	-

is, however, of secondary importance, as these agents cannot be used on
seed potatoes.

The administration of benzimidazoles at the time of harvesting is
found to counteract propagation in the form of mycelium growth during
storage, but the dose recommended at harvesting is quite insufficient to
inactivate the sclerotia. The sclerotia can, however, be killed (at least
if they are not too thick) by dipping the seed potatoes in an organomercury bath. The 'five-minute method' is customary in the Netherlands, u-
sing a solution of 3 g/l or alternatively immersion for 20 to 30 min in
a solution of 1.5 g/l. The compound Lirotectasol (150 g thiabendazole +
150 g 8-hydroxyquinoline per litre of solution in organic acid) has recently been approved for this purpose in the Netherlands. Five minutes'
immersion in a solution of 7.5 ml/l is recommended.

An antibiotic based on validamycin has recently come on to the market
and has a good suppressant action when sprayed on to the tubers in the
planting machine. In addition, for the growing of both table and industrial potatoes, there are a number of agents administered at the time of
planting either in powder form or sprayed in the planting machine. The
'Rhizotox bomb' is also used in some parts of the Netherlands. These
smoke bombs contain trioxymethylene, which is converted into formaldehyde
vapour by heating. This vapour can kill sclerotia. Other fungus diseases
can in principle also be controlled in this way. However, it is essential
for the vapour to be well distributed throughout the location where the
planting trays filled with seed potatoes must stand for 48 h. This is not
always feasible in practice, and the results therefore are often disap-
pointing. One smoke bomb for every 15 m³ is recommended.

For the sake of completeness, it is also pointed out that *Rhizoctonia*
disease can also be controlled by soil treatment with PCNB at a dose rate
of 20-30 kg/ha.

6.1.5 Dry rot *(Fusarium spp.)*

Affected tubers exhibit rather sunken patches on the outside, on which numerous white-pink fungal cushions can be seen (Fig. 6.4). The skin shrivels locally and more or less clearly defined concentric rings are often evident. On cutting through, the soft, rotten patches are coloured light to dark brown and cavities with a bluish-coloured fluff of fungus are often visible. The tubers generally rot very slowly, so that the affected patches remain quite dry. The tuber then eventually shrivels up. In conditions favourable to the fungus, however, the rotting process may progress very quickly. The rotten patches are then moist and soft, so that they can readily be pushed in with the tumb ('thumb rot').

Every year, tubers affected with *Fusarium* are found in most lots of potatoes - usually more in potatoes from sandy soils than in ones from clay soils. The extent of the attack is closely bound up with tuber damage and susceptibility. The storability of a lot largely depends on whether or not this fungal condition is present. This becomes evident particularly where potatoes are re-stored after grading.

The *Fusarium* fungi are wound parasites which occur in all types of soil, but particularly in sandy and peat soils. In the Netherlands, potatoes are primarily affected by *F. solani* var. *coeruleum* and *F. sulphureum*.

The fungus infects the tubers through wounds caused during lifting, transport, and grading or through broken-off sprouts. Favourable growth conditions for the fungus are high atmospheric humidity and high temperature (15 to 20 °C). In this disease again, the largest number of affected

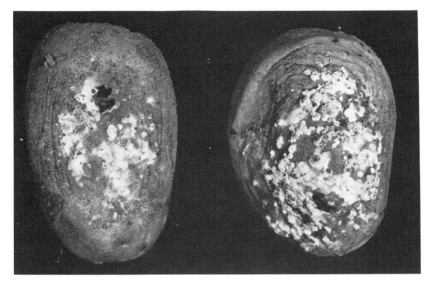

Fig. 6.4. Dry rot.

tubers are to be found in the top of the potato stack. An important factor in the occurance of *Fusarium* is tuber susceptibility. Resistance to
this disease is at a maximum at the time of harvesting (Boyd, 1972). For
this reason wounds occurring during harvesting, particularly if they heal
rapidly, do not generally lead to *Fusarium* attack.

However, susceptibility increases during storage. An important cause
of this disease is grading. Even the very small wounds which then arise,
coupled with the increasing susceptibility, make further storage of potatoes after grading a very risky business. The risk of rot increases the
later grading is carried out. With seed potatoes, which are often graded
in autumn, the effects are therefore not usually too serious. However, if
the potatoes are graded only just before planting, this may give rise to
serious infection of the tubers and poor emergence after planting (Boyd,
1972). Ware potatoes are almost always consumed within two or three weeks
of grading; little or no problems of *Fusarium* attack are then likely to
occur. If the potatoes are re-stored for a relatively long period after
grading, the likelihood of rot is then also greatly increased. This re-
storage after grading occurs occasionally with ware potatoes, when a
stock of big potatoes is kept for chipping in June and July.

There is a simple cutting test to determine the extent of *Fusarium*
contamination and susceptibility of the tubers (Nielsen & Johnson, 1972).
This gives an indication of the likelihood of rot in the event of re-storage after grading. In this test, a sample of 50 tubers per lot is taken.
The tubers are cut through, placed in a clean, multiple-ply paper bag and
well mixed. The cut surfaces thus come into contact with the outside of
various other tuber halves and become dirty. The paper bags are folded
for sealing and stored for two weeks at 14 to 16 °C, after which they are
inspected for *Fusarium*. The cut surface is cleaned by scraping to facilitate inspection. In the event of *Fusarium* attack, the tissue of the potato will be seen to have a dark brown discoloration. If the percentages
of cut surface affected are grouped in a small number of classes, an average percentage of *Fusarium*-affected tuber area per sample can be calculated. The result is called the *Fusarium* index, which may range between 0
and 75 (% affected cut surface).

This cutting test usually shows only slight attack shortly after harvesting owing to the high resistance of the tubers at this time (indices
of less than 5), but increasing susceptibility is observed after a few
months (Table 6.4). However, badly affected lots can be detected early on
by this test.

Differences can be demonstrated between growing areas.

The correlation between *Fusarium* index and the percentage rot found
later after re-storage emerges clearly from the results of a storage test
using thiabendazole carried out in 1974/75 (Tabel 6.5).

146

Table 6.4 Average Fusarium indices at different dates, 1974/1975 season, ware potatoes.

Growing area	Number of samples	19 December	11 February	7 April	6 June
I	4	1.2	5.1	24.4	41.2
II	12	0.9	1.9	6.3	37.4

Table 6.5 Fusarium index in March and percentages of Fusarium-affected tubers in July with different forms of application of thiabendazole; test with Bintje variety in the 1974/75 season.

Application of thiabendazole	Dose in g active ingredient/ tonne	Fusarium index, March	rot (kg/tonne) July
Untreated	-	70	279
Flowable - pulsfog apparatus	10	46	189
Flowable - pulsfog apparatus	25	22	151
Flowable - pulsfog apparatus	50	7	117
Flowable - pulsfog apparatus; 3 weeks after harvesting	25	27	191
Smoke tablets	10	33	156
Flowable - sprayed	10	11	87

The primary methods of controlling *Fusarium* are prevention of tuber damage and cool, dry storage.

In addition, it is found that *Fusarium* can readily be controlled by treating the tuber with benzimidazoles (Table 6.5). A good treatment immediately after harvesting is sufficient for the entire storage season, although it is interrupted by grading, as in the case of seed potatoes. This rot-inhibiting effect after treatment on harvesting is still clearly evident on cutting seed material shortly before planting.

6.1.6 Gangrene (Phoma spp.)

This fungus disease, which greatly resembles dry rot, is usually known as *Phoma* in the Netherlands. Two varieties of this fungus are known. *P. exigua* var. *exigua* commonly occurs in the Netherlands as a soil fungus, but is not very pathogenic. *P. exigua* var. *foveata* is much more dangerous than the first variety, but fortunately occurs only occasionally in the Netherlands. The condition caused by this fungus is regarded as the most serious storage disease occurring in England (Boyd, 1972). The fungus of-

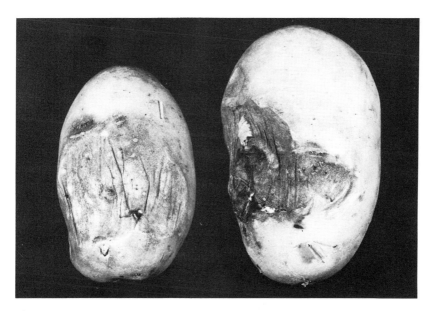

Fig. 6.5. Gangrene.

ten enters the tuber from the soil through wounds, but infection is also possible through lenticels.

Affected tubers have brown-black, sunken, often initially round patches, with numerous pycnidia if conditions are damp. The fungus cushions characteristic of *Fusarium* do not occur (Fig. 6.5). On cutting through, the affected tissue is at first brownish, and later more grey-black in colour

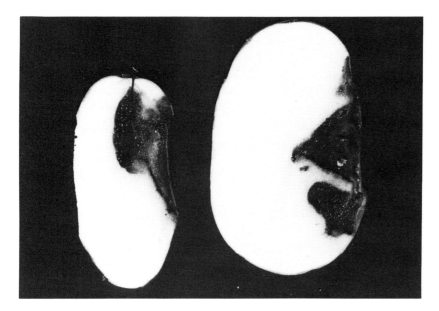

Fig. 6.6. Potato tissue affected by Grangrene.

(Fig. 6.6). The boundary with healthy tissue is quite sharply defined. A lot may be infected with *Phoma* without rot being visible (latent infection). If wound healing after damage is delayed by low temperatures, this fungus is given a chance to spread. As in the case of dry rot, tuber damage must be avoided as far as possible, and dry, cool storage following the observance of a satisfactory curing period is desirable. Susceptibility to this disease increases during storage.

This disease is well controlled in England by fumigation with 2-aminobutane shortly after harvesting. The liquid compound is heated to form a vapour, which is then blown on to the potato stack with a fan. The potatoes are often treated in cases in specially equipped rooms, but they can also be treated in bulk. The recommended dose is 200 ml/tonne. The use of 2-aminobutane is not allowed in the Netherlands.

The benzimidazoles also have a clear effect. To make it possible to detect latent infection of seed potatoes, the tubers must not be treated with compounds of this type before sampling. For further suppression of this disease, it is recommended that the seed potatoes be disinfected at an early date with organomercury or treated with Rhizotox bombs.

6.1.7 Skin spot (*Polyscytalum pustulans*)

This fungus disease is virtually unknown in the Netherlands, but in England and Scotland some varieties are often badly affected.

Affected tubers display small pustules, 1 to 2 mm in diameter and depth. These pustules are sometimes spread right over the tuber, but may also occur in small groups. The tissue under the pustules is darker in colour, giving rise in ware potatoes to somewhat larger peel losses. In seed potatoes, however, this disease may have much more serious consequences, because the fungus kills the eyes. After planting, the tuber thus fails to sprout or produces only a few stems.

The fungus enters the tuber via the lenticels, eyes or surface wounds. Infection takes place in the field, but the condition only becomes visible a few months after harvesting.

The spread of this disease is greatly encouraged by storage at low temperatures (less than 5 °C) anf high relative atmospheric humidity (over 90 %). Observance of a curing period at temperatures of about 15 °C shortly after harvesting has an insufficient effect; such a period with optimum storage conditions would have to last at least a few months for a substantial effect to be obtained (Boyd, 1972).

Treatment with compounds based on propham and chlorpropham, as is commonly carried out with ware potatoes, often gives rise to an increase in the number and diameter of the pustules, because these agents also inhibit wound healing.

Apart from dry, not excessively cool storage, the best methods of con-

trolling this disease are to treat the tubers on harvesting with one of
the benzimidazoles or to fumigate them with 2-aminobutane shortly after
the beginning of storage.

6.2 Bacterial diseases

6.2.1 Soft rot

Certain fungi and bacteria can very rapidly rot potato tubers, whose
substance is then transformed into a foul, evil-smelling, slimy mass.

Soft rot in western Europe is generally caused by bacteria of the *Erwinia* complex. Where plants are affected by soft rot of the stem *(E. carotovora* var. *carotovora)* or black leg *(E. carotovora* var. *atroseptica)*,
the diseased mother tuber rots in the soil. This releases a mass of bacteria into the soil; these spread in water through the soil and many infect the new tubers through lenticels or growth cracks.

Soft rot due to *Erwinia* spp. is often observed in fields which have
been flooded or waterlogged.

Potato lots which have become wet owing to rain after lifting are
known not to keep well. The tubers are then often coated with a film of
water, so that it takes a long time for such a lot to be dried by forced
draught. Such tubers are often badly contaminated with soil after unloading. This gives rise to relatively anaerobic conditions, in which bacterial infection occurs through lenticels or wounds.

Bacteria frequently also occur secondarily, e.g., after freezing of
tubers, rotting of mother sets or infection with dry rot or potato
blight.

Rotting due to *Pythium* spp. may also occur in warm summers in early-
lifted tubers. The fungus enters the tuber through the often badly damaged skin. The tuber contents then turn into a brown-black, watery paste
(Fig. 6.7).

Pink rot *(Phytophtora erythroseptica)* is also occasionally observed.
This fungus changes the colour of the tuber flesh, as seen on cutting
through, quite quickly to brick-red and later black.

The rotting process in the diseases described above takes place very rapidly in warm, humid conditions. Lots including tubers with soft rot are
not readily storable if more than 1 % of the tubers are affected. The
rotten tubers and mother tubers must as far as possible be eliminated before storage. Affected lots and ones which have become wet from rain must
be stored separately (e.g., in crates). The lot must then quickly be
blown dry, while avoiding any rise in the storage temperature. Dry, cool
storage is necessary. Nests of rotten tubers quickly arise in warm, humid
storage. As a result, the tubers on top can no longer be ventilated, thus
accelerating the rotting process. The tubers below are then also infected

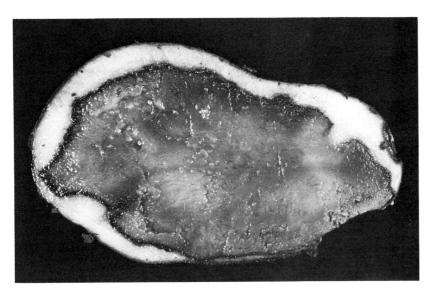

Fig. 6.7. Watery wound rot.

by the release of moisture. The rotting process is accompanied by a considerable temperature increase and local subsidence of the potato stack. The rotting can readily be smelt, and small flies can also be seen in the store. To prevent further rotting, there is usually no other course but to eliminate the rotten part. To date, no chemical agents capable of controlling bacterial rotting during storage are known.

6.2.2 Ring rot (Corynebacterium sepedonicum)

This highly infectious bacterial condition does not occur in the Netherlands, but is one of the principal tuber diseases in such countries as the USA, the USSR and Japan.

Ring rot has also been reported in some Scandinavian countries.

Because ring rot is so greatly feared, many countries, including the Netherlands, lay down very stringent requirements to prevent the import of infected potatoes.

The bacteria enter the tuber's ring of vascular bundles through wounds or the stem end, no external symptoms being evident. When cut through, affected tubers exhibit a cheesy, grey, cream-coloured or light to red-brown rotting of the ring of vascular bundles. Light pressure on the cut half of the tuber causes a jelly-like substance to be exuded from the vascular bundle ring. Cavities are visible between the medulla and the cortical parenchyma in badly affected tubers.

Ring rot is transmitted through seed. It is also disseminated by infected transport material (including sacks), planters, graders and knife blades. In normal conditions, the bacterium can survive for months on infected surfaces.

In particular, the use of cut seed has greatly facilitated the spread of this disease in some countries.

Satisfactory results have not hitherto been achieved with chemical methods of control. Apart from the disinfection of contaminated equipment and transport facilities, the best way of combating this disease will be to use seed which is truly free of ring rot.

Affected lots are best steamed and used for cattle feed.

6.2.3 Brown rot or bacterial wilt (Pseudomonas solanacearum)

This bacterial disease is liable to threaten the potato crop mainly in certain tropical and subtropical regions, although one strain of the bacterium can also live in cooler climates. Brown rot does not occur in the Netherlands.

The bacteria enter the tuber through the stems and stolons. The condition closely resembles ring rot. Affected tubers, when cut through, initially show a brown discoloration of the vascular bundle ring at the apical and stem ends. Characteristic pearl-like slimy lumps arise on this brown ring. Badly affected tubers are completely rotten even before harvesting, thus infecting the soil.

Slightly affected tubers, however, will keep for a considerable time in storage under cool, dry conditions.

The best methods of control are the use of disease-free seed, ample rotation of crops (combined with good weed control) and the planting of less susceptible varieties.

6.3 Potato tuber moth *(Phthorimaea operculella)*

This moth is a dreaded parasite in the countries around the Mediterranean Sea and in various other, tropical countries. The tuber moth is sometimes seen in western Europe when potatoes are imported from these countries. If the weather conditions are favourable, the tuber moth can cause some damage to potatoes for a short time after importation (i.e., in summer), but this is usually negligible. The Dutch climate is too cool for the moth to become permanently established.

It is the caterpillars which cause the damage to the tubers. The damage is somewhat similar to that caused by wireworm, but is usually much worse.

At first the caterpillars eat away surface corridors under the skin (Fig. 6.8). Later the white-yellow caterpillars (9 to 11 mm long when fully grown) penetrate deeper into the tuber, making large numbers of

Fig. 6.8. Potato tubers affected by potato tuber moth.

passages. There may be as many as ten caterpillars in one tuber. Badly affected tubers often rot.

Incipient attack may be detected the caterpillars betray their presence by their black-brown grains of excreta. The lifecycle from egg to moth is only three or four weeks at temperatures of 25 to 30 °C. Three to six generations may therefore occur in warm countries.

The caterpillars pupate on the outside of the tuber and also in the seams of sacks, in chinks, in corners of stores, etc.

In the last few decades, a variety of chemical agents have been used to combat the tuber moth in the field and in the potato store. The moth has developed a resistance to some of these. Apart from the public health aspects, the use of chemical agents in the potato store sometimes adversely affects the taste. The tuber moth cannot develop at temperatures of 10 °C or lower. Such temperatures may occur in refrigerated stores. Where refrigerated stores are not available in tropical countries, apart from the use of permissible efficient chemical agents, the principal methods of control will be regular cleaning of the store and careful inspection to remove affected tubers before they are brought into the store.

6.4 Defects

6.4.1 Mechanical damage

In addition to blue discoloration, this is the most common defect. Increasing mechanization in harvesting, tranport to and from the store and all operations associated with grading and marketing have resulted in a considerable increase in tuber damage. The following clearly demonstrable causes may be mentioned: incorrectly equipped or adjusted lifting machines, excessive dropping heights, high belt speeds and failure to coat the grading riddles with rubber. Dropping heights must be limited to 30 to 40 cm, while conveyor speed must not exceed 40 m/min.

The damage - several different types can be distinguished - often only becomes visible after several days or weeks. A typical form is hard, dry, grey-white mass of starch from the damaged cells, evident on cutting. Tuber damage gives rise to an increase in the respiration rate and in evaporation losses. In addition, the quality of the lot is reduced and skin and flesh losses are greatly increased. Again, these damaged areas frequently constitute a point of entry for microorganisms. This may also occur with less conspicuous damage, of the kind occurring during grading.

6.4.2 Blue discoloration or black spot

6.4.2.1 Occurrence of blue discoloration

Tubers with this defect display local blue-grey discoloration of the potato tissue on cutting. This discoloration is almost always to be found just below the skin around the vascular bundle tissue (Fig. 6.9). However, the blue colour may go much deeper in tubers which are very susceptible to this condition ('worn-out' tubers). The discoloration occurs principally at the stem end.

The condition is usually not visible externally; only if the tuber is very seriously affected can the discoloration be observed through the skin below the often rather sunken patch. To see the discoloration, the patch must be cut into or the tubers peeled. It is obviously impossible, or virtually so, to pick out all the tubers affected with this defect, which is particularly common in ware potatoes.

The discoloration of the potato tissue is caused by oxidation of certain phenols by the enzyme phenol oxidase. Until a few years ago it was

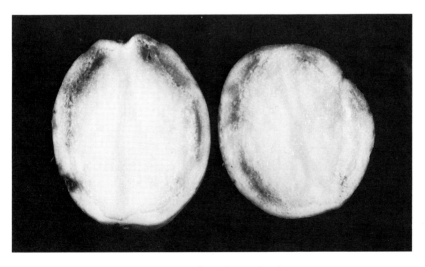

Fig. 6.9. Black spot (blue discoloration).

154

thought that this discoloration was attributable solely to the amino acid tyrosine, but it is now considered that not only tyrosine but also other phenols (including chlorogenic acid and caffeic acid) are involved (Müller, 1979). In these reactions, the blue-black pigment melanin is formed via the red-coloured intermediate product dopachrome. Oxygen is required for this process, but can only be supplied after the cells have been damaged. Shortly after the damage occurs, a red discoloration of the tissue occurs first; the blue coloration only becomes visible a few hours or even one or two days later. High storage temperatures after the damage accelerate the development of the blue coloration (Dwelle & Stallknecht, 1976).

If no cells are damaged, black spot also does not occur. On the other hand, not every instance of damage results in black spot.

There are big differences in susceptibility to black spot, not only between varieties but also within one and the same variety and even within a single lot. The fact that susceptibility to black spot exists does not necessarily mean that the lot must in fact exhibit the condition, either severely or slightly, because little or no black spot will arise given careful treatment. Even so, such a lot is extremely dangerous, because as soon as the lot is handled roughly anywhere along the line between the grower and the consumer or processor, black spot will occur. On the other hand, rough treatment may give rise to more black spot in a lot which is essentially insusceptible than would occur in a susceptible lot treated with due care. For this reason, the proper indicator of the degree of susceptibility to black spot of a lot is the increase in the condition occuring given comparable treatment.

The blue patches must be removed for both fresh consumption and industrial processing. This often involves substantial pith losses and much additional manual labour. Because the discoloration is not visible immediately after the damage, any complaints are only made some time after delivery. By then, considerable expense in packaging and transport has already been incurred.
Black spot often also constitutes grounds for export rejection.

Although this condition has long been known and has been the subject of a large volume of research, our knowledge of the factors involved in the occurrence of blue discoloration is still very incomplete.

It is clear that tuber susceptibility to black spot is largely determined by growth conditions. One of the main factors is certainly the dry matter content of the tubers: it can in general be stated that the tubers are more susceptible to black spot the higher the dry matter content, although there are exceptions, probably related to the cell size of the potato tissue and the distribution of the dry matter in the tuber. Tubers with large cells are more susceptible to black spot than ones with small cells (Van Es et al., 1975b).

The dry matter content of the tubers is influenced by fertilization, particularly with N and K, the lenght of the growing period, the moisture supply to the plants and the time of destruction of the haulm. The tissue (turgor) of the tubers, the soil temperature at the time of lifting and the degree of care taken during transport are also relevant. Since the tubers at the time of harvesting are not yet as susceptible to black spot as after a certain period of storage, the proportion of affected tubers shortly after lifting is usually still small (20 to 30 kg/tonne) in normal years. The biggest problems with black spot arise after storage. Important factors here are tuber temperature during grading and transport, weight losses and bruising.

6.4.2.2 Tuber temperature

Particularly after storage, the temperature at which the tuber is transported and graded is found to be of the greatest importance. At low temperatures the tubers are much more susceptible to damage (Baganz, 1968). The susceptibility of the tubers to black spot can be greatly reduced by warming the potatoes before tuber damage can occur. The effect of warming (and indeed also cooling) is clearly brought out by a test with the Bintje variety (Table 6.6).

Table 6.6 Effect of storage temperature and warming on potato susceptibility to black spot (Bintje variety), observed on various dates in 1969/1970.

Storage temperature (°C)	Warming or cooling to stated temperature (°C) 1	% tubers with moderate and severe black spot:					
		11/11	15/12	20/1	9/3	20/4	1/6
3	-	87	85	84	80	86	74
3	10	20	24	37	45	62	54
3	20	1	7	21	23	35	17
10	3	40	22	28	32	55	70
10	-	9	7	15	8	29	45
10	20	1	1	2	2	9	21

1. During one week

Warming the tubers from the initial storage temperature of 3 °C to 10 °C resulted, particularly at the beginning of the storage season, in an appreciable decrease in susceptibility to black spot. The result of warming to 20 °C is even better. The effect of the warming declines the longer the period of storage. 'Warm' storage at a constant 10 °C proved

Table 6.7 Black spot indices 1) before store emptying and 3-5 days after grading; Bintje variety; test period 1972 to 1975.

Warmed to 12 °C	Sold before 1 April	Before emptying of store	After grading	Number of samples
No	Yes	7.8	8.8	103
No	No	7.3	8.6	34
Yes	Yes	7.4	6.4	224
Yes	No	9.2	9.2	278
Average		8.2	8.1	639
Not warmed		7.7	8.8	137
Warmed		8.4	8.0	502

1. Range of indices: 0-50

Fig. 6.10. Shaker equipment.

to be extremely favourable. The effect of the preceding storage temperature is also evident from the result of cooling from 10 to 3 °C; the relevant tubers were less susceptible to black spot on all observation dates than those stored at a constant 3 C°. Other research has shown that as soon as the tubers have reached the desired temperature, no further significant decline in susceptibility to black spot is to be expected in the short term. The fact that this does seem to occur in long-term 'warm' or 'cold 'storage suggests the existence of other, still unknown factors.

For practical purposes, it is recommended that the lots, depending on their susceptibility to black spot, be warmed before grading to a minimum of 12 to 15 °C. However, lots which are extremely susceptible to this condition must always be warmed to 18 to 20 °C.

Comprehensive practical tests have shown that sampling shortly before the stores are emptied, followed by application of the IBVL 'shaking method', can provide extremely good impression of the degree of black spot to be expected after normal grading (Table 6.7) (Meijers & Van Loon, 1978). In this shaking method (Fig. 6.10), a sample of 100 tubers is shaken for 30 s on an approximately 1 m² shaker plate (at a rotational speed of 290 rev/min). This method is currently used in the Netherlands to determine susceptibility to black spot to allow the grower to be paid by quality.

6.4.2.3. Weight losses

Table 6.6 clearly shows that the susceptibility of the tubers to blue discoloration increases during storage. This must be attributed to loss of moisture and tissue tension (turgor) due to evaporation.

The tubers at the bottom of the store are the most susceptible to blue discoloration, because this is where the highest moisture loss occurs (Meijers, 1966). As it happens, the relation between the degree of moisture loss and susceptibility to blue discoloration is non-linear. If the tuber has not yet sustained any moisture loss, the tissue tension will be optimal. As the tuber increasingly loses moisture, the tissue tension declines and susceptibility to blue discoloration increases (Kunkel et al., 1965).

However, very soft tubers are not damaged so readily because of the concomitant elasticity of the cell walls. On the other hand, tubers in the soil in extremely wet conditions again become very susceptible to blue discoloration, apparently because their turgor becomes too high. It should be pointed out that little is yet known about the susceptibility of the cells to damage and such factors as turgor, cell wall structure and elasticity.

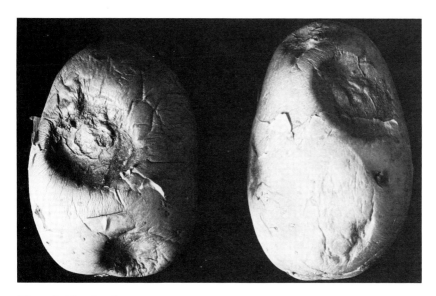

Fig. 6.11. Bruises.

6.4.2.4 Bruising or pressure spots

One of the consequences of modern storage using stack heights of 3.5 to 4.0 m is the occurrence of bruising. Where tubers have been in contact with each other during storage, the surfaces may be flattened and indented (Fig. 6.11). These indentations are known in practice as bruises or pressure spots because they result from the pressure exerted by the potatoes on each other (Table 6.8).

Table 6.8 Weight losses and bruising at different heights in the potato stack with (A) and without (B) air humidification; variety Bintje; storage temperature 3-5 °C.

Height above ground (m)	Weight losses (kg/tonne)		Bruising 1 (% tubers)	
	A	B	A	B
0.25	29	37	24	64
0.50	22	31	23	51
1.00	20	27	19	39
1.50	18	28	12	32
2.00	23	26	7	11
2.50	18	23	2	10
3.00	17	27	0	1
Average	21	28	12	30

1. Percentage tubers with moderate and severe bruises

159

The flesh under a bruise is softer and can be cut rather less easily. Discoloration under the bruise is rarely observed immediately after the store is emptied. The smaller bruises disappear almost entirely after a few days, and the deeper indentations partially so. Depending on the severity of the defect, the tissue under a bruise is more or less badly deformed and damaged.

A deformed and damaged tissue is illustrated in Fig 6.12. Undamaged tissue is shown for comparison in Fig. 6.13 (both electron microscope pictures).

In very bad cases the starch grains are cemented together (Van Es et al., 1975a). When the pressure is removed on emptying of the stores, the tissue partially springs back, giving rise to small cavities in the tissue in the case of severe bruises. The deformed and sometimes damaged tissue is particularly sensitive to dropping and impact, so that a blue-grey discoloration under the bruises may be observed very soon after grading. It is precisely this characteristic - the high sensitivity to blue discoloration - which makes bruising such a badly feared defect. The fact that discoloration can be seen under a bruise very rarely when the store is emptied is probably attributable to expulsion of all air, and hence also oxygen, from the tissue by the pressure. When the pressure is relieved, and if cavities form, air can return and the discoloration can then arise (see Section 6.4.2.1).

Research has shown that not only pressure but also weight loss can play a very important part (Meijers, 1965). Not only pressure but also weight losses are highest at the bottom of the store (Table 6.8), and it is therefore clear that this combination will often give rise to a very large number of bruised tubers particularly in the bottom metre of the store.

There are not only varietal differences but also clear differences from year to year. This defect is worse after dry summers or considerable ventilation. This problem is generally more serious in seed potatoes (often already in October and November) than in better-matured ware potatoes, where bruising is usually observed only in March or later.

The discoloration under the bruises is also related to the susceptibility of the lot to blue discoloration. In ware potatoes, a high proportion of the blue discoloration observed from April onwards may be attributed to bruising.

One approach to prevention of this condition would be to reduce the stacking height, but this is not practicable. It is better to start with well-hardened tubers on harvesting; these should then be ventilated as little as possible and then only at high atmospheric humidity, followed by careful grading and transport at tuber temperatures which are not too low. Humidification of the ventilation air (Table 6.8) has a favourable effect, greatly reducing the proportion of tubers with severe bruises.

160

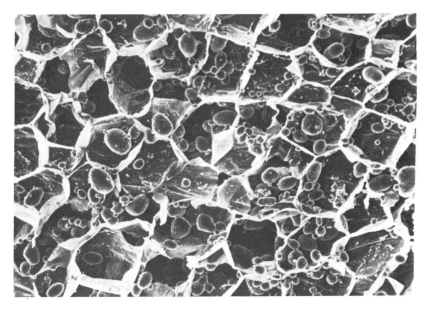

Fig. 6.12. Undamaged potato tissue (Micrograph obtained with a Scanning Electron Microscope; magnification x 110).

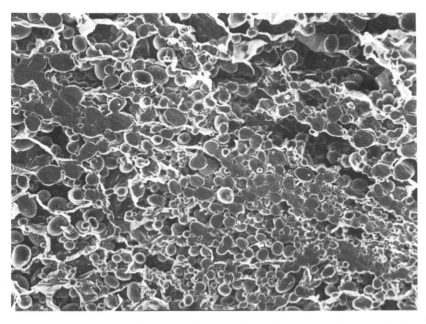

Fig. 6.13. Potato tissue under bruises (Micrograph obtained with a Scanning Electron Microscope; magnification x 110).

Where potatoes are stored in crates under comparable conditions, bruising is, of course, less of a nuisance, because the stack height is only about 1 m.

6.4.3 Glassiness; 'water bags'

A long period of warm, dry weather during the growing season may give rise to second growth. Owing to the high soil temperature, the tubers will then sprout and different forms of second growth may occur. The degree of second growth depends on the time and length (intensity) of the warm spell. One form of second growth is the occurence of secondary tubers formed on the sprout of the primary tuber. The latter passes the assimilates formed in the haulm on to the new tuber. However, if the haulm is destroyed this is no longer possible, but the secondary tuber, if still insufficiently mature, will then withdraw assimilates from the primary tuber. The dry matter content of the latter is thereby reduced, and this eventually becomes visible in the form of glassiness of part of the tuber. The cells of the glassy part often contain virtually no more dry matter and are filled solely with cell moisture. This glassiness begins at the stem end and becomes increasingly visible the more assimilates are withdrawn. The entire tuber may become glassy or spongy (Fig. 6.14).

As long as the plant is still green, glassy tubers are found only seldom. Glassiness generally commences after destruction of the haulm. The process is interrupted on lifting breaking the link between the old and the new tuber.

To limit glassiness, the period between haulm destruction and lifting must thus be as short as possible. However, it is very difficult to give any general recommendation as to whether or when the haulm should be des-

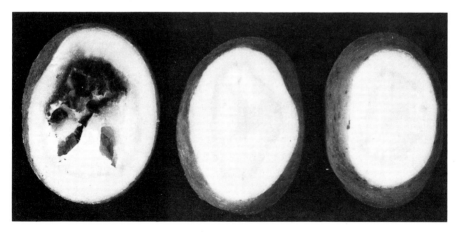

Fig. 6.14. Glassiness.

troyed. This depends on the date, expected yield and degree of second growth.

Clearly, however, lifting shortly after haulm destruction inevitably means that a part of the tubers (the newly formed ones) will be either not fully or not at all hardened, with all the resulting consequences (abrasions, high weight losses).

Tuber glassiness does not usually progress further during storage (Krijthe & Hulstein, 1959). However, 'water bags' may develop from the very glassy or partially spongy tubers during the first few weeks of storage. The entire contents of the tuber then consist of a watery substance held together by the skin. Under pressure or during handling, these tubers fall to pieces and the tubers below them are contaminated. Damaged or abraded tubers may then rot, partly owing to the presence of bacteria. If it is found on harvesting that the lot includes very glassy tubers or even 'water bags', every effort should be made to keep the lot dry, firstly by forced-draught drying and then by more than normal ventilation. In extreme conditions (presence of large amounts of soil and 'water bags'), it may be justifiable to heat this air somewhat. But since the conditions for secondary bacterial infections also become more favourable at higher temperatures, the air must not be heated by more than 5 °C. This will inevitable involve some additional weight loss. To minimize these extra losses, such lots should preferable be sold as quickly as possible as soon as they are thoroughly dry. Cool storage (temperatures 4 to 7 °C) are preferable for rot control, and intense heating at the end of the storage period should be avoided. This does not matter very much, because the susceptibility of such lots to black spot will usually be less.

To eliminate the less glassy tubers which are nevertheless not fit for consumption, the tubers should be passed after washing through a salt bath with a specific gravity of 1.055 to 1.065. The bath salt concentration required is determined partly by the variety and the required degree of elimination of glassy tubers.

6.4.4 Mother tubers

A large number of mother tubers are sometimes harvested together with the crop and placed in store, particularly when seed potatoes are lifted. This is an increasingly serious problem, particularly in drier years. In the past, the mother tuber was eliminated at the time of lifting, but this is often no longer possible with modern methods of lifting potatoes.

These mother tubers can be compared to the 'water bags' discussed earlier. They are squashed flat after a few weeks of storage and the watery contents spread over the tubers below. To prevent rotting of the healthy tubers, additional ventilation is recommended in the first few weeks, as in the case of 'water bags'. The grower will not be inclined to provide much ventilation in dry summers, when the lot will have been dried very quickly because little damp soil will have been clinging to the potatoes. However, the presence of mother tubers calls for extra care if subsequent surprises with nests of tubers affected by soft rot are to be avoided.

6.4.5 Black heart

Tubers with black heart initially show no external symptons, but when cut through, the heart of the tuber is found to be coloured blue-black (Fig. 6.15). These discoloured patches are sharply delineated. A crack-like cavity is then often observed in the centre, due to shrivelling of dead tissue. The tubers may remain intact for a long time, but will eventually rot. Black heart may be caused by lack of oxygen or excessive CO_2 concentration, e.g., at high temperatures or with insufficient air renewal. High temperatures (over 35 °C) may cause this defect in summer where tubers are exposed to substantial heating, e.g., after lifting.

Such high temperatures are virtually unknown in the Netherlands, while modern methods of lifting and transport obviate long-term exposure to intense sunshine, so that black heart seldom occurs in summer in the Netherlands. Insufficient air renewal may occur if badly abraded tubers are

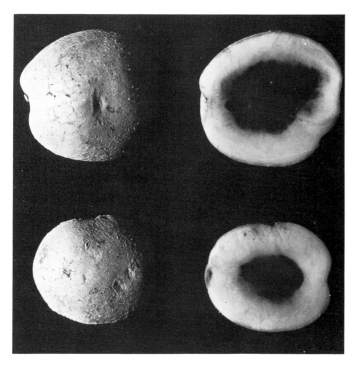

Fig. 6.15. Black heart.

164

placed in store in warm weather, rapidly stacked to a height of 3 to 4 m and not immediately provided with regular ventilation.

However, a few lots with black heart are encountered every year in the Netherlands following warming to control blue discoloration. The affected potatoes are those in the immediate vicinity of the fan and air ducts. This indicates that the heating was excessive. The air should preferably not be heated to more than 20 to 22 °C.

Old stores are generally anything but airtight, so that oxygen deficiency will be very rare even after a long period of lack ventilation. Modern stores constructed with sandwich panels are more dangerous in this respect, because they are more airtight.

In stores with total mechanical cooling, where internally cooled air is used constantly, some air renewal is required to prevent this defect. However, an air renewal of 10 m³/tonne · 24 h is sufficient.

Inadequate ventilation in clamps or stacks covered for a long period with plastic may also give rise to black heart. It is difficult to specify the oxygen level at which black heart problems may arise, because this depends on a variety of factors (temperature, respiration rate, air leaks and storage time). Lack of air renewal in long-term storage (e.g., in frosty periods) may constitute a hazard even to man in reasonably well sealed stores, as the oxygen level may have fallen excessively. If it is observed, for example, that a cigarette will not continue to burn, this should be taken as a warning.

References

Baganz, K., 1968. Untersuchungen über den Temperatureinfluss auf verschiedene Festigkeitskennwerte der Kartoffeln. Albrecht Thaer-Archiv, 12. Band, Heft 3.

Boyd, A.E.W., 1972. Potato storage diseases. Rev. Pl. Path. 51 (5).

Dwelle, R.B. & G.F. Stallknecht, 1976. Rates of internal black spot bruise development in potato tubers under conditions of elevated temperatures and gas pressure. Am. Pot. J. 53: 235-244.

Es, A. van, K.J. Hartmans & C.P. Meijers, 1975. Onderzoek naar de diepergelegen oorzaken van de blauwgevoeligheid van aardappelen II. IBVL-Publikatie 280.

Es, A. van, K.J. Hartmans & M.H. van Calker, 1975. Onderzoek naar de dieper-gelegen oorzaken van de blauwgevoeligheid van aardappelen III. (De invloed van de celgrootte). IBVL-Publikatie 288.

Krijthe, N. & G. Hulstein, 1959. Onderzoek aan pootgoedpartijen waarin 'glas' voorkomt. IBVL-Rapport Serie A No. 30.

Kunkel, R. & W.H. Gardner, 1965. Potato tuber dehydration and its effects on the black spot of Russet Burbank potatoes in the Columbia Basin of Washington. Am. Potato J. 41: 109-124.

Labruyère, R.E. & C.P. Meijers, 1965. De uitbreiding van Rhizoctonia tijdens de bewaring II. IBVL-intern rapport 240.

Meijers, C.P., 1964. Zilverschurftaantasting op aardappelen, de invloed daarvan op de blauwgevoeligheid van de knollen en de uitbreiding tijdens de bewaring. IBVL-Jaarboek, p. 72-81.

Meijers, C.P., 1965. Drukplekken op aardappelen. IBVL-Publikatie Jaarboek 139.

Meijers, C.P., 1966. De invloed van bewaarkondities op het optreden van bewaargebreken bij aardappelen. IBVL-Jaarboek, p. 77-89.

Meijers, C.P. & C.D. van Loon, 1978. De blauwaktie 1972-1976. Bedrijfsontwikkeling, 898-902.

Mooi, J.C., 1957. Zilverschurft bij aardappelen. IBVL-Publikatie 17-1957.

Mooi, J.C., 1959. A skin necrosis occurring on potato tubers affected by black dot (*Colletotrichum atramentarium*) after exposure to low temperature (preliminary communication). Eur. Pot. J. 2: 58-68.

Mooi, J.C., 1968. De aantasting van de aardappel door zilverschurft (*Helminthosporium solani*). IPO-Mededeling 482.

Müller, K., 1979. Chemisch und physiologisch bedingte Ursache von Blaufleckigkeit, Rohbreiverfärbung und Kochdunkelung der Kartoffel. Der Kartoffelbau 11: 404-407.

Nielsen, L.W. & J.T. Johnson, 1972. Seed potatoes contamination with fusarial propagules and their removal by washing. Am. Pot. J. 49: 391-395.

PRINCIPLES OF POTATO STORAGE

7 Storage losses

A. Rastovski

7.1 Introduction

Potato tubers are living organisms and as such are unavoidably subject
to losses during their autonomous life - i.e., after the tuber has been
seperated from the plant. This is because the life processes require
energy and the tuber has to supply this from its own reserves. During
storage, therefore, the tuber sustains a continuous weight loss and
constantly undergoes changes in chemical composition which may adversely
affect its quality, depending, of course, on the duration of storage.

Potatoes are also perishable products. Microorganisms (fungi and
bacteria) can cause potatoes to rot, resulting in substantial losses.
Nevertheless, the potato is a product which can be stored, since all the
losses mentioned are greatly dependent on the storage conditions and can
be limited by storing the potatoes under favourable conditions.

However, the storability of potatoes is already determined before the
beginning of storage, by such factors as variety; growing techniques;
type of soil; weather conditions during growth; disease before harvesting; maturity of potatoes at the time of harvesting; damage to tubers
during lifting; transport and filling of the store; etc.

Hence three variables determine the storage losses, viz., the potato,
storage conditions and storage duration. It must be realized that potato
quality cannot be improved even by the best storage. Good storage can
merely limit storage losses in a good product over relatively long periods of storage. Bad storage results in high storage losses, even in an
originally good product.

Storage losses are often specified as weight losses and losses in the
quality of potatoes, although the two cannot always be distinguished.
Storage losses are caused by the following processes:
a. Respiration
b. Sprouting
c. Changes in the chemical composition of the tuber
d. Spread of diseases
e. Damage by extreme temperatures
f. Evaporation of water from the tubers

All these processes are influenced by the storage conditions.

7.2 Respiration

As stated in Chapter 4, respiration provides the energy required to maintain the life processes in the tuber. In respiration, the sugars of the tuber are converted into water and carbon dioxide by absorption of oxygen from the environment, heat energy being evolved. Sugars are formed by hydrolysis of starch. Starch is lost during respiration, giving rise to losses of dry substance.

The respiration rate depends greatly on temperature and other factors. Fig. 4.1 (Chapter 4) clearly shows that the lowest respiration rate is obtained at temperatures in the region of 5 °C. The respiration rate increases slowly up to about 15 °C, above which respiration begins to increase sharply. Reducing the temperature below 3 °C also results in a sharp increase in respiration; at 0 °C, the rate of respiration is the same as at 20 °C. Respiration results directly in losses of dry substance in potatoes. These losses are relatively low in the range 5 to 10 °C and seldom exceed 1.5 % of the fresh weight of the potatoes in a storage period of six to eight months. However, this is equivalent to a loss of 6 to 7 % of the total dry substance of the potatoes. These losses are substantially greater at higher temperatures.

Since a part of the dry substance is converted into water which re- mains in the potato, the weight loss due to respiration is, however, appreciably lower, not exceeding 0.5 to 0.6 % of the fresh weight of the potatoes at temperatures of 5 to 10 °C over a storage period of six to eight months.

Nevertheless, respiration is an important indirect source of weight losses during storage. To maintain the temperature of the potatoes at a specific level, the heat evolved by the potatoes in the process of res- piration must be removed - i.e., the potatoes must be cooled. As descri- bed later, cooling always causes water to evaporate from the tubers, resulting in weight loss. This evaporation water loss is responsible in good potatoes for 90 % of the total weight losses during storage, and may also adversely affect potato quality (e.g., giving rise to sensitivity to blue discoloration, bruising, etc.).

It is therefore important to keep the respiration rate low - i.e. by preferably storing potatoes at temperatures in the region of 5 °C.

7.3 Sprouting

Sprouting of potatoes can result in relatively high weight losses. First of all, the sprout itself is a direct loss in the amount of fresh potatoes available for sale. But much greater losses occur as a result of intensive evaporation of water from the sprout surface.

Sprouting and sprout inhibition are discussed in detail in Chapters 3 and 21.

There are two methods of keeping potatoes sprout-free during storage:

1) Storage at temperatures of 2 to 4 °C.

2) Use of sprout suppressants.

7.4 Changes in the chemical composition of potatoes

The main changes in the chemical composition of potatoes caused by storage conditions and liable adversely to affect potato quality are the formation of solanine and an increase in the sugar content (Chapter 1 and 2).

To prevent intensive sweetening of ware potatoes, the storage temperature must be 7 °C or higher. Solanine formation is prevented by storing the potatoes in the dark.

7.5 Spread of diseases

In certain circumstances, diseases may give rise to substantial losses during potato storage. To counteract the spread of diseases in the store, curing must first be stimulated at the beginning of the storage period and, if the potatoes are wet when placed in the store, they must immediately be blown dry. The potatoes must then be stored at low temperatures and kept dry (Chapters 6 and 19).

7.6 Damage by extreme temperatures

Both extremely high and extremely low temperatures damage potato tubers.

A potato tuber freezes at a temperature of -1 to -2 °C. Frozen tubers quickly become spoilt and are no longer usable. In some varieties, however, the tuber tissue can already be damaged if the potatoes are stored for long periods at below 2 °C. For this reason the storage temperature should not be allowed to fall below 2 °C for prolonged periods.

Potatoes begin to respire strongly at a temperature of 30 °C or higher; the tuber requires a great deal of oxygen and develops large amounts of CO_2. At a certain temperature respiration may become so intensive that the cells deep inside the tuber can no longer obtain sufficient oxygen and the carbon dioxide formed cannot be released. These cells then die, giving rise to 'black heart' (Chapter 6).

7.7 Evaporation of water from tubers

In evaporation, water is lost from the potatoes, so that the amount (weight) of product remaining for sale is smaller. Water loss is thus principally an economic loss; the original food value of the potatoes is virtually unaffected. However, large water losses may adversely affect the quality of potatoes. Tubers which have lost a lot of water are more susceptible to mechanical damage, such as bruising and blue discoloration. High water loss also leads to greater peeling losses, reduction of culinary quality, etc. In economic terms, it is therefore very important to limit water loss. The mechanism of water loss in potatoes is analysed in Chapter 9.

At this point it is sufficient to state that water loss during potato storage depends on heat production in the potatoes, the temperature of the potatoes, the relative humidity of the air, the quality of the potato skin (suberization), sprout growth and the duration of ventilation. Since water loss in badly suberized and damaged potatoes may be very high, it is important to stimulate suberization and wound healing in the tubers right at the beginning of the storage season by keeping the potatoes at a temperature of 15 to 20 °C and a relative atmospheric humidity of 95 % or more. Minimum possible ventilation is required during this seven- to 14-day curing period. After this, the potatoes must be cooled to the required storage temperature as quickly as possible. In addition, the potatoes must be prevented from sprouting throughout the storage season. Since the water loss depends on the heat production of the potatoes, it will be at a minimum at storage temperatures of about 5 °C (Section 7.2).

Very humid air (95 % RH or higher) should preferably be used for ventilation, and since water loss depends strongly on the period of ventilation, the potatoes must be ventilated solely for drying or cooling.

8 Storage conditions

It is clear from the foregoing (Chapter 7) that the storage conditions required to limit different forms of storage losses are mutually exclusive. Hence the optimum storage conditions will have to be a compromise between these contradictory requirements for the relevant situation.

It still remains to define what actually counts as a storage loss. The definition will depend on the use to which the potatoes are to be put. Rotten potatoes always constitute a loss. Losses of dry substance represent losses in the amount of food. Sprouts also constitute a loss in ware potatoes. For this reason the prevention of rotting and sprouting must remain the main aim in the storage of ware potatoes.
However, sprouting is not a loss in the case of seed potatoes.

Sugar accumulation in potatoes intended for processing as potato products constitutes a loss of quality. In seed potatoes, the sugar content is irrelevant as far as quality is concerned, and it is of secondary importance only in potatoes intended for fresh consumption.

Water loss is largely an economic loss. It always represents a loss in potatoes intended for sale. However, for a processing firm or an individual storing potatoes for its or his or her own use, the water loss is only important if the potato quality thereby suffers.

For this reason the optimum storage conditions must always be determined by the relevant situation. The costs and benefits of storage will always be crucial determinants here.

It is therefore difficult to specify optimum storage conditions in general terms. However, the following conditions may be specified as a general guide for long-term storage:
a. Storage temperature:

Seed potatoes	2 - 4 °C
Potatoes for fresh comsumption	5 - 6 °C
Potatoes for crisping	7 - 10 °C
Potatoes for chipping	6 - 8 °C

Potatoes for granulation (mashed potatoes)   7 °C
Ware potatoes must be treated with sprout inhibitors at temperatures above 4 °C.

b. The atmospheric humidity must in general be as high as possible. A favourable value for the relative humidity of the storage atmosphere is 95 % or more.

c. The CO_2 concentration in the store must not exceed 2 % by volume for prolonged periods. The oxygen concentration in the storage atmosphere must be kept at 20 to 21 % by volume.

d. Ware potatoes must be stored in the dark.

9 Cooling of potatoes and water loss

A. Rastovski

Cooling is one of the most important processes in the storage of potatoes. The required storage temperature is usually lower than the temperature of the potatoes on lifting. To obtain the required storage temperature, the potatoes must therefore be cooled. However, potatoes are living
products which produce heat through respiration. If the required temperature is to be maintained, this heat must be continuously evacuated, as
the temperature of the potatoes would otherwise steadily increase. This
means that the potatoes must be constantly cooled to obtain and then maintain the required storage temperature. The potatoes must thus be cooled
throughout the storage period.

However, cooling not only reduces the temperature of the potatoes but
also unavoidably causes water to be lost from the product. In other
words, when the potatoes are cooled, heat and moisture are exchanged between the potatoes and the cooling air. Cooling results in a fall in the
potato temperature and moisture loss from the product, together with a
concomitant increase in the temperature and moisture content of the air.

To understand the mechanism of heat and moisture exchange between potatoes and air, a knowledge of the physical characteristics of humid air
is required. These characteristics will be analysed in Section 9.1.

9.1 Humid air

Air is a mixture of gases, chief among which are nitrogen and oxygen.
However, atmospheric air always also contains a certain amount of water.
The water is present in the air in the form of water vapour and is thus
invisible; it only becomes visible in foggy air.

The principal parameters of humid air - i.e., of a mixture of water
and air - relevant to heat and moisture exchange between potatoes and air
are as follows: partial vapour pressure, moisture content, relative humidity, heat content, dry and wet bulb temperature, dew point, specific heat
and density (specific gravity).

9.1.1 Partial vapour pressure, moisture content and relative humidity

Moisture enters the air by evaporation of water from a water surface

in contact with the air. Like every material, water consists of molecules. Since water is a liquid, these molecules can move freely; this they
do in random criss-cross motions throughout the medium. The same is true
of a gas, but in this case the molecules are very much further apart.

In a liquid, the molecules are influenced by each other's force of attraction to a much greater extent than in a gas. They collide with and
scrape past each other, so that their individual velocities are highly
variable. Molecules which happen to have a high velocity may thus, notwithstanding this force of attraction, leave a water surface and emerge
from the liquid; in other words, they 'evaporate'. They then mingle with
the molecules of, for example, air. In the air, oxygen and nitrogen molecules are in constant random motion and their mutual force of attraction
is, as stated, much less. Hence the water molecule obtains nitrogen and
oxygen molecules as neighbours.

While some water molecules 'evaporate' in this way, the converse is
also happening. Water molecules moving in the air which happen to have a
high velocity in the direction of the water surface may enter it and
'condense'.

If the air space above a water surface is enclosed, the traffic of water molecules from and to the water surface will continue until an equilibrium condition is achieved, when the number of 'evaporating' and 'condensing' water molecules per unit time will be the same. When this equilibrium condition has been attained, the air above the water level is
stated to be *saturated* with water vapour. As stated, the humid air consists of a mixture of various gases and water vapour. The pressure of the
air which contains water vapour is equal to the sum of the pressures
which each of the separate constituent substances would have had if they
had been present alone in this space.

The pressure of the water vapour in this air is only a fraction of the
total pressure of the air. The pressure of the water vapour is called the
partial vapour pressure. The partial vapour pressure is determined by the
vapour content in the air. In the case here assumed, where the water is
in equilibrium with the humid air above it, the partial water vapour
pressure is equal to the 'saturated vapour pressure' of the air at a specific temperature and to the vapour pressure of the water at the same
temperature.

All substances have a specific vapour pressure at a specific temperature. In liquids, the vapour pressure depends on temperature. For example, above a sheet of water, immediately on the surface, there is always
a water vapour pressure whose magnitude depends on the water temperature.
This is equal to the partial vapour pressure of saturated air having the
same temperature as the water. The amount of water vapour present in the
air at saturation pressure is called the saturation moisture content.
This is the highest amount of water vapour the air can contain at a given

Table 9.1 Saturation pressure and saturation moisture content in air at atmospheric pressure (101 kPa).

	Air temperature (°C)					
	0	5	10	15	20	25
Saturation pressure P_s (Pa)	610.7	872	227.0	1704	2337	3167
Saturation moisture content X_s (g/kg dry air)	3.85	5.50	7.78	10.86	15.5	20.5

temperature.

The saturation pressure and saturation moisture content of air at a number of different temperatures are set out in Table 9.1.

If the water temperature is 25 °C, the corresponding vapour pressure will be 3167 Pa. Under equilibrium conditions, the partial vapour pressure is also 3167 Pa. If it can be assumed that the enclosed space above the liquid can be enlarged, for example by a piston, in such a way that the total pressure remains 101 kPa, then the pressure in the humid atmosphere of the air itself at a total pressure of 101 kPa will thus have become 101 - 3.167 = 97.833 kPa.

Consider an enclosed volume of this saturated air (25 °C; vapour pressure 3167 Pa); if now water vapour at 25 °C is admitted to the space from elsewhere, this additional amount cannot be absorbed by this air, which, as stated, was saturated at 25 °C. The excess vapour will condense. The *relative humidity* of the air was 100 %. This could not be higher.

Now consider a volume of air at 101 kPa and 25 °C containing an amount of water vapour such that the partial vapour pressure is only half of 3167 Pa - i.e., 1583.5 Pa - the *relative humidity* of this air is stated to be 50 %. The relative humidity thus indicates the percentage of the saturation pressure actually prevailing in the air at the given temperature. Alternatively, it indicates the ratio of the actual vapour pressure (P) to the saturation pressure (P_s) *at a given air temperature*:

$$RH = \frac{P}{P_s} \cdot 100 \ (\%) \tag{1}$$

The relative humidity can be determined by dividing the actual vapour pressure in the air by the saturation pressure at the same air temperature.

Example 1

The vapour pressure is 1300 Pa in air at 15 °C. What is the relative humidity (RH) of the air?

Solution: Saturation pressure of water vapour at 15 °C (see Table 9.1) is 1704 Pa.

Actual pressure is 1300 Pa.

According to the equatation, the relative humidity is:

$$RH = 100 \frac{P}{P_s} = 1300 \div 1704 \cdot 100 = 76.29 \ \%$$

Example 2

Air from Example 1 is heated to a temperature of 25 °C without any change in the vapour content. What is the RH of this air at 25 °C?

Solution: The vapour pressure in the air remains constant on heating, and equal to P = 1300 Pa. The saturation pressure at 25 °C is 3167 Pa. The relative humidity at 25 °C becomes:

$$RH = 1300 \div 3167 \cdot 100 = 41 \ \%.$$

Example 3

Air from Example 1 is cooled to 10 °C without changing the moisture content.

What is the RH at 10 °C?

Solution: Saturation pressure at 10 °C is 1227 Pa.

Vapour pressure in the air: 1300 Pa.

The relative humidity at 10 °C becomes: RH = 1300 ÷ 1227 · 100 = 105.9 %. However, the RH cannot be greater than 100 %. In this example, condensation therefore occurs and the air becomes foggy.

It can be concluded from these examples that when air of constant moisture content is heated the relative humidity falls: 41 % RH at 25 °C compared with 76.29 % RH at 15 °C (Examples 1 and 2). When air is cooled, the relative humidity increases. At a specific, lower temperature the RH becomes 100 % and if the air temperature falls further the air becomes foggy - in other words, water vapour condenses in the air.

9.1.2 Heat content of air

The heat content is often called enthalpy. The enthalpy of the mixture 'dry air + water vapour' is defined as the heat content of humid air per unit weight of dry air. It is measured in joules per kilogram of dry air or J/kg. The heat content of the air increases with temperature. At constant air temperature, the enthalpy increases with the moisture content of the air.

This is due to the heat content of the added water vapour. Heat is required to convert liquid water into water vapour. A quantity of heat of

178

2500 kJ is needed, for example, to evaporate 1 kg of water in air at atmospheric pressure. However, the extra energy which ends up in the vapour is not 'sensible'. During evaporation, the temperature of the vapour remains equal to the water temperature. If the water is 30 °C, then the vapour is also 30 °C. The heat in the vapour is stated to be present in 'latent' form. If this vapour at 30 °C enters air at 30 °C, the temperature of the air/water vapour mixture will not be changed, but the heat content of the humid air will nevertheless increase as a result. The latent heat of the air increases, while the sensible heat content remains the same.

The sensible heat changes only with the temperature of the humid air and increases at high temperatures.

To determine the change in the heat content of the air, it is therefore insufficient to measure the change in air temperature alone. In addition to temperature, the change in the vapour content of the air must also be determined.

9.1.3 Dry bulb temperature

The dry bulb temperature in the air is measured with an ordinary thermometer. Unqualified references to the temperature of the air always mean the dry bulb temperature.

9.1.4 Wet bulb temperature

The wet bulb temperature of the air is measured by a thermometer whose bulb is covered with a wet wick. The air velocity along the bulb covered with the wet wick must be at least 2.5 m/s.

If unsaturated air is allowed to flow along a wet cloth and the vapour pressure of the cloth is higher than the partial vapour pressure of the unsaturated air, evaporation will occur. The cloth is thereby cooled and the vapour pressure of the cloth decreases. This process continues until equilibrium is attained - an equilibrium at which the cloth will assume a temperature such that the heat for evaporation per unit time will correspond to the heat received from the air (as long as the cloth is still sufficiently wet). This temperature is called the wet bulb temperature of the relevant air.

It must be remembered that the warm air contains a certain amount of 'sensible heat'. Now heat is required to convert water into vapour. When the vapour has arisen, it contains a quantity of heat of evaporation, but in the 'latent' condition; in other words, the heat is there but is not sensible. On saturation of the air to the wet bulb temperature, the air has lost a certain amount of 'sensible' heat, but has in return received an equal amount of 'latent' heat.

The wet bulb temperature of saturated air is thus equal to the dry
bulb temperature because the saturated air can no longer absorb any more
vapour.
However, the wet bulb temperature of unsaturated air will always be lower
than the dry bulb temperature, and the difference between the two temperatures will be greater the lower the partial vapour pressure in the air
becomes - i.e., the lower the relative humidity of the air. The relative
humidity can be determined by measuring the dry and wet bulb temperatures. The instruments used for this purpose are called psychrometers, and
they consist of a dry and a wet bulb thermometer and the necessary facilities to obtain an air flow of at least 2.5 m/s along the wet bulb.

9.1.5 Dew point

The dew point is the temperature at which the water vapour begins to
condense if the air is cooled at constant moisture content. As stated
earlier, the air can contain less vapour at lower than at higher temperatures.
Cooling causes the temperature of humid air to fall, and since the moisture content does not change, the saturation point will be reached at a
specific temperature. If the temperature falls further, condensation will
occur.
This temperature, at which 100 % RH is reached, is known as the dew
point.

9.1.6 Specific heat

Specific heat is the amount of heat which must be added to a mass of
1 kg of air to increase the air temperature by 1 °C. The specific heat of
atmospheric air depends on the moisture content of the air and on temperature; the specific heat increases at high moisture contents and high
temperatures.

9.1.7 Density (specific gravity)

Density indicates the mass of air in kilograms per unit volume
(kg/m^3). At a given air pressure, density falls with increasing air temperature and moisture content. Warm air is thus lighter than cold air,
and at a given temperature the air becomes lighter the more vapour it
contains.

There is a fixed mutual relation between the above parameters of humid
air. For precise definition of the condition of the air, at least two parameters have to be known - e.g., temperature and RH; dry and wet bulb

180

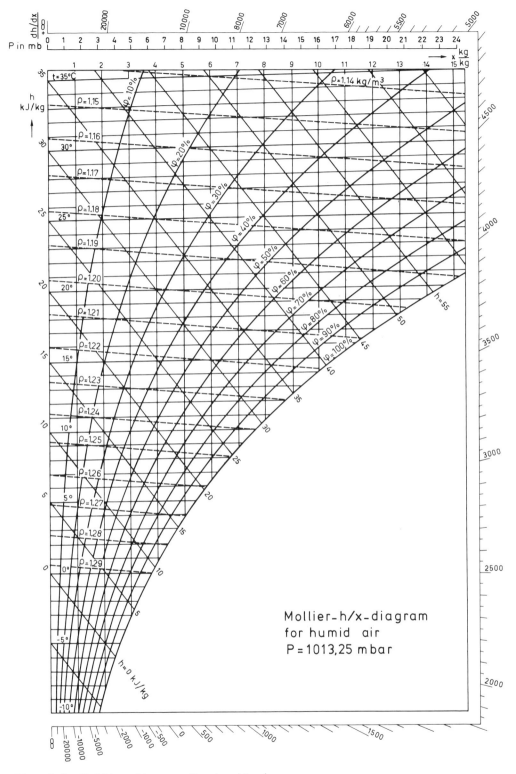

Fig. 9.1. Mollier-diagram for humid air.

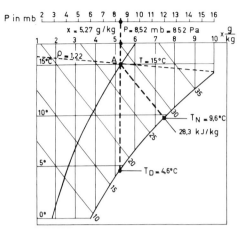

Fig. 9.1a. Reading the air conditions off the Mollier-diagram.

temperatures; dry bulb temperature and dew point; etc.
A single parameter does *not* unequivocally define the condition of the
air. The parameters of humid air have been determined experimentally and
presented in tables or graphs, such as the Mollier diagram (Fig. 9.1).
The Mollier diagram is very suitable for the analysis of various processes which take place during storage. The moisture content of the air (x)
in g/kg dry air is presented on the horizontal axis of the Mollier diagram, with the heat content (enthalpy) h in joules per kg dry air (J/kg)
along the vertical axis. The diagram shows the curves for air temperature
T (in °C), relative humidity RH (%), vapour pressure P (in pascals (Pa))
and sometimes also the vapour density ρ (in kg/m^3). The saturation curve
- i.e. the 100 % RH curve - indicates the position of the wet bulb temperature and dew point.

    The value $\Delta h/\Delta x$ is also given in the diagram. This parameter indicates
the increase or decrease in the heat content of the air per 1 kg increase
or decrease respectively in the moisture content of the air.

    If two of the above parameters are known, the point in the diagram
which determines the condition of the air has been indentified, and all
the other parameters of the air can be read off the diagramm. For example, in the Mollier diagram shown in Fig. 9.1a, the condition of the air
at a temperature of 15 °C and 50 % RH is indicated by point A. The following values can be read off the diagram for point A:

    Enthalpy h = 28.3 kJ/kg
    Moisture content x = 5.27 g/kg
    Wet bulb temperature (point B) T_N = 9.6 °C
    Dew point (point C) T_D = 4.6 °C
    Air density ρ = 1.222 kg/m^3
    Vapour pressure (point D) P = 852 Pa.

182

As already stated, the Mollier diagram is very suitable for analysing the changing in air conditions due to various processes occuring during storage. A number of processes in the Mollier diagram are analysed below.

9.1.8 Cooling and heating of air at constant moisture content

This process is represented in the Mollier diagram in Fig. 9.2 by curve A-B.

Since the moisture content of the air does not change during these processes, the change in the condition of the air must run along the vertical line - i.e., along the line x = constant. Heating the air from point A to point B, or cooling it from point B to point A, changes only the following parameters of the air: dry and wet bulb temperature, enthalpy, density and relative humidity. The moisture content, vapour pressure and dew point of the air, however, remain unchanged.

As stated earlier, the relative humidity decreases when the air is heated and increases if it is cooled.

The amount of heat that must be added to a mass of 1 kg of dry air to increase its temperature from T_A to T_B is given by the difference in enthalpy between points B and A - i.e., by $h_B - h_A$. This amount of heat $h_B - h_A$ must also be withdrawn from each kg of dry air to reduce the air temperature form T_B to T_A. Since only the temperature of the air changes in these processes and there is no evaporation or condensation of water vapour, they are referred to as *sensible cooling* and *sensible heating* respectively.

Sensible heating of the air as illustrated in Fig. 9.2 can, however, only occur on a surface where no water is present - i.e., in cooling products which cannot give up any moisture.

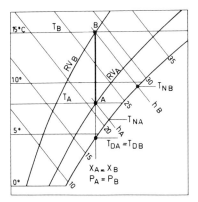

Fig. 9.2. Cooling and heating of air at constant moisture content.

9.1.9 Simultaneous heating and humidification of air

This process takes place when potatoes are cooled. When cold air is passed through a stack of warm potatoes the air is heated and the moisture content of the air increases owing to evaporation of water from the potatoes. This process is illustrated in Fig. 9.3. Points A and C represent the initial and final conditions of the air respectively.

The process is characterized by a simultaneous increase in the enthalpy (Δh) and the moisture content of the air (Δx). If the air conditions change from, for example, point A to point C, the increase in enthalpy Δh is $h_C - h_A$ and the increase in the moisture content Δx is $x_C - x_A$. The diagram clearly shows that for a given temperature difference, the increase in enthalpy Δh becomes larger the more water evaporates - i.e., the larger the increase in the moisture content Δx becomes. This increase in enthalpy is exclusively due to the increasing latent heat of the air: since the temperature increase remains the same ($T_e - T_A = T_B - T_a$), the increase in the sensible heat is also the same. The cooling capacity of the air is thus increased by the evaporation of water. In an extreme case - i.e., if so much water evaporates from the potatoes that the air becomes saturated at the same final temperature (point D) - the cooling capacity (the increase in the enthalpy of the air Δh) will be at its maximum, viz., $h_D - h_A$. However, the amount of water evaporated from the product, or the increase in the moisture content of the air Δx, will also be maximum, viz., $x_D - x_A$.

In the cooling of agricultural produce, evaporation of water from the product is an undesirable side-effect.

The relative increase in the heat and moisture content of the air is indicated by $\Delta h / \Delta x$.

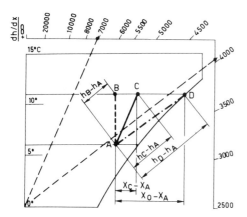

Fig. 9.3. Simultaneous heating and variation of moisture content of the air.

The magnitude $\Delta h/\Delta x$ in the Mollier diagram determines the slope of the line linking the initial and final conditions of the air, i.e., the slope of the line A-B, A-C and A-D relative to the horizontal axis. Where the air undergoes sensible heating - i.e., process A-B - there is no increase in the moisture content of air and $\Delta h/\Delta x$ becomes infinitely large. This process proceeds along a vertical line. The diagram shows that the slope of the process lines, or $\Delta h/\Delta x$, decreases the larger the increase in the moisture content Δx. At the specified air and product temperatures, $\Delta h/\Delta x$ is smallest if the air coming from the product is satured. A large $\Delta h/\Delta x$ thus means that the increase in the moisture content of the air is relatively small compared with the increase in the heat content during the cooling process - i.e., that relatively little water is evaporated during the cooling of potatoes. In other words, a large $\Delta h/\Delta x$ means that a relatively small water loss occurs during cooling of the product, while a small $\Delta h/\Delta x$, on the other hand, signifies that water loss from the product during cooling is relatively high. The aim in the cooling of agricultural produce is to minimize water loss - i.e., to maximize $\Delta h/\Delta x$. The value of $\Delta h/\Delta x$ can be read off the scale in the Mollier diagram. If the change in the condition of the air proceeds, for example, along the line A-C, $\Delta h/\Delta x$ can be read off the scale by drawing a line parallel to A-C from the point $h = 0$, $x = 0$ (the dotted line in Fig. 9.3).

9.1.10 *Cooling and variation in the moisture content of the air*

This process takes place when the potatoes are heated and often also by cooling of the air on the store walls or on the surface of an air cooler (Fig. 9.4).

When air is heated its moisture content can only either remain unchanged or increase; when air is cooled, however, it is also possible for its moisture content to be reduced - i.e., water vapour may condense on the

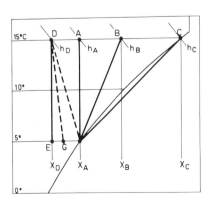

Fig. 9.4. Simultaneous cooling and variation of moisture content of the air.

cold surface. In the diagram the surface temperature is indicated by T_O and the air temperature by T_L. The saturation moisture content of the air at temperature T_O is given by the moisture content at point O (x_O). If the moisture content of the air is higher than x_O - e.g., point B or point C - water vapour will always condense on the cooling surface when the air is cooled. This condensation will result in a reduction of the moisture content of the air. Reduction of the moisture content of the air by cooling the air from point B or point C to temperature T_O (point 0) is represented by $x_B - x_O$ and $x_C - x_O$ respectively. This amount of water will be precipitated on the cooling surface for each kg of dry air flowing along the surface.

If the air condition is represented by point A or D, however, no change in the moisture content will occur if the air is cooled - i.e., there will be no condensation on the surface. In this case the temperature of the cooling surface is equal to viz., lower than the dew point of the air. Hence the moisture content will be reduced during cooling of the air *only if the dew point of the air is higher than the temperature of the cold surface.* If the dew point of the air is equal to or less than the tempereature of the cold surface (e.g., points A and D), no condensation will take place. Cooling through the walls and roof of the store or by a dry air cooler at a temperature T_O will then take place along the line A-O or D-E.

However, if the air at point D is cooled by the cold water at temperature T_O, the change in the air conditions will proceed along line D-O and the moisture content of the air will increase. The increase will be equal to $x_O - x_E$. If the vapour pressure in the cooling water of temperature T_O is higher than the partial vapour pressure in the air at point E, water will evaporate during the process, thus increasing the moisture content of the air. But the moisture content will only increase as the air cools if water is present on the cooling surface and the dew point of the air is lower than the temperature of the wet surface. However, cooling of air on dry surfaces may cause the moisture content either to remain unchanged or to fall. On cooling of the air on the surface of potatoes at temperature T_O, the air conditions of the cooled air will come to be between points E and O - e.g., at point G - because the potatoes can give up only a limited amount of moisture.

The graph shows that the reduction in the heat content of the air becomes larger the greater the decrease in the moisture content; for example, $h_C - h_O$ is larger than $h_B - h_O$ because $x_C - x_O$ is also larger than $x_B - x_O$. This is due to the release of heat of evaporation by the condensation of water vapour from the air. The decrease in the moisture content increases the heating capacity of the air, but condensation occurs on the cold surface. However, to re-evaporate this condensation in order to obtain a dry product surface, the same amount of heat is theoretically ne-

186

cessary as the amount released by condensation, and the net heating capacity of the air remains independent of the moisture exchange during the heating process.

9.1.11 *Mixing of two air streams*

Two air streams are often mixed in the storage of potatoes in cold climates. The desired cooling air temperature can be obtained by mixing very cold outside air with air from the potato stack. This process is illustrated in Fig 9.5.

If the conditions of the two air streams are represented by, for example, points A and B, point M, which indicates the conditions of the mixed air, must lie on the line linking A and B. The position of point M on the line A-B is determined by the relative quantities of the air streams L_A and L_B, as follows:

$$\overline{AM} = \overline{AB} \cdot \frac{L_B}{L_A + L_B}$$

For example, if L_B = 100 kg of outside air (point B) is mixed with L_A = 300 kg of inside air (point A), the distance A-M is determined by

$$\overline{AM} = \overline{AB} \cdot \frac{100}{300 + 100}$$

and the distance B-M by

$$\overline{AB} \cdot \frac{300}{300 + 100}$$

Where the same quantities of air in conditions A and B are mixed, point M will lie on the line linking A and B equidistant from A and B.

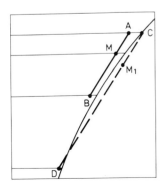

Fig. 9.5. Mixing of two air streams.

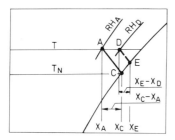

Fig. 9.6. Humidification of air by water spray.

Fig 9.5. shows that the mixing of two air streams - e.g., C and D - can also cause condensation.

9.1.12 Air humidification by water spray

The air is sometimes humidified to minimize water loss from the potatoes during storage. A water spray is generally used for humidification. The variation of the air conditions during humidification of this kind is illustrated in Fig. 9.6.

The change in the air conditions proceeds in parallel with the line $\Delta h/\Delta x = T_W$, where T_W is the temperature of the sprayed water. However, if water at low temperatures (8 to 15 °C) is used for humidification, this is practically equivalent to a change in the air conditions along the line $\Delta h/\Delta x = 0$, or h_A = constant, i.e., from A to C. By evaporation of the quantity of water ($x_C - x_A$) for each kg of air, the air becomes saturated with water vapour and the air temperature falls from T_A to T_C. The air can thus attain the wet bulb temperature by humidification. If more water than $x_C - x_A$ per kg of air is sprayed, the excess water remains present in the air in the form of a mist. The fine mist is readily entrained by the air flow and thus reaches the potatoes, which become wet. The same may occur if the air conditions change in time to, for example, point D and the amount of sprayed water remains unchanged. This air cannot evaporate more than $x_E - x_D$ kg of water per kg of air and a larger amount of water ($x_C - x_A$) is sprayed. Part of this water spray will thus be unable to evaporate and will fall on the potatoes as liquid water.

Clearly, the amount of water sprayed for air humidification must always be matched to the changing conditions of the air to prevent the potatoes from becoming wet.

9.2 Heat and vapour transfer

During storage the potatoes must be cooled, first in order to reach the required storage temperature and then to maintain this temperature.

Before the compartments are emptied, the temperature of the potatoes must often be increased again to limit susceptibility to mechanical damage (blue discoloration). Air is used for cooling and heating potatoes.

In both these processes there is an exchange of heat between the potatoes and the air. Heat is given up by the potatoes to the air or absorbed from the air. However, during this process of heat transfer, vapour is also transferred. When potatoes are cooled, the water evaporates from the product and this water vapour is given up to the air. During heating, on the other hand, the water can evaporate from the product or water vapour from the air may condense on the product surface. This vapour transfer also affects heat exchange. The heat exchanged between the potatoes and the air is thus partly sensible and partly latent.

Final aim of cooling or heating potatoes, however, is to obtain the required product temperature - i.e., to modify the sensible heat of the potatoes.

Vapour exchange occurring simultaneously and causing the potatoes to lose water by evaporation or become wet by condensation, is an undesirable side-effect. This vapour exchange, or transfer of latent heat, must therefore be minimized. The relative amount of latent heat exchanged between potatoes and air when the former are cooled or heated is influenced by such factors as the method of cooling and heating used. To optimize these processes, the mechanisms of heat and vapour transfer must be understood.

9.2.1 Transfer of sensible heat

As a result of heat transfer, the heat content of the materials concerned is modified. Every change in the sensible heat content is reflected in a change in temperature. The supply of a specific amount of heat will increase the temperature. The temperature increase will depend on the amount of material to which this heat is supplied and on its specific heat. For example, to heat a mass of 5 kg of potatoes from 5 to 10 °C, five times as much thermal energy is required than to heat 1 kg of potatoes from 5 to 10 °C. Similarly, less heat is required, for example, to heat a mass of 1 kg of air from 5 to 10 °C than to heat 1 kg of potatoes from 5 to 10 °C, because the specific heat of potatoes is 3.6 kJ/kg while that of air is only 1 kJ/kg.

Hence, the greater the mass and the specific heat of a material, the more heat will have to be supplied to the material to obtain a specific temperature increase.

The change in the heat content is thus proportional to the mass of the material (m), the specific heat (c) and the temperature change (ΔT). This change can be calculated as follows:

$$Q = m \cdot c \cdot \Delta T \quad (J) \tag{2}$$

189

The amount of heat is measured in joules (J).

For determination of the amount of heat supplied or evacuated, the mass
and specific heat, for instance, of the material must be known and the
temperature change must be found by measurement.

Each of the magnitudes in Equation 2 can be determined if the other
three are known, as follows:

Mass of material: $\quad m = \dfrac{Q}{c \cdot \Delta T} \quad$ (kg) $\qquad\qquad$ (3)

Temperature change: $\quad \Delta T = \dfrac{Q}{m \cdot c} \quad$ (K) $\qquad\qquad$ (4)

Specific heat: $\quad c = \dfrac{Q}{m \cdot \Delta T} \quad$ (J/kg $\cdot$ K) $\qquad\qquad$ (5)

Example 1

What is the amount of heat that must be removed from 10 kg of potatoes
to cool them from 10 to 5 °C?

Specific heat of the potatoes is c = 3.60 kJ/kg $\cdot$ K.

From Equation 2:

$Q = m \cdot c \cdot \Delta T$

$Q = 10 \cdot 3.60 \cdot (10-5)$

$Q = 180$ (kJ)

Example 2

The amount of heat in Example 1 (Q = 180 kJ) is evacuated by the air
and the air is thereby heated by 5 °C, so that ΔT_2 = 5 °C.

The specific heat of the air is c_2 = 1 kJ/kg.

How much air must be blown through the potatoes?

The mass of air is determined from Equation 3:

$$m = \frac{Q}{c_2 \cdot \Delta T_2} = \frac{180}{1.5} = 36 \text{ kg}$$

If the temperature change is measured, Equation 2 makes it possible to
determine the amount of heat supplied to or removed from the specified
mass of material. However, this equation gives no indication of the rate
or mechanism of heat transfer.

Heat transfer entails a movement 'flow' of heat. Just as a mass can only
be put in motion by a force - e.g., a car by the power of the engine or a
mass of water by pressure - motive power is also necessary to move heat.
This motive power which puts the heat in motion is the temperature difference. Heat will thus only be transferred if there is a temperature
difference between the two points, and the heat will always flow from a
point of higher to a point of lower temperature. The larger the tempera-

ture differences, the greater the heat flow will be. No heat flow will arise between two points at the same temperature, and there will be no heat transfer between these points.

However, each flow experiences resistance. The greater the resistance to a heat flow, the less heat flows for one and the same temperature difference.

Heat flows are measured in joules per second (J/s) or watts (W). The heat flow through an area of 1 m² is known as the heat flux density or heat flow per unit area. The heat flux density represents the amount of heat transported per second through an area of 1 m²; it is measured in joules per second per m² (J/s · m²) or in watts per m² (W/m²). It can therefore be stated that the heat flux density is proportional to the temperature difference between the potato and the air (ΔT) and inversely proportional to the resistance to the heat flow (R).

The heat flux density is calculated by the following equation:

$$q = \frac{\Delta T}{R} \qquad\qquad (J/m^2 \cdot s) \qquad\qquad\qquad (6)$$

The amount of heat flowing in a specific time t (seconds) through an area A (m²) is then:

$$Q = A \cdot \frac{\Delta T}{R} \cdot t \qquad (J) \qquad\qquad\qquad (7)$$

The heat exchange between the potatoes and the air can be determined by means of Equations 6 and 7. The larger the temperature difference between the potatoes and the air and the smaller the resistance to heat transport, the faster the heat exchange will be. Heat transfer from a potato tuber to an air flow can be analysed by Fig. 9.7.

If the air is colder than the tuber - i.e., $T_L < T_A$, a heat flow will arise from the surface of the tuber to the air (qc). As a result the temperature of the tuber surface will begin to fall. Since the surface temperature has now become lower than that in the centre of the tuber, a heat flow will arise inside the tuber from the centre to the surface (qa). Both heat flux densities are here referred to the tuber surface. According to Equation 6, qc and qa can be determined as follows:

$$qc = \frac{T_W - T_L}{R_c} \qquad\qquad qa = \frac{T_A - T_W}{R_a}$$

These two heat flux densities must be the same during heat transfer, i.e., qc = qa.

If more heat is removed from the surface by the air than can be sup-

plied by the tuber to the surface - i.e., qc > qa, the surface temperature (T_W) begins to fall. The temperature difference between the air and
the surface thus steadily decreases, while the temperature difference inside the tuber (T_A - T_W) increases. As a result the heat flux density
through the tuber (qa) increases and that from the surface to the air
(qc) falls, until equilibrium between the two heat flows is re-establish-
ed. The heat flow inside the tuber is thus equal to that from the tuber
surface to the air.

Hence, owing to the temperatures difference between the centre of the
tuber and the air, a heat flow arises from the inside of the tuber to the
air.

This heat flow meets with two resistances on its way from the centre of
the tuber to the air: first the resistance through the tuber R_a and then
that from the tuber surface into the air R_c. The total resistance to the
air flow thus becomes $R = R_a + R_c$. If there is a difference between the
tuber temperature (T_A) and the air temperature (T_L) of $\Delta T = T_A - T_L$, the
heat transfer per m² of tuber area will be as follows according to Equation 6:

$$q = \frac{\Delta T}{R} = \frac{T_A - T_L}{R_a + R_c} \qquad (W/m^2) \qquad (8)$$

The rate of the heat flow between the potatoes and the air is determined
by the temperature difference between the potatoes and the air and by the
sum of the two resistances R_a and R_c.

It can be concluded from this equation that the rate of cooling or
heating of the tuber in a given air flow falls during the process. For if
the air temperature remains unchanged during the cooling process, the
temperature difference between the tuber and the air (T_A - T_L) during
the process will become smaller and smaller as the tuber cools. The heat
flow thus steadily decreases and the cooling proceeds at an ever slower
rate.

The rate of heat transfer is also influenced by the resistance encountered by the heat flow. However, the heat transfer between the tuber and

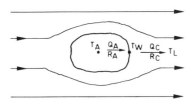

Fig. 9.7. Heat transfer from a potato tuber to an air flow; Q_a is the
conductive heat transfer through the tuber and Q_c is the convective heat
transfer from the tuber to the air.

the air flowing past it (Fig. 9.7) is of two different forms: *conductive heat transfer* and *convective* heat transfer.

The process of heat transfer by conduction takes place inside the tuber. The heat is exchanged between the particles of tuber material in contact with each other. The resistance to this type of heat transfer depends only on the physical characteristics of the material - in particular, the coefficient of thermal conductivity of the material (λ) and the thickness of the material layer (s) in the direction of the heat transfer. A high coefficient of thermal conductivity coupled with low material thickness result in a lower resistance to conductive heat transport. The resistance R_a in Equation 8 can be determined by the following equation:

$$R_a = \frac{s}{\lambda} \qquad (9)$$

Since the coefficient of thermal conductivity is a property of the material, the resistance to conductive heat transfer inside the tuber will be independent of external influences, such as the air velocity around the tuber.

In the case of a potato tuber, this resistance depends solely on its diameter. Rao et al. (1975) found an average coefficient of thermal conductivity for various potato varieties of $\lambda = 0.55$ W/m $\cdot$ K. The resistance R_a in Equation 8 is thus constant for a given lot of potatoes.

The process of heat transfer by convection generally takes place in a moving fluid - e.g., in a flow of air or water. Owing to the rapid motion of the particles of material constituting the fluid, more particles are mixed with each other and more come into contact with the heat transfer surface, thus also accelerating the process of heat transfer.

Convective heat transfer takes place between the surface of the tuber and the air. This form of heat transfer depends substantially on the air velocity and proceeds faster at high air velocities. Convective heat transfer is determined by the heat transfer coefficient (α). The resistance to convective heat transfer is then:

$$R_c = \frac{1}{\alpha} \qquad (10)$$

The resistance to convective heat transfer between the tuber surface and the air thus decreases with increasing air velocity. According to measurements by McAdams (1954), the heat transfer coefficient of a spherical body to the air can be determined by the equation:

$$\alpha = 7.8 \cdot \frac{v^{0.6}}{D^{0.4}} \qquad (11)$$

This equation can also be used to give an indication of the coefficient for a potato tuber in an air flow. The heat transfer coefficient for a tuber 0.05 m in diameter is then:

$$\alpha = 25.8 \cdot v^{0.6}$$

This equation indicates that the heat transfer coefficient doubles if the air velocity is tripled, or that the resistance R_c is halved if the air velocity is tripled (see Equation 10).

The resistance to the heat flow from the tuber to the air thus consists partly of a constant and partly of a resistance which varies with the air velocity: the air velocity is the only factor which can influence the total resistance to heat transfer from a given tuber to the air. The effect of the air velocity on the heat transfer process will depend on the proportion of the total resistance to heat transfer accounted for by convective resistance - i.e., on R_c: $(R_a + R_c)$. For instance, if the resistance to convective heat transfer R_c is 80 % of the total resistance R - i.e., R_c = 0.8 R - a reduction of R_c to 50 % of its original value will result in a change in the total resistance equal to R · 0.8 · 0.5 100 = 40 % R. The total resistance has thereby been reduced by 40 %, although it still amounts to 60 % of its orginal value. If the convective resistance R_c, however, is only 40 % of the total resistance - i.e., R_c = 0.4 R - the result of a reduction of R_c to 50 % of its original value is a reduction in the total resistance of R · 0.4 · 0.5 · 100 = 20 % R. The same 50 % reduction in the convective resistance thus has a much greater effect on the change in the total resistance the higher the proportion of the total resistance for which it accounts.

To investigate the effect of air velocity on the cooling time of a spherical tuber of diameter D = 50 mm, the cooling times were calculated by Fourier's equation and using graphs due to Grigull (1964). A coefficient of thermal conductivity of λ = 0.55 W/m · K was used and the heat transfer coefficient α was calculated by Equation 11. The results are shown in Fig. 9.8.

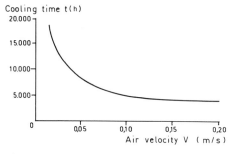

Fig. 9.8. Time necessary to cool the potato tuber of a diameter d = 50 mm at various air velocities around the tuber, to approx. air temperature.

Fig. 9.8 shows that an increase in the air velocity has a positive effect on the rate of heat transfer from a tuber to the air, even at air velocities of about 0.33 m/s. However, air velocities exceeding 0.16 m/s are seldom observed in potato storage.

The conclusion is that the transfer of sensible heat between potatoes and air is substantially influenced by the air velocity. The rate of sensible heat transfer is increased the higher the air velocity.

9.2.2 Mass transfer; water evaporation

As described in Section 9.9.1, evaporation takes places on the water surface as long as there is a difference between the vapour pressure in the water and the partial vapour pressure in the air. Hence a difference in vapour pressure gives rise to a flow of vapour from the water to the air. This flow depends on the vapour pressure difference and increases as the difference between the vapour pressure in the water and that in the air increases. The vapour flow, however, experiences a resistance which tends to counteract it. The higher this resistance, the smaller the vapour flow becomes and the less water evaporates into the air at the same vapour pressure difference. The rate of water evaporation, or vapour flow density, is thus directly proportional to the vapour pressure difference between water and air (ΔP) and inversely proportional to the resistance (R_d) encountered by the vapour flow.

The rate of water evaporation can be determined by the following equation:

$$m = \frac{\Delta P}{R_d} \qquad (kg/m^2 \cdot s) \qquad (12)$$

The vapour pressure difference is determined by the temperature of the water and the temperature and relative humidity of the air. Vapour pressure differences between water and air at different conditions of water and air are given in Table 9.2.

Table 9.2 and Equation 12 clearly show that, for a given relative air humudity and a given temperature difference between water and air, evaporation takes place faster the higher the temperature of the water and air respectively.

Equation 12 gives the amount of vapour flowing into the air per second from a water area of 1 m² under a vapour pressure difference ΔP (N/m²). The amount of vapour M which will flow into the air from a given area A (m²) in a given time t (s) under a vapour pressure difference ΔP (N/m²) can be determined as follows:

$$M = A \cdot \frac{\Delta P}{R_D} \cdot t \qquad (kg) \qquad (13)$$

Table 9.2 Vapour pressure between water and air (N/m^2).

Temperature difference water/air (°C)	Relative humidity of air (%)	Water temperature (°C)		
		5	10	20
0	80	174.0	245.0	467.4
	90	87.0	122.7	233.7
	95	43.5	61.35	116.85
2	80	265.9	369.4	686.6
	90	190.15	262.2	480.3
	95	152.2	208.6	377.15

This general theory also applies to the evaporation of water from a potato tuber into the air.

According to Equations 12 and 13, a vapour flow, or moisture loss from
potatoes, will occur if there is a positive vapour pressure difference
between the tuber and the air.
A positive vapour pressure difference exists between potatoes and air as
long as the air temperature is lower than the temperature of the potatoes,
or at the same temperature of the air and the potatoes if the relative
humidity of the air is less than 100 %.

When potatoes are cooled, the air temperature is always lower than the
potato temperature. The cooling of potatoes is thus unavoidably accompanied by evaporative moisture loss. The higher the temperature difference
between the potatoes and the air and the lower the relative humidity of
the air, the larger the vapour pressure difference becomes. But even the
cold saturated air - i.e., air at 100 % RH at a temperature lower than
that of the potatoes - will be able to withdraw moisture from the potatoes. This air is first heated by contact with warmer potatoes, so that
its relative humidity falls, after which evaporation can occur.

However, since the potatoes produce heat in respiration, the tuber
temperature will always be higher than the air temperature - i.e., there
will always be a positive vapour pressure difference between the potatoes
and the air. The magnitude of this vapour pressure difference depends on
the heat production of the potatoes, which in turn depends on the potato
temperature. Because of the heat produced in respiration, the potato temperature increases (see Equation 4) - i.e., the potatoes become warmer
than the air. As a result, heat is transferred from the potatoes to the
air.
The temperature of the potatoes will increase until equilibrium has been
established between this heat production and the heat transfer from the
potatoes to the air. According to Equation 8, the temperature difference

196

in the equilibrium condition for a given heat production q is given by:

$$\Delta T = q \cdot R \qquad\qquad (14)$$

Hence the temperature difference between potatoes and air increases the more heat is produced by the potatoes in respiration and the higher the resistance to heat transfer to the air. However, this temperature difference determines the vapour pressure difference between potatoes and air: a high temperature difference also signifies that the vapour pressure difference will be large. Thus the vapour pressure difference generally becomes larger the more heat has to be removed and the lower the air velocity becomes. But there is always a positive vapour pressure difference between potatoes and air, so that the potatoes will sustain some moisture loss in all conditions. For instance, the moisture loss from potatoes packed in plastic bags at constant ambient temperature is visible in the form of drops of water on the bag walls.

Since the potatoes produce more heat at high temperature, the moisture loss will also be greater at high temperatures.

Now the air can only absorb moisture present on the surface of the tuber. But in a dry tuber, the entire moisture contained in the tuber is present in the tuber cells. This moisture first pass through the tuber to the surface before it can be absorbed by the air. The moisture loss from potatoes is thus determined by two moisture flows: one flow through the tuber to its surface and one from the surface to the air. Like the heat flows described earlier, these two moisture flows must be equal.

The two moisture flows encounter specific resistances. The moisture flow through the tuber experiences an internal resistance R_{Di} and that from the surface to the air an external resistance R_{De}. The total resistance to the moisture flow in Equation 12 thus becomes $R_D = R_{Di} + R_{De}$. The internal resistance R_{Di} is a biophysical constant of the potatoes. However, this internal resistance is influenced by the vapour pressure difference between the surface of the tuber and the air, (Villa and Bakker Arkema, 1974 and Rastovski and Van Vliet, 1981). The higher the vapour pressure difference, the larger the resistance R_{Di} becomes. The internal resistance is also greatly affected by the general condition of the potato skin. In potatoes with damaged or badly suberized skin, or in sprouted potatoes, the internal resistance to moisture loss is substantially lower than in well suberized and non-sprouted potatoes. Such potatoes therefore lose more moisture. The internal resistance, however, is not affected by the air velocity.

The external or convective resistance R_{De}, on the other hand, is very dependent on the air velocity, falling as the latter increases. The external resistance R_{De} is influenced by the air velocity to the same extent as the resistance to the convective heat flow R_c. Since only the ex-

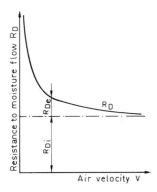

Fig. 9.9. Influence of air velocity on overall resistance to moisture
transfer from the potato tuber to the air.

ternal resistance, and not the internal resistance, is affected by the
air velocity, the effect of the latter on the total resistance will depend on the proportion of the total accounted for by the external resistance. At high velocities, the external resistance becomes so small that
its effect on the total $R_D = R_{Di} + R_{De}$ becomes extremely limited, as
Fig. 9.9 clearly shows.

R_{De} is relatively large at low air velocities and its variation with air
velocity greatly affects the change in the total resistance. It has, however, a decreasing effect at high velocities because R_{De} becomes relatively small.

R_D tends towards the value of R_{Di} as the air velocity increases. The total resistance to the moisture flow from the potatoes to the air is often
expressed by the transpiration coefficient k_D.

The transpiration coefficient gives the amount of moisture flowing into the air per second from 1 kg of potatoes at a vapour pressure difference of 1 N/m². The total resistance R_D is then equal to the reciprocal
of the transpiration coefficient k_D, i.e.:

$$R_D = \frac{1}{k_D} \tag{15}$$

The rate of water evaporation in accordance with Equation 12 then becomes:

$$m = k_D \cdot \Delta P \tag{16}$$

The moisture loss was determined experimentally at the IBVL for well
suberized, unsprouted, healthy Bintje potatoes at approaching air velocities ranging between 0 and 0.2 m/s.

The average moisture loss obtained from a number of tests is shown in
Fig. 9.10.

198

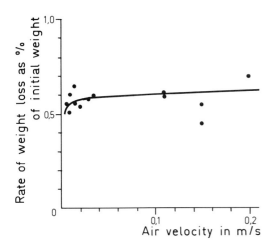

Fig. 9.10. Average moisture loss from Bintje-potatoes at various air velocities - air temperature 10 °C and relative humidity of air 85 %.

Fig. 9.10 shows that the degree of moisture loss is greatly affected
by air velocity in the velocity range 0 to 0.01 m/s. Above 0.01 m/s, a
further increase in air velocity has only a very limited effect on the
rate of moisture loss from the potatoes. These results are in good agreement with the findings of Burton (1966). However, moisture loss reaches a
minimum in non-ventilated potatoes, i.e., when the air velocity is nil;
see also Hunter (1974).

A maximum rate of evaporation from non-sprouted, well suberized potatoes is thus attained at an air velocity of about 0.01 m/s. A further
increase in air velocity has practically no further effect on the rate of
evaporation. Hence it may be concluded that the internal resistance of
these potatoes to moisture loss is relatively large compared with the external resistance.

In unripe and freshly lifted potatoes, which, like sprouted or damaged
tubers, have a substantially lower internal resistance to moisture loss,
the effect of air velocity will in general be greater and will be observable even at higher velocities (Burton, 1966).

Stimulation of suberization and wound healing before the potatoes are
cooled, and prevention of sprouting throughout the storage period, are
thus highly efficient measures to limit moisture loss from potatoes.
Moisture loss from unsprouted and well suberized potatoes (Equation 13)
thus depends only on the vapour pressure difference between potatoes and
air and on the duration of ventilation. The effect of air velocity on
moisture loss from potatoes is in general small and is confined to the
velocity range 0 to 0.01 m/s.

However, evaporation of free moisture from the tuber surface - i.e.,
the rate of drying of wet potatoes - depends greatly on the air velocity.

In this case the water is present on the surface of the tuber and can evaporate direct to the air, so that there is only one moisture flow, that from the surface to the air. The only resistance to this flow is the external resistance, which is extremely dependent on air velocity. Wet potatoes will therefore dry faster the higher the air velocity and the greater the vapour pressure difference between the potatoes and the air.

9.2.3 Simultaneous heat and moisture transfer between potatoes and air

Potatoes are cooled by air. Since the partial vapour pressure in cold air is always lower than the vapour pressure in warm potatoes, a positive vapour pressure difference always exists between potatoes and air during cooling and water evaporates from the potatoes. The tubers thus lose moisture during cooling - i.e., simultaneous heat and moisture transfer takes place between the potatoes and the air. The moisture from the potatoes, given a constant vapour pressure difference between potatoes and air, largely depends on the duration of ventilation and is only slightly dependent on air velocity. In cooling, however, the duration of ventilation is determined by the rate of cooling of the potatoes and the amount of heat to be evacuated from them. The potato cooling rate is strongly dependent on the air velocity and increases at high velocities. The duration of cooling (and ventilation) will thus be shorter the higher the air velocity. Hence the moisture loss during potato cooling wiļl be smaller the higher the air velocity and the less the amount of heat.

The moisture loss during potato cooling can be determined from Equations 6, 7, 12 and 13, allowing for the fact that the moisture loss is accompanied by latent heat transfer during cooling. The heat transfer is thereby increased, being as follows according to Equation 7:

$$Q = A \cdot \frac{\Delta T}{R} \cdot t + M \cdot r \qquad (17)$$

in which r represents the amount of heat necessary to evaporate 1 kg of water and M stands for the amount of water evaporated during cooling.

The amount of water evaporating from potatoes (i.e., their moisture loss) during cooling is determined from Equation 13:

$$M = A \cdot \frac{\Delta P}{R_D} \cdot t$$

Since this moisture loss M arises during cooling, the duration t in Equations 13 and 14 must be the same.

Substitution of t from Equation 14 in Equation 13 gives the following equation for determination of the moisture loss during potato cooling:

$$M = \frac{Q}{\frac{\Delta T}{\Delta P} \cdot \frac{R_D}{R} + r} \quad (kg) \qquad (18)$$

The amount of heat necessary for the evaporation of 1 kg water is r = 2500 kJ/kg, and Equation 15 can be written:

$$M = \frac{Q}{\frac{\Delta T}{\Delta P} \cdot \frac{R_D}{R} + 2.5 \cdot 10^6} \qquad (19)$$

Hence the moisture loss during cooling (M) falls with increasing R_D/R and $\Delta T/\Delta P$ and decreasing Q. Since R_D is only slightly affected by the air velocity and since the resistance to heat transfer R falls sharply with increasing air velocity, R_D/R becomes larger as the air velocity increases. The value of $\Delta T/\Delta P$ increases with increasing temperature difference ΔT and relative air humidity; see Fig. 9.11.

Increases in ΔT and in air velocity result in faster cooling or heat transfer. Hence the moisture loss during cooling falls with increasing heat transfer rate, the increase in the latter being due to the increase in air velocity and/or the increase in the temperature difference between potatoes and air; see Lerew (1978), Misener and MacDonald (1975) and Ophuis (1957). In the cooling of potatoes and other agricultural products, the aim is always to minimize moisture loss from the product - i.e., to obtain as low a moisture loss as possible during the removal of a specific quantity of heat. These processes can therefore be assessed on the

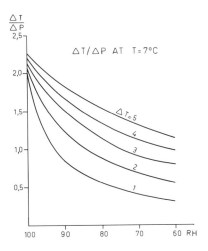

Fig. 9.11. The value of $\frac{\Delta T}{\Delta P}$ (Eq. 19) as a function of temperature difference between potato and air (ΔT) and relative humidity of air at 7 °C potato temperature.

basis of the factor Q/M, which expresses the amount of heat evacuated per kg of water evaporated from the product. The higher Q/M, the lower the moisture loss from the product during cooling.

It follows from Equation 16 that:

$$\frac{Q}{M} = 2.5 \cdot 10^6 + \frac{\Delta T}{\Delta P} \cdot \frac{R_D}{R} \tag{20}$$

However, because the heat and water vapour are evacuated by the air, Q and M must be equal to the increase in the heat content Δh or the increase in the moisture content Δx of the air flow, i.e.:

$$Q/M = \frac{\Delta h}{\Delta x}$$

$\Delta h/\Delta x$ can be determined in the Mollier diagram on the basis of measurements as shown in Fig. 9.12. During cooling, thermometers and hygrometers must be used only to measure the temperature and relative humidity of the fresh cooling air (T_o and RH_o) and the air from the potato stack (T_A and RH_A). These parameters define the points A and B in the Mollier diagram in Fig. 9.13. The value of $\Delta h/\Delta x$ is determined by linking A and B can be read off the scale as described in Section 9.1.11. A high value of $\Delta h/\Delta x$ thus signifies low moisture loss during potato cooling. Under the cooling air conditions represented by point A in Fig. 9.13 and at the specified temperature of the potatoes T_A, $\Delta h/\Delta x$ reaches a minimum if the cooling process proceeds along the dotted line A-C. The moisture loss during cooling is thus at a maximum if the air from the potatoes is saturated with water vapour. However, for a given temperature difference between potatoes and air, the moisture loss during cooling will be lowest if the cooling air enters the potatoes saturated with water vapour (100 % RH) - i.e., if the condition of the cooling air is characterized by point D

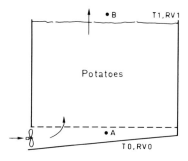

Fig. 9.12. Points in the store at which temperature and relative humidity of air should be checked.

202

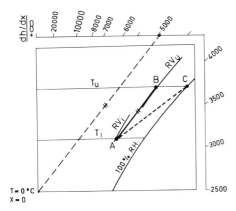

Fi. 9.13. Reading Δh/Δx off the Mollier-diagram.

in Fig. 9.13. The vapour pressure difference between potatoes and air
then reaches a minimum ($\Delta P = P_C - P_D$) and the moisture transfer M according to Equation 13 is also at its lowest. This fully agrees with conclusions drawn earlier.

Hence moisture loss during cooling can be limited by high air velocities, high relative humidities of the cooling air and large temperature
differences between the potatoes and the cooling air. Since the moisture
loss depends strongly on the amount of heat to be removed from the potatoes, the aim must be to minimize heat production or accumulation in the
potatoes (see Equation 16).

9.2.4 *Cooling of a potato stack*

When tall stacks of potatoes are cooled by an air flow as illustrated
in Fig. 9.14, cooling is not uniform throughout the stack. The potatoes
which come into contact with the cold air flow first are also cooled
first.
The air flow is heated by absorption of heat from these potatoes, so that
the temperature of the air flow increases.

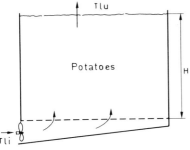

Fig. 9.14. Cooling of a deep pile of potatoes by air.

This heated air then comes into contact with potatoes in the next layer. Since the air temperature has meanwhile risen, the temperature difference between the air flow and the potatoes (ΔT) will also have fallen.

According to Equation 6, heat transfer in this layer thus takes place more slowly than in the first layer and the air is heated less (Equation 4). The same then applies in each succeeding layer, until the air temperature in a given layer becomes the same as the original temperature of the potatoes.

No further heat transfer then takes place in the subsequent layers and the temperature of the potatoes and of the air remains temporarily unchanged.

After a given time τ_1 of ventilation, the variation of temperature through the stack will have become as shown by the line 'a' in Fig. 9.15. The potatoes up to a given height 1-1 have been partially cooled, while those above this line still have the original temperature T_A. The line 1-1 is called the 'cooling front'.

The following volume of air blown through the stack will cool the potatoes further. However, since the potatoes in the lowest layers have already been partially cooled, the heat transfer in these layers will be smaller and the air temperature will increase less, so that the potatoes in the subsequent layers will also be cooled. The cooling front thus moves upwards, i.e., in the direction of the air flow. After a certain time the temperature in the stack will vary as indicated by line 'b'.

Part of the stack at the bottom will then already have cooled to the air temperature T_O. This part is called the 'cold region'. There follows a

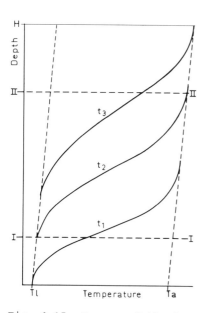

Fig. 9.15. Course of the temperature in the pile during cooling.

zone in which the actual heat transfer takes place - the 'cooling zone'. Above this, the potatoes are still totally uncooled and this is the 'warm region'. The stack has been cooled when the cooling zone has passed through the entire stack - i.e., when the trailing edge of the cooling zone has reached the top of the stack. The lower the partial vapour pressure in the air flow - i.e., the lower the RH of the air - the more water will evaporate from the potatoes, thus increasing the cooling rate.

The speed of advance of the cooling front depends on the air velocity, the original temperature difference between the potatoes and the air and the rate of evaporation in the stack. However, the depth of the cooling zone depends mainly on the air velocity, increasing with the latter.

The temperature of the potatoes will not be the same throughout the cold and warm regions, but will always increase in the direction of the air flow. This increase is due to the heat produced by the potatoes in respiration. The temperature increase will increase with increasing potato heat production and decreasing air velocity (see Equation 4).

The graph in Fig. 9.16 can be used as a guide to the variation of

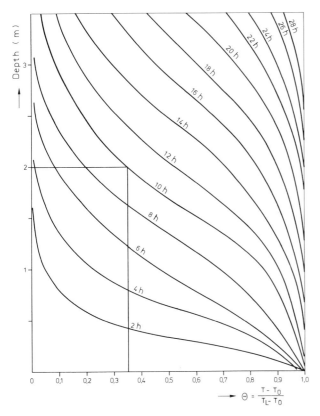

Fig. 9.16. Change of dimensionless temperature θ during cooling or heating of deep beds of potatoes by the air flux density 0.1 $m^3/m^2 \cdot s$.

temperature during the cooling or heating of bulk potatoes. This graph was drawn by Ophuis (1957) in the basis of a method of calculation developed by Bussinger (1954). This graph assumes that the potatoes initially have the same temperature in all layers and that air at constant temperature is used for ventilation throughout the cooling or heating process. Bussinger's calculation method is based on the theory of heat exchange between potatoes and air without moisture transport. However, Ophuis's graph has been experimentally tested and is found to be in good agreement with experimental observations. The dimensionless temperature θ is set out on the horizontal axis of the graph. Before cooling commences, the temperature of the potatoes and the air is equal everywhere in the stack to the initial temperature T_{Ao} - i.e., $T_L = T_{Ao}$, and $\theta = 0$. When the potatoes have cooled to the air temperature T_o, T_L also becomes equal to T_o and the dimensionless temperature $\theta = 1$. The air has then withdrawn the maximum possible quantity of heat from the potatoes. The dimensionless temperature θ thus indicates what proportion of the maximum possible amount of heat has been evacuated by the air, this amount being defined by $T_{Lo} - T_{Ao}$.

To limit the duration of ventilation, the cooling process is usually terminated when 90 % of the maximum amount of heat has been evacuated - i.e., when the dimensionless temperature $\theta = 0.9$. The graph in Fig. 9.16 is drawn for an air flow of 0.1 m³/s . m² floor area (350 m³/m² . h). For example, after 10 hours' ventilation the dimensionless temperature $\theta = 0.35$ applies at a stack height of 2 m. If the potato temperature at the beginning of ventilation was $T_{Ao} = 15$ °C and air at $T_{Lo} = 7$ °C is used for ventilation, the potato temperature can be determined as follows after 10 hours' ventilation:

$$T_L - T_{Ao} = 0.35 \; (T_{Lo} - T_{Ao})$$

$$T_L - 15 = 0.35 \; (7-15)$$

$$T_L = 15 - 0.35 \cdot 8 = 15 - 2.8$$

$$T_L = 12.2 \; °C$$

In the case of a stacking height of 1 m, $\theta = 0.866$ can be read off at the same time - i.e., the potatoes have been cooled to $T_a = 8.07$ °C. Cooling is only just beginning to be observable at a stacking height of 3.5 m. The dimensionless temperature will only reach $\theta = 0.9$ after 27 hours' ventilation in the topmost layer - i.e., at a height of 3.5 m.

206

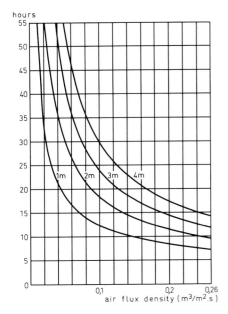

Fig. 9.17. Time needed to reach θ = 0.9 at various air flux densities.

The cooling and heating time required to reach θ = 0.9 when ventilating with different rates of air flow are shown in the graph reproduced
in Fig. 9.17, which shows that the rate of air flow has a great effect on
the rate of cooling or heating of potatoes. If rapid cooling or heating
is required, high rates of air flow are necessary. Since the lowest layers of potatoes - i.e., those which come first into contact with cold or
warm air - reach the air temperature very quickly, the air temperature T_o
must not be higher or lower than the required temperature of the potatoes.

Example
A 3.5 m tall stack of potatoes with an initial temperature of T_{Ao} = 15 °C
is to be cooled to T = 5 °C. The stack is ventilated with air at T_{Lo} =
-2 °C and the air velocity is 0.1 m³/m² · s. The dimensionless temperature
in the top layer at the end of cooling is then:

$$\theta = \frac{5 - 15}{-2 - 15} = \frac{10}{17} = 0.588$$

The duration of cooling is obtained form the graph in Fig. 2.3.16:
    τ = 20 hours
At the same time the potatoes up to a height of 1.2 m have already been
cooled to -2 °C - i.e., the potatoes are frozen up to a height of 1.2 m.
For this reason, not only the potato temperature in the top layer but also the temperature of the ventilation air T_{Lo} must alsways be measured du-

ring the cooling or heating of the stacks of potatoes. For rapid cooling or heating of the potato stack, a large volume of air must be used for ventilation and not extremely cold or extremely warm air.

As stated, the graphs in Figs. 9.16 and 9.17 can only be used as a rough guide, but they do, however, give a good qualitative impression of the processes involved.

There are also other mathematical models which do allow for moisture exchange between the potatoes and the air: Lerew (1978), Misener and MacDonald (1975) and Beukema (1980). These models could be used to quantify the heat and moisture exchange, but unfortunately the necessary parameters of heat and moisture transport in potatoes are not adequately known *in quantitative terms* and generally show considerable variation. The trend of the variations in heat and moisture transport relative to the ambient conditions has, however, been clearly established.

References

Beukema, K.J., 1980. Heat and mass transfer during cooling and storage of agricultural products as influenced by natural convection. Pudoc, Wageningen.

Burton, W.G., 1966. The potato. Veenman, Wageningen.

Bussinger, J.A., 1954. Luchtbehandeling van produkten in gestorte toestand. Meded. Dir. Tuinb. 17, no. 8/9.

Grigull, U., 1964. Temparaturausgleich in einfachen Körpern. Springer-Verlag, Berlin.

Hunter, J.H., 1974. A basis for computer simulation of the potato in storage. Research in the life sciences 22, no. 3. University of Maine.

Lerew, L.E., 1978. Development of a temperature-weight loss model for bulk stored potatoes. Dissertation for the Degree of Ph.D. Michigan State University.

McAdams, W.H., 1954. Heat transmission. McGraw-Hill Book Company Inc. New York.

Misener, G.C. & M.L. MacDonald, 1975. Simulated moisture loss and cooling time for bulk potatoes. Can. Agric. Eng. 17, no. 2.

Ophuis, B.G., 1957. De invloed van de ventilatiecapaciteit op de gewichtsverliezen bij luchtgekoelde bewaring van aardappelen. IBVL-Publikatie Serie A no. 17.

Rao, M.A., J. Barnard & J.F. Kenny, 1975. Thermal conductivity and thermal diffusivity of process variety Squash and white potatoes. Transactions of the ASAE 1188-1192.

Rastovski, A. & W.F. van Vliet, 1981. The influence of relative humidity of the air on moisture loss of potatoes. (Not yet published). IBVL, Wageningen.

Villa, L.G. & F.W. Bakker Arkema, 1974. Moisture losses from potatoes during storage. Paper 74-6510 for winter meeting ASAE.

10   Heat balance in a potato store

A. Rastovski

In a store filled with potatoes, a certain amount of heat is continuously produced and heat evacuation also takes place.

The temperature at which the potatoes are placed in the store is usually higher than the required storage temperature, so that the potatoes
first have to be cooled to that temperature. More heat than is being produced in the store has to be evacuated during the cooling period. Once
the storage temperature is reached, heat evacuation must be equal to the
heat production in the store if the required storage temperature is to be
maintained. Fig. 10.1 shows the heat supply or heat production and heat
evacuation in a store.

The heat supply thus stems from the following heat sources:
a. Heat content of the potatoes - i.e., field heat Q_1
b. Respiration of potatoes Q_2
c. Heat flow through walls, roof and floor Q_3
d. Heat production by fans Q_4
e. Heat supplied by air renewal Q_5
f. Heat produced by lighting, machinery and people and heat supplied
   through leaks in the building structure, open doors, etc.

a. Heat content of the potatoes
   The amount of heat to be evacuated to cool a given quantity of pota-

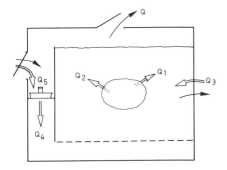

Fig. 10.1. Heat sources in the store.

toes from the initial temperature of the storage temperature can be calculated as follows:

$$Q_1^x = m \cdot Ca \cdot 1000 \, \Delta T \, (J/day)$$

in which

ΔT = cooling of potatoes per day (°C)
Ca = specific heat of potatoes (J/kg · K)
m = weight of potatoes (tonnes)

Since the specific heat of potatoes is approximately 3.600 kJ/kg · K, the
required evacuation of heat is:

$$Q_1 = m \cdot 3600 \cdot \Delta T \cdot 1000 \, (J/day)$$

If a small quantity of potatoes m is brought into the store every day,
the storage temperature having already been reached in the store, then
the above amount of heat is the heat supplied per day. The quantity of
potatoes m is then given in tonnes/day.

b. Respiration of potatoes
    The heat of respiration of the potatoes depends on the potato tempera-
ture and the factors mentioned in Chapter 7. In healthy potatoes some
time after harvesting, this heat may range from 0.01 J/kg · s at 5 °C to
0.05 J/kg · s at 30 °C. Three to six times as much heat may, however, be
developed in unripe and damaged potatoes. The heat produced by respiration is then:

$$Q_2 = m \cdot 1000 \cdot qa \cdot 3600 \cdot 24 \, (J/day)$$

in which

m = weight of potatoes (tonnes)
q = heat of respiration (J/kg · s)

c. Heat flow through walls, roof and floor
    The heat flow through the walls, roof and floor of the store arises
owing to the difference between the ambient and storage temperatures. If
the former is higher than the latter, there will be a heat flow from the
outside to the inside. If the outside temperature is lower, heat will
flow in the opposite direction - i.e., heat will be removed from the
store. The amount of heat exchanged depends on the temperature difference

210

between the outside and the storage temperatures, the area of walls, roof and floor and on the resistance to the heat flow. According to Equation 13, the rate of heat flow is:

$$Q_3 = A \cdot \frac{\Delta T}{R} \cdot 3600 \cdot 24 \text{ (J/day)}$$

The resistance is then:

$$R = \frac{1}{k}$$

and k is the heat transfer coefficient of the relevant surface in $J/m^2/s \cdot k$ or $W/m^2 \cdot K$.

The temperature difference is usually calculated on the basis of the average outside temperature during the warmest storage period. However, insulation must also be allowed for in sunny areas. Since the temperature differences are usually not the same for different parts of the structure, the heat transfer must be calculated separately for each part and all these individual heat flows must then be added together, as follows:

$$Q_3 = \Sigma_1^i A_i \cdot \frac{\Delta T_i}{R_i} \cdot 3600 \cdot 24 \text{ (J/day)}$$

The heat flow into or out of the store can thus be limited by insulating the walls, roof and floor, i.e. by increasing R_i.

d. Heat production by fans

A fan produces heat while operating. The total power of the electric motor which drives the fan is converted into heat. Hence the heat supplied by the fan is:

$$Q_4 = 1000 \cdot N \cdot t \text{ (J/day)}$$

in which

N = installed power of electric motor (kW)
t = duration of ventilation (s/day)

The heat production can be determined as follows for a given fan capacity and a given pressure increase:

$$Q_4 = \frac{V \cdot \Delta P}{\eta} \cdot t \text{ (J/day)}$$

in which

V = volume of air (m³/s)
ΔP = pressure increase through the fan (N/m² or Pa)
η = overall fan efficiency (about 0.5)
t = duration of ventilation (s/day)

e. Heat supplied by air renewal
Fresh air is required to provide the potatoes with the necessary oxy-gen and to remove the CO_2 produced from the store. Air renewal supplies heat to the store if the fresh (external) air is warmer than that in the store, but removes heat from the store if the outside air is colder.

A volume of air equal to the fresh air supplied to the store is also removed from it. The temperature and relative humidity of this discharg-ing air are those prevailing in the store. Hence V m³/day of fresh air with a heat content i_1 is supplied to the store while the same amount of air with a heat content i_2 is removed from it. The amount of heat is then:

$$Q_5 = V \cdot (i_1 - i_2) \cdot \rho$$

or

$$Q_5 = V \cdot \Delta i \cdot \rho$$

in which

V = amount of fresh air (m³/day)
Δi = difference in enthalpy between storage air and outside air
ρ = air density (kg/m³)

The enthalpy and air density can be obtained from the Mollier diagram at known air temperatures and relative humidities.

f. Heat produced by lightning, machinery, etc.
The heat produced in a store by leaks in the stucture, lighting, ma-chinery, people and open doors is not easy to determine. This amount of heat is usually added as a percentage to the sum of the components of the total heat supplied in accordance with items a) to e). This is 5 % for large stores and 10 % for small ones; hence:

$$Q_6 = 0.05 \text{ to } 0.1 \sum_{i=1}^{i=5} Q_i$$

The total heat supply or heat production in the store is then:

$$Q_{tot} = Q_1 + Q_2 + Q_3 + Q_4 + Q_5 + Q_6 \ (J/day) \qquad (21)$$

This amount of heat has to be evacuated from the store in order to reach
and maintain the required storage conditions. This heat is therefore
equivalent to the cooling requirement of the store.

However, the installed cooling capacity in a mechanically cooled store
is always greater than Q_{tot} for safety reasons, because:
- The calculated cooling requirement may differ from the actual require-
  ment (incorrect estimation).
- Extra heat must be evacuated to cool the walls, roof, floor and soil
  under the floor.
- Allowance must be made for necessary repairs to the cooling system.
- The insulation efficiency of the walls and roof may be reduced if the
  insulation is wet.
- The efficiency of the compressor falls; etc.
For the above reasons the installed cooling capacity becomes:

$$Q_K = 1.2 \cdot Q_{tot} \ (J/day)$$

When the potatoes have been cooled to the required storage temperature, part of the cooling requirement - viz., Q_1 - is no longer necessary. Less cooling is then needed to maintain the required temperature in
the store and the cooling system can operate for a shorter period or the
cooling capacity can be reduced.

The heat balance is the same in a store cooled with outside air, except that the heat is removed by ventilation with cold, fresh air. This
means that the heat evacuation (Q_5) in Equation 21 must be equal to the
rest of the heat supply, as follows:

$$Q_5 = Q_1 + Q_2 + Q_3 + Q_4 + Q_6 \qquad (22)$$

The amount of heat Q_5 is determined by:

$$Q_5 = V \cdot \Delta i \cdot \rho \ (J/day) \qquad (23)$$

However, fresh outside air can only be used for cooling if its temperature is lower than that in the store. The ventilation periods will
therefore be limited to a given time t per day, so that Equation 23 becomes:

$$Q_5 = V \cdot \Delta i \cdot \rho \cdot t \ (J/day) \qquad (24)$$

in which

Δi = difference in enthalpy between store air and external air
ρ = air density (approx. 1.27 kg/m³)
V = fan capacity (m³/s)
t = ventilation time (s/day)

With Equation 24 and ρ = 1.27 kg/m³, Equation 22 becomes:

$$Q_1 + Q_2 + Q_3 + Q_4 + Q_6 = 1.27 \cdot V \cdot \Delta i \cdot t$$

or

$$Q = 1.27 \cdot V \cdot \Delta i \cdot t \tag{25}$$

in which

Q = heat production in the store (J/day)

The fan capacity can be determined from Equation 25:

$$V = \frac{Q}{1.27 \cdot \Delta i \cdot t} \ (m^3/s) \tag{26}$$

Equation 26 shows that more fan capacity is required to remove a given quantity of heat Q the smaller the difference in enthalpy Δi and the shorter the available ventilation time t.

214

CONSTRUCTION AND TECHNICAL FACILITIES OF POTATO STORES

11 Purpose of storage and store requirements

A. Rastovski

Upon harvesting the crop, the entire supply of potatoes becomes available at once. This supply normally exceeds the current demand. The demand for potatoes continues throughout the year. To satisfy this continuing demand, the supply of potatoes must also be spread over the year. Hence those potatoes not sold immediately after harvesting must be stored. It is obviously only worth growing potatoes if there is sufficient storage capacity to accommodate most of the crop. This is the only way to satisfy the demand for potatoes, which remains more or less constant until the next harvest. If the demand for potatoes increases and production is raised accordingly, storage capacity must also be enlarged.

The storage period is thus determined by the frequency of harvesting. In climates where there is only one crop per year, the potatoes must be stored for eight to ten months. However, in a warm climate where two or three crops per year are possible, a storage period of only three or five months respectively may suffice.

Fig. 11.1. Filling a ventilated potato bin.

Fig. 11.2. Potato heap with ventilation duct.

In any case, the aim of storage is always the same: the best possible preservation of both the quantity and the quality of the potato crop.

Factors which may limit the storage time are sprouting, drying-out, rotting or undesirable changes in the chemical composition of the potatoes. These processes are strongly affected by the storage conditions -in particular, the temperature of the potatoes and the relative humidity of the storage environment. Since the presence of free moisture on the tuber surface encourages the spread of diseases and rot, the tuber surfaces must be kept as dry as possible during storage.

Efficient storage thus involves control of potato temperature and relative humidity in the store while ensuring that the tuber surfaces remain dry. The necessary equipment must from an integral part of any efficient potato store.

The recommended conditions for long-term storage are set out in Chapter 8. Under these conditions, good potatoes can be kept for a period of ten months or longer. The less favourable the storage conditions, the shorter the storage period will be. However, the ambient conditions are variable and usually differ substantially from the desired storage conditions. The following are therefore necessary for efficient potato storage:
a. An insulated building, to limit environmental effects on storage conditions.

218

b. A cooling or heating system to allow the temperature of the potatoes to be kept at the required level.
c. A system for drying wet potatoes; the cooling system is often used for this purpose.
d. A system for controlling the relative humidity of the store atmosphere.
   This is usually provided for sufficiently by good insulation of the building and an efficient cooling system, although air humidification facilities are sometimes used.
e. Equipment for efficient control of items b) to d), often wholly or partially automated. However, supervision by the store manager always remains crucial to the succes of storage.

The equipment of a storage facility of this kind will obviously be relatively expensive, but this high capital investment is necessary if the potatoes have to be stored for extensive periods, e.g. longer than three or four months or if special requirements are laid down in respect of the quality of the stored produce.
For shorter storage periods, the potatoes may also be kept in clamps, simple sheds or cellars. Since efficient control of the storage conditions is virtually impossible with these forms of storage, produce intended to be stored in this way should preferable be carefully selected beforehand; the storage period depends, however, greatly on the prevailing ambient conditions. These methods of storage are also relatively labour-intensive but are nevertheless used as temporary measures, even in the industrialized world, owing to the low capital costs.

Fig. 11.3. Modern farm store; capacity: 1,000 tonnes of potatoes.

Fig. 11.4. Storage bin with 3,000 tonnes of potatoes.

The facilities required for efficient control of storage conditions will be discussed in detail in Chapters 12 to 17.

12 Potato store construction

A. Rastovski

12.1 Method of storage and store design

Potatoes can be stored loose (in bulk), in bags or in crates resp. boxes. The density of a bulk of potatoes amounts to 650 to 700 kg/m^3. The specific volume of a bulk thus averages 1.5 m^3/tonne of potatoes. The required volume for a known quantity of potatoes can then be determined as follows:

$$V_a = G \cdot 1.5 \qquad\qquad (m^3) \qquad\qquad (35)$$

in which G is expressed in tonnes.

The bulk density also determines the vertical pressure of potatoes which is 650 to 700 kg/m^2 per metre of stacking height. This pressure limits the height to which potatoes can be stacked, as the tubers at the bottom of a heap must withstand the total pressure exerted by the potatoes on top of them. Since high pressure damages the tubers, causing bruising, the pressure must be limited by restricting the stack height to 3 to 4 m depending on the quality of the potatoes. The weight of potatoes which can be stored per m^2 of floor area is then:

$$G_a = \frac{H}{1.5} \qquad\qquad (tonnes/m^2) \qquad\qquad (36)$$

in which H is the stack height in metres.
With a stacking height of 3 m, therefore, 2 tonnes of potatoes per m^2 can be stored, increasing to 2.67 tonnes/m^2 for a height of 4 m.
Hence the required floor area A to store G tonnes of potatoes is:

$$A = \frac{G}{G_a} = \frac{G \cdot 1.5}{H} \quad (m^2) \qquad\qquad (37)$$

In this way both the floor area of a store, when potatoes are stored in bulk, and the bottom area of a box or container can be determined. The floor area required for bulk storage of 1000 tonnes of potatoes stacked to a height of 3 m is thus:

$$A = \frac{1000 \cdot 1.5}{3} = 500 \ m^2$$

When potatoes are stored in bags, the loading capacity of the store is lower, because there is always some empty space between the bags. With bag storage the loading capacity of a store is likely to be 500 to 550 kg/m³, or the required volume of the store becomes 1.8 m³/tonne. To store 1000 tonnes of potatoes in bags stacked to a height of 3 m, the required store floor area is thus:

$$A_2 = \frac{1000 \cdot 1.8}{3} = 600 \text{ m}^2$$

Compared with loose storage, bag storage requires 20 % more floor area or store volume respectively.

In the case of box storage, the loading density of the stack is determined by the box construction and how the boxes are stacked. In the Netherlands, boxes with a capacity of 1 tonne of potatoes are generally used. Their standard dimensions, including pallet, being 1.39 m long by 1.09 m wide by 1.24 m high (Fig. 12.1). The loading density per box is thus 530 kg/m³. Since there is always free space between the boxes when they are stacked, the loading density of a stack of boxes is reduced to an average of 500 kg/m³ in a solid stack of boxes.

Since the pressure exerted by the potatoes when stored in boxes is determined only by the box height, the risk of potato damage no longer constitutes a limiting factor to the height of the box stack, and the boxes can thus be stacked five or six high. With stacking five-high, 3.1 tonnes of potatoes can be accommodated per m² of floor area, increasing to as much as 3.70 tonnes/m² with six-high stacking. However, the volume of a stack of boxes is always 35 % more than that of the same quantity of bulk potatoes. Hence, for a given floor area, the height of the box stack exceeds that of the same amount of loose potatoes.

However, the height of a store must always be greater than the pile or stacking height. A clearance is required above the heap or stack to enable the boxes or bags to be stacked or potatoes to be heaped to the required height, and to allow also for air circulation during cooling or drying of the potatoes.

The minimum height of this clearance is about 0.5 m, but it may be 1 to

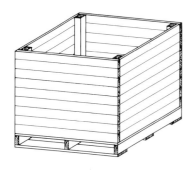

Fig. 12.1. Box containing 1 ton of potatoes.

1.5 m or even more depending on the type of equipment used to fill the store and the apparatus to be accommodated above the pile or the stack (e.g., air coolers with mechanical cooling), as well as the potato inspection requirements.

The size or loading capacity of a store or compartment is greatly affected by the manner of storage as well as other factors. For instance, where potatoes are stored in bulk, all the potatoes in any one heap must be of the same variety, and preferably of consistent quality. A small lot of bad potatoes - especially if seriously affected by disease - may give rise to substantial losses even in good potatoes. If such a lot of potatoes begins to rot, it must be removed from the store as quickly as possible to limit the damage. If this lot happens to be in the middle of the stack, at least half the store must be emptied. This has adverse economic effects as regards sale of the potatoes, the financial loss being greater the larger the store.

Another important factor determining the size of the store (or compartment) is the rate of arrival of the potatoes, which determines how long it takes to load the store. The storage conditions cannot easily be efficiently controlled during loading and a long loading period may thus adversely affect the quality of the stored produce. The loading period of a compartment must therefore be limited to two or three weeks.
Hence the size of a heap of loose potatoes is determined by the amount of potatoes of a given variety grown and the growing techniques used; the latter determines the quality of the potatoes.

Apart from the factors mentioned above, the store size also depends on the rate of arrival of the potatoes; it must be possible to load the store within a period of two or three weeks.

The capital investment required for the construction of a store, however, increases with the number of separate compartments to be used to accommodate the total volume. The same considerations apply to the design of a bag or box store, except that the potato variety is then less important.

The foregoing explains the great variety of potato store designs, with compartment capacities ranging from 20 tonnes to 10,000 tonnes or more.

Typical potato store designs are illustrated in Fig. 12.2 to 12.4.

The design shown in Fig. 12.2 is very common for bag or loose stores. The central passage is often used for grading and packing the potatoes before despatch. This passage is usually 4 to 12 m wide depending on its purpose. In this design, the storage conditions in the compartments can be controlled as required.
Owing to the low capital cost, the design illustrated in Fig. 12.3 is now also commonly used. The store is built as a single compartment in which the potatoes can be stored in boxes, in bags or loose. For loose storage, different consignments of potatoes are separated by boxes filled with po-

tatoes or by means of lightweight, movable partitions (Fig. 12.4). The pressure of the potatoes on the bottom prevents the lateral thrust from bringing down the partition.

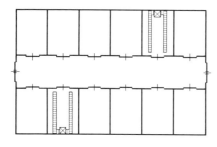

Fig. 12.2. General design of a multi-compartment store.

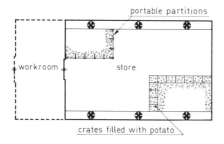

Fig. 12.3. Single compartment store.

Fig. 12.4. (a and b) Movable thrust resisting partition.

224

However, in this design the storage conditions are the same for all consignments. If necessary, a workroom can be built on to the store as illustrated in Fig. 12.3.

12.2 Store construction requirements

An efficiently constructed potato store has to satisfy a number of specific requirements, viz.:
a. It must be possible to control the conditions in the store. The required temperature in the store ranges between 2 and 10 °C during storage and between 15 and 20 °C when the potatoes are heated. The relative humidity of the air in the store should be 90 to 100 %, but the potatoes must remain dry throughout the storage period. To satisfy these requirements, the store must be well insulated and as airtight as possible.
b. The construction must withstand all the mechanical thrusts and loads exerted by the potatoes, wind, snow, etc.
c. The store must be large enough to accommodate the required quantity of potatoes and must be suitable for the method of storage chosen
   - loose, boxes, bags, crates, etc.
d. It must be possible to perform operations such as the reception of the potatoes, the loading and unloading of the store and delivery of potatoes without difficulty, the necessary mechanization being provided. There may also have to be sufficient room for carrying out certain operations on the potatoes prior to marketing - e.g., cleaning, grading to size and by quality, bagging, packing in boxes etc.

It is obvious from this list of requirements that each store must be individually designed.

The principal factors determining the design of the store are the local climate, the quantity of potatoes to be stored, the manner of storage - i.e., loose, in bags, in boxes or in crates - daily amounts of incoming and outgoing potatoes, operations to which the potatoes are to be subjected and the type of mechanization used for these operations.

12.3 Store insulation

The prime requirement for control of the storage conditions is insulation of the store. The purpose of insulating the store can be summarized as follows:
a. Limitation of heat exchange between the store and the environment
   - i.e., conservation of heat in the store.
b. Prevention of condensation on the walls and ceiling or roof of the store during periods of low ambient temperature.
   Intensive heat exchange takes place between the store and the environ-

ment through badly insulated walls and ceilings. Much heat is then lost through the structure of the store when the weather is cold. If more heat is lost through the structure than the potatoes can produce at a given temperature, the potato temperature will begin to fall, in extreme cases as far as freezing point. To prevent this temperature drop, additional heating would be necessary in the store.

When the weather is warm, on the other hand, much heat would be supplied to the store, so that more heat would have to be removed to keep the store temperature at the required level. The capacity of the refrigeration system would then have to be higher.

Hence poor insulation of the store results in extra energy consumption for heating or cooling the potatoes and in additional capital costs for the necessary heating or cooling equipment. Storage thus becomes more expensive. A badly insulated store has, however, even more disadvantages, because the insulation also affects produce losses.

Poor insulation reduces the surface temperature of the walls and ceiling in cold weather. When the ambient temperature is extremely low, the walls may become so cold that the potatoes in contact with them freeze or become excessively chilled. This may cause condensation on the tuber surfaces, so that the potatoes become wet and rot. Under certain conditions condensation may also form on the surfaces of walls and the roof. The amount of water vapour condensing on to these surfaces comes from the air in the store. Since the temperature in the store is kept constant by heating, this condensation means that the relative humidity of the air in the store is reduced, so that there is more evaporation from the potatoes, which lose more moisture. Condensation on the walls and the roof is thus in fact water extracted from the potatoes. This condensation, already constituting a loss in itself, may, however, lead to even greater losses in potatoes. When serious condensation occurs, drops of water form on the roof surface and fall back on to the potatoes; the moisture loss then also causes the potatoes to become wet, with all the resulting adverse consequences.

The structure of the store may also be damaged by condensation.

To prevent water dripping on to the potatoes, special measures will be necessary, involving additional costs. No condensation will form on the walls and roof in hot weather, but more heat will have to be dissipated from the potatoes owing to the additional heat supplied to the store. Since water loss from potatoes greatly depends on the amount of heat to be removed from the potatoes (Section 9.2), the weight loss will be further augmented. Hence insulation not only affects the capital and running costs of the store but also losses in the stored potatoes. Insulation of a store is therefore a matter of economics.

12.3.1 Heat conservation

The ambient temperature differs from the required storage temperature for most of the storage period, so that heat exchange takes place between the store and the environment during storage. The heat will always flow from the higher- to the lower-temperature location. Depending on the ambient temperature, the heat will therefore flow either from the outside into the store or from the store to the outside. The rate of heat flow will depend on the temperature difference between inside and outside and on the resistance to the heat flow presented by the walls and roof. The higher the resistance of the walls or roof, the less heat will flow between the store and the environment for a given temperature difference. The resistance to the heat flow in this case is the reciprocal of the 'k-value' or heat transfer coefficient of the walls and roof. Hence a high resistance to heat flow means a low k-value.

Since a heat flow arises only when there is a temperature difference between two points, the temperature in the direction of the heat flow must fall constantly.

The variation of temperature through an insulated wall or roof structure is illustrated in Fig. 12.5.

In this case the temperature in the store (T_i) is higher than the ambient temperature (T_o). At constant temperatures T_i and T_o, the temperature at each point of the wall will also eventually be stabilized and will remain unchanged as heat transfer proceeds further. The *steady-state condition* has then been attained, when the heat flow at any point in the structure is equal and constant. The rate of heat flow arising in the case of a temperature difference T_i - T_o is as follows according to Equation 6:

$$q = \frac{T_i - T_o}{R}$$

However, this heat flow meets with the following resistances in

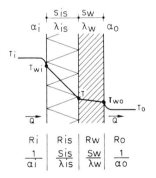

Fig. 12.5. Temperature process through an insulated wall and roof structure.

succession on its way from the store to the outside (Fig. 12.5):

- Convective resistance on the inside of the wall $R_i = \dfrac{1}{\alpha_i}$
  (Equation 9)

- Resistance to heat conduction through the insulation $R_{is} = \dfrac{S_{is}}{\lambda_{is}}$
  (Equation 10)

- Resistance to heat conduction through the wall $R_w = \dfrac{S_w}{\lambda_w}$
  (Equation 10)

- Convective resistance on the outside of the wall $R_o = \dfrac{1}{\alpha_o}$
  (Equation 9)

Hence the total resistance to the heat flow is:

$$R = R_i + R_{is} + R_w + R_o$$

or

$$R = \frac{1}{k} = \frac{1}{\alpha_i} + \frac{S_{is}}{\lambda_{is}} + \frac{S_w}{\lambda_w} + \frac{1}{\alpha_o} \qquad (27)$$

The k-value, or overall heat transfer coefficient, can be determined from Equation 27, in which s is the thickness of the relevant structural component in m and λ is the coefficient of thermal conductivity of the re-levant material in W/m · K.

The resistances to convective heat transfer R_i and R_o depend on the air velocity along the wall. The following values may be used for calcu-lation under normal conditions:

a. Wall

$$R_i = \frac{1}{\alpha_i} = 0.12 \qquad (m^2K/W) \qquad \text{or } \alpha_i = 8.1 \qquad (W/m^2 \cdot K)$$

$$R_o = \frac{1}{\alpha_o} = 0.043 \qquad (m^2K/W) \qquad \text{or } \alpha_o = 23 \qquad (W/m^2 \cdot K)$$

b. Roof or ceiling $R_o = 0.043$ m^{2}K/W   or $\alpha_o = 23$ W/m^2 K

- roof warmer than $R_i = 0.17$ m^{2}K/W   or $\alpha_i = 5.8$ W/m^2 K
  air in store

- roof colder than $R_i = 0.12$ m^{2}K/W   or $\alpha_i = 8.1$ W/m^2 K
  air in store

However, most of the total resistance to the heat flow, and hence also

228

to the rate of heat flow, depends on the construction of the store -
i.e., on the coefficients of thermal conductivity and the thicknesses of
the structural components. The coefficients of thermal conductivity of a
number of construction and insulation materials are set out in Table 12.1.

Table 12.1 Coefficients of thermal conductivity of construction materials.

Material	Density	Coefficient of thermal conductivity λ
	kg/m^3	(W/m · K)
Brick	1600	0.93
	1900	1.16
Sand-lime brick	1900	1.5
Concrete	2200	1.62
	2400	2.32
Gas concrete	500	0.24
	650	0.31
Wood fibre concrete	530	0.08
	720	0.12
Timber	400	0.17
Plywood	700	0.23
Hardboard	1000	0.29
Cement plaster	1900	1.5
Insulating materials		
Mineral wool	35	0.041
Flax boards	110	0.12
Foam polystyrene	15	0.035
	20	0.035
	25	0.035
Extruded foam polystyrene	35	0.027
Foam polyurethane	40	0.023
Expanded cork	150	0.045

The total resistance to the heat flow (R) and the overall heat transfer coefficient (k) for different store structures can be determined from
Equation 27 and Table 12.1. The method of calculation will be demonstrated by some examples.

EXAMPLE 1
What is the total resistance and total heat transfer coefficient of a
24 cm thick wall made of gas concrete blocks? The gas concrete has a specific gravity of 500 kg/m^3.
Table 12.1 gives for this gas concrete: λ = 0.24 W/m^2 K.

According to Equation 27, the resistance is then:

$$R = R_i + \frac{S}{\lambda} + R_o$$

Now

$$R_i = 0.12 \ m^2K/W$$
$$R_o = 0.043 \ m^2K/W$$

Hence the total resistance is:

$$R = 0.12 + \frac{0.24}{0.24} + 0.043$$
$$R = 1.163 \ m^2K/W$$

The heat transfer coefficient is then:

$$k = \frac{1}{R} = \frac{1}{1.163}$$

$$k = 0.859 \ W/m^2 \cdot K$$

EXAMPLE 2
The total heat transfer coefficient of the wall in Example 1 must be re-duced by insulation to $k_1 = 0.40W/m^2 \cdot$ K. Foam polystyrene of a density of 25 kg/m^3 is used for the insulation. What must be the thickness of the insulation? The heat transfer coefficient of the wall in Example 1 is k = 0.859 W/m^2 $\cdot$ K. This is equivalent to a total resistance R = 1.163 m^2 K/W. This resistance must be increased to $R_1 = \frac{1}{k_1} = \frac{1}{0.40} = 2.50 \ m^2 \cdot$ K/W
The difference between R_1 and R then gives the resistance which the insu-lation must provide. This resistance must therefore be:

$$R_{is} = R_1 - R = 2.50 - 1.163$$
$$R_{is} = 1.337 \ m^2 \cdot K/W$$

The resistance through the insulation is determined by the following equation:

$$R_{is} = \frac{S_{is}}{\lambda_{is}}$$

and the thickness of the insulation is then:

$$S_{is} = R_{is} \cdot \lambda_{is}$$

230

Table 12.1 shows that λ_{is} = 0.025 W/m · K. The required insulation thickness is then S_{is} = 1.337 · 0.035 = 0.046 m. The insulating panels must therefore be 5 cm thick.

For a known wall or roof construction and known temperatures in the store (T_i) and in the outside environment (T_o), the temperature at any position in the structure can also be determined in the steady state, since the heat flow is equal and constant at any point in the structure.

Hence, for example, the heat flow from the air to the wall inside in Fig. 12.1 must be equal to the heat flow through the entire construction; i.e.

$$\frac{T_i - T_{wi}}{R_i} = \frac{T_i - T_o}{R}$$

or

$$\alpha_i \, (T_i - T_{wi}) = K \, (T_i - T_o)$$

Hence

$$T_i - T_{wi} = \frac{K}{\alpha} \, (T_i - T_o) \tag{28}$$

or

$$T_{wi} = T_i - \frac{K}{\alpha} \, (T_i - T_o) \tag{29}$$

The temperature of the inside of the wall can be determined from Equation 29 if the k-value of the wall is known.
For the wall in Example 1, with a store temperature T_i of 7 °C and an outside air temperature T_o of -10 °C, the temperature of the inside of the wall is thus:

$$T_{wi} = 7 - \frac{0.859}{8.10} \, (7 - (-10))$$

$$T_{wi} = 7 - \frac{0.859}{8.10} \cdot 17 = 7 - 1.8$$

$$T_{wi} = 5.2 \, °C$$

For the wall in Example 2, this temperature is as follows in the same conditions:

$$T_{wi} = 7 - \frac{0.4}{8.1} \cdot 17 = 7 - 0.24$$

$$T_{wi} = 6.16 \ °C$$

The temperature at any point in the structure can be determined in the same way. For instance, the temperature on the outside of the insulation in Fig. 12.1 is determined by the equation:

$$\frac{T_i - T}{R_i + R_{is}} = \frac{T_i - T_o}{R}$$

or

$$T = T_i - \frac{R_i + R_{is}}{R} (T_i - T_o)$$

Hence the store insulation not only affects the degree of heat exchange with the environment but also influences the surface temperature of the walls and roof. The poorer the insulation of the store, the greater the difference between the storage temperature and the surface temperature of the store.

The temperature of the air and of the potatoes in direct contact with the store surface will also be affected. Poor insulation thus gives rise to temperature variations in the store, possibly resulting in condensation on the surface of the potatoes and the surfaces of the store.

As stated earlier, this may have disastrous consequences for the stored produce. However, this risk can be minimized by good insulation of the store.

12.3.2 Condensation in the store

Water vapour condenses from the air if the latter is cooled below its dew point. The dew point is determined by the temperature and relative humidity of the air.

Table 12.2 sets out the dew points for different temperatures and relative humidities of the air. The table also gives the 'dew point depression' or difference between the air temperature and dew point.

Table 12.2 shows that the dew point depression depends mostly on relative humidity of air and very little on the air temperature. The dew point depression falls as the relative humidity of the air increases. The dew point depression falls to nil at 100 % RH - i.e., condensation occurs always when the surface temperature is lower than the air temperature. At

Table 12.2 Dew point of the air.

Air temperature	Relative humidity of air	Dew point	Dew point depression
T (°C)	(%)	T_D (°C)	$(T - T_D)$ (°C)
	80	6.7	3.3
	85	7.6	2.4
10	90	8.4	1.55
	95	9.2	0.8
	98	9.7	0.3
	80	4.75	3.25
	85	5.6	2.4
8	90	6.45	1.55
	95	7.25	0.75
	98	7.7	0.3
	80	2.8	3.2
	85	3.7	2.3
6	90	4.5	1.5
	95	5.25	0.75
	98	5.7	0.3
	80	0.9	3.1
	85	1.7	2.3
4	90	2.5	1.5
	95	3.3	0.7
	98	3.7	0.3

the relative humidities normally occurring in a potato store - i.e., around 95 % RH - the dew point depression is 0.7 K, falling to only 0.3 K at 98 % RH. The margins are thus extremely limited.

In principle, condensation may occur on the surface of the potatoes or on surfaces of the store.

Condensation on the roof is much more dangerous than on the walls, as it may drip and make a large quantity of potatoes wet. To prevent condensation, the surface temperature T_{wi} in Fig. 12.1 must be not lower than the dew point of the air T_D, or the temperature difference between the air and the surface must be not more than the dew point depression. The temperature difference between the air and the surface of the structure can be determined from Equation 28. To prevent condensation, T_{wi} in Equation 28 must, however, be not lower than T_D. The critical condition for condensation is thus given by the following equation:

$$T_i - T_D \leq \frac{k}{\alpha_i^*} (T_i - T_o) \tag{30}$$

$T_i - T_D$ is the dew point depression of the air in Equation 30; it must be less than or equal to the right-hand side of the equation if condensation on the surface is to be prevented. The critical value of the overall heat transfer coefficient k can be determined from Equation 30:

$$k \leq \alpha_i^* \frac{T_i - T_D}{T_i - T_o} \tag{31}$$

The critical overall heat transfer coefficient is thus determined by the internal heat transfer coefficient α_i^*, the dew point depression $T_i - T_D$ and the difference between the storage and ambient temperatures $T_i - T_o$.

Two mechanisms are, however, operative in the transfer of heat on the surface of the store, viz., convection and radiation.

In radiation, the heat between two surfaces at different temperatures is exchanged by electromagnetic waves; this heat exchange hardly affects the air temperature. Radiative heat exchange arises between the free surface of a potato stack and the roof. Hence radiation increases the rate of heat transfer at the roof surface for a given temperature difference between the air and the roof. The internal heat transfer coefficient α_i^* in Equations 30 and 31 is therefore $\alpha_i^* = \alpha_i + \alpha_s$, in which α_i determines the heat transfer by convection and α_s that by radiation. As stated in Section 9.2.1, α_i depends mainly on the air velocity along the roof surface, increasing as the air velocity becomes higher.

The heat transfer coefficient α_s, however, depends largely on the radiation coefficient E of the surfaces participating in the heat exchange. In organic substances, including potatoes, the radiation coefficient is large, viz., $E = 5$ W/m^2 · K^4. In polished metals it is generally small: $E = 0.15$ to 2 W/m^2 · K^4. Thus the heat transfer coefficient α_s, and hence also the internal heat transfer coefficient α_i^*, is higher on the surface of an organic material than on a metal surface.

The internal heat transfer coefficient α_i^* is therefore affected by the material of the surface and the air velocity along the surface.

The effect of the radiation coefficient of the roof surface and of the air velocity along the surface on the critical heat transfer coefficient k is set out in Table 12.3.

Table 12.3 sets out, for a number of k-values of the roof structure, the temperature differences $T_i - T_o$ at which no condensation yet forms on the roof surface of the relative humidity of the air in the store is 95 % or less. The table shows that condensation forms at a bigger temperature difference $T_i - T_o$, if the air velocity along the surface and the radia-

234

Table 12.3 Critical difference between outside and inside temperature at 95 % RH in the store.

(W/m² K)	v m/s	$T_i - T_o$ (K)	
		Shining metal surface (E = 0.17 W/m²K⁴)	Organic material (E = 5.1 W/m²K⁴)
0.58	Small	10	15
	1	12	17
	2	16	21
0.4	Small	14	21
	1	17	24
	2	23	30
0.3	Small	19	29
	1	23	32
	2	30	40

tion coefficient of the surface increase. For example, at T_i = 6 °C and 95 % RH in the store and a roof structure insulation value of k = 0.4 W/ m²K, condensation will already occur on an internal polished steel sur- face (Σ = 0.17) and without forced air movement when the outside air tem- perature is below -8 °C - i.e., at $T_i - T_o$ = 14 K. On a roof surface made of organic material (Σ = 5), this will only happen when the outside tempe- rature falls below -15 °C. However, if the air flows along the roof sur- face at a velocity of v = 1 m/s, condensation will only begin at an out- side temperature below -9 °C on the steel surface or below -18 °C on the surface of an organic material. The occurrence of condensation on the roof can be retarded by intensive air flow under the roof, as shown in Fig. 12.6.

Note that the extremely low radiation coefficient of a metal surface given in Table 12.3 applies only if the surface is clean. In a store, the surface will quickly become soiled with dust, so that the radiation coef- ficient will increase and condensation will be delayed. Even so, it is best to line the roof surface with timber or another porous organic mate- rial, as these materials not only have a higher radiation coefficient but are also able to absorb moisture, thus limiting the risk of drops of con- densation.

It was assumed in the calculation of the data in Table 12.3 that the temperature of the potato surface and the roof surface remains constant, but this is not always the case. The temperature of the topmost layer of potatoes falls owing to radiation of heat to the roof. This reduces the

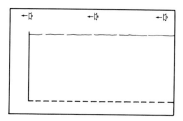

Fig. 12.6. Ventilation under the roof
to retard condensation.

temperature difference between the potatoes and the roof, so that the
heat radiation falls constantly, and the risk of condensation on the roof
surface is again increased.

However, this cooling of the potatoes can be prevented by internal
ventilation. If internal ventilation is carried out, the heat of the entire potato stack is used to warm the topmost layer and thus keep it at
constant temperature.

Internal ventilation in cold weather also serves to prevent condensation on the surface of the potatoes themselves. Potatoes in the top layer
and along the walls become wet if unventilated for a long period, precisely because the potatoes cool, as explained above, owing to heat radiation to the roof and walls and contact between the potatoes and the cold
wall surfaces. This gives rise to temperature differences through the potato stack, resulting in convective air flows: cooled air along the roof
and walls become heavier and flows downwards. The place of the cooled air
is taken by the warm air from the potato stack. The cold air flowing down
the walls in turn has to take the place of the upward-flowing air from the
potato stack. An air flow caused exclusively by temperature differences
thus arises. The rate of this air flow is affected by the temperature
difference.

However, the warm air flow from the potato stack is virtually saturated
with water vapour withdrawn from the potatoes by evaporation. A part of
this water vapour condenses on the cold surfaces of the potatoes in the
top layers and along the walls and roof and wall surfaces of the store.
The extent of this condensation depends on the convective air flow -
i.e., on the temperature differences within the potato stack. But substantial temperature differences can be prevented by regular internal
ventilation, thus also limiting the degree of condensation.

If very low outside temperatures occur regularly during the storage

236

period, the store must first of all be well insulated to limit condensation. A low k-value of the walls and roof is the most efficient way of
preventing serious condensation. For instance, given a storage temperature of 6 °C and 95 % relative humidity in the store, if condensation is
still to be avoided at -14 °C - i.e., at $T_i - T_o = 20$ K in Table 12.3 -
the structure must have a k-value of at least 0.4 W/m²K. However, if the
outside air temperature falls to -29 °C for extended periods, k = 0.3 W/
m²K is necessary if condensation is still to be prevented under the storage conditions described above.

Last but not least, condensation is also affected by the dew point depression $T_i - T_D$, which depends greatly on the relative atmospheric humidity. Table 12.2 shows that the dew point depression at 90 % RH is twice
as high as at 95 % RH. However, at 98 % RH the dew point depression is
only half that at 95 % RH. This means - Equations 30 and 31 - that for
one and the same k-value the temperature difference between inside and
outside $T_i - T_o$ at 90 % RH may be twice as high, and at 98 % RH only half
as much, as the temperature difference at 95 % RH. Condensation can thus
be delayed also by reducing the relative humidity of air.

The relative humidity can be reduced by ventilating with cold outside
air. Some degree of ventilation with cold outside air is essential to
prevent condensation on the surfaces of the store. It was tacitly assumed
in the foregoing that the relative humidity in the store is less than
100 %. However, if outside air ventilation is not carried out, the RH in
the store will very quickly rise to 100 %, as the potatoes constantly lose moisture (one need only think of the condensation on the inside of
plastic bags containing potatoes). Since the RH in the stores is usually
less than 100 % although there is no outside air ventilation, this means
that most stores are not absolutely airtight. Some uncontrolled ventilation with outside air thus arises through leaks in the building structure. For efficient control of condensation, however, effective outside air
ventilation is recommended. A ventilation system is illustrated in
Fig. 12.7.

The purpose of this ventilation is dissipation of the moisture withdrawn from the potatoes by the air in the store. For this purpose a certain volume of cold outside air with a low moisture content is supplied

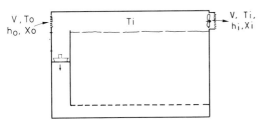

Fig. 12.7. Ventilation with fresh air above the pile of potatoes.

to the store and the same amount of air with a higher moisture content is removed from it. The amount of moisture removed from the store by ventilation is given by the formula $V (\rho_i X_i - \rho_o X_o) \cong V \cdot \rho_i (X_i - X_o)$, in which x_i and x_o are determined by the temperature and relative humidity of the inside and outside air respectively. Hence the amount of moisture removed under specified conditions is influenced by the amount of ventilation air. The degree of moisture loss from the potatoes is represented by G_D, which must be equal to the degree of moisture removal if the moisture content x_i of the store air is to be kept constant. The required amount of ventilation air follows from this. For instance, if the relative humidity is to be kept at 95 % in the store at a temperature of $T_i = 6\ °C$, x_i will be 5.5 g/kg air and ρ_i will be 1.261 kg/m³. If the outside air temperature T_o is -10 °C and the relative humidity is 100 %, x_o will be 1.62 g/kg air.

Under the above storage conditions, the moisture loss from potatoes averages 0.25 % of the fresh weight per month, corresponding to G_D = 83 g/tonne · day. The volume of air required to remove this amount of moisture is then:

$$V = \frac{83}{1.261\ (5.5 - 1.62)} \cong 17\ m^3 \cdot tonne \cdot day$$

At higher outside air temperatures, x_o increases and more air will be necessary to remove the moisture released. Hence, under the storage conditions specified above and at an outside temperature of 0 °C, a ventilation capacity of 38.4 m³/t · day will be required.

However, this ventilation removes not only moisture but also heat from the store. The amount of heat removed is given by:

$$Q = V \cdot \rho \cdot (i_i - i_o)$$

At T_i = 6 °C and 95 % RH, the ambient conditions being T_o = - 10 °C and 100 % RH, i_i = 19.7 kJ/kg and i_o = -6.2 kJ/kg. The heat removed by the ventilation is then Q = 17 · 1.261 (19.7 + 6.2) = 555 kJ/t · day. This heat loss must be allowed for when calculating the heat balance of the store. Where the temperature difference $T_i - T_o$ exceeds 15 K, the ventilation air will usually have to be heated by an additional air heater.

To sum up, the following measures are necessary for effective limitation of condensation on the store surfaces and those of the potatoes:

- Ventilation with cold outside air, for example as illustrated in Fig. 12.7, to maintain the dew point and relative humidity of the air at the required level. To maintain 95 % RH in the store, 17 m³ of outside air per tonne of potatoes per day will be sufficient.

238

- The store must be insulated in such a way that the surface temperature of the walls and roof does not fall below the dew point of the air in the store.

- The roof or ceiling surface should preferably be clad with a porous organic material, such as wood, heraklit, etc., to delay condensation and limit the risk of dripping.

- Condensation can also be delayed by installing fans below the roof, to increase the air velocity along the surface.

- Regular internal ventilation will prevent high temperature differences within the potato heap, thus delaying condensation on the surfaces of the store and on those of the potaoes.

12.3.3 *Insulation capacity required*

The thickness of the insulation or k-value of the roof and walls of the store is generally a matter of the economics of storage. In determination of the storage costs, allowance must also be made for losses of stored produce.
This clearly shows that the amount of insulation justified on economic grounds greatly depends on the prices of the equipment used to control the storage conditions, on the cost of energy and of insulation, and on the market price of the potatoes. The period of storage is also relevant to the economic considerations. For this reason it is only possible to give a rough guide for determination of the required insulation.
In warm climates where the ambient temperature is always higher than the storage temperature, no condensation forms on the internal surfaces of the store. In this case the heat flow through the structure largely determines the capital and operating costs of the store. As a guide to determination of the optimum insulation, a heat flow of $Q = 9$ to 11 W/m² through the walls and roof may be assumed. This heat flow may occur at the mean maximum ambient temperature during the storage period. For instance, if the storage temperature T_i is 7 °C and the mean maximum ambient temperature occurring during storage T_o is 40 °C, the optimum insulation or k-value is given by:

$$k = \frac{Q}{T_o - T_i} = \frac{11}{40-7} = 0.33 \text{ W/m}^2\text{K}$$

However, in a climate where the ambient temperature during the storage period falls considerably below the storage temperature, insulation of the store is required to prevent cooling of the potatoes and the formation of condensation on the store surfaces.

Determination of the required insulation capacity of the store in such a case will be illustrated by an example.

EXAMPLE

The parameters of the store are as follows:

Storage capacity : 2000 tonnes of potatoes

Height of bulk heap: 3.5 m

Store dimensions: 43 m long by 20 m wide by 5 m high

Total area of walls and roof: A = 1490 m²

Storage conditions: T_i = 7 °C; 95 % RH; i_i = 21.6 kJ/kg

Ambient conditions: T_o = -10 °C; 100 % RH; i_i = -6.2 kJ/kg

Heat production of potatoes: 10 W/tonne

Ventilation with outside air to maintain 95 % RH: 17 m³/tonne · day or 34,000 m³/day.

Heat produced by the potatoes: Q_a = 2000 · 10 = 20,000 W = 20 kW

Heat loss by ventilation with outside air:

Q_V = V · (i_i - i_o) = 34,000 · 1.26 (21.6 + 6.2)

Q_V = 1,191,000 kJ/day = 13.8 kW

The heat produced in the store is then still:

Q = Q_a - Q_V = 20 - 13.8 = 6.2 kW

This heat may be lost through the structure to keep the temperature in the store constant. The k-value of the structure can be determined from this:

$$k = \frac{Q}{(T_i - T_o) \cdot A} = \frac{6200}{17 \cdot 1490} = 0.245 \text{ W/m}^2\text{K}$$

According to Table 12.3, no condensation will form on the surface of the store at this k-value and at 95 % RH in the store. However, according to the table, k = 0.4 W/m² · K is already sufficient to prevent condensation on a surface of organic material. But in this case the outside air would have to be heated to prevent cooling of the potatoes. The capacity of the air heater required at k = 0.4 W/m²K would be:

Q_H = k. · A · (T_i - T_o) - 6200 = 0.4 · 1490 · 17 - 6200

Q_H = 3932 W ≅ 4 kW

The mean minimum ambient temperature of the coldest period must be taken as the basis for determining the store insulation required and the volume of outside air. The mean minimum ambient temperature in the Netherlands is 0 °C and the required insulation capacity of the structure is k = 0.4 W/m²K for the roof and 0.5 W/m²K for the walls. The required volume of outside air, as shown in Fig. 12.7, is 25 m³/tonne · day. At extremely low ambient temperatures, a heating of ventilation air may be required to prevent cooling of the potatoes.

240

12.3.4 Requirements to be satisfied by the insulation

The insulation must be applied continuously to the walls and
roof - i.e., on the 'darkroom' principle. There must not be any uninsulated and highly heat conductive structural parts passing through the insulation to the store. This applies equally to heavy structural parts and
to hardware such as screws, bolts, nails, etc. Where such a structural
part unavoidably has to be passed through the insulation, the part must
be insulated over a length of at least 1.5 m from the penetration, which
must itself be properly sealed. The penetration of structural parts
through the insulation must, however, be kept to a minimum. Uninsulated
and badly insulated penetrating components give rise to intensive heat
exchange with the environment, as a result of which it may become difficult if not impossible to maintain the required temperature in the store.
A much greater danger is, however, presented by the condensation occurring at these points in cold weather.
Insulation material itself must also not become wet, because the insulating capacity of an insulating material is based on a large number of
small air spaces within it; if these spaces become filled with water, the
material loses its insulating power.

Insulating material may become wet by condensation of water vapour
which diffuses through the insulation. Diffusion of water vapour through
the structure occurs as a result of the difference in the partial vapour
pressure of the air on either side of the wall or roof. The diffusion
flux density - i.e., the amount of vapour passing through 1 m² of the
surface per second - depends on the difference between the partial vapour
pressures on either side of the wall or roof and on the resistance of the
relevant component to vapour diffusion. Hence vapour diffusion will occur
even if the air pressure on either side of a structural component is the
same if the partial vapour pressure on each side is different. This is
mostly the case in potato stores. Since the vapour pressure in warm air
is usually higher than in cold air, the vapour will also diffuse in the
direction from the warm to the cold side of a component.

The diffusion flux density can be determined from Equation 12:

$$\dot{m} = \frac{\Delta P}{R_D}$$

Since there is always a resistance to vapour diffusion through each part
of a structural component, the vapour pressure will decline in the direction of the vapour flow, falling more slowly the lower the resistance of
a part to vapour diffusion. The total pressure drop through a component
is determined by the vapour pressure in the air on either side of the
structure.

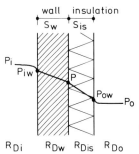

wall insulation

Fig. 12.8. Process of vapour pressure through the wall and roof structure.

The variation of the vapour pressure through a structural component in the steady-state condition is plotted in Fig. 12.8. In the steady-state condition the diffusion flux density is equal throughout the component. The total resistance to the vapour flow in Equation 12 is then:

$$R_D = R_{Di} + R_{DW} + R_{Dis} + R_{Do}$$

The resistances to vapour diffusion can be determined as follows:

Internal resistance to vapour flow R_{Di} = 9700 m²Pa · h/kg

External resistance to vapour flow R_{Do} = 1300 m²Pa · h/kg

Resistance to vapour diffusion through the wall: $R_{DW} = 1.56 · 10^6 · \mu_w · Sw$

Resistance to vapour diffusion through the insulation:

$$R_{DW} = 1.56 · 10 · \mu_{is} · Sis$$

Table 12.4 Diffusion resistance factors of construction materials.

Material	Specific gravity ρ (kg/m³)	Diffusion resistance factor μ
Concrete	1300-1800	4-10
Gas concrete	600	3.5- 5.5
	800	5.5- 7.5
Cement mortar	1980	16.5
Asbestos cement panels	1690	37
Asbestos cement panels with		
decompression layer	1885	1030
Deal	400	200
Brick	1500-1900	9.3-10
Foam polystyrene	10	15- 50
	20	40-100
	40	80-210
Glass wool and rock wool	100-300	1.17-1.27
Glass foam	149	tight
Aluminium foil		practically tight
Polyvinyl film	259/m²	32600-65000

242

The factor μ in the equations is the 'diffusion resistance factor', a physical property of the relevant material. The diffusion resistance factors
for a number of construction materials are set out in Table 12.4.

With the usual wall and roof structures in potato stores, the internal
and external resistances to moisture transmission R_{Di} and R_{DE} are very
small compared with the vapour diffusion resistances through the structure itself, and can therefore be neglected in calculations.
The diffusion resistance is then:

$$R_D = 1.56 \cdot 10^6 \, (\mu_1 S_1 + \mu_2 S_2 + \mu_n S_n) \tag{32}$$

The total resistance to vapour diffusion through a wall or roof structure can thus be determined from Equation 32 and Table 12.4. If the air
conditions inside and outside the store are known, Equation 12 can then
be used to determine the amount of vapour passing through each m² of the
area of the structure per second. Obviously, under specific internal and
external conditions, less vapour will flow the higher the resistance of
the structure. In the steady-state condition, the total resistance also
defines the variation of the vapour pressure through the structure. The
vapour pressure loss through each structural part in Fig. 12.8 can be determined as follows:

$$P_i - P = \frac{R}{R_w} \, (P_i - P_o)$$

or

$$P - P_o = \frac{R}{R_{is}} \, (P_i - P_o) \tag{33}$$

The previous considerations on heat transport show that there is also
a temperature drop through the structure in the direction of the heat or
vapour flow. However, the temperature determines the saturation pressure
of water vapour, which is the highest pressure at which water can exist
in vapour phase.
If the vapour pressure in the diffusion flow at a given position in the
structure thus becomes higher than the saturation pressure corresponding
to the temperature at that position, part of the water vapour will inevitably condense at this point. The variation of the temperature and saturation pressure of water vapour and of the vapour pressure in the diffusion flow through a component is illustrated in Fig. 12.9.
In this case the condensation occurs in the shaded area of the insulating material. To prevent this condensation, the vapour diffusion resis-

243

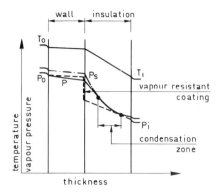

Fig. 12.9. Variation of temperature, saturation vapour pressure and actual vapour pressure through the structure.

tance on the warm side of the insulation must be increased so that the vapour pressure in the diffusion flow everywhere remains lower than the saturation pressure. This can be achieved by placing an additional resistance to vapour flow between the wall and the insulation.

The addition of this extra resistance to the structure reduces the diffusion flow and, as Equations 32 and 33 show, also changes the course of the variation of vapour pressure, as indicated by the dashed curve in Fig. 12.9. See Cammerer (1962).

Hence condensation in the insulation material can be prevented by applying a layer of high resistance to vapour flow, viz., a vapour barrier on the *warm side* of the insulation. However, the cold side of the insulation should preferably remain open, or, if it has to be covered, only a *material permeable to vapour* may be used to cover it. A structure of this kind is very suitable for a climate where the outside temperature remains constantly higher or constantly lower than the inside temperature throughout the whole or most of the storage period, as in the tropics or in cold regions. If the direction of the heat and/or vapour flow during the storage period reverses, as usually occurs in a temperate climate, this vapour barrier will find itself on the cold side of the insulation and condensation will unavoidably occur in the insulating material. The variation of temperature and pressure in such a case is plotted in Fig. 12.10.

Since the vapour pressure in the diffusion flow cannot become higher than the saturation pressure, condensation occurs in this case between points A and B - i.e., within the insulating material.

The amount of condensed vapour can be determined from Equations 6 and 33, as follows:

$$M_k = \frac{P_o - P_a}{R_a} - \frac{P_R - P_i}{R_{DR} + R_W} \tag{34}$$

244

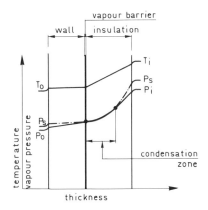

Fig. 12.10. Process of vapour pressure when vapour barrier is placed on the cold side of the insulation.

Since the diffusion resistance of the vapour barrier (R_{DR}) is very high, the second term on the right-hand side of Equation 34 becomes small, so that the rate of condensation may be very high. This will always be the case in insulating materials with low diffusion resistance, such as glass wool or rock wool. As a result, the insulating capacity of these materials may fall very sharply.

Condensation formed during vapour diffusion in one direction can, however, be re-evaporated if the direction of vapour diffusion changes, thus drying the insulating material again. In situations where the direction of vapour diffusion changes during the storage period, the insulating capacity of the structure can thus be retained without using a diffusion resistant layer. But it is then preferable to use an insulating material of high diffusion resistance, such as polystyrene or foam polyurethane, to minimize condensation in each case. This will also limit the temporary decline in the insulating capacity. However, if glass wool or rock wool is used for insulation, at least one diffusion resistant layer must for the same reason be present on both sides of the insulation, to limit the degree of condensation. In this way the insulating capacity can be retained for a long time. However, if condensation is to be prevented where the direction of vapour diffusion is variable, a *vapour-tight* layer must be applied on both sides of the insulation - e.g., a metal sheet - or else a vapour-tight insulating material such as foam glass must be used.

When diffusion resistant and vapour-tight layers are used, it is essential to avoid scratching these materials during construction, as this may give rise to serious condensation in the insulating material and rapid loss of the insulating capacity of the structure.

12.4 Construction of walls, roof and floor

12.4.1 Wall construction

Potatoes are often stored loose. This means that considerable lateral thrust is exerted on the walls (Fig. 12.11), which must be capable of withstanding it. This thrust must be transmitted to the main structure of the building. In addition to the pressure on the walls, the nature of the ground underneath the building is an important determining factor in its construction. The ground must ultimately be capable of supporting the building. Due allowance must be made for these points in design and calculation.

The silo calculations of Marcel and André Reimbert can be used for calculating the expected wall thrust pressures exerted by the potatoes. These are in good agreement with the thrusts measured by the IBVL in practice in different stores and with measurements carried out in the USA (United States Department of Agriculture) (Fig. 12.11).

No lateral thrust is exerted on the structure where potatoes are stored in pallet boxes or in bags on pallets, so that the store structure can be lighter in such cases. This partially offsets the cost of the boxes or bags and pallets. Even where the potatoes are stored in bulk heaps, the lateral thrust can be limited or even prevented by reducing the height of the bulk heap along the wall or by allowing the potatoes to ta-

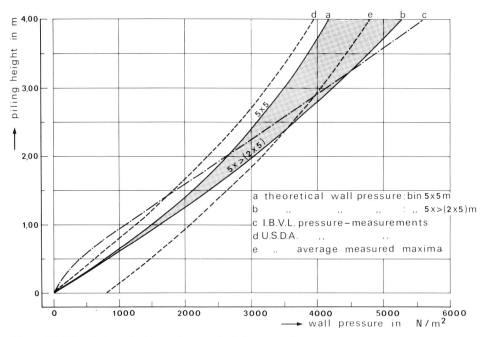

Fig. 12.11. Lateral thrust exerted by potatoes.

ke up their natural angle of repose down to the floor at the periphery of the building. However, the angle of repose of clean potatoes is 35 to 40 °C relative to a horizontal surface, and the storage capacity of the building will be reduced at the natural angle of repose.

Brick is still often used for store construction. For all this material's good properties, it is not so suitable for the construction of stores, as a brick or stone structure cannot withstand any significant tensile forces, and reinforcements are then necessary - e.g., timber, steel, reinforced masonry or concrete and other structures.

One of the oldest types of wall structures is the 'box wall' (Fig. 12.12). This consists of an ordinary cavity wall with a double-skinned, pressureresistant wooden lining on the inside with a 5 cm clearance from the masonry.

Another type of wall structure commonly used is the reinforced hollow brick wall (Fig. 12.13). Depending on the insulating materials to be used, the heavy timber construction may in this case be wholly or partially omitted. Where loose insulating materials are used, the wooden internal structure is partially retained, mainly to keep the insulating material in position. The wooden internal structure may be completely omitted where solid insulating materials, such as cork, polystyrene or polyurethane, are used (Fig. 12.13b). Reinforced gas concrete blocks are often used instead of brick.

The types of structures described above, with the associated traditional working methods, are highly labour-intensive with a great deal of un-

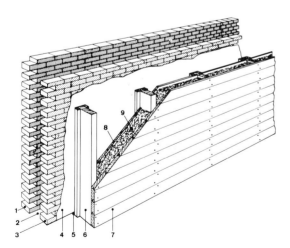

Fig. 12.12. Wooden case-wall construction. 1. Outer wall of half a brick's thickness; 2. air space; 3. inner wall of half a brick's thickness; 4. plaster; 5. distance between posts and wall (5 cm); 6. posts; 7. wooden inner wall (3 cm thickness); 8. wooden back wall (1.5. cm thickness); 9. insulation (loose material).

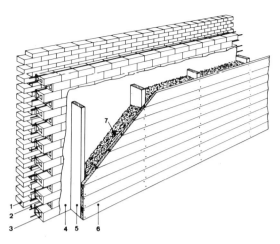

Fig. 12.13a. Reinforced hollow brick wall construction with loose insulating material. 1. Outer wall of half a brick's thickness; 2. air space; 3. inner wall of reinforced hollow bricks; 4. plaster; 5. posts; 6. wooden inner wall; 7. loose insulating material.

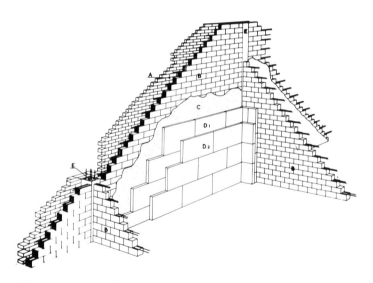

Fig. 12.13b. Reinforced hollow brick wall construction with solid insulating material. A. Outer wall of half a brick's thickness; B. inner wall of reinforced hollow bricks; C. plaster; D1-D2. solid insulating material; E. reinforced concrete columns.

productive working time involved, for example, in the placing of a large number of sections, formwork and other structures. The capital cost is therefore also relatively high.

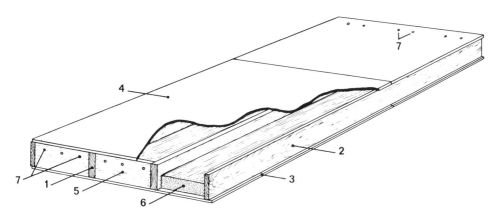

Fig. 12.14. Wooden box panel. 1. Main posts; 2. side posts; 3. plywood (16 mm thickness); 4. plywood (10 mm thickness); 5. intermediate plank between posts; 6. insulating material; 7. ventilation holes.

A cheaper method of construction was therefore sought, using prefabricated wall panels strong enough to withstand the pressure of the potatoes and at the same time having sufficient heat transfer resistance. The wooden 'box panel', (Fig. 12.14) is an example. These panels weigh some 40 kg/m², a saving of about 300 kg per m² of wall area compared with traditional masonry structures. Owing to the weight saving of the new structure, the foundations can also be lighter. The main structure is of steel with this construction system.

To erect the wall panels (Fig. 12.15), a ring beam is mounted on the foundation beam and the bottom of the wall panels is secured to this. The panel is supported at the top by a steel beam and it is terminated by an angle iron on the inside of the building. The panels are protected from the weather by a lightweight cladding such as corrugated asbestos cement panels. Experience with this modular system has been good. However, the timber structure is suitable only for storage at low temperatures (about 4 °C). The storage temperature for potatoes to be processed is 10 to 12 °C, and the storage season is then also longer. As a result, the wood of a store has less opportunity to dry out after a period of storage, and its moisture content increases to 27 % or more. All the wood used in the interior of a store where potatoes are kept at a temperature above 4 °C must therefore be impregnated. Because of the nature of the stored produce, the only wood preservatives that can be used for this purpose are boron compounds, but these do not provide sufficient protection from deterioration. In many stores, wood rot fungi have been encountered after a single storage season at high temperature.

For this reason attempts were made to find a more universal prefabricated structural component, which had to have sufficient insulating capa-

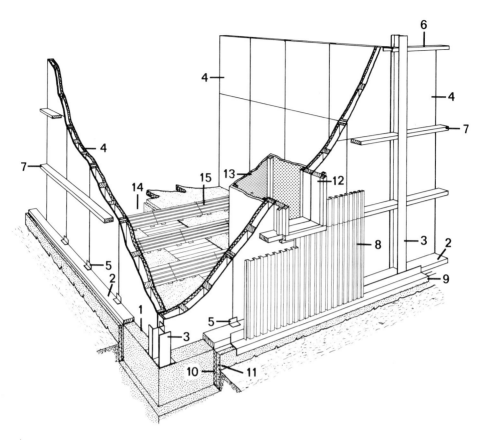

Fig. 12.15. Erection of the structure with wooden box panels. 1. Foundation beam; 2. wooden beam; 3. steel column; 4. wall elements; 5. corner profile for fastening; 6. U-profile; 7. horizontal wall beam; 8. wall sheating; 9. Z-profile; 10. insulation; 11. protection of insulation; 12. air inlet; 13. internal ventilation shaft; 14. underground air duct; 15. air distribution system.

city as well as being vapour-tight on both sides and pressure-resistant. It also had to conform to the international modular system (basic module 10 cm). Another equally important requirement was that the modules should require minimum maintenance and be easy to clean. These properties were found in sandwich wall units, which consist of two metal panels with insulation between them (Fig. 12.16).

These prefabricated units are very narrow - only 30 cm (0.3 m) - offering great freedom in the shaping of buildings. The panels consist of enamel-coloured sheets of an aluminium-magnesium alloy with very high corrosion resistance.
The panels are firmly secured together by a core of foam polyurethane. They are assembled by double tongue-and-groove joints giving a dimensional tolerance of 3 mm. The wall dimensions can thus readily be adapted to

250

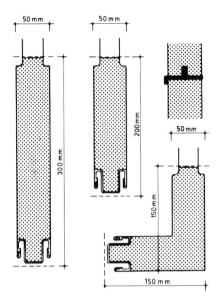

max. length   : 10 m
K-value   : 0,5 W /m^2 °C
weight of panel: ± 70 N /m^2

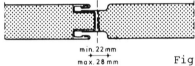

min. 22 mm
max. 28 mm   Fig. 12.16. Prefabricated sandwich wall panels.

make up for dimensional inaccuracies in other parts of the structure. An
additional sectional neoprene seal is placed on the outside of the double
tongue and groove. A T-shaped neoprene section is also available for sealing butt joints between the panels, so that there is no limit to the
wall height. Walls with the following characteristics can be made from
these panels:
a. good insulation without heat bridges combined with low thickness and
   light weight,
b. pressure resistance,
c. simple and rapid assembly; can be re-erected elsewhere without loss,
d. vapour-tightness.
These panels are made in insulation thicknesses of 4, 5, 7.5 and 10 cm,
giving insulation values of k = 0.5, 0.3 and 0.23 W/m^2 K respectively.
Since these units are absolutely vapour-tight, their insulation capacity
remains unchanged even after the store has been in use for many years.
    Similar sandwich panels are available, using galvanized steel or hard-
board sheets instead of aluminium. Foam polystyrene can also be used for
the insulation.

When building with sandwich panels, it is best to position the main steel structure on the outside of the panels, when the passage of heavy structural components through the insulation can be avoided.

The use of sandwich panels combined with a main steel structure also has the advantage of drastically reducing construction time on site. A store of this kind can be erected in a few weeks.

The price of the different types of wall structure will determine the eventual choice.

12.4.2 Roof construction

The requirements to be satisfied by the roof structure can be summarized as follows:
- The structure must be capable of withstanding the loads presented by wind, snow, water, its own weight and the suspension of equipment.
- The structure must protect the interior of the building from heat and moisture exchange with the surrounding atmosphere.
- The structure must be permanent and require little maintenance.

The main structure of the roof is usually of timber or steel, covered preferably with materials having a low thermal radiation factor; the materials used must, of course, be watertight. A low thermal radiation factor is necessary to prevent large fluctuations in the roof temperature due, for example, to heating of the roof in the sun and cooling due to thermal radiation into the cold atmosphere. Metal or asbestos cement sheets are very suitable for roofing, but the sheets must be able to expand freely when their temperature varies. A well ventilated space should preferably be left between the roof panels and the insulation, to limit the amount of condensation on the cold roof sheets in cold weather. The extreme temperatures of the roof panels caused by thermal radiation will then also have less effect on the storage conditions.

As stated in Section 12.2.4, there is always some vapour diffusion through the insulation unless the latter is provided with a vapour-tight layer on both sides. This vapour will condense on the cold surface of the panels in cold weather and the condensation will drip back on the insulation below.

To prevent this water from ultimately dripping on to the potatoes, the entire surface of the insulation must be watertight. Particular attention

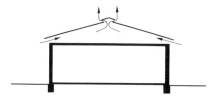

Fig. 12.17. Roof structure.

252

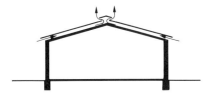

Fig. 12.18. Roof structure.

must be devoted to sealing the seams between the insulating panels. The risk of leaks through the insulation is also reduced if this water can drain away freely to the gutter. The clearance required between the insulation and the roof panelling for efficient ventilation is 5 to 15 cm. Examples of good roof structures are shown in Fig. 12.17 and 12.18.

12.4.3 Floor construction

Concrete or earth floors are used in potato stores. A concrete floor is necessary if an underground ducting system is used to distribute the ventilation air or if the store is emptied by fluming. An earth floor must always be hardened before the potatoes are loaded into the store, usually by making the earth wet a few times and tamping it. These operations are repeated in the first two or three years to obtain a hard surface. A drainage system must be incorporated in an earth floor.

Concrete floors are used almost exclusively in potato stores in Europe. Apart from their higher load-bearing capacity, concrete floors also have hygienic advantages, as they can be easily cleaned and if necessary also disinfected.

The floor must be capable of withstanding the load presented by the machinery and the stored potatoes. The potatoes exert a pressure of 700 kg/m² on the floor per metre of bulk height - i.e., the pressure on the floor is 2800 kg/m² for a height of 4 m.
However, the maximum concentrated load on the floor is exerted by forklift trucks (as much as 1500 kg in some cases).

In temperate climates the floors of potato stores seldom have thermal insulation. However, if the groundwater temperature is 20 °C and the average water table is high (1 m or less below floor level), the storage temperature being 8 to 10 °C, floor insulation is advisable. Insulation with 4 to 6 cm of foam polystyrene is always sufficient.

If the floor is uninsulated, the wall insulation should preferably be continued to 0.6 to 1 m below floor level. This limits heat exchange along the periphery of the floor and prevents freezing or overheating of the potatoes along the periphery of the store. The same effect is obtained by insulating a 1 to 1.5 m wide strip of floor around the edge of the store.

Reference

Cammerer, J.S., 1962. Der Wärme- und Kälteschutz in der Industrie.
4. Auflage. Springer-Verlag, Berlin.

13 Cooling systems in potato stores

A. Rastovski

Stored potatoes have to be cooled to keep them at the required storage
temperature. If they are not cooled, their temperature will increase
owing to the heat produced in respiration.
Temperature is one of the most important factors affecting the quality of
potatoes during storage. Cooling is therefore necessary to maintain the
quality of the stored potatoes. However, cooling always involves a certain loss of weight from the potatoes due to water evaporation. This
weight loss must be controlled during cooling. An efficient cooling system must thus satisfy the following requirements:
a. Maintenance of the required potato temperature and prevention of substantial temperatue variations in the mass of stored produce.
b. Limitation of weight losses due to evaporation of water.
It is usually aimed to limit the maximum temperature difference within
the heap of stored produce to 1 to 1.5 °C, as shown in Fig. 13.1.
   Air is commonly used for cooling potatoes during storage. The temperature of the cooling air must therefore obviously be lower than that of
the potatoes.
However, the cooling rate and temperature fluctuations through a mass of
stored produce greatly depend on the rate of the air flow through the
stack of potatoes. The higher the rate of air flow, the faster the cooling process - i.e., the shorter the cooling time - and the smaller the
temperature fluctuations in the stored potatoes. Since evaporative water
loss greatly depends on the cooling time and is hardly at all affected by
the air velocity resp. the rate of air flow, water loss from the potatoes
is also reduced the higher the rate of air flow.
   Hence a forced flow of cold air through the produce is essential for
efficient cooling of potatoes. The relative humidity of the cold air

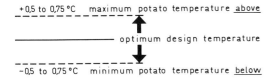

Fig. 13.1. Usual temperature difference within the potato pile.

should, however, be kept as high as possible to minimize water loss from the potatoes during cooling.

The temperature of potatoes can be controlled by:
a. Outside air cooling, or
b. Mechanical refrigeration
Both forms of cooling are used in potato storage.

13.1 Outside air cooling

Outside air cooling is an efficient and relatively inexpensive method, which is therefore often used in potato storage. However, it can be used only if the ambient temperature during the storage period regularly falls below the required storage temperature. Outside air can be used to cool the potatoes only during such periods. Low ambient temperatures regularly occur in temperate and cold climates, where external air cooling is therefore frequently used.

An outside air cooling system is illustrated in Fig. 13.2.
The standard components of an outside air cooling system are as follows:
- Fan
- Air supply and discharge openings
- Dampers, viz.
  1. Inlet damper
  2. Oulet damper
  3. Mixing damper
- Air ducting for uniform air distribution through the stored produce
- Controls and instrumentation

The principle of outside air cooling is as follows. A thermometer in the stored potatoes measures the temperature of the produce. If it rises above the required storage temperature, the potatoes must be cooled. However, cooling is only possible if the ambient temperature is lower than that of the potatoes. Hence the ambient temperature must also be known;

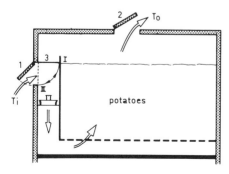

Fig. 13.2. Outside air cooling system. 1. Inlet damper; 2. outlet damper; 3. mixing damper.

it is measured by a second thermometer outside the store. If the ambient temperature falls below that of the potatoes, cooling can commence. The inlet and outlet dampers are opened and the fan is switched on. As long as the ambient temperature does not fall below the minimum acceptable temperature shown in Fig. 13.1, the mixing damper remains in the bottom position (position 1). Fresh outside air is now aspirated by the fan and blown through the ducting and the potatoes; the air leaves the store through the outlet opening. Since the air temperature is lower than that of the potatoes, the latter are cooled by this ventilation. In principle cooling ends when the potatoes have reached the required temperature.

However, if the ambient temperature rises above that of the potatoes during ventilation, the fan must immediately be stopped to prevent the potatoes from being heated again. The inlet and outlet dampers must be closed at the same time. Ventilation (cooling) continues as soon as the ambient temperature has again fallen below the potato temperature as shown in Fig. 13.1.

But if the ambient temperature falls below the minimum acceptable temperature shown in Fig. 13.1 during ventilation, mixed-air ventilation must be used to prevent chilling or even freezing of the potatoes. Section 9.1.11 shows that when two air flows of different temperatures are mixed, the combined flow will assume a temperature between those of the two air flows. This temperature depends on the relative volumes of air mixed. In this way the required cooling air temperature can be achieved by mixing the heated air from the potato heap with low-temperature outside air.

The relative volumes of these two air masses are determined by the position of the mixing damper in Fig. 13.2. With the damper in position 1, only outside air is aspirated by the fan, while in position II all the ventilation air is internal. In any position of the damper between I and II, the fan aspirates both outside and inside air. The correct position of the mixing damper for a given ambient temperature is determined by the required air temperature in the main duct behind the fan - i.e., by the required cooling air temperature. The latter can be measured by a thermometer placed in the main duct. The mixing damper must therefore be set so as to give the required temperature in the duct. To maintain this temperature, the damper position must be regularly varied during ventilation to conform to changes in the outside air temperature. Hence the temperature in the delivery duct must be continuously monitored.

If the air from inside the store is mixed with the outside air, the produce can be cooled in any period when the outside air temperature is *lower* than the required storage temperature. However, if outside air alone is used for ventilation without mixing with internal air, cooling is possible only when the outside air temperature is *equal* to the minimum cooling air temperature shown in Fig. 13.1. However, the ambient temperature varies both from hour to hour during the day and over the storage period as a whole. Any given temperature will normally prevail only for very short times. On the other hand, very long periods of low temperature may occur. Mixing thus makes it possible to cool (ventilate) the store for long periods.

Since heat production in the store remains virtually the same in both cases, the same amount of heat will need to be removed from it. The rate of heat removal is determined by the rate of air flow through a stack of potatoes, the duration of ventilation and the temperature rise of the air on its passage through the store. During storage, however, heating of the air is limited by the acceptable temperature variation in a heap of stored potatoes - i.e., by $T_{max} - T_{min} = 1$-1.5 K (Fig. 13.1).

The cooling effect then depends solely on the rate of air flow through a heap of stored produce, or the fan capacity and period of fan operation. For a given rate of cooling, the fan capacity must be larger the shorter the period of fan operation. Since a longer period of ventilation is possible with a mixed air system than with all-outside-air cooling, a smaller fan capacity will be sufficient in a mixed air system (Chapter 15).

The cooling requirement can be determined from Equation 24:

$$Q = V \cdot \Delta i \cdot \rho \cdot t \qquad \qquad (kJ/day)$$

The difference in enthalpy can also be expressed as follows:

$$\Delta i = C_p \cdot \Delta T \qquad \qquad (kJ/kg)$$

Equation 24 thus becomes:

$$Q = V \cdot \rho \cdot C_p \Delta T \cdot t \qquad \qquad (38)$$

in which

   V = fan capacity (m³/s)
   ρ = 1.26 kg/m³ (specific gravity of air at normal storage temperatures)
   C_p = 2.0 kJ/kg K (apparent specific heat of air - i.e., specific heat including heat of evaporation withdrawn by the air when potatoes are cooled)
   ΔT = temperature difference between fresh air and potatoes
   t = period of fan operation (s/day)

Equation 38 then becomes:

$$Q = 2.52 \cdot V \cdot \Delta T \cdot t \qquad \qquad (kJ/day) \qquad \qquad (39)$$

258

During storage at the required temperature, however, ΔT is determined by $T_{max} - T_{min} = 1-1.5$ K (Fig. 13.1), and the cooling effect becomes:

$$Q = 3.7 \cdot V \cdot t \qquad\qquad (kJ/day) \qquad\qquad (40)$$

As stated earlier, the cooling effect of an outside air cooling system is thus determined by the fan capacity and the period of fan operation.

For efficient cooling of potatoes, the air flow must be distributed uniformly through the entire mass of stored produce (Chapter 16).

The cross-sectional area of the air inlet and outlet openings must be sufficient to pass the required air flow without causing serious losses of pressure in that flow. The air velocity through these openings is therefore usually limited to 4 to 5 m/s.

The required cross-sectional area of the openings can be determined as follows:

$$A = \frac{V}{w} \qquad\qquad (m^2) \qquad\qquad (41)$$

in which

V	= fan capacity (m^3/s)
w	= 4 to 5 m/s air velocity through opening
A	= a $\cdot$ b (m^2) cross-sectional area of opening

The air inlet and outlet openings must be fitted with tightly closing dampers to avoid unwanted air flows when the fans are not operating. Like the walls and roof of the store, the dampers must be well insulated. Since the cooling periods are substantially limited in a system with outside air cooling by ambient conditions, good insulation of the store is very important for efficient control of the storage conditions - i.e., to prevent major fluctuations in the storage temperature.

13.2 Mechanical refrigeration

Unlike systems with outside air cooling, mechanical refrigeration systems operate independently of the ambient temperature. In other words, the temperature in a mechanically refrigerated space can be maintained at any desired level regardless of the ambient temperature. Of course, this independence of nature has to be paid for. The capital cost of the equipment and the running costs (energy) in this system are considerably higher than with a comparable outside air cooling system. Hence storage with mechanical refrigeration is more expensive. However, mechanical refrigeration is necessary for long-term storage of potatoes and other perishable natural produce in climates where the ambient temperature never falls below the acceptable storage temperature, as in the tropics and subtropics. It is also used in temperate climates to store potatoes right into the summer months.

Here again, the potatoes are cooled with air, but in this case one and the same volume of air is used not just once, as in an outside air cooling system, but over and over again. As Fig. 13.3 clearly shows, air recirculation is the basic principle of a mechanically refrigerated store. The cooled air flows first through the potato stack and, since it is colder than the potatoes, it withdraws heat from them; the potatoes are thus cooled and the air heated. The heated air then passes through the air cooler, whose surface temperature is lower than the required storage temperature.

The air gives up the heat withdrawn from the potatoes to the cooler and is thus recooled to the desired temperature; the cycle can then begin again. The air thus recirculates constantly.

However, while the potatoes are being cooled, water also evaporates from them. This vapour is absorbed by the air, whose moisture content thus increases. The humidified air then comes into contact with the cold surface of the cooler. If the dew point of the warm air becomes higher than the surface temperature of the cooler owing to moisture absorption, water vapour will inevitably condense on the surface of the cooler. In the steady-state condition, the degree of condensation on the cooler surface will become equal to the degree of water evaporation from the potatoes. A mechanical refrigeration system thus controls both the heat and the moisture balances of a store. The water loss from the potatoes is thus determined by the amount of water removed from the store by the cooler.

The same volume of air cannot, however, continue to recirculate without limitation, as the potatoes use up oxygen from the air during respiration and at the same time release carbon dioxide (CO_2). The air in the store must thus be renewed to supply oxygen and remove CO_2. In most cases,

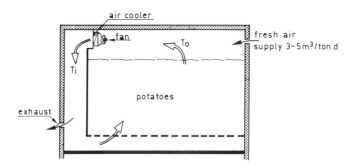

Fig. 13.3. Mechanically refrigerated store.

260

the volume of air exchanged with the environment through leaks in the store is already sufficient.

Even so, a mechanically refrigerated store must have an efficient air renewal system for safety reasons. Air renewal of 3 to 5 m³ of fresh air per tonne of stored potatoes per day is sufficient to provide the potatoes with the necessary oxygen and to keep the CO_2 concentration in the store below 1 % vol.

For efficient temperature control in a heap of stored produce it is very important with this system, as in outside air cooling systems, for the air to flow *through* the heap and not round it. For efficient cooling there must always be a positive air flow *around each tuber*. If not enough attention is paid to this requirement when the store is designed and constructed, even an intrinsically excellent refrigerating system will give poor results.

Although the potatoes are cooled with air in both systems, the rate of air flow in a mechanical refrigeration system is entirely different in its significance from that in an outside air cooling system. In the latter case, the rate of air flow determines the cooling capacity of the system as a whole because the heat is removed from the store together with the air flow through the air outlet.

In the mechanical system, on the other hand, the heat is removed by the air cooler. Obviously, therefore, the cooling rate of the entire system is determined by that of the air cooler, or the rating of the refrigeration equipment. For a given air cooler rating, the fan capacity then determines only the temperature drop of the air through the air cooler.

The temperature drop of the air through the cooler can be determined from Equation 38:

$$\Delta T = \frac{Q}{V \cdot C_p \cdot \rho} \tag{42}$$

in which Q is expressed in kJ/s and T = 1 s.

Hence, in Fig. 13.4: $T_1 - T_2 = \dfrac{Q}{V \cdot C_p \cdot \rho}$

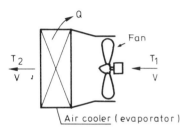

Fig. 13.4. Process of air temperature through the air cooler.

The temperature drop of the air through a cooler of given capacity thus becomes smaller the higher the rate of air flow, but the cooling capacity of the air flow remains unaffected. Fig. 13.4 shows that fan capacity, viz., the rate of air flow alone influences the variation of temperature in the store. According to Fig. 13.1, however, the latter must not exceed 1 to 1.5 K. The fan capacity for a given air cooler rating can be determined as follows from Equation 42:

$$\dot{V} = \frac{Q}{\Delta T \cdot C_p \cdot \rho} \tag{43}$$

and since ΔT_{max} = 1.5 K, the required fan capacity becomes:

$$\dot{V} = \frac{Q}{\Delta T \cdot C_p \cdot \rho} \qquad (m^3/s) \text{ or} \tag{44}$$

$$\dot{V} = 0.27 \ Q \qquad (m^3/s)$$

in which Q is the rating of refrigeration expressed in kJ/s or kW. The fan capacity in a mechanically refrigerated store is thus determined by the rating of the refrigeration system installed.

13.3 Refrigeration system

A refrigeration system allows the temperature in a store to be kept at a low level. This means that the heat produced in the cooled space is removed at low temperature. To remove this heat, refrigeration systems use the heat of evaporation of refrigerants, which are liquids with specific characteristics.

All liquids begin to evaporate when a given temperature is reached. The temperature at which evaporation commences is known as the boiling point of the liquid. The boiling point depends on the pressure of the liquid. For instance, water at atmospheric pressure (98.1 kPa) begins to evaporate at 100 °C. If the pressure is reduced to 49 kPa, it will already begin to evaporate at 81 °C. At 196 kPa, however, the water will only start to evaporate at 120 °C. Hence boiling point varies with pressure, and becomes higher at high pressure. If the water temperature rises to 119 °C and the pressure is 196 kPa, no evaporation will take place. But if the pressure is abruptly reduced to 98.1 kPa, a certain amount of water will evaporate and the temperature of the remainder will fall to 100 °C - i.e., to the boiling point of water at 98.1 kPa. Liquid water can thus no longer exist at a temperature higher than its boiling point at the relevant pressure. The temperature of the liquid phase can thus be varied by modifying the pressure.

262

If heat is added to water at 100 °C under a pressure of 98.1 kPa, the water will evaporate, but notwithstanding the addition of heat the temperature will remain 100 °C until the last drop of water has evaporated. The amount of heat which must be supplied to evaporate 1 kg of liquid is called the heat of evaporation. The heat of evaporation of water at a pressure of 98.1 kPa is 2258 kJ/kg. The water can thus absorb a relatively large amount of heat by evaporation without any change in its temperature.

If the water vapour then condenses on to a cold surface, the entire heat of evaporation is released again and liquid water again forms. A small quantity of water can thus absorb and release a relatively large amount of heat by evaporation and condensation respectively without any change in the temperature.

The same applies to all liquids. By using the heat of evaporation in refrigeration systems, the temperature of the refrigerant can be kept constant during heat transfer and only a limited quantity of refrigerant has to be transported through the system. This facilitates temperature control and allows the refrigeration system to be of compact construction.

The refrigerants most commonly used in potato storage are ammonia (NH_3) and the freons F-12 and F-22. These liquids evaporate at very low temperatures and relatively low gauge pressures, and can also be condensed at relatively high temperatures and low gauge pressures.

A refrigeration system is illustrated in Fig. 13.5.
The refrigerant recirculates through the system and undergoes the following changes of state in each cycle: evaporation, compression, condensation and expansion.

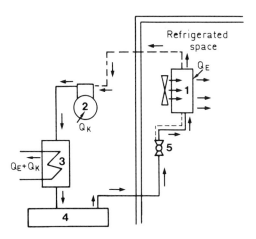

Fig. 13.5. Refrigeration system. 1. Evaporator - air cooler; 2. compressor; 3. condensor; 4. refrigerant receiver-tank; 5. expansion valve.

Evaporation takes place in the evaporator, which is often used as an air cooler. Predominantly liquid refrigerant with a small quantity of refrigerant vapour is fed to the evaporator. The pressure in the evaporator is kept so low that the boiling point of the refrigerant falls below the required temperature in the refrigerated space. Since the evaporator is colder than the air in that space, the air flowing through the evaporator (air cooler) is cooled. The heat withdrawn from the air is supplied to the refrigerant, causing it to evaporate. The low-pressure vapour forming in the evaporator is aspirated by the compressor.

Compression increases the pressure and temperature of the vapour. At higher pressure, the boiling point is also raised. The refrigerant vapour can thus condence at a temperature higher than the ambient temperature. The compressor pumps the high-pressure vapour to the condenser, through which ambient air or water flows. Since the boiling point of the refrigerant is higher, a heat flow will arise in the condenser from the refrigerant to the air or water, thus condensing the refrigerant vapour. Liquid refrigerant under high pressure thus flows out of the condenser and is collected in a receiver tank. The liquid refrigerant is conveyed from the reservoir to the expansion valve.

This valve expands the refrigerant, reducing its pressure. This pressure reduction causes a small quantity of refrigerant to evaporate, so that the temperature of the liquid falls to the boiling point at the resulting low pressure. This mixture of liquid and vapour flows to the evaporator and the cycle can then begin again. Hence a refrigerating system pumps the heat from the cooled space to the environment - i.e., from a low to a high temperature level.

Energy is, of course, necessary for this. This energy is used for compression of the refrigerant vapour, viz., for increasing both the pressure and the temperature of the refrigerant vapour. The mechanical energy necessary to drive the compressor is finally converted into heat. This heat must be removed by the condenser to condense the refrigerant vapour. The amount of heat to be removed by the condenser is thus determined by the sum of the heat removal from the cooled space (Q_E) and the heat of compression (Q_K) - i.e., by $Q_E + Q_K$ (Fig. 13.5).

The refrigeration capacity of a given refrigeration system depends on the evaporation and condensation temperatures or the evaporation and condensation pressures of the refrigerant respectively. The refrigeration capacity of a given system falls with increasing difference between the evaporation and condensation temperatures. For this reason the refrigeration capacity of a refrigeration system must always be specified at stated refrigerant evaporation and condensation temperatures.

The energy consumption of a refrigerating system is determined by the refrigeration capacity and the difference between the condensation and evaporation temperatures. Energy consumption at a given refrigeration capacity increases the bigger the difference between the condensation and evaporation temperatures.

The evaporation and condensation temperatures strongly depend on the required temperature in the refrigerated space and the ambient air temperature or cooling water temperature respectively. But heat transfer can only take place if the evaporation temperature is lower than the temperature in the cooled space or if the condensation temperature becomes higher than the temperature of the ambient air or cooling water. The necessary temperature differences depend on the size of the evaporator or condenser and on their design. The air or water flow velocity over the surface of the heat exchanger is also an important factor.

In general, for a given refrigeration capacity, the temperature difference required will be smaller the larger the cooling surface area and the higher the air or water flow velocity over the surface.
This is clear from the heat transfer equation:

$$Q = A \cdot k \cdot \Delta T \qquad\qquad (J/s) \qquad\qquad (45)$$

According to Equation 45, the required temperature difference becomes:

$$\Delta T = \frac{Q}{A \cdot k} \qquad\qquad (K) \qquad\qquad (46)$$

in which
ΔT = difference between evaporation or condensation temperature and air or water temperature
Q = refrigeration capacity (W)
A = area of heat exchanger (m^2)
k = heat transfer coefficient (W/m^2 K)

In Equations 45 and 46, k varies with the air or water flow velocity, increasing at high velocities. A relatively large evaporator or condenser area and forced air or water circulation over the area thus tend to save energy.

However, the relative size of the evaporator surface also affects weight loss in the potatoes.
In potato storage, the evaporator of the refrigerating system is normally used as an air cooler (Fig. 13.3). As stated earlier, when the humid air from the potatoes is cooled, condensation occurs on the cooler surface if the surface temperature falls below the dew point of the air. The lower the surface temperature, the more condensation will form. However, the amount of condensation determines the water loss from the potatoes. Hence potato weight loss during storage can be limited by providing a larger evaporator area in the store.

For this reason it is recommended that the difference between the storage temperature and the refrigerant evaporation temperature in the evaporator/air cooler be limited to 7 K. This determines the area of the evaporator (Equation 46). The rating of the refrigeration system is determined by the heat produced in the store (Equation 21).
The required refrigeration capacity is then:

$$\dot{Q} = \frac{1.2 \cdot Q_{tot}}{t} \qquad (w) \qquad (47)$$

in which

Q_{tot} = heat produced (J/day) in accordance with Equation 21
t = refrigeration time per day (s)

A larger installed refrigeration capacity will result in shorter refrigeration periods, thus reducing the weight loss (Chapter 9). But since a higher-capacity system is more expensive, the optimum refrigeration capacity must always be determined by cost-benefit considerations.

14   Temperature control in potato stores

A. Rastovski

The temperature of potatoes during storage is subject to variations
due to heat production and heat losses in the store. The temperature will
increase or decrease in accordance with the relative amount of heat produced or lost respectively in a store. However, temperature is one of the
principal determinants of potato quality during storage. Temperature control during storage is thus the prime condition for preservation of potato quality.

For efficient temperature control, a store must have a cooling and/or
heating system with the relevant control equipment and also facilities to
measure temperature. The principle of temperature control is illustrated
in the block diagram in Fig. 14.1.
The temperature of the potatoes is measured by a temperature sensor
placed in the potato stack and read off a measuring instrument. The measured temperature is then compared with the required, set potato temperature. In accordance with the result, a decision is then taken as to
whether the potatoes should or should not be cooled or heated. If the
measured temperature differs from the required temperature, the cooling
or heating system must be switched on.

The relevant controls are operated and the cooling or heating system
is started up. To prevent the temperature in the bottom layers of a stack
of potatoes from falling too low or rising too high, the air temperature
in the supply duct is also sensed and measured. On the basis of this tem-

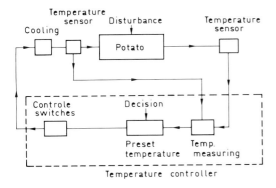

Fig. 14.1. Block-diagram for temperature control.

perature measurement, the relevant controls are set so as to maintain the
required duct temperature. The temperatures are measured continuously during cooling or heating. When the potato has again reached the desired
value, the cooling or heating system is switched off. The control process
is repeated whenever the potato temperature changes.

The temperature controller represented by the dashed line in Fig. 14.1
thus performs the following operations: temperature measurement, comparison of measured and set temperatures, decision as to whether the temperature should or should not be controlled, and actuation of the control
switches.

The function of the temperature controller can be performed by a human
being - i.e., the storekeeper - or by automatic equipment or by a combination of both. Automatic temperature control is always used in mechanically refrigerated stores, but all three systems are commonly used in
stores with outside air cooling. Even in the latter, however, automatic
temperature control is increasingly coming to be used.

14.1 Mechanically refrigerated stores

The process of temperature control in a mechanically refrigerated
store is illustrated in Fig. 14.2. A temperature sensor in the potato
stack measures the temperature of the potatoes. The controller includes a
thermostat set to the required storage temperature. If the potato temperature rises above that set on the thermostat, the latter switches the
refrigeration system and the air cooler fan on. Refrigeration continues
until the set temperature is reached in the potato stack. When this temperature has been reached, the thermostat automatically switches off the
refrigeration system and the fan. To prevent the air temperature in the
supply duct falling from too low - e.g., owing to freezing of the air
cooler - another temperature sensor is positioned in the supply duct and
is connected to a second thermostat. If the air temperature falls below
the relevant thermostat setting, the second thermostat switches off the
entire refrigeration system. The second thermostat thus acts as a safety device. The same control cycle is also performed if the temperature
in the potatoes increases.

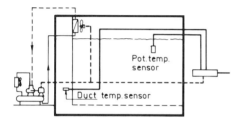

Fig. 14.2. Temperature control in a mechanically refrigerated store.

In an automatic control system of this kind, the thermostat thus performs the following functions: temperature measurement, comparison with the set value, decision and operation of controls (in accordance with the block diagram given in Fig. 14.1). This automatic temperature control system is relatively simple; the temperature is controlled solely by switching the refrigeration system and the air cooler fan on and off.

14.2 Stores with outside air cooling

In a store with an outside air cooling system, the fan, the fresh air inlet and exhaust oulet dampers and the mixing damper must be operated for cooling or control of the potato temperature.

These control operations can in principle be performed by the storekeeper himself. In the past, store temperatures were indeed generally controlled manually. For this purpose, only three thermometers are required: one in the potatoes, one outside and one in the supply duct behind the fan (Fig. 14.3). If the potato temperature rises too high and the outside air temperature is lower than the potato temperature, the fan is switched on, the air inlet and outlet dampers are opened and the desired temperature in the supply duct is set with the aid of the mixing damper. Both the temperature in the duct and that of the potatoes must be measured at regular intervals during fan operation: the ventilation must be stopped as soon as the desired potato temperature is reached or if the outside air temperature rises above that of the potatoes.

However, favourable outside air temperatures often occur only at night or very early in the morning. This is, of course, most inconvenient for the storekeeper if he has to control the temperature in the store manually. For this reason, automatic temperature control even in stores cooled with outside air has recently been introduced.

To reduce the cost of an automatic control system, the damper system has also been simplified. The most common types of damper systems are illustrated in Fig. 14.4.

Damper 1 in systems A and C takes the form of a pressure damper, whose design is illustrated in Figs. 14.5 and 14.6 for horizontal and vertical

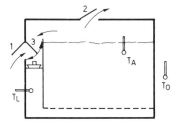

Fig. 14.3. Manual temperature control in stores with outside air cooling.
1. Air inlet damper; 2. air exhaust damper; 3. mixing damper.

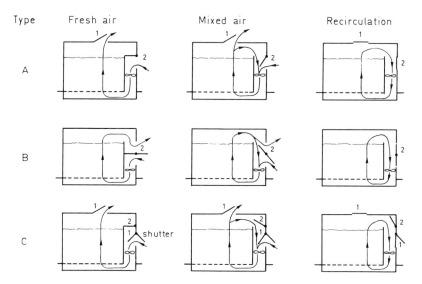

Fig. 14.4. Damper systems in stores with outside air cooling.

installation respectively. The dampers are made up of foam polystyrene and move with virtually no friction. The movement is initiated by the difference in pressure on either side of the damper. The outlet damper is opened by the excess pressure prevailing in the store if outside air is used for ventilation.

Similarly, the air inlet damper is also opened because there is a pressure deficit in the air duct. However, with internal air ventilation, both dampers remain closed, because there is then a small pressure deficit under both dampers in the store, not enough to open the inlet damper and, of course, also holding the outlet damper shut. Hence both dampers remain closed if the fan is not operating.

If the fan is in operation and the mixing damper is set to a mid-position - i.e., if ventilation is being carried out with mixed air - both pressure dampers also open partially because the excess pressure or pressure deficit is now reduced. The pressure dampers are thus operated by the fan and the mixing damper.

The air inlet in system C must be provided with a damper which closes with a highly efficient seal, as it is shut during periods of frost when the fan is not opreating, to prevent freezing of the potatoes. This damper can be operated manually. In system B, however, the ventilation can be fully controlled by means of a butterfly valve type of damper.

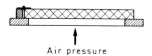

Fig. 14.5. Pressure operated exhaust damper for roof mounting.

Fig. 14.6. Pressure operated damper for wall mounting.

In all three damper systems illustrated in Fig. 14.4 therefore, only one damper has to be actuated by the automatic temperature control facilities. To control the temperature in the store, only the fan and the mixing damper have to be actuated by the automatic control system in this case.

The temperature is controlled by the thermostats as shown in Fig. 14.7. The fan is operated by a control circuit incorporating three thermostats. Thermostat TH_A controls the potato temperature and is set to the required potato storage temperature. At a potato temperature higher than that set, the termostat switches the circuit on. The thermostat disconnects the circuit again when the required temperature is reached or at a lower potato temperature.

Differential thermostat TH_D is set to a specific temperature difference between the potatoes and the outside air - usually 1 to 2 °C. If the temperature difference rises above 1 to 2 °C, the thermostat switches on the control circuit. It disconnects it again at a smaller temperature diffe-

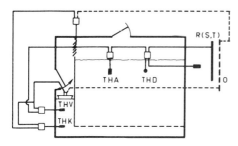

Fig. 14.7. Automatic temperature control in stores cooled with mixed air.

rence or if the outside air temperature rises above the temperature of
the potatoes. This thermostat thus ensures that the fan operates only if
it is possible to cool the potatoes.

The control circuit operating the fan also includes the safety thermostat
TH_V. This thermostat is set to the minimum acceptable temperature of the
potatoes - usually 1 to 2 °C lower than the required storage temperature.
If the temperature in the duct falls below the set temperature, this
thermostat disconnects the control circuit to prevent chilling of the potatoes.

Since all three thermostats are connected in series in the fan control
circuit, the fan can only operate if all three thermostats so allow. Ventilation (i.e., cooling of the potatoes) can thus only take place if the
following conditions are met simultaneously:
- The potato temperature is higher than the required storage temperature
  (thermostat TH_A on)
- The outside air is colder than the potatoes (thermostat TH_D on)
- The duct temperature does not fall too low (thermostat TH_V on).

The mixing damper is driven by a servomotor, which, however, is operated
by the duct thermostat TH_K via a changeover switch. The duct thermostat
is set to a temperature usually 0.75 to 1.0 K below the required storage
temperature. If the duct temperature rises above the set temperature during ventilation, the thermostat switches the power to the pole of the
changeover switch which causes the servomotor to close the mixing damper.
As a result, relatively more outside air is aspirated by the fan and the
duct temperature falls. Once the desired duct temperature is reached, the
thermostat disconnects the control circuit and the flap remains in the
relevant position.

If, however, the temperature in the duct falls below the set temperature,
the thermostat switches the servomotor so that it begins to open the
mixing damper. This motion is halted when the temperature in the duct has
again reached the set value.

This process continues as long as the fan is in operation. When the fan
is not operating, the mixing damper remains open, thus preventing venti-

lation with excessively cold air when the fan is switched on. As stated earlier, the mixing flap at the same time also controls the positions of the pressure dampers for air inlet and outlet.

The temperature is thus controlled by two control circuits, one of which actuates the fan and the other the mixing damper. This damper must in this case be machanically controlled with a continuous range of adjustment.

The control system shown in Fig. 14.7 is fully automated and can be used everywhere for temperature control with outside air cooling.

In a temperature climate, as in the Netherlands, where the outside air temperature during the storage period regularly falls to the required storage temperature, the automatic temperature control system can be further simplified. In such cases pure outside air cooling becomes possible during most of the storage period. Automatic control of the mixing damper then becomes superfluous and the operation of the fan also becomes simpler. A system of the type illustrated in Fig. 14.8 will then be sufficient. The fan is operated by a control circuit including only a differential thermostat and an outside air thermostat in series. The differential thermostat TH_D is set to a difference of 1 to 1.5 °C between the potato and outside air temperatures.

The differential thermostat switches the control circuit on if this temperature difference is reached or if the temperature difference rises above the set value. The outside air thermostat, however, is set to a temperature 1.5 to 2 °C lower than the required storage temperature. This thermostat switches the control circuit on if the outside air temperature is not below the set value.

The mixing damper is normally closed, so that the store can be ventilated with outside air only. The store will thus be cooled only if the outside air temperature is higher than the temperature set on thermostat TH_O and if the outside air is 1 to 1.5 K colder than the potatoes.

For instance, if the potatoes are to be stored at 7 °C, the outside air thermostat TH_O must be set to 5 °C. If the differential thermostat has then been set to a difference of 1.5 K, the fan will operate only at times when the outside air temperature is 5 to 5.5 °C. The temperature

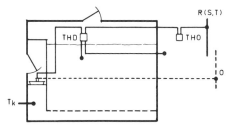

Fig. 14.8. Automatic temperature control in stores cooled with pure outside air.

difference within a heap of stored potatoes will then not exceed 1.5 to 2 °C - i.e., 7 - 5.5 = 1.5 K or 7 - 5 = 2 K.

However, if the outside air temperature remains below the set outside air temperature day and night for a long period and the potato temperature nevertheless rises, mixed-air ventilation will be required during the daytime. For this purpose, the fan has to be switched on manually and the mixing damper set manually so that the required temperature is obtained in the air duct. For this purpose all that is necessary is to place a thermometer T_K in the supply duct. This semiautomatic temperature control system is often used in Europe.

Electrical or electropneumatic control systems are generally used in potato stores.

The aim with an automatic system is to control the temperature from a central point - i.e., to position the controller at a central point. Even where the temperature is controlled manually, the fans are often operated from a central point or control panel.

For temperature monitoring, the controller or control panel must in both cases be provided with remote temperature measuring equipment.

However, all automatic control systems are liable to failure or loss of correct adjustment. Automatic control systems must therefore incorporate facilities for manual temperature control in the event of faults. There must be a 3-position switch with the settings 'automatic', 'manual' and 'off'.

Incorrect adjustment or faults may also occur in a remote temperature measuring system. Local thermometers must therefore be installed in the store even where such a system is fitted.

Efficient control of the temperature of the stored product thus calls for constant supervision by the storekeeper, whether the temperature is controlled automatically or manually.

14.3 Thermometers and thermostats in potato stores

14.3.1 Thermometers

Thermometers are essential for efficient potato temperature control. Various types of thermometers are available, although two main types are used in potato stores, viz., mercury thermometers and bimetal thermometers.

Glass mercury thermometers are generally used to measure the air temperature, or alternatively maximum-minimum thermometers (Fig. 14.9). The latter also measure the minimum and maximum temperatures during a given measuring period. Mercury thermometers are reliable and accurate.

Bimetal insertion-type thermometers are usually used to measure the temperature in a potato stack. The temperature of the potatoes is highest

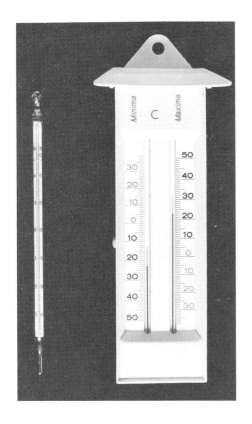

Fig. 14.9. Mercury thermometers.

Fig. 14.10. Bimetal thermometers.

275

Fig. 14.11. Glass mercury thermometers used for checking temperature in the potato pile.

0.5 to 0.75 m below the top of the stack, so that this is the point at which the temperature must be measured. Hence insertion-type thermometers as illustrated in Fig. 14.10 are used to measure the potato temperature. As stated, these are mainly bimetal thermometers, but insertion-type mercury thermometers may also be used. The latter are usually glass mercury thermometers inserted into the potato stack in a plastic or steel tube (Fig. 14.11). The mercury thermometers are generally more accurate and less subject to error. Nevertheless, bimetal insertion-type thermometers are often used because they are robust. The thermometers must be calibrated regularly - i.e., at least once a year and then preferably before the beginning of the storage period.

The potato temperature is usually measured at a number of points in the stack. Resistance sensors are normally used for remote temperature measurement and are positioned at different points. The temperature at each point is then read off a central instrument by means of a selector switch (Fig. 14.12). This system must also be a calibrated regularly.

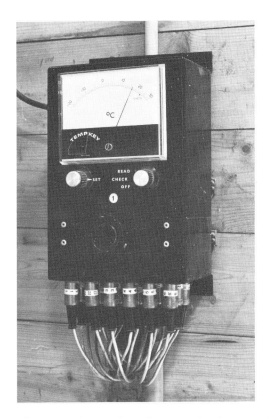

Fig. 14.12. Device for remote temperature measurement.

14.3.2 Thermostats

Thermostats are instruments for automatic temperature control. In temperature control in potato stores, the thermostat is always a component of a control circuit which actuates the electric control switch. As shown in the block temperature control diagram in Fig. 14.1, the thermostat performs the following functions together with the temperature sensor: temperature sensing, temperature measurement, comparison of measured and set temperatures and decision as to whether or not the control switches are to be actuated.

Thermostats are divided into two groups, viz., mechanical and electronic, according to the method of temperature measurement.

In mechanical thermostats, the temperature is measured by means of the vapour pressure of a known liquid, while the temperature determinant in an electronic thermostat is the electrical voltage or resistance to an electric current. The electrical resistance of a conductor varies with temperature.

In a mechanical thermostat, the temperature sensor consists of a small vessel filled with a known liquid or vapour and linked to the thermostat by a capillary tube (Fig. 14.13). The vapour pressure in the capillary tube depends on temperature. The vapour pressure acts on a diaphragm which is loaded on the other side by a spring. If the force of the pressure rises above that of the spring, the diaphragm moves in the direction of the pressure force, thus operating a switch linked to the diaphragm and switching the control circuit on or off. The temperature setting is thus determined by the spring force. A mechanical thermostat therefore operates on the vapour pressure difference principle.

An electronic thermostat, on the other hand, operates on a principle of the difference in electrical voltage or resistance in a circuit. The sensor of an electronic thermostat contains an electrical resistance which changes with temperature. The sensor is connected to a specific voltage by a cable, so that an electric current flows through the sensor. The voltage in a circuit always decreases through a resistance, the voltage drop depending on the size of the resistance. Hence the voltage drop in the sensor depends on its temperature.
A known resistance is connected to the same voltage source by another cable, and is made equal to the resistance in the sensor at the required temperature. If the sensor temperature departs from the required temperature, a difference in voltage arises at the end of the two cables.
If a winding is connected between the two cables, the voltage difference causes a magnetic field to arise in the winding, and this can be used to operate a switch in the control circuit.

A thermostat thus operates by differences in vapour pressure or electrical voltage. The control circuit is switched on or off if the measured temperature is somewhat higher of somewhat lower than the set temperature. This difference between the set and the measured temperature, required to operate a thermostat, is called the *switching differential* of the thermostat. This is an important thermostat characteristic, as it also determines the temperature fluctuations in the store. A good thermostat must therefore be capable of operating with a small and constant

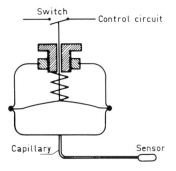

Fig. 14.13. Mechanical, viz., pressure operated thermostat.

switching differential. The temperature sensor must also have a quick response to temperature changes at the measuring point. This rate of response largely depends on the mass of the sensor. Electronic thermostats with PT-100 sensors usually satisfy these two requirements better than mechanical thermostats.

The main advantage of an electronic thermostat is that the distance between the temperature sensor and the thermostat is not limited. This distance, however, cannot exceed a few metres in a mechanical thermostat. An electronic thermostat can thus always be positioned in the central controller, so that the temperature in the entire store can be set from a single point. This is not possible with mechanical thermostats in large stores, thus complicating setting of the required temperature.

For all these reasons, electronic thermostats are preferred for temperature control in potato stores.

An electronic thermostat must satisfy the following requirements:
- The thermostat setting must be adjustable by scale with scale divisions of not more than 0.2 °C.
- Resetting of the thermostat must give rise to a corresponding change in the setting of the switching point.
- The setting must not change as a result of temperature variations in the environment of the thermostat.
- The temperature of the material controlled or stored must be displayed on the thermostat.
- The thermostat must have indicator lamps to show whether it is on or off.
- Simple temperature correction must be possible on the thermostat.
- The thermostat's intrinsic switching differential must be less than 0.5 °C.

A well designed and constructed automatic temperature control system can thus maintain the set temperature very accurately if the appropriate conditions are satisfied. However, ventilation may be necessary during the storage of perishable produce such as potatoes, not only for temperature control but also, for example, to dry the produce, to localize decay areas, etc. An automatic temperature control system will not perform these functions. The temperature control system itself may also fail, as any automatic system is liable to faults.

Since, even where an automatic temperature control system is present, the quality of the stored produce largely depends on the vigilance and expertise of the storekeeper.

15 Fans

A. Rastovski

15.1 Fan characteristics

For efficient cooling, heating and drying of potatoes, a certain volume of air has to be passed through the produce. Fans are used to move this volume of air. Hence the main requirement for a fan installed in a store is that it should move the desired volume of air.

However, a flow of air always meets with resistances, which reduce the pressure in the air stream, giving rise to a certain head loss. For the desired air flow to be obtained, the fan must therefore build up a head equal to the head losses in the ventilation system as a whole.

Consequently, a pressure difference must arise between the suction and delivery sides of a fan equal to the head losses in the ventilation system at the desired rate of air flow. This pressure difference is called the *static pressure differential* (Δps) or the *static pressure* (ps) of the fan.

The air leaves the fan not only at higher pressure but also with a certain velocity. To make the air move at a given velocity however, a certain pressure, or pressure difference, is also necessary, viz., the pressure can be transformed into air velocity. The air velocity is then equivalent to a given static pressure, which is called the *velocity pressure* or *dynamic pressure* (Pd).

Both the static and dynamic pressure thus increase through the fan. The sum of the static and dynamic pressures is called the *total pressure* (P_{tot}) of the air flow, i.e.:

$$P_{tot} = P_s + P_d \quad \text{(Pa)} \tag{48}$$

The dynamic pressure is determined by the air velocity:

$$P_d = \frac{\rho}{2} \cdot v^2 \qquad \text{(Pa)} \tag{49}$$

$\rho \cong$ specific gravity of the air (kg/m^3)
v = air velocity (m/s)

The total pressure of the air flow after the fan is then:

280

$$P_{tot} = P_s + \frac{\rho}{2} v^2 \qquad \text{(Pa)} \qquad (50)$$

The air velocity v is generally determined by the rate of air flow and the cross-sectional area of the duct perpendicular to the direction of flow, as follows:

$$v = \frac{\dot{V}}{A} \qquad \text{(m/s)} \qquad (51)$$

in which

$\dot{V}$ = volume air flow (m³/s)

A = cross-sectional area (m²)

For example, if the static pressure differential of a fan is ΔP_s = 150 Pa at a rate of air flow of $\dot{V}$ = 6 m³/s, and if the cross-sectional area of the discharge orifice of the fan is A = 1.0 m², the air velocity through the orifice is:

$$v = \frac{\dot{V}}{A} = \frac{6}{1} = 6 \text{ m/s}$$

and the total pressure increase through the fan if the specific gravity of the air is ρ = 1.26 kg/m³ becomes:

$$\Delta P_{tot} = \Delta P_{st} + \rho/2 \ v^2 = 150 + \frac{1.26}{2} \cdot 6^2$$

$$\Delta P_{tot} = 150 + 22.68 = 177.68 \text{ Pa}$$

The velocity pressure Pd = 22.68 Pa could in principle be converted into the static pressure by, for example, fitting a diffuser behind the delivery orifice of the fan. In this case the total head of the fan can be used to overcome resistances in the ventilation system. Diffusers are, however, not normally used in potato stores.

Most of the velocity pressure is then lost in turbulence, and only the static pressure of the fan is used to move air through the ventilation system.

Hence the principal parameters of a fan are:

$\dot{V}$ = fan capacity (m³/s)

ΔP_s or Ps = static pressure differential or static pressure (Pa)

N_m = rating of drive motor (kW)

However, the fan capacity varies with variations in the pressure differential ΔP_s or ΔP_{tot}. The relationship between the fan capacity and the fan pressure difference produced is known as the *fan characteristic* (Fig. 15.1).

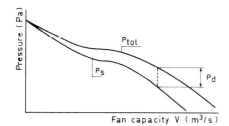

Fan capacity V (m³/s)   Fig. 15.1. Fan characteristic.

The characteristic of a fan is determined experimentally. Each type of fan has its own characteristic. In general, however, the higher the pressure differential ΔP_s, of a given fan, the lower its capacity. Since the fan capacity always follows the characteristic, it is essential when choosing a fan to know its characteristic. Characteristics are specified by manufacturers in tables or graphs, as in Fig. 15.1.

The characteristic of a given type of fan varies with the rotational speed and the diameter of the blade unit. Both the air delivery and the pressure differential usually increase with increasing blade unit diameter and increasing fan rotational speed.

The power, or energy consumption, required to drive the fan greatly depends on the volume of air moved and the increase in head through the fan.

The energy increase in the air flow through the fan is determined as follows:

$$N_{th} = \dot{V} \cdot \Delta P_{tot} \qquad \text{(W)} \qquad (52)$$

For this reason N_{th} is known as the theoretical, or useful, power of the fan, as this amount of energy is used to move the volume of air $\dot{V}$ against a pressure ΔP_{tot}.

However, losses always arise through the fan, and these increase the required power or energy consumption to drive the fan, as follows:

$$N_a = \frac{N_{th}}{\eta v} = \frac{\dot{V} \cdot \Delta P_{tot}}{\eta v} \qquad \text{(W)} \qquad (53)$$

N_a is called the *shaft power* of the fan and ηv is its *efficiency*. The efficiency ηv is also a characteristic of the fan - i.e., ηv varies from one type of fan to another. ηv, however, also varies with air delivery in one and the same fan.

In each fan, there is therefore a specific air delivery at which ηv is maximum. The larger ηv becomes, the less energy the fan consumes for the same air delivery and the same pressure differential. The fan efficiency ηv seldom exceeds 0.75, but it may also be much less.

Fans in potato stores are usually driven by electric motors. However,

282

an electric motor also does not operate without losses. By virtue of these losses, the energy consumption of the motor becomes even greater than
the necessary shaft power of the fan. The motor power is determined as
follows:

$$N_m = \frac{Na}{\eta m} = \frac{\dot{V} \cdot \Delta P_{tot}}{\eta m \cdot \eta v} = \frac{\dot{V} \cdot \Delta P_{tot}}{\eta} \qquad (54)$$

Nm is the energy consumption of the electric motor and vm its efficiency. The total efficiency η of the fan and the motor determines the actual energy consumption for ventilation at a given fan capacity and a given head loss through the ventilation system.

The efficiency ηm of an electric motor is seldom higher than 0.8, but
may be considerably less, particularly at low loads.

The total efficiency of the fan and motor (η) is therefore seldom
higher than 0.6, but it may be as low as 0.3 or even less.

If $\dot{V}$, ΔP_{tot} and Nm are specified for a fan, the total efficiency can
be calculated as follows from Equation 54:

$$\eta = \frac{\dot{V} \cdot \Delta P_{tot}}{N_m} \qquad (55)$$

A fan drive motor clearly consumes appreciably more energy than is required for moving the air. However, this additional energy consumption is
not lost but is converted into heat owing to friction in the fan and the
motor. Hence the difference $N_m - N_{th}$ is used directly for heating the air.
As a result, the temperature of the air flow after the fan is higher than
that of the aspirated air.

Owing to friction in the air ducts and in the potato heap, the useful
energy N_{th} is also converted into heat. Finally, therefore, the total
energy consumption of the drive motor is converted into heat, thus heating the air flow. Consequently, the energy consumption during ventilation must be regarded as a heat source in the store and must be taken into account as such in the compilation of the store heat balance (see
Chapter 10).

Hence the energy consumption directly determines energy costs during
storage, as well as influencing the required refrigeration capacity in
the store. The higher refrigeration capacity in a mechanically refrigerated store entails extra costs for the expensive refrigeration plant.
However, the extra equipment costs are very limited in stores cooled with
outside air.

As the air is heated, its relative humidity falls, so that weight losses, especially in the lowest layers of potatoes, may increase substantially.

The increase in the air temperature is directly proportional to the pressure differential ΔP_{tot} and inversely proportional to the total efficiency η. For these reasons it is essential when choosing a fan to pay adequate attention to its efficiency η. The ventilation system must also be designed so as to minimize head losses within it. Since most of the dynamic pressure of the fan is lost, a larger fan generally uses less energy for a given air delivery and a given static pressure. But a larger fan has also a higher capital cost.

The fan capacity must also be limited to what is essential for efficient temperature control in the store and for drying wet potatoes.

15.2 Head losses through the ventilation system

The static pressure differential of the fan must be equal to the head losses in the ventilation system at the desired rate of air flow.

The head loss in the ventilation system greatly depends on the air velocity or the rate of air flow through the system. Head losses arise both in the air ducts and in the heap of stored potatoes.

Head losses in a ducting system are caused by friction along the walls of the straight ducts, by changes in the air velocity and by changes in the direction of flow.

All these losses can be determined from the following general equation:

$$\Delta P = \zeta \frac{\rho}{2} \cdot v^2 \qquad (Pa) \qquad (56)$$

in which ζ = resistance factor of a part of the duct.

The resistance factors for different parts of a ducting system have been determined experimentally and published in the literature; see, for example, VDI-Wärmeatlas (1963) and Sprenger (1964).

Equation 49 clearly shows that the head losses depend strongly on the air velocity or on the dynamic pressure of the air flow. The relationship

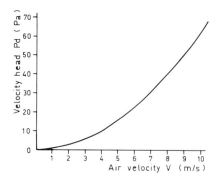

Fig. 15.2. Dynamic pressure of the air, viz., pressure loss by ζ = 1.

284

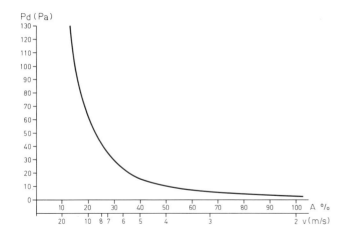

Fig. 15.3. Relation between head loss and the cross-sectional area of a duct by $\xi = 1$.

between the air velocity and the dynamic pressure or head losses through the ducting system is illustrated in Fig. 15.2.

The air velocity also affects the dimensions or cross-sectional area of a duct. The cross-sectional area can be determined as follows using Equation 51:

$$A = \frac{\dot{V}}{v} \qquad\qquad (m^2) \qquad\qquad (57)$$

Hence, the higher the air velocity, the smaller (and cheaper) the duct. As shown above, however, head losses are thereby increased. For instance, if the air velocity is doubled, the cross-sectional area can be halved (Equation 57), but the head loss is then quadrupled (Equation 56).

The relation between head loss and the cross-sectional area of a duct is illustrated in Fig. 15.3.

The cross-sectional area and air velocity are set out on the horizontal axis and the dynamic pressure on the vertical axis. A value of 100 has been assigned to the cross-sectional area at an air velocity v = 2 m/s. The graph shows that a reduction in the cross-sectional area from 100 to about 35 is accompanied by a relatively small increase in the dynamic pressure; the air velocity thereby increases from 2 m/s to 5 to 6 m/s.

However, if the cross-sectional area is further reduced, the dynamic pressure increases sharply. For example, if the cross-sectional area is reduced from 35 to 25, the increase in the dynamic pressure is just as large as that caused by the reduction from 100 to 35. The air velocity then increases from 6 to 8 m/s. At an air velocity of 10 m/s, the dynamic pressure is tripled as compared with 6 m/s and the cross-sectional area is reduced only from 35 to 20.

For these reasons the air velocity through the ducting should preferably be limited to 5 to 6 m/s.

If the air velocity through the duct is known, the head loss can be
determined by Equation 56, if the resistance factor is known. The resistance factor of a straight duct depends on its length, the roughness of
its walls and the size and shape of the cross-sectional area. A round or
cylindrical duct has the optimum shape. Compared with a cylindrical duct,
a square duct of the same length, wall smoothness and cross-sectional
area has a resistance factor about 15 % larger, while the resistance factor of a triangular duct is as much as 30 % larger.

In general, head losses through well designed straight ducts in potato
stores are, however, relatively small.

The largest head losses are caused by changes in the cross-sectional
area of the ducts and changes in flow direction. Duct air inlets and outlets, sharp bends and abrupt increases or decreases in the duct cross
section cause the largest head losses. Rounded bends and gradual changes
in duct cross section can substantially reduce the head loss.

The head loss through the ducting of a potato store, assuming a maximum air velocity of 5 to 6 m/s, is usually limited to 80 to 100 Pa.

Head losses in a heap of stored potatoes greatly depend on the air velocity through the heap, the height of the potato heap, the amount of
soil in it and the extent of sprouting of the potatoes. Head losses are
lowest in a heap of clean and unsprouted potatoes. Accumulations of soil
at certain positions in the heap present a considerable resistance to the
air flow, obstructing the flow of air in these positions. Local accumulations of soil (soil cones) must therefore be avoided. The head loss in a
heap of potatoes was determined experimentally by Ophuis, (1958), and
Cloud (1976). The head loss in a heap of clean, unsprouted potatoes is
shown in Fig. 15.4.

The specific volume flow (the volume of air in m³ moved per second per
m² of floor area) is set out on the horizontal axis. The head loss
through a 1 m deep layer of potatoes at a specific volume flow of 0.083
m³/m².s (300 m³/m².h) is thus 11 Pa. At 0.027 m³/m².s (100 m³/m².h), the
head loss in only 2 Pa/m. The specific volume flow in potato storage is
seldom higher than 0.08 to 0.10 m³/m².s (290 to 360 m³/m².h).

The head loss through a 3.5 m deep layer of potatoes is thus 3.5 x
11 = 38.5 Pa at 0.083 m³/m².s (300 m³/m².h) and 3.5 x 2 = 7 Pa at
0.027 m³/m² s (100 m³/m² h). However, the head loss becomes appreciably
higher through a heap of potatoes which have sprouted considerably or
have a great deal of soil clinging to them.

The head loss through the ventilation system as a whole - i.e.,
through the air ducts and the stored potatoes - will normally be in the
range 100 to 160 Pa in stores with outside air cooling. In mechanically
refrigerated stores, there is also a head loss through the evaporator

286

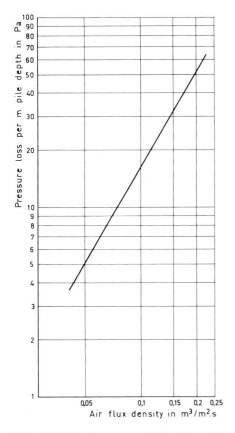

Fig. 15.4. Pressure loss in a 1 m deep pile of clean and unsprouted potatoes.

(air cooler), so that the total head loss through the ventilation system is larger. The head loss in a mechanically refrigerated store will therefore be in the range 200 to 250 Pa.

15.3 The fan capacity

The fan capacity strongly influences both the cooling and the drying rate in the store, and cannot therefore be chosen arbitrarily. The fan capacity must be determined on the basis of the required cooling and drying rate in the store.

The air flow required to store potatoes at a given temperature can be determined from Equation 40, as follows:

$$\dot{V} = \frac{Q}{3700 \cdot t} \qquad (m^3/s) \qquad (58)$$

in which:

Q = heat production in the store (J/day)

t = cooling time (s/day)

It is assumed in Equation 58 that the temperature rise of the air flow
is 1.5 °C and that half of the total heat dissipation (Q) is dissipated
as latent heat, i.e., by evaporation of water from the potatoes. These
assumptions will be correct if the relative humidity of the air is
90 to 95 %.

If the relative humidity of the air is lower, the relative amount of
latent heat will be larger, thus also increasing the cooling capacity at
a given air flow and temperature increase. If the air is dry, the cooling
time is thus reduced, or, if the same ventilation time is retained, a
smaller air flow will be sufficient. However, this will give rise to
greater moisture losses from the potatoes.

At a given air humidity and temperature increase through the potato
heap, the needed air flow is determined solely by the heat production in
the store and by the ventilation or cooling time.

The heat produced by the fan and electric motor, however, depends on
the air flow and on the duration of fan operation.

The cooling capacity of the air flow is reduced by this heat production and can be calculated as follows:

$$V \quad 3700 - V \frac{\Delta P_{tot}}{\eta} = \frac{Q*}{t} \qquad (59)$$

In Equation 59, Q* is the heat produced by respiration of the potatoes
and heat transmission through the store walls, floor and roof (see
Chapter 10).

The volume air flow can then be calculated as follows:

$$V = \frac{Q*}{t \, (3700 - \frac{\Delta P_{tot}}{\eta})} \qquad (m^3/s) \qquad (60)$$

The volume air flow $\dot{V}$ is plotted against the cooling time t in
Fig. 15.5 for a heat production Q* = 1000 kJ per tonne of potatoes per
day (i.e., Q* = 1000 kJ/day · tonne), on the basis of Equation 60. An efficiency of η= 0.5 and a head loss in the ducting system ΔP_k = 100 Pa
were assumed for the calculation. The head losses in 3 m and 4 m potato
heaps were taken from Fig. 15.4. The specific volume flow in $m^3/m^2 \cdot s$
is set out on the horizontal axis and the cooling time per day on the
vertical axis.

288

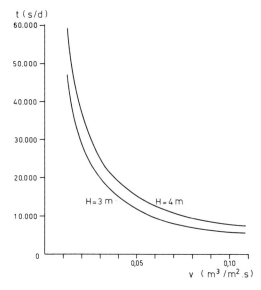

Fig. 15.5. Cooling time as a function of the rate of air flow through the pile; heat generation $Q = 1.000$ kJ/day.

Fig. 15.5 shows that the rate of air flow is dependent on the duration of ventilation or cooling.

Increasing the rate of air flow from 0 to about 0.05 $m^3/m^2 \cdot s$ (180 $m^3/m^2 \cdot h$) quickly reduces the cooling time. The ventilation time decreases more slowly as the rate of air flow increases further. But even an increase in the rate of air flow above 0.1 $m^3/m^2 \cdot s$ (360 $m^3/m^2 \cdot h$ still has a positive effect in reducing the cooling periods.

Fig. 15.5 clearly explains the big differences in rates of air flow in different parts of the world when potatoes are cooled with outside air. Climate greatly affects the required rate of air flow with outside air cooling. For instance, if the ambient temperature remains below the desired storage temperature for 11 to 12 hours per day, a rate of air flow of 0.015 $m^3/m^2 \cdot s$ (55 $m^3/m^2 \cdot h$) is sufficient to maintain the storage temperature. This is the case in certain parts of the USA and northern Europe. However, if the ambient temperature during a given storage period falls below the desired storage temperature for an average of only one or two hours per day, a rate of air flow of 0.1 $m^3/m^2 \cdot s$ (360 $m^3/m^2 \cdot h$) or even higher will be necessary.

In a well insulated store, it is usually possible to maintain the storage temperature at the level of the mean minimum ambient temperature with a rate of air flow of 0.1 $m^3/m^2 \cdot s$.

The lower the rate of air flow, the longer will be the ventilation time required - i.e., potatoes will have to be ventilated with air at a higher temperature, which means that the storage temperature will also be higher.

However, the ventilation system is used not only for cooling but also to dry wet potatoes. Drying relates to the elimination both of any free water on the surface of the tubers and in the soil clinging to them, and of the moisture released by rotting of potatoes. In both cases, efficient drying is essential to limit the spread of disease. However, like cooling, drying depends on the rate of air flow through the potato heap. With outside air ventilation, therefore, both cooling and drying of the potatoes will be faster the greater the air flow through the potato heap. Consequently, the rate of air flow through a potato heap must be large enough not only to allow the required temperature to be maintained, but also to remove any free moisture on the surface of the tubers. If a decay area arises in the potato heap during storage although the required temperature is maintained, moisture severely contaminated with disease organisms emerges from the rotten tubers. If this moisture comes into contact with the surface of healthy tubers, they will also be infected and the rot will spread. This spread of diseases can be limited by rapid elimination of moisture released from rotten tubers. The rate of air flow required for this may sometimes be considerably greater than that needed to maintain the desired temperature in the store. This is usually the case in areas where the ambient temperature remains low throughout the storage period. In these situations, the drying rate thus becomes the critical factor determining the rate of air flow.

Weight losses from the potatoes are reduced by increasing the rate of air flow or reducing the ventilation time. However, the capital cost of a store with outside air cooling is influenced only to a relatively small extent by the rate of air flow, so that there is little reason to limit the fan capacity to a very low level in a store cooled with outside air. A more generously scaled fan facilitates maintenance of the required temperature in the store and reduces the risk of the spread of disease in the stored produce.

This last point, of course, greatly depends on the quality of the potatoes - i.e., the extent to which they are infected with diseases and their resistance to disease.

For all these reasons, the following rates of air flow are recommended with outside air cooling in the Netherlands (where the ambient temperature varies as shown in Fig. 21.2):
- V = 0.1 $m^3/m^2 \cdot s$ (360 $m^3/m^2 \cdot h$) for the storage of ware potatoes at 7 to 10 °C until the end of May and the storage of seed potatoes at 4 °C until the end of March.
- For the storage of ware potatoes at 7 to 10 °C until the end of April, however, a volume air flow of V = 0.05 $m^3/m^2 \cdot s$ (180 $m^3/m^2 \cdot h$) may be sufficient.

In mechanically refrigerated stores, the cooling period is not determined by the ambient temperature, and refrigeration can usually proceed

for a much longer time. The required rate of air flow in mechanically refrigerated stores is therefore obviously appreciably lower. The air flow
or the fan capacity is determined by the refrigeration capacity of the
refrigeration plant and the acceptable temperature difference through the
potato heap, as follows:

$$V = \frac{\dot{Q}}{\rho \cdot C_L \cdot \Delta T} \tag{61}$$

in which

Q = refrigeration capacity of refrigeration plant (J/s or W)
ρ = specific gravity of air (kg/m³)
C_L = specific heat of air including heat of evaporation (J/kg K)
ΔT = acceptable temperature difference through the potato heap (°C).

For ΔT = 1.5 °C, ρ = 1.26 kg/m³ and C_L = 2 kJ/kg K, the rate of air flow
is determined as:

$$\dot{V} = \frac{\dot{Q}}{3700} = 0.00026 \ Q \ (m^3/s) \tag{62}$$

in which $\dot{Q}$ is equal to Q/t in Equation 58. Hence the air flow in fact depends on the cooling capacity of refrigeration plant or the heat production in the store and the period of cooling respectively.
    In contrast to the situation with an outside air cooling system, the
refrigeration capacity in a mechanically refrigerated store substantially
affects the capital cost of the store. For this reason every effort is
made to reduce the installed refrigeration capacity, and hence also the
fan capacity to what is strictly necessary for efficient control of the
storage conditions.

15.4 Choice of fan

    The required volume air flow and the pressure ps needed for this flow
determine the 'working point' of a ventilation system. If the fan is to
transport this volume of air through the system, the working point must
lie on the fan characteristic, as shown in Fig. 15.6.
    If the fan produces a higher pressure than the resistance of the sys-
tem at the required volume air flow, a larger volume of air will be
transported through the system, as shown in Fig. 15.7a.
    However, if the fan pressure at the desired volume air flow is less
than the system resistance, the fan will move less air, as shown in Fig.
15.7b.
    The changes in fan capacity caused by variations of the pressure loss

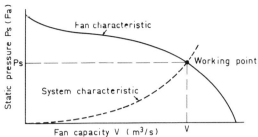

Fig. 15.6. Working point of a fan.

through the system depend on the shape of the fan characteristic. One and the same pressure discrepancy will result in smaller changes in the fan capacity the steeper the fan characteristic (Fig. 15.8).

The characteristics of two different fans, A and B, are shown in Fig. 15.8. The same pressure discrepancy Δp from the required pressure ps of the fans gives rise to a smaller reduction in the volume of air moved with fan A, which has a steep characteristic ($V-V_A$), than with fan B, which has a flat characteristic ($\dot{V}-V_B$). This may be important when choosing a fan for a potato store.

Accurate determination of the resistance of the ventilation system in a store is difficult. The resistance of the potato heap depends on the degree of sprouting of the potatoes and on the amount of soil and other impurities clinging to them. The resistance may also be substantially increased by settlement of the potatoes during storage.

The resistance of the ducting system may also become much higher if the air ducts are badly designed - e.g., with structured components perpendicular to the direction of flow of the air.

By virtue of all these factors, the actual resistance or head loss in the system may be greater than the calculated resistance. If the fan is selected on the basis of the required rate of air flow and the calculated head loss, it may be found that this fan in fact has a much lower capacity. Fig. 15.8 shows that this reduction in the volume air flow depends on the fan characteristic.

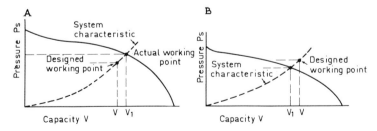

Fig. 15.7. Shifting of the working point as influenced by the fan size. a. Size of the fan too big; b. size of the fan too small.

292

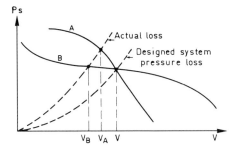

Fig. 15.8. Shifting of the working point by change in head loss through the ventilation system as influenced by the fan characteristic.

The fan chosen for a potato store should therefore be one in which the calculated working point of the system lies on the steeply sloping part of the characteristic, even if the fan efficiency is thereby reduced by a few percent.

This is particularly important in stores used not only for potatoes but also for other produce, such as onions, which present a greater resistance to the air flow.

15.5 Fan types

Two types of fans are normally used in potato stores, viz.:
- Axial-flow fans or screw fans
- Centrifugal fans

In an axial-flow fan (Fig. 15.9), the air is moved by the blade assembly in the direction of the shaft (i.e., axially).

In centrifugal fans (Fig. 15.10), the impeller moves the air radially. Axial-flow fans are suitable for transporting large volumes of air at relatively low pressures, while centrifugal fans can build up much higher pressures. Axial-flow fans are usually more efficient than centrifugal types. Since relatively small head losses occur in the ventilation systems of potato stores, axial-flow fans are usually used for this application.

The noise level of the fan is also an important parameter, especially in stores located close to residential areas.

The noise level generally depends on the fan capacity and the pressure of the fan. The higher the capacity and the pressure of the fan, the higher the noise level generally is. However, the human ear is more sen-

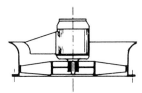

Fig. 15.9. Axial-flow fan.

Fig. 15.10. Centrifugal fan.

sitive to high-pitched than to low-pitched sounds - i.e., it is more sensitive to high frequencies. The frequency of the noise of a fan strongly
depends on its rotational speed. The fans in the stores should therefore
preferably not be run at faster speeds than 1450 rev/min or 24 rev/s
($24s^{-1}$). However, if the store is located in a built-up area, special
measures will often be necessary, such as the use of acoustic insulation.
This must be designed and installed by specialists.

References

Anon., 1963. VDI-Wärmeatlas. Berechnungsblätter für den Wärmeübergang.
    Verein Deutscher Ingenieure. VDI-Verlag, Düsseldorf.
Cloud, H.A., 1976. Design Criteria for the air handling and distribution
    system for potato storages. The potato storage; design, construction,
    handling and environmental control. Editor: B.F. Cargill. Michigan
    State University.
Ophuis, B.G., 1958. De invloed van de ventilatiekapaciteit op de ge-
    wichtsverliezen bij luchtgekoelde bewaring van aardappelen. Publikatie
    Serie A no. 17, IBVL, Wageningen.
Sprenger, E., 1964. Taschenbuch für Heizung, Lüftung und Klimatechnik.
    R. Oldenbourg, München-Wien.

16   Ventilation systems in potato stores

A. Rastovski

16.1 Introduction

Ventilation is necessary when potatoes are stored in order to control the storage conditions - i.e., for the cooling, heating and drying of potatoes.

These processes, of course, depend very much on the air velocity - i.e., the rate of air flow over the tubers.

Sprout inhibitors (IPC-CIPC) are now often applied to the potatoes by way of the air flow. In this case, the degree of treatment of the potatoes with sprout suppressant also depends greatly on the rate of air flow through the pile of produce. To maintain uniform conditions in stored potatoes, it is therefore insufficient for the store merely to be supplied with the necessary volume of air at the required temperature and humidity; this volume of air must also be distributed evenly over all the potatoes. Uniform air distribution through the potatoes is thus an important aspect of an efficient ventilation system in the store.

Very often, it is precisely uneven air distribution through the stored potatoes that causes many problems during storage, generally giving rise to inferior storage results.

The following types of ventilation systems are used in potato stores:
a. Space ventilation
b. Forced-draught ventilation through the heap of stored potatoes.
These two systems are illustrated in Fig. 16.1.

In forced ventilation through the potato heap (Fig. 16.1a), the volume of air moved through each point in the heap depends solely on the total volume of air moved by the fan and on the air distribution. The storage

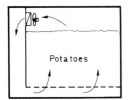
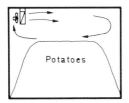

Fig. 16.1. Ventilation systems. a. Forced ventilation through the pile; b. space ventilation - unventilated heap.

conditions in a homogeneous heap of potatoes can be controlled very efficiently and accurately by choice of the correct fan and an efficient air distribution system beneath the heap.

However, since air distribution in forced ventilation is independent of the size of the heap, this ventilation system also allows potatoes to be stored in large heaps, so that optimum use can be made of the capacity of the store.

In this way the size of the store and the capital cost of the building per unit of stored potatoes can be minimized. On the other hand, additional capital investment is required for the air distribution system.

In space ventilation, the air is usually blown freely into the store by the fan (Fig. 16.1b). Since the resistance to air movement through a heap of potatoes is many times higher than the resistance of the free space in the store, the blown-in air will be moved almost exclusively through the free space. This air will pass along the surface of the heap, only a thin upper layer of the potatoes coming into contact with it. The potatoes deep down in the heap will be hardly, if at all, affected by this air flow in the room - at least, not directly.

With space ventilation, air movement through the heap is thus uneven, so that the storage conditions of the potatoes differ. Since the potatoes constantly produce heat, the uneven ventilation will inevitably give rise to temperature differences within the heap. These temperature differences cause a natural draught, as a result of which the room air is after all moved through the heap, although to a lesser extent. The processes taking place in an unventilated potato heap will be described in more detail in Section 16.2.

By virtue of the natural draught, the temperature in the heap will never be equal throughout. The temperature deep within the heap will always remain higher than that in the room around the heap. This temperature difference depends greatly on the size of the potato heap.

To contain these temperature differences within acceptable limits, where space ventilation is used, the potatoes must be stored in relatively small units - e.g., crates, boxes, etc. - with adequate free space around the stacks.

This method of storage involves relatively poor utilization of the store, the space required per unit of stored potatoes being larger and the capital investment in the building thereby being increased. However, the capital cost of the air distribution system is minimized.

Clearly, therefore, efficient ventilation of stored potatoes always involves additional capital costs, either for the building or for the air distribution system. The total capital investment in the store is usually lower in the case of forced potato ventilation. Forced ventilation also has the advantages, mentioned earlier, of very accurate and rapid control of the storage conditions in the stored potatoes, whereby storage losses

296

can be minimized. For these reasons, the forced ventilation system is generally used in potato stores.

16.2 Space ventilation or natural draught ventilation of potatoes

In an analysis of the processes taking place in a lot of potatoes ventilated without forced draught, it must be remembered that the potato is a living organism which constantly produces heat by respiration. If this heat is not eliminated, the temperature of the potatoes inevitably rises. When a single tuber lies in a space, the heat produced can easily be removed by the air and the temperature of the tuber will differ little from that of the air. However, when potatoes are stored in a heap, as shown in Fig. 16.1b, the air has free access only to a relatively thin layer of potatoes on the surface of the heap. The temperature of these potatoes will relatively quickly become equal to the ambient temperature. The potatoes lower down in the heap, however, have no direct contact with the air in the room, and therefore cannot give up the heat produced directly to the ambient air; they are therefore heated. Regardless of their original temperature, self-heating will always eventually raise the temperature of these potatoes deep inside the heap and of the air around them to a level higher than the ambient temperature.

Air movement
However, a change in temperature is accompanied by a change in the specific gravity of the air. The specific gravity of the warm air in the heap falls below that of the colder, ambient air. This difference in specific gravity gives rise to the familiar chimney effect. The cold, heavier ambient air flows towards the heap and displaces the lighter, warm air out of the heap. The cold air is heated in the heap, becomes lighter and can in turn be displaced from the heap by the heavier ambient air. The temperature difference between the heap and the ambient air thus causes the heap to be ventilated.

This form of ventilation is known as natural draught ventilation or ventilation by free convection.

Since the temperature of the air leaving the potato heap is higher than that of the air entering it, this ventilation removes heat from the heap - i.e., the potatoes are cooled. The amount of heat removed by the air is proportionate to the air velocity and the temperature difference between the incoming and discharging air - i.e., $Q \approx v \, (T_A - T_O)$, in which Q represents the amount of heat removed per m^2 of floor area.

The motive power for this air movement is the pressure, or pressure head caused by the difference in weight between the colder ambient air and the warmer air in the heap. This pressure head is proportionate to the difference between the temperature of the air in the heap and the ambient air and to the height of the heap - i.e., $\Delta p \approx H \ (\bar{T}_A - T_O)$, in which $\bar{T}_A$ is the average temperature in the heap.

However, the air movement through the heap gives rise to a certain pressure drop. At low air velocities, this pressure drop is almost linearly proportionate to the air velocity (v), the resistance to air movement (K) and the height of the heap (H) - i.e., $\Delta p \approx K \cdot H \cdot v$.

Since the pressure drop is always equal to the prevailing pressure head it follows from the two relations given above that the temperature difference $\bar{T}_A - T_O$ must be proportionate to the air velocity v and the resistance through the heap K - i.e., $(\bar{T}_A - T_O) \approx v \cdot K$.

Hence the larger the difference in temperature becomes, the more air will be moved through the heap. More heat will therefore be removed from the heap, the temperature in the heap falling relatively quickly. The temperature difference thus constantly decreases, so that less and less air is moved through the heap and less heat is eliminated. At a given temperature difference, the air will remove just as much heat as the potatoes produce. At this temperature difference, the steady-state condition will be attained, and the temperature in the heap will no longer change.

Temperature differences between the potatoes and their environment at steady state.

This temperature is determined by the heat and pressure balance within the heap - i.e., the relations $Q \approx (T_A - T_O) \cdot v$ and $(\bar{T}_A - T_O) \approx v \cdot K$. However, the amount of heat removed Q in the steady state is equal to the heat production of the potatoes per m^2 of horizontal area of the heap $Q_a \cdot H$; i.e., $Q = Q_a \cdot H$, in which Q_A is the heat production per m^3 of potatoes. The temperature T_A is proportionate to the average temperature in the heap $\bar{T}_A$. It follows from the relations $Q_a \cdot H \approx (\bar{T}_A - T_O) \cdot v$ and $(\bar{T}_A - T_O) \approx v \cdot K$ that the temperature difference between the heap and the environment in the steady state is exponentially proportionate to the heat production of the potatoes and to the resistance and height of the heap, viz., $(\bar{T}_A - T_O) \approx \sqrt{Q_a \cdot H \cdot K}$. This relation was verified experimentally by Beukema (1980) and Burton et al. (1955).

An unventilated potato heap is thus continuously ventilated by natural draught or free convection. As a result, even the potatoes deep down in the heap are after all cooled with ambient air.

The temperature difference between the heap and the environment with this form of ventilation depends on:
a. the height of the potato heap;
b. the resistance to air movement through the heap;
c. the heat production of the potatoes.

a. The temperature difference in a 2 m high heap will be 40 to 50 %

298

greater than in a 1 m high heap of the same lot of potatoes given the same ambient air conditions. In a 3 m high heap, however, the temperature difference will be 70 to 80 % more than in the 1 m case.

b. An equally large temperature increase takes place in a heap of the same height if the resistance to air movement is doubled or tripled. Hence the temperature difference will usually be larger the more the potatoes have sprouted and/or the more soil and folialge is present among the potatoes as these increase the resistance to air movement. The temperature difference is thus smallest if the potatoes are clean and sprout-free.

c. The heat production of the potatoes influences the temperature to the same extent as the pile height and resistance. A number of factors determine heat production in potatoes. Heat production is usually many times greater immediately after harvesting than a few weeks later. Tuber damage, intense sprouting and disease also substantially increase heat production (Burton et al., 1955).

However, heat production in healthy potatoes a few weeks after lifting is largely determined by the temperature of the potatoes. The increase in heat production is very limited in the temperature range 5 to 15 °C, averaging 0.4 W/tonne · °C. At temperatures above 15 °C, heat production increases considerably faster, averaging 2 W/tonne · °C. The temperature of the potatoes in an unventilated heap depends on the ambient temperature. The potato temperature is always a few degrees higher than the ambient temperature. Because heat production increases sharply at higher potato temperatures, the difference between the temperature of the potatoes and that of the environment will be larger at high ambient temperatures.

However, these high temperatures also promote sprouting and rotting in potatoes. This also increases the resistance to air movement through the heap, resulting in a further increase in temperature. At high ambient temperatures and/or in deep potato piles, there is therefore a danger of excessive temperatures in the heap and even of overheating of the potatoes. The equilibrium or steady-state condition is achieved only at excessively high temperatures, or not at all. Hence the pile height must be limited to avoid overheating of freshly lifted or sprouted potatoes and of potatoes stored at higher ambient temperatures.

The volume of air moved by natural draught is usually relatively small, so that it takes a long time for the equilibrium condition to be attained. It is therefore the average ambient temperature which determines the temperature of the potatoes. The temperature in a heap of this kind will therefore always be higher than in a heap with forced-draught ventilation. But the temperature is not the same right through the heap.

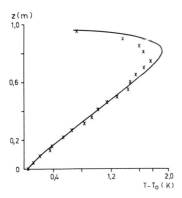

Fig. 16.2. Temperature variation through a 1 m deep pile at 20 °C and relative humidity of ambient air of 76 % RH. (from Beukema, 1980).

The characteristic temperature variation in the centre of large heaps of
potatoes ventilated by natural draught is shown in Fig. 16.2.

In a humid environment the air always moves upwards through the pile
and the lowest temperature is attained in the lowest layers of potatoes.
The temperature increases from the bottom towards the top, peaking at a
height of approximately 0.8 H, above which level it falls again. This
fall in temperature in the upper layers is due to intense mixing of the
air flow from the heap with the ambient air and to the elimination of
heat by conduction (Beukema, 1980).

The same occurs on all surfaces of the potato heap which are in direct
contact with the ambient air. This intense heat removal from the surface
may also influence the temperature in the middle of the heap. This influence, of course, depends on the size of the heap. Burton et al. (1955)
found that this influence was evident as long as the length or width of
the heap was less than twice the height - i.e., L < 2H or W < 2H. In
these heaps of limited horizontal size, the maximum temperature in the
middle of the heap was also appreciably lower than in larger-sized heaps
at the same ambient temperature. The length and/or width of the heap thus
also affect the maximum temperature difference between the heap and the
environment.

This temperature difference is also affected by the manner in which
the air can gain access to the heap (Beukema, 1980). Fig. 16.3 depicts
two heaps of equal size. The air has free access to the bottom of heap A,
while heap B is ventilated from above only.
The arrows show the direction of air movement through the two heaps.
Since the air in heap A is moved principally in one direction - i.e., upwards - while it is moved in heap B first downwards and only then upwards, more air will flow through heap A, so that the temperature of
these potatoes will be lower.

300

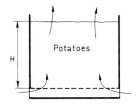 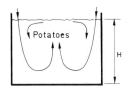

Fig. 16.3. Heaps with different air access. a. Free air access to the
bottom of the heap; b. air access only from above.

In a 3.7 m high heap ventilated only from above (type B), Burton
et al. (1955) observed the largest temperature difference $T_{ma} - T_o$ =
4.5 °C at ambient temperatures of 6 to 10 °C, The highest temperature was
measured at a height of 3 m. The temperature of the lowest layer of potatoes was then 1 °C higher than the ambient temperature. The measurements ware carried out a few weeks after the harvest in unsprouted potatoes with relatively little clinging soil.

Beukema (1980) measured a maximum temperature of 21.8 °C in a 1 m high
heap of clean, unsprouted potatoes with type A vetilation, the ambient
conditions being T_o= 20 °C and 96 % RH. This temperature was measured at
a height of 0.85 m. The temperature of the lowest layer of potatoes was
virtually the same as the ambient temperature - viz., 20 °C. Given the
same ambient conditions and with the same lot of potatoes piled to a
height of 3 m, a maximum temperature of about 24 °C could be expected in
a type A heap. However, the potatoes would sprout intensively at these
high temperatures, thus after a relatively short time increasing the resistance to air movement again, so that the temperature in the heap might
increase sharply. Heap size must therefore be limited to a minimum at
these high ambient temperatures to avoid overheating of the potatoes.

At lower humidities of the ambient air the lowest temperature does not
occur at the very bottom of a pile but somewhat higher, as shown in
Fig. 16.4(a); the initial temperature drop being caused by intensive evaporative cooling of potatoes.

At very low humidities of ambient air the evaporative cooling becomes
predominant and the temperature of potatoes remains lower than the ambient temperature throughout the pile as shown in Fig. 16.4(b). In that
case there occurs a downward movement of air through the pile.

Dimensions of potato heap
It is clear from the foregoing that the temperature in an unventilated
heap of potatoes can be reasonably well controlled by limiting the size
of the heap. If the requirements as to temperature uniformity are not
critical, healthy, clean potatoes can be stored in this way even in large
heaps (up to 3 m high) at an average ambient temperature not exceeding

301

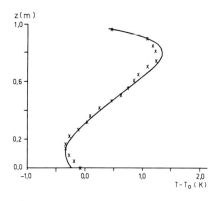
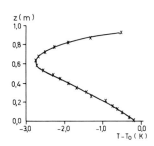

Fig. 16.4. Temperature variation through a 1 m deep pile of 20 °C and a relative humidity of the ambient air of: a. 76 % RH; b. 45 % RH. (from Beukema, 1980).

6 to 8 °C. The maximum temperature in the heap will then be limited to about 10 to 13 °C.

At higher ambient temperatures and/or if the temperature uniformity requirements for the potatoes are more critical, the heap size - in particular, its height - must be limited. In this case the potatoes are usually stored in boxes or crates, as illustrated in Fig. 16.5, or bulk-piled in clamps as shown in Fig. 16.6.

Potatoes to be stored without forced ventilation must be dry and reasonably clean - i.e., with little clinging soil and foliage. Large quantities of soil and foliage impede air movement, causing the temperature of the potatoes to rise. The potatoes must also be treated with sprout suppressants to prevent intense sprouting. The volume of air moved by natural draught is usually very small, so that the wet potatoes dry slowly. There is therefore a relatively high risk of rotting in wet potatoes.

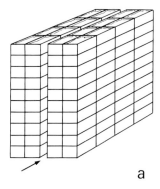
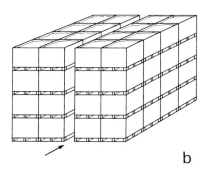

a   b

Fig. 16.5. Stacking of crates (a) and boxes (b) in space ventilated stores.

302

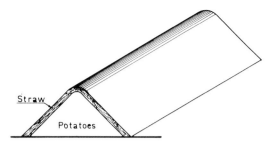

Straw

Potatoes

Fig. 16.6. Storage of potatoes in unventilated clamps.

Condensation

Since the temperature deep within the heap is higher than the surface temperature, water vapour from the air will condense on the surface of the heap. The amount of moisture precipitated depends on the amount of air moved through the heap and the difference between the temperature in the heap and on the surface. Hence more moisture will precipitate on the surface of large, tall heaps, thus also substantially increasing the risk of rotting of the potatoes. Since the moisture released by rotten potatoes cannot be efficiently evaporated, the disease rapidly spreads. This is one of the main disadvantages of natural draught ventilation.

Condensation on the surface layers of large heaps can, however, be prevented by covering them with straw. The highest temperature is then attained in the top layer of potatoes and the condensation occurs in the straw where the temperature is lower.

Because the spread of rot in unventilated heaps cannot be efficiently counteracted, this method of storage is relatively little used. Space ventilation is usually employed only for temporary storage is boxes, crates, sacks on pallets and in above-ground clamps.

In developing countries, however, potatoes, like many other agricultural produce, are usually stored without forced ventilation. It is then preferable for the potatoes to be carefully selected for storage; the heaps should be kept small and above all not too high (not more than 1 to 1.5 m), and they should be covered with straw or other air-permeable insulating materials. Losses can be substantially reduced by periodic inspection of the stored potatoes and elimination of rotten tubers from the heap.

16.3 Forced ventilation of the potato heap

16.3.1 Air distribution

In forced ventilation, the fan moves the air directly through the heap. The ventilation of the heap is then determined by the volume air flow of the fan. Unlike natural draught ventilation, forced ventilation allows accurate control of the volume air flow through the heap and hence also the storage conditions of the potatoes. To avoid major differences between the storage conditions in different parts of a heap, the heap must, however, be ventilated uniformly - i.e., the volume of air moved by the fan must be distributed evenly through the heap.

The air is always moved through the heap vertically. A system of air ducts underneath the potato heap is therefore required for even air distribution through it. A typical air distribution system is illustrated in Fig. 16.7. The air supplied by the fan or fans is distributed from the main duct to the lateral ducts, which have openings through which the air can be blown into the heap.

The air is distributed through the heap by the laterals, which are therefore also called distribution ducts. The system must be so designed that the air supplied by the fan can be distributed uniformly to the laterals, the same volume of air being discharged through all the openings in the laterals. Air distribution through the heap then depends solely on the distance between the discharge openings - i.e., the distance between the ducts and between the discharge openings in the ducts. In forced ventilation, the movement of air through a homogeneous heap of potatoes is thus fully determined by the fan and the air distribution system. Ventilation is, however, completely independent of both the horizontal dimensions and the height of the heap. The smaller the spacing between the discharge openings, the more uniform the air distribution becomes.

The widest spacing between discharge openings is usually determined by the distance between the distribution ducts. The openings in a duct can be positioned very close together without substantially increasing the cost of the duct. Ducts are often made with a gap along their entire

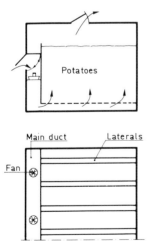

Fig. 16.7. Air distribution system in the potato store.

length. However, narrow duct spacing results in a larger number of ducts,
so that the air distribution system becomes more expensive. With above-
ground ducts, the useful floor area is also reduced as the duct spacing
becomes closer. The work of filling and emptying the store is thereby
impeded.

Hence the duct spacing is always a compromise between the air distribution, the system cost and the obstruction to working in the store.

16.3.2 *Spacing between distribution ducts*

The effect of the spacing between the discharge openings of air ducts
on air distribution through the heap will now be analysed (Fig. 16.8).

A given pressure P, which is higher than the pressure P_o above the
potato heap, is present in the duct. Owing to the pressure difference
$P - P_o$, the air is moved through the heap at a given velocity. The pressure drop through the heap must be equal to the prevailing pressure difference $P - P_o$. However, since the pressure drop through the heap depends
on the air velocity and the distance to be travelled by the air, the air
velocity will be lower the longer this distance. For this reason the air
velocity along the path $\overline{KA}$ will be higher than that along the path $\overline{KB}$.
The heap will thus not be ventilated uniformly.

The potatoes directly above the duct will always be better ventilated
than those at a greater horizontal distance from the duct. In general,
the air distribution will depend on the ratio between the distances to be
travelled by the air through the heap - i.e., on $\overline{KB}/\overline{KA}$. Since $\overline{KB}$ depends both on the height of the heap (H) and on the distance between the
air ducts (L) - or on (H + L) - $\overline{KA}$ being defined solely by the height of
the heap (H), the air distribution will also depend on the ratio of the
duct spacing to the heap height - i.e., on L/H. The smaller the duct
spacing relative to the heap height, the more uniform the air distribution becomes.

However, since the pressure drop through the heap at high air veloci-

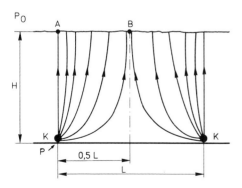

Fig. 16.8. Air distribution between two ducts.

305

ties is influenced more by the air velocity than by the distance to be travelled by the air (Fig. 15.4), the air distribution will not be linearly proportionate to L/H but approximately to $(L/H)^{0.55}$. At a duct spacing L equal to the height of the heap H (i.e., L = H), the air velocity through the potatoes exactly between the ducts will be about 80 % of that directly above the duct.

At a duct spacing of L = 2H, the air velocity exactly between the ducts will be equal to about 68 % of the maximum velocity above the duct, i.e., $v_{\overline{KB}}$ = 0.68 $v_{\overline{KA}}$. At the bottom of the heap, between the ducts, however, a cone of very poor ventilation arises, its size depending on L/H.

Uneven air distribution also increases the pressure drop in the heap, so that the fan can move less air. This is because the fan is chosen on the basis of uniform air distribution through the heap - i.e., for an average air velocity through the heap of v_g m³/m² · h and the pressure drop Δ_{P_1} · H associated with this velocity (Δ_{P_1} being the pressure drop per metre of height of the potato heap at the average velocity of v_g). Since uneven air distribution causes the velocity over $\overline{KA}$ to be higher than v_g, the pressure drop in the heap will also be increased and the fan will not be able to move so much air. The ventilation of the potatoes at a large horizontal distance from the duct will thereby be further impaired.

The conditions of the less well ventilated potatoes will always be behind those of well ventilated potatoes. A longer ventilation time will therefore be necessary to bring the entire heap to the same temperature or to dry it uniformly. As a result, weight losses in non-uniformly ventilated heaps of potatoes will increase. Since the temperature of the potatoes in the badly ventilated cone between the ducts generally remains higher after termination of ventilation, air movement by natural draught arises in the heap. This air movement eliminates the temperature differences in the heap but also leads to condensation on the surface of the colder potatoes. The amount of condensation depends on the quantity of badly ventilated potatoes - i.e., on the duct spacing.

It is difficult to define precisely the maximum distance between ducts. In general, the distance between the ducts must be reduced:
- the less air is moved by the fan per tonne of stored potatoes;
- the lower the height of the potato heap;
- the poorer the quality of the potatoes.

Ideal air distribution is obtained by a grating-type floor, the distance between the gaps being extremely limited. Where air is distributed through separate underfloor ducts, their spacing should preferably be limited to L = 0.8 H between centres. Experience shows that the condition of all potatoes can still be efficiently controlled at this duct spacing. Control of the storage conditions becomes more difficult if the duct spacing is wider, the risk of unexpected losses being increased.

The distance between ducts above floor level should be limited to a maximum of L = H between centres. If the air distribution ducts are spaced the recommended distance apart, the air is well distributed through the potatoes between the ducts. However, if the entire heap is to be uniformly ventilated, the air must also be blown uniformly into the heap over the entire length of the duct.

16.3.3 Air distribution through the duct

The air must be uniformly distributed over the entire length of the duct. For this purpose an air distribution duct is provided with discharge openings a relatively short distance apart. Each discharge opening in a duct must then discharge approximately the same volume of air.

The volume of air discharged by an opening is determined by the latter's cross-sectional area (A) and the air velocity (v) - i.e., $V = A \cdot v$ (m³/s).

However, the air is moved only by the agency of a pressure or a pressure difference. To move the air through an opening at a velocity v, a pressure of $\Delta ps = \xi \rho/2 \cdot v^2$ is necessary. The air velocity through the opening of an air duct is thus determined by the static gauge pressure in the duct Δps and the resistance factor of the opening ξ - i.e., $v = \sqrt{\frac{2 \; \Delta ps}{\xi \cdot \rho}}$. The discharge velocity through the opening will thus increase the higher the static gauge pressure in the duct. The volume of air discharged through an opening is then determined by the static gauge pressure in the duct and the cross-sectional area of the opening - i.e., $V = A \sqrt{\frac{2 \; \Delta ps}{\xi \cdot \rho}}$.

Uniform air distribution through a duct can thus be obtained in two ways, viz.:
a. keeping the static pressure in the ducts and the cross-sectional areas or dimensions of all openings the same, or
b. allowing the static pressure in the ducts to change and modifying the dimensions of the discharge openings in the duct in such a way that the volume of air moved through all openings is the same.

The air distribution ducts usually have equal-sized discharge openings. For uniform air distribution through the duct, the static pressure over its entire length must then remain approximately the same.

In an air flow through the duct there is always a static pressure Ps and the air is moved at a specific velocity v. To move the air at a specific velocity a static pressure is necessary.

The static pressure can thus be converted into air velocity, but the air velocity can also be converted into static pressure.

An example of this is the windmill. The wind arises as a consequence of a pressure difference in the atmosphere. The static pressure is thus converted into wind (or air) velocity. However, the wind exerts a pressure on the sails of the mill, setting it in rotation. The wind velocity

is thus reconverted into static pressure on the sails of the windmill.
The same conversion can take place in an air duct. Hence the air velocity
determines a pressure, which is known as the velocity pressure or dynamic
pressure of the air flow, $P_d = \frac{\rho}{2} \cdot v^2$ (Chapter 15).

The total pressure in the air flow is then the sum of the static and
dynamic pressures - i.e., $P_{tot} = P_s + P_d = P_s + \rho/2 \cdot v^2$. At a specific
total pressure P_{tot} of an air flow, the static pressure thus declines as
the air velocity increases. However, the static pressure increases as the
air velocity falls. But the total pressure P_{tot} is never equal throughout
an air duct. The total pressure declines constantly in the direction of
the air flow owing to pressure losses in the duct.

The static pressure, however, may fall, remain the same or increase
according to the change in velocity in the duct. This will be illustrated
by an example. Fig. 16.9 represents a segment of an air distribution
duct. An equal volume of air V_0 is discharged through the discharge
openings. As a result the volume of air moved through the duct falls from
V_1 before the opening to $V_1 - V_0$ after the opening, the air velocity also
changing from v_1 to v_2.
The movement of air from A to B gives rise to a pressure loss of ΔP. The
total pressure P_{t_2} at B is then ΔP less then the total pressure P_{t_1} at
A - i.e.:

$$P_{t_2} = P_{t_1} - \Delta P \qquad\qquad (63)$$

However, the total pressures at A and B can be determined as follows:

$$P_{t_1} = P_{s_1} + \rho/2 \; v_1^2$$
$$P_{t_2} = P_{s_1} + \rho/2 \; v_2^2$$

Equation (63) can thus be written as follows:

$$P_{s_2} + \rho/2 \; v_2^2 = P_{s_1} + \rho/2 \; v_1^2 - \Delta P$$

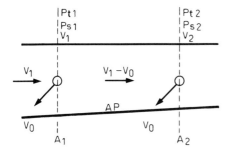

Fig. 16.9. Variation of static pressure through the duct.

The difference in static pressure between A and B is then:

$$P_{S_1} - P_{S_2} = \Delta P - \frac{\rho}{2} (v_1^2 - v_2^2) \tag{64}$$

Since pressure losses always arise when the air velocity changes, the velocity pressure will not be entirely converted into static pressure but only a part η of it. Equation 64 then becomes:

$$P_{S_1} - P_{S_2} = \Delta P - \eta \frac{\rho}{2} (v_1^2 - v_2^2) \tag{65}$$

In air ducts, η will usually vary between 80 % and 90 % - i.e., η = 0.8 to 0.9.

The air velocity, however, is determined by the volume air flow and the cross-sectional area of the duct - i.e., $v = \frac{V}{A}$.

Equation (64) can thus be written as follows:

$$P_{S_1} - P_{S_2} = \Delta P - \eta \frac{\rho}{2} \left[(\frac{\dot{V}_1}{A_1})^2 - (\frac{\dot{V}_1 - \dot{V}_0}{A_2})^2 \right] \tag{66}$$

It is clear from Equation 65 that the change in static pressure through the duct is greatly affected by the change in its cross-sectional area.

ΔP always represents a pressure loss (Equations 64 to 66) - i.e., ΔP entails a decrease in static pressure. The change in the velocity pressure $\rho/2$ ($v_1^2 - v_2^2$) may, however, result in a corresponding pressure loss or pressure gain according to the change in air velocity. If the air velocity constantly increases - i.e., if v_2 becomes larger than v_1 - the static pressure in the duct declines correspondingly. However, if the air velocity in the direction of flow constantly decreases - i.e., v_2 less than v_1 - the pressure in the duct increases correspondingly. It therefore depends on the shape of the duct whether the static pressure in the duct increases, decreases or remains the same.

The static pressure in the duct remains unchanged - i.e., $P_{S_1} - P_{S_2} = 0$ - if the velocity in the direction of flow declines in such a way that the resulting pressure gain is equal to the pressure loss ΔP in the duct. According to Equation 66, this requirement is satisfied if:

$$\Delta P = \frac{\rho}{2} \eta \left[(\frac{\dot{V}_1}{A_1})^2 - (\frac{\dot{V}_1 - \dot{V}_0}{A_2})^2 \right] \tag{67}$$

A duct which conforms to Equation 67 is known as an equal-pressure

duct. The air is distributed uniformly through the heap of potatoes
through an equal-pressure duct having equal-sized discharge openings.

The cross-sectional area of an equal-pressured duct declines constantly in the direction of the air flow.

However, ducts of equal cross-sectional area are also used in potato
stores. Since the volume air flow in a distribution duct constantly declines, the air velocity will also decrease in a duct of equal cross-
section. The pressure loss in the duct depends greatly on air velocity,
declining with decreasing air velocity. The pressure gain, however, will
increase substantially with falling air velocity. This will usually give
rise to an increase in the static pressure in the direction of the air
flow. The static pressure at the end of a duct of this kind may be considerably higher than the pressure at the beginning. This pressure difference depends very much on the air velocity at the beginning of the duct.

A duct of equal cross-section, having equal-sized discharge openings,
will thus not distribute the air absolutely uniformly through the potato
heap. Even so, reasonable air distribution can be obtained with a duct of
this kind subject to certain conditions.

16.3.3.1 Equal-pressure ducts

An equal-pressure duct can be scaled on the basis of Equation 67. For
this purpose the duct must be divided into short segments. For the first
segment, at the beginning of a duct, all data are known except for the
cross-sectional area A_2. This can be calculated from Equation 67. This
also fixes the initial cross-section of the second segment, and the final
cross-section of this segment can be determined. The variation of the
cross-sectional area of the entire duct can be determined in the same
way.

The characteristic variation of the cross-sectional area of an equal-
pressure duct is represented by the full line in Fig. 16.10.

The air distribution through the equal-pressure duct, having equal-
sized discharge openings, is independent of the air velocity at the duct
inlet and of the air discharge velocity. Air distribution remains uniform
even at very high air velocities at the beginning of the duct and low
discharge velocities. As a result the duct size and the static gauge

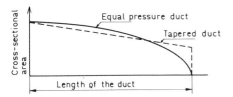

Fig. 16.10. Cross-sectional area of an equal-pressure duct.

pressure inside the duct can be kept small. However, since the high air
velocity necessitates a considerable increase in the fan size and influences the duct dimensions to a much lesser extent, it is preferable to
limit the air velocity at the duct inlet to 6 m/s.

An equal-pressure duct as illustrated in Fig. 16.10 is much too complicated and expensive for potato storage. Air distribution ducts are
therefore made with a tapered configuration as indicated by the dashed
line in Fig. 16.10. If the cross-section of the duct is rectangular, the
width is usually kept constant throughout its length, the height varying
in proportion to its cross-sectional area.

Table 16.1 Inlet/end cross-sections of distribution ducts of
different lengths.

Duct length (m)	Inlet/end cross-sectional ratio
5	4:1
10	7:1
15	10:1
20	13:1

Table 16.1 sets out the recommended ratios between the inlet and end
cross-sections of distribution ducts of different lengths. It applies
only to smooth-walled distribution ducts.

The static pressure through a duct of this kind changes only to a limited extent. To achieve even air distribution, the discharge velocity
should preferably not be allowed to fall below 4 m/s. The maximum effective cross-section of all discharge openings is then determined as follows:

$$A_0 = \frac{V}{4} \ (m^2) \quad V \ in \ m^3/s$$

This corresponds to a maximum effective cross-section of the discharge
openings of 0.25 m^2 per m^3 of air blown through the duct per second.
However, since about three quarters of the cross-sectional area of the
discharge openings is covered by potato tubers when stored in bulk heaps,
this area must be made three or four times larger than stated above –
i.e., 0.75 to 1 m^2 per m^3/s of discharging air.

The air distribution through a duct can best be tested when the store
is empty. If major irregularities are found, these can be eliminated
before the store is filled. If, however, the air distribution proves to
be reasonable, it will be even more uniform in the filled store. Serious
problems during storage can be avoided by a check of this kind.

16.3.3.2 Ducts of equal cross-section

The static pressure at the end of an equal-section duct will usually be higher than at the inlet. Since the cross-section of the duct is the same over its entire length and the volume of air moved continuously declines owing to the air discharge, the velocity will also fall continuously, reaching nil at the end of the duct. This means that the total velocity pressure at the duct inlet is converted into static pressure at the end of the duct. Equation 67 can then be written as follows:

$$P_{s_e} - P_{s_i} = \eta v_i^2 \cdot \frac{\rho}{2} - \Delta P = \eta \left(\frac{V_i}{A_K}\right)^2 \cdot \frac{\rho}{2} - \Delta P$$

The pressure loss ΔP in the duct is usually smaller than the velocity pressure at the inlet. The static pressure will therefore increase continuously in the duct, reaching its highest value at the end of the duct. The static pressure, or gauge pressure relative to the environment, however, determines the air velocity through the discharge openings, $\Delta P_s = \frac{\rho}{2} v_0^2 \cdot \xi$.

Hence the discharge velocity will increase continuously in the direction of the air flow, reaching a maximum at the end of the duct. The air distribution through a duct with equal discharge openings therefore becomes non-uniform.

This non-uniformity is determined by the ratio between the static pressures at the end and at the inlet of the duct. If the duct is designed for a specific average discharge velocity v_0, the static gauge pressure at the inlet is determined by $\Delta P_i = \xi \frac{\rho}{2} v_0^2$. The static gauge pressure at the end of the duct is then:

$$\Delta P_e = \xi \frac{\rho}{2} v_0^2 + \eta \frac{\rho}{2} v_i^2 - \Delta P.$$

The ratio between the static pressures at the end and at the inlet of the duct becomes:

$$\frac{\Delta P_e}{\Delta P_i} = \frac{\xi\, \rho/2\, v_0^2 + \eta\rho/2\, v_i^2 - \Delta P}{\xi\, \rho/2\, v_0^2} = 1 - \frac{\Delta P}{\Delta P_i} + \frac{v_i^2}{v_0^2} \frac{\eta}{\xi}$$

Since the velocity is equal to $\frac{V}{A}$, this ratio can be written as follows:

$$\frac{\Delta P_e}{\Delta P_i} = 1 - \frac{2\Delta p \cdot A_0^2}{\xi\, \rho\, v^2} + \left(\frac{A_0}{A_K}\right)^2 \cdot \frac{\eta}{\xi} \tag{68}$$

in which: A_0 = cross-sectional area of all discharge openings (m²)
A_k = cross-sectional area of duct (m²)
V = volume air flow at duct inlet (m³/s)
ΔP = pressure loss in duct (Pa)

The static pressures ΔP_e and ΔP_i determine the discharge velocities at the end and at the inlet of the duct respectively, i.e.:

$$\Delta P_e = (\frac{V_e}{A_o})^2 \cdot \frac{\rho}{2} \xi$$

$$\Delta P_i = (\frac{V_i}{A_o})^2 \cdot \frac{\rho}{2} \xi$$

Equation 68 then becomes:

$$(\frac{V_e}{V_i})^2 = 1 + (\frac{A_0}{A_k})^2 \cdot \frac{\eta}{\xi} - \frac{2\Delta P}{\xi\rho} \cdot (\frac{A_0}{V_i})^2 \qquad (69)$$

in which: V_e = volume of air discharged at the end of the duct (m³/s)

V_i = volume of air discharged at the inlet (m³/s)

In a smooth-walled duct, the pressure loss in the duct ΔP is usually relatively small and the value $(\frac{A_0}{V_i})2 \frac{2\Delta P}{\xi \rho}$ can be disregarded.

The resistance factor for the discharge openings is approximately $\xi \cong 1$.

The air distribution through the duct is then largely determined by the ratio between the area of the air discharge openings and the cross-sectional area of the duct A_o/A_k. The air distribution becomes more uniform the smaller A_o/A_k becomes - i.e., the smaller the area of the discharge opening becomes relative to the cross-section of the duct.

For example, if the total area of the air discharge openings is twice the cross-sectional area of the duct ($A_o/A_k = 2$), about twice as much air will be discharged at the end of the duct as at the inlet ($V_e/V_i \cong 2$). At a ratio $A_o/A_i \cong 1$, about 35 % more air is discharged at the end of the duct, i.e., $V_e/V_i \cong 1.35$, and at $A_o/A_i \cong 0.5$ about 13 % more, i.e., $V_e/V_i \cong 1.13$.

This air distribution is obtained by a duct which blows the air into a free space, i.e., if the back-pressure on the outside of the duct is constant. However, in a duct covered with potatoes, the back-pressure varies in proportion to the pressure loss involved in the motion of air through the heap. This pressure loss depends greatly on the volume air flow. Hence the largest pressure drop will arise at the end of the duct, where the largest volume of air is moved. The back-pressure at the end of the duct thus becomes larger than at the inlet, so that $\Delta P_e/\Delta P_i$ in Equation 68 becomes smaller - i.e., the air is distributed more uniformly through a duct covered with potatoes.

In general, the air distribution through a duct of equal cross-section at any ratio A_o/A_k will become more uniform the higher the pressure losses through the potato heap - i.e., the higher the static pressure at the duct inlet. The air distribution will thus become more uniform the higher the heap of potatoes and the greater the air flow per tonne of stored potatoes per hour.

In the case of an equal-section duct, it is recommended that the effective area of the discharge openings should be kept equal to or smaller than the cross-section of the duct - i.e., $A_o/A_k \leq 1$. If the air velocity at the duct inlet is thus limited to 5 to 6 m/s, reasonable air distribution can be achieved with an equal-section duct without excessive pressure loss, as the pressure loss through the discharge openings in this case remains limited to about 16 and 23 Pa respectively.

However, if the air velocity at the duct inlet is 10 m/s, the pressure loss through the discharge openings will rise to about 64 Pa.

Since some 65 to 75 % of the discharge area is blocked by potatoes, the duct will need to have a total area of discharge openings about three times its cross-section.

The rules set out in Sections 16.3.3.1 and 16.3.3.2 also apply to the securing of uniform air distribution from the main duct to the air distribution ducts.

16.3.4 Air duct construction

Both underfloor and above-floor ducts (in the floor and on the floor respectively) are used in potato stores. A ventilation system often comprises a combination of both types of ducts.

An underfloor distribution duct is illustrated in Fig. 16.11.

Underfloor ducts are made entirely of concrete (Fig. 16.11a) or partly of concrete and partly of brick (Fig. 16.11b). The walls are often finished with cement mortar to provide a smooth surface. Underfloor ducts are covered with wooden or concrete beams or metal sheets.

In the case of the air distribution ducts, the space between the covering beams must be left free for the air outlet (Fig. 16.12). The

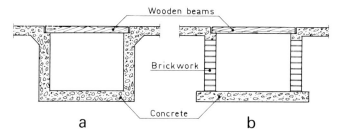

Fig. 16.11. Underfloor duct.

314

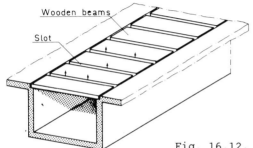

Fig. 16.12. Air discharge from underfloor ducts.

area of the air discharge gaps must be determined as explained in Sections 16.3.3.1 and 16.3.3.2.

The beams or panels covering over the ducts must be capable of withstanding the pressure exerted by potatoes, equipment and machinery. If underfloor air ducts are used in the store, the floor must be of concrete. Above-floor ducts, however, may ne installed on either a concrete or a hardened earth floor.

Above-floor ducts are made of timber or metal. Galvanized steel is usually used in the latter case.

Examples of above-floor ducts are illustrated in Fig. 16.13.

Above-floor ducts are usually cheaper to buy and are often used for this reason. However, the operating costs of above-floor ducts are higher because they usually need more maintenance and must be replaced more

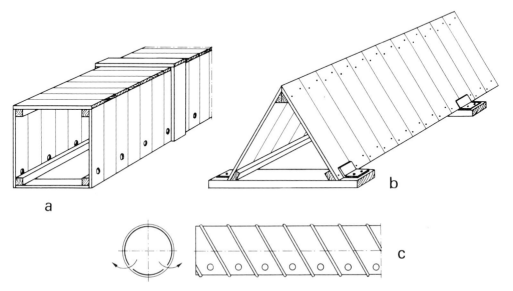

Fid. 16.13. Examples of above-floor ducts. a. Rectangular duct made of timber; b. triangular duct made of timber; c. steel tube ducts.

frequently. They also require more labour, as they are placed in position
when the store is filled and have to be removed again for unloading.

One advantage of underfloor ducts is also that they are of universal
application - i.e., they can be used for bulk storage, storage in boxes,
storage in sacks and sacks on pallets. Above-floor ducts are suitable
only for bulk and sack storage.

In terms of ventilation of the potatoes, however, there is no difference between the two types of ducts. The ventilation depends solely on
the design and construction of the system.

16.3.5 Air distribution systems

Uniform air distribution through the stored potatoes and minimum obstruction of operations during loading and unloading of the store are the
two principal requirements which must be satisfied by a good air distribution system.

Since the potatoes are stored in different ways - viz., loose, in
sacks, boxes, sacks on pallets, etc. - appropriate air distribution systems must be used in the stores concerned. A ventilation or air distribution system usually comprises a manifold or main duct, to which one or
more distribution ducts are connected. If the potatoes are cooled with
outside air, the ventilation system must be designed so that the potatoes
can be ventilated with fresh outside air, ambient air or a mixture of the
two. The main duct with the fan(s) must therefore communicate with the
space above the potato heap and with the surrounding atmosphere. This is
necessary in mechanically refrigerated stores only if outside air ventilation is used for drying wet potatoes.

Air distribution systems for loose storage are illustrated in Figs.
16.14, 15, 16 and 17.

Both above-floor and underfloor air distribution ducts may be used for
the system illustrated. The air distribution depends solely on the duct
spacing and on the air distribution through each duct. If the duct spacing is limited to 80 % of the height of the bulk heap - i.e., 0.8 H

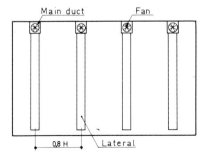

Fig. 16.14. Each lateral provided with a fan.

between centres - and the ducts are scaled as described in Sections 16.3.3.1 and 16.3.3.2, good air distribution will be obtained with all systems illustrated.

Ideal air distribution is obtained with the system depicted in Fig. 16.17. This system is, however, also the most expensive. Its advantage is its universal applicability: it is suitable for all forms of storage, including boxes and sacks on pallets.

In small stores, underfloor distribution ducts are also used for unloading the store. For this purpose a conveyor belt is placed in the duct

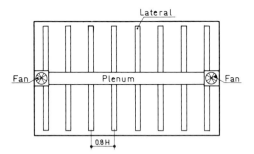

Fig. 16.15. Plenum in the middle.

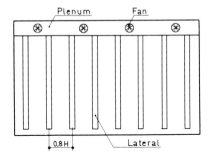

Fig. 16.16. Plenum among the side wall and laterals.

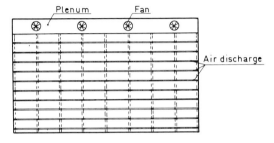

Fig. 16.17. Air distribution through slatted floor.

317

and transports the potatoes out of the store to the outside of the building (Fig. 16.18).

In this case the duct dimensions must be matched to those of the conveyor belt.

Where potatoes are stored in boxes, the air distribution system illustrated in Fig. 16.17 may be used. The systems shown in Figs. 16.19 and 20 may also be used for box storage.

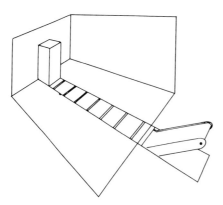

Fig. 16.18. Lateral used for unloading the store.

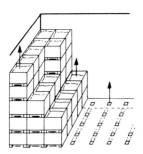

Fig. 16.19. Stack of boxes ventilated through an underfloor duct.

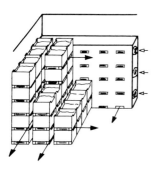

Fig. 16.20. Separate ventilation of each box.

318

In the system illustrated in Fig. 16.19, the boxes must be stacked as close together as possible to prevent air from flowing around them. In the system in Fig. 16.20 the distribution duct is formed by the pallets of the boxes; the pallets must then have a solid wall on two sides (Fig. 16.21).

The boxes in a given row must be stacked very close together to minimize air losses. Since the 'distribution duct' has an equal cross-section in this case, both this cross-section and that of the discharge openings being determined by the construction and the number of boxes, the number of boxes per discharge opening in the main duct must be limited if uniform air distribution is to be obtained.

The number of boxes in a row is determined by the requirement that the total discharge area of all boxes in a row must be equal to or smaller than 3 to 4 times the cross-section of the pallet - i.e., in accordance with Fig. 16.21:

$$n \leq 3 \, \frac{A_K}{A_o} \tag{70}$$

n = number of boxes in a row.

Since the distribution duct is not absolutely airtight in this case (as air can leak between the boxes), high pressure cannot be built up in it. For this reason the air velocity through the discharge openings of filled boxes must be limited to 3 to 4 m/s.

For this reason the velocity on admission to the pallet of the first box must not exceed 4 m/s. Assuming an air loss of 20 %, the number of boxes in a row can be determined as follows:

$$n = 3.3 \cdot \frac{A_K}{\dot{V}_0}$$

$\dot{V}_0$ = volume air flow through each box (m³/s)

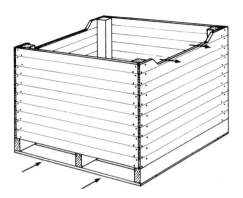

Fig. 16.21. Box type to be used for the ventilation system in Fig. 16.20.

The boxes used in, for example, the Netherlands have a free pallet cross-section of $A_K \simeq 0.11$ m², and each box has a storage capacity of one tonne of potatoes. If an air flow of 0.041 m³/s per box is required, the permissible number of boxes in a row is n = 3.3 $\frac{0.11}{0.041}$ = 8.85 ≈ 9.

The area of the gap in the bottom of the box is given by Equation 70:

$$A_o \leq \frac{3A_K}{n} = \frac{3 \cdot 0.11}{9} = 0.037 \text{ m}^2.$$

The number of boxes in a row can be determined in the same way for any type of box and any desired volume air flow through the box.

The main ducts of ventilation systems usually have equal cross-sections throughout their length. For good air distribution through all the distribution ducts connected, the cross-section of the main duct must then be equal to or larger than the cross-section of all connections.

However, there are no limitations on the cross-section of equal-pressure main ducts.

References

Beukema, K.J., 1980. Heat and mass transfer during cooling and storage of agricultural products as influenced by natural convection. Doctoral thesis. Agricultural University, Wageningen.

Burton, W.G., G. Mann and H.G. Wager, 1955. The storage of ware potatoes in permanent buildings. II The temperature of unventilated stacks of potatoes. J. Agric. Sci., 46.

17 Air humidification

A. Rastovski

The weight losses caused by evaporation of water from potatoes depend greatly on the difference in vapour pressure between the potatoes and the air. This vapour pressure difference is determined by:

a. the temperature of the potatoes;
b. the difference in temperature between the potatoes and the air;
c. the relative humidity of the air.

If the difference in temperature between the potatoes and the air is considerable, the humidity of the air has relatively little effect on the vapour pressure difference. However, if the potatoes and the air are at the same temperature, the relative humidity is the only factor (apart from the temperature) which determines the vapour pressure difference. The vapour pressure difference becomes nil at any temperature at a relative humidity of 100 % if the potatoes and the air are at the same temperature.

In theory, therefore, no water should evaporate under these conditions - i.e., there should be no moisture loss from the potatoes. As stated earlier, the temperature of the potatoes is nevel equal to that of the ambient air owing to the heat produced by the potatoes. Some moisture loss will therefore also occur under the conditions mentioned, but will be the minimum possible.

However, any fall in relative humidity below 100 % will give rise to a considerable increase in the vapour pressure difference or moisture loss. For instance, if the relative humidity falls from 99 % to 96 %, the vapour pressure difference is quadrupled ($\frac{100-96}{100-99} = 4$) and the moisture loss will increase by about the same factor. If a quantity of moisture is added to air at 96 % RH, sufficient to raise the relative humidity to 99 %, the moisture loss can thus be reduced to about a quarter. The same relative reduction in vapour pressure difference would occur if the relative humidity were increased, for example, from 84 % to 96 % ($\frac{100-84}{100-96} = 4$).

These examples show that if the potatoes and the air are at the same temperature, any increase in relative humidity substantially reduces the vapour pressure difference. If the air is very humid, a relatively small increase in relative humidity can reduce the vapour pressure difference to a fraction of its original value. Of course, this involves a drastic reduction in a small quantity.

When tall potato heaps are cooled, the potatoes which come into contact with the cold air first - i.e., the lowest layers - are cooled very quickly to the air temperature. After this, it takes a long time before the entire heap is cooled. During all this time, the temperature of the lowest potatoes is equal to the air temperature and the moisture loss from these potatoes is greatly affected by the relative humidity of the air.

Potatoes higher up in the heap attain these conditions later, and remain so for a shorter time. In the lowest layers of potatoes, therefore, the relative humidity has the strongest effect on moisture loss. The moisture loss in the lowest layers of potatoes can be minimized by ventilation with saturated or very humid air. This low moisture loss may also result in reduced losses due to pressure damage or bruising in the potatoes at the bottom, thus enhancing the economic value of the potatoes.

For this reason it is advantageous to ventilate the potatoes with very humid air. The aim is usually to ventilate with air of 95 % or higher relative humidity. The air which has to be used for ventilation is often drier, and it is then advantageous to humidify it.

The air can usually be humidified by supplying water vapour or by evaporating water into the air. In the former case, the air temperature increases relatively little and the heat content or enthalpy of the air increases substantially. However, if water is evaporated into the air, the air temperature falls and the enthalpy remains virtually unchanged (Section 9.1.2).

If the air is saturated by evaporation of water, its temperature falls (practically) to the wet bulb temperature. As a result of this falling temperature, the cooling capacity of the air increases. For this reason humidification by water evaporation is generally used in potato storage. To accelerate the evaporation process, the air must come into contact with a large area of water, as the degree of evaporation is directly proportional to the area of water on which evaporation occurs.

The area of a given quantity of water can be increased in two ways, viz.:
a. atomizing the water in fine drops
b. dividing the water into thin layers.

The first principle is used in water atomizers and the second in air washers.

Particularly with the former, it is essential to be aware of the danger of overhumidifying the air and wetting the potatoes during ventilation. The more the potatoes are diseased and the longer the ventilation periods, the greater the danger of serious rotting of potatoes due to overhumidification of the air. With the ventilation capacity used in the Netherlands (100 to 150 m^3 of air per hour per tonne of potatoes), the ventilation time averages 150 to 200 hours in a storage period of seven

months. Overhumidification of the air during these short ventilation periods has no effect on potato rotting.

Compared with ventilation without air humidification, weight losses
can, however, be reduced by an average of 15 to 20 % if the air is humidified. Air humidification has a much greater effect with regard to pres-
sure-bruising of the lowest potatoes (Buitelaar, 1980), which it limits.

The benefits of air humidification will be even greater where potatoes
are ventilated with outside air in drier climates.

In mechanically refrigerated stores in warm countries, weight losses
during cooling of the potatoes to the desired storage temperature can be
limited by air humidification. In these countries the potatoes enter the
store at high temperatures (30 °C or higher). At these temperatures the
vapour pressure difference between the potatoes and the air becomes much
greater at one and the same relative humidity of the air than at the lower temperatures in temperate climates. The effect of air humidity on potato moisture loss is thereby substantially increased.

Once the potatoes have been cooled to the required temperature, air
humidification in a mechanically refrigerated store has relatively little
effect on moisture loss from the potatoes. In a well insulated store filled with potatoes, the relative humidity will seldom fall below 95 %. The
risk of high losses due to rot, caused by overhumidification of the air
for relatively long periods, must in this case be weighed against a relatively small gain from lower moisture losses.

17.1 Water atomizers

Water atomizers divide the water into very fine drops, thus increasing
the water area by several tens of thousands of times. These fine drops
are entrained by the air flow and rapid evaporation takes place. An atomizer is illustrated in Fig. 17.1. The atomizers are positioned in the
main duct after the fan, as shown in Fig. 17.2.

If sufficient atomized water is added to the air flow, the air can be
saturated to the wet bulb temperature before it is blown into the potato
heap. In this way the air is cooled and saturated with water vapour. The
amount of atomized water which must be added to 1 m³ of air to saturate
it ot the wet bulb temperature is determined by the temperature and the
relative humidity of the air. For example, in the case of air at 7 °C and
80 % RH, about 0.58 g of water per m³ of air must be added to saturate
the air to the wet bulb temperature, which is then 5.45 °C.

However, if the relative humidity at the same temperature becomes
90 %, only 0.38 g of water per m³ of air is necessary for saturation to
the wet bulb temperature, which in this case is about 6.3 °C.

If the same amount of water is added to air at 7 °C and 90 % RH as to
air at 7 °C and 80 % RH (viz., 0.58 g/m³), this water will not be able to

Fig. 17.1. Centrifugal water atomizer.

evaporate completely, as this air is saturated already by the addition of 0.38 g of water per m³ of air. Hence 0.58 to 0.38 = 0.2 g/m³ of water will remain present in the air flow in the form of drops. Since the fine drops are readily entrained by the air flow, this water will be blown into the heap of potatoes with the air, thus wetting the potatoes. The presence of free water on the surface of the tubers may, however, encourage the spread of diseases.

The same will occur if the temperature of the air falls during ventilation. The temperature and relative humidity of the air vary not only during the storage period but also during ventilation. If the potatoes are not to become wet, the quantity of water atomized must be continuously controlled.

Water atomizers are usually relatively simple and efficient devices, but they all have the deficiency that the quantity of water atomized can-

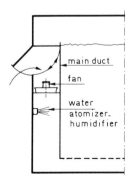

main duct

fan

water
atomizer-
humidifier

Fig. 17.2. Air humidification by water atomizers.

not be accurately controlled. The other problem is the control instrumentation. Reliable equipment for practical measurement of relative humidity at levels in excess of 95 % does not exist. For this reason the capacity of water atomizers is predominantly controlled manually, the atomizer being switched on and off together with the fan. The result is in most cases that the air is overhumidified, so that the potatoes get wet during ventilation.

17.2 Columns filled with evaporation elements (air washers)

Overhumidification of the air can be prevented by the use of an air washer as illustrated in Fig. 17.3.

Compared with water atomizers, the difference is that the active water evaporation area is enlarged in this case by dividing the water into thin layers. This is carried out in a column filled with elements having a relatively large area per unit volume, such as short cylinders or ribbed plates.

Sufficient space must be left between the elements for the air to flow through the column.

The water is distributed over the elements by a system of perforated pipes and then spreads evenly over the surface of the elements, which is thus covered with a film of water. The air is blown in at the bottom of the column and comes into contact with the wet surfaces of the elements as it flows upwards. Since the wet surfaces are large in area, the evaporation process takes place relatively fast and the air is efficiently humidified.

The air can be humidified to an RH of approximately 98 % using this equipment. A lower air humidity can be obtained by supplying less water to the column: in this case only a part of the elements becomes wet, thus reducing the evaporation area and the amount of water evaporating. For

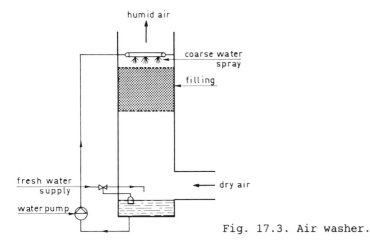

Fig. 17.3. Air washer.

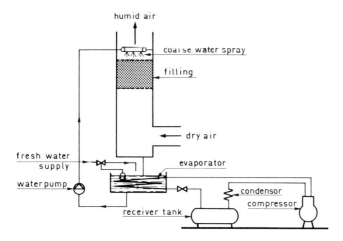

Fig. 17.4. Cooling and humidifying of air by air-washer.

maximum relative humidity, more water is admitted to the column than evaporates into the air. The surplus water falls into a reservoir and is re-
cycled to the column. In this way the air is humidified so that it tends
towards the wet bulb temperature. Only the amount of fresh water evaporated by the air is fed to the reservoir.

Since fine drops of water are not formed in this humidification process, there is no danger of drop formation in the air flow at the usual
air velocities through the column. The air flow thus leaves the humidifier at high relative humidity without drops of water. The moisture loss
can be reduced in this way without the potatoes becoming wet.

The same system can be used for simultaneous cooling and humidification of the air. In this case cooled water must be fed to the column, a
refrigeration unit being used to cool it. This system is illustrated in
Fig. 17.4 and it can be used in mechanically refrigerated stores.

The column here replaces the evaporator/air cooler. The temperature
and humidity of the air can be controlled accurately by a cooling system
of this kind.

Air washers are more expensive than water atomizers, and are therefore
less frequently used for air humidification in potato storage.

Reference

Buitelaar, N., 1980. De invloed van luchtbevochtiging tijdens het venti-
    leren op de bewaarresultaten van consumptie-aardappelen. IBVL-Publi-
    katie 332.

POTATO STORAGE PRACTICE

18 Inspection of store and arrival of potatoes

C.P. Meijers

18.1 Inspection of store

Before the harvest season begins, a check must be carried out to ensure that the store is in order, attention being devoted to the following points:
- The storage compartments must be clean; they should preferably be cleaned as soon as possible after emptying. Old potatoes and residual soil and sprout inhibitor powder must be removed. If the compartment contained a lot with a large number of rotten tubers (e.g., soft rot or *Fusarium*) in the previous season, it may be worth while to disinfect it by spraying with a solution of formalin (20 g/l). A gas mask should be worn as formalin vapour is a powerful eye irritant. Undiluted commercial formalin can also be applied with a Swingfog unit (0.5 to 1 l/100 m³ of volume), or else the material can be heated in a pan or on an electric hotplate. In the latter case, formaldehyde flakes could perhaps also be used.
- In a new store or after repair or maintenance, check that the fan operates satisfactorily. The correct sense of rotation can be determined by holding a handkerchief in front of the rotating fan, which should be shielded, or by using smoke. When sprout suppressants are applied with a Swingfog unit, some of the agent precipitates on the fan and its housing and may cause unbalance in the fan. This precipitate also attacks metal parts of the fan. The fan should therefore preferably be cleaned annually and if necessary repainted (using aluminium paint).
- The condition of the ducts and dampers should be examined, for example with a torch.
- The reliability of the insertion-type thermometers to be used should be checked with a calibrated thermometer. This should be done at various temperatures, for example in water at temperatures of 0, 5, 7, 10, 15 and 20 °C. It is important to note the errors observed. It is not very serious if the thermometers have an error provided that the correction to be applied at different temperatures is known. Good insertion-type thermometers have an adjusting mechanism to correct the error. Thermostats are best inspected by an expert, who can at the same time check the control panels and thermal safety devices.

- Seed potatoes should never be stored in compartments where a sprout inhibitor has previously been used, especially a liquid sprout inhibitor (Swingfog method), as the seed potatoes may then sprout less readily. Appreciably delayed sprouting and inferior emergence are likely even if the store concerned was last treated as long as two or three years previously. Reduced sprouting potential is also likely if, for example, grass seed was dried in the store.
- Seed potatoes should also not be stored in compartments also used for fruit, vegetables or bulbs, as these products produce ethylene, which may adversely affect sprouting. A period of two or three weeks should be allowed between the storage of such produce and of seed potatoes, during which the store should be regularly ventilated to eliminate the ethylene.

18.2 Reception of potatoes

Seed and ware potatoes in the Netherlands are lifted primarily with harvesters with an accompanian trailer, although bunker-type harvesters are also used. With these types of lifting machines, the potatoes are loaded on to a truck either direct or by way of a bunker. These trucks are usually tippers, which deposit the potatoes through a hatch on to a conveyor belt, or in a bulk hopper, from which they are fed to the conveyor. Few potatoes have hitherto been harvested direct into boxes in the Netherlands.

It is best for the first potatoes in a store to be placed on bags filled with straw or similar material. As soon as a small heap has formed, this is no longer necessary, and the conveyor belt (box filler) is always adjusted so that the height of fall is limited to a maximum of 40 cm, the belt speed at the same time not exceeding 30 to 40 m/min.

Large quantities of fine, loose soil between the potatoes impede ventilation. Loose soil (and any clods and stones) should therefore preferably as far as possible be removed with a preliminary cleaner, but without damaging the tubers. Provided that it is evenly distributed, a small quantity of loose soil between the potatoes (100 to 200 kg/tonne) is not important. To achieve this even distribution, the belt which conveys the potatoes into the store must be moved regularly to and fro, either automatically or manually. This prevents the formation of soil cones - i.e., local accumulations of large quantities of soil, often accompanied by a few small tubers. These cones are hardly if at all accessible to air, so that the tubers are dried more slowly, the temperature is locally higher, sprouting occurs sooner and diseases such as silver scurf and *Rhizoctonia* can spread faster here. Of course, the presence of large amounts of soil between the potatoes also facilitates the spread of these diseases. On the other hand, the weight losses are usually somewhat less if considerable soil is present. For this reason store managers favour the presence of a certain amount of soil, which also has a buffering effect and tends to prevent damage or black spot.

Lots affected with *Phytophthora* require additional care and should if possible be stored separately. Success in the storage of such lots depends on whether they can be blown dry quickly and then kept dry. If there is also a great deal of soil between the potatoes, good storage becomes more difficult. Given good management, lots containing 5 to 10 % tubers affected with *Phytophthora* will keep well.

However, the situation is more difficult if the lot contains many tubers affected with soft rot. Such lots often keep much less well and the permissible limit is lower than for *Phytophthora* control (less than 1 % tubers). The same applies to lots including frozen tubers (check for this by cutting through a few tubers or scratching a tuber with a fingernail: frozen tubers do not make a snapping noise) or many glassy tubers ('water bags'). Such lots should if possible be stored separately and rapidly blown dry. Rapid drying can be facilitated, for example, by not stacking the potatoes up to the usual height.

Lots of potatoes which have become wet from rain after harvesting must never be stored with other potatoes even if there is no rot in them. These lots must always be stored separately, given intense ventilation and sold as quickly as possible; the keeping quality of such lots is very limited. In moving along the conveyor belt, the tubers become completely coated with wet soil and therefore often rot quickly. In changeable weather, trucks loaded with potatoes should preferably be covered with tarpaulins, particularly if the potatoes have to be transported over long distances.

It will not always be possible to avoid successive arrivals of wet and drier lots of potatoes over a short period. The consequences are usually not evident, but very wet lots with a great deal of soil clinging to them should preferably not be stored in the same compartment as dry lots. The air seeks out the path of minimum resistance, which will always tend to be through a dry lot with little soil adhering to the potatoes. This is likely to occur with the normal shape of the potato stack in a compartment. Where the store as a whole is loaded horizontally, this disadvantage does not arise.

The storage height of bulk seed potatoes must be limited to 3.0 to 3.5 m owing to the greater weight losses, which give rise to bruising problems at greater heights.

Ware potatoes can be stored to a height of 4 m given good management, but if substantial ventilation is necessary (e.g., to prevent soft rot or 'water bags'), the likelihood of bruising increases here too, especially in the spring. The same bulk height should be observed throughout the compartment. If there are 'hills and valleys', drying ('sweating points') and cooling are bound to be irregular.

If different lots of a single variety are combined, lots of the same quality should be stored together. For this purpose, the quality of the lots (dry matter content, susceptibility to black spot, etc.) must have been determined prior to lifting.

19   Drying of potatoes

P.H. Sijbring

19.1 Introduction

The drying of potatoes here means the elimination of surface water
from the tubers - i.e., the water present on the outside of the potato or
in the soil clinging to and other trash between the potatoes. This water
has to be eliminated because microorganisms can readily multiply in a wet
environment, thus potentially spreading rot and other storage diseases.
However, drying must be conducted in such a way as to minimize water loss
from the tubers.

19.2 The drying process

Drying entails simultaneous physical processes which influence each
other - viz., evaporation of water and heat transport.

19.2.1.   Evaporation of water

The water present on the tubers can usually be eliminated as water
vapour. The water is transformed into vapour and is removed as such with
the air. The degree of water evaporation is proportional to the difference between the vapour pressure of the water on the tuber and that of the
water in the air. The vapour pressure of the free water on the tuber surface depends solely on the water temperature. The higher the temperature,
the higher the pressure. The water vapour pressure of the air is proportional to the amount of water vapour in the air.

The term 'relative humidity' is often used. This indicates the quantity of water contained in the air as a percentage of the maximum quantity
of water which the air could hold. This latter quantity in turn depends
on the air temperature. The quantity of water vapour in the air is not
changed if the air is heated. The vapour pressure is also not changed.
However, the maximum quantity of water which the air can contain does
change. Warmer air can contain more water than cold air, so that the relative humidity of the air also changes.

When water is transported into the air, the water must first evaporate, after which it is absorbed by the air. A resistance to this process

has to be overcome. Since the water enters the air, the quantity of water in the air is increased, and so also is the water vapour pressure. The vapour pressure differential becomes smaller, causing the process to slow down. The faster the water is eliminated with the air, the faster the water will evaporate.

Heat is required to evaporate water. This heat of evaporation is drawn from the environment, thus causing the temperature to fall. The temperature of a wet surface may fall to a level far below the air temperature.

19.2.2 Heat transport

The air and the tubers usually have different temperatures. Because of this temperature difference, heat will flow from the tuber to the air or vice versa. The quantity of heat transported depends on the magnitude of the temperature difference. There is also a resistance to heat transport. The heat flux causes the temperature difference to become smaller, so that less heat flows. The faster the heat transferred to the air is eliminated, the more heat can be transmitted.

19.2.3 Relationship between heat and water transport

It is evident from the description of water and heat transport that both phenomena obey the same laws. The resistances to water and heat transport also vary to the same extent if conditions change. They both greatly depend on the air velocity around the tuber.
Once the free water has disappeared from the tuber, so that the latter is dry, the resistance to the transfer of water to the air will be greatly increased. Hence water evaporating from already dried potatoes must come from the tuber. The tubers have a natural resistance to excessive drying-out. Evaporation of water will not cease entirely, but will be greatly reduced.

19.2.4 Temperature distribution in the tuber

If heat is supplied to or withdrawn from a tuber, this occurs on the surface. The temperature on the surface changes. A heat flow from the inside of the tuber arises by virtue of this temperature difference. If a tuber is cooled, the outside of the potato will have a lower temperature than the centre of the tuber. The surface of the potato has a lower temperature than the average temperature of the inside of the tuber. The faster the rate of cooling, the larger this difference will be.

Potatoes are normally dried in the store, where they are piled in very thick layers. When air passes through a layer of potatoes, the air temperature and humidity will change. Each consecutive layer of potatoes is treated with air in which these parameters differ. The temperature and water content of the air change constantly on passage through the potato heap. The situation is also constantly changing in time, as the air absorbs or gives up heat and water in its passage.

19.3 Quantity of water eliminated

The quantity of water eliminated with the air is proportional to the quantity of ventilation air and the difference in water vapour content between the incoming and discharging air. The quantity of water contained in the incoming air is determined by the latter's temperature and relative humidity. With relatively thick layers of potatoes, the discharging air will, at least to start with, have the same temperature as the potatoes and will be almost saturated with water.
It makes no difference during this period whether the incoming air is heated or not, as the quantity of water in the air is not changed by heating and the discharging air retains the same temperature and humidity. Eventually the temperature of the air from the potatoes will change owing to the cooling of the potatoes. The relative humidity will remain virtually unchanged as long asthe potatoes are wet. If the relative humidity of the discharging air falls, this indicates that the potatoes are almost dry.
As long as the tubers are wet and the air is not saturated with water, or the air is heated by the potatoes, evaporation of water (drying) will take place. Heat is required for water evaporation. This heat is withdrawn from the tuber, which will therefore be cooled.
Cooling also occurs if the surface temperature of the tuber becomes lower than the air temperature. In this case, heat flows from the air to the tuber, which gives up heat required for evaporation of the water.
If the air is saturated with water, no evaporation will occur and the tuber will be heated by the air if the former is colder than the latter. Warm air can contain more water than cold air. Slight evaporation of water will occur in this case.

19.4 Examples of drying processes

In view of the difficulty of taking measurements in thick layers of potatoes, an attempt has been made to combine all the relevant processes in a mathematical model so as to calculate the course of the drying process.

Two cases have been compared. In both cases the initial temperature of the potatoes is 15 °C, the quantity of free water on the tuber being 5 g per kg of potatoes. The pile height is 2 m and the volume of ventilation air used is 150 m³/m³ potatoes · h. (This air volume is rather high. It results in the same air velocity as e.g., 100 m³ air/m³ potatoes · h for a pile with a height of 3 m. The examples have to be considered as the lower part of a thicker layer of potatoes with a lower rate of air.) The available ventilation air has a temperature of 5 °C and a relative humidity of 90 %. It is assumed that evaporation of water from the tuber (once the surface water had disappeared) is 1/50 of what it would be if there were free water on the surface of the tuber.

Example 1 (Figs. 1 and 2)

The ventilation air used is not heated in this example. The lowest potatoes have very quickly assumed the temperature of the air and are soon dry. These potatoes are ventilated with cold air of high humidity for the remainder of the drying period. They experience little drying-out. It is also found that the potatoes cool more slowly when the surface water has disappeared. There is a very evident kink in the cooling curve of the tubers at the point where the tubers become dry. The tubers are dry in about 6.3 hours. Water loss from the tubers is low (0.4 g per kg of potatoes). The average tuber temperature at the point when the tubers become dry is 8.25 °C.

Example 2 (Figs. 3 and 4)

In this example, the temperatures and humidities are the same as in Example 1, but the ventilation air has been heated to 15 °C. Here again, the temperature of the potatoes falls owing to evaporation of the surface water. The tubers are cooled. When the tubers have been rid of their free water, evaporation of water from them is only a fraction of its previous value, so that the tuber is reheated by the air. The already dried tubers are ventilated with warm air of low relative humidity for the remainder of the drying period.

Drying-out will be much greater in this case than without heating of the air. All the tubers are dry after about 7.1 hours. The average temperature of the potatoes at this point is 12.05 °C. Water loss from the tubers is much greater than in Example 1 - viz., 1.4 g per kg of potatoes. After drying, the tubers will have to be cooled for satisfactory storage, involving further water loss.

These examples show that it is preferable to dry the potatoes with unheated air. Cooling and drying can then be combined, thus minimizing

336

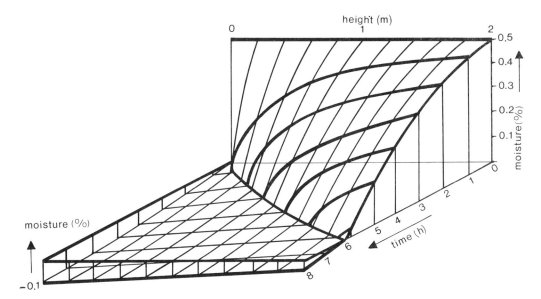

Fig. 19.1. Moisture content of potatoes during drying with air at 5 °C and 90 % relative humidity. The positive moisture contents represent water on the surface, while the negative values indicate water loss from the potatoes.

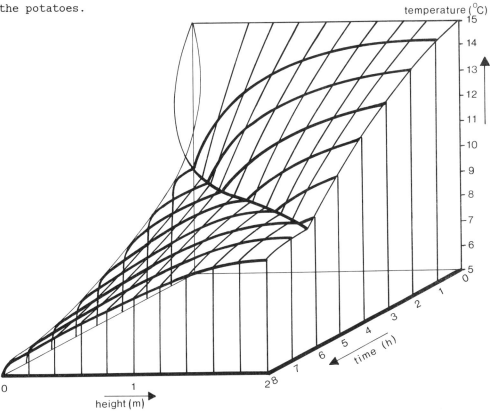

Fig. 19.2. Temperature of potatoes during drying with air at 5 °C and 90 % relative humidity.

337

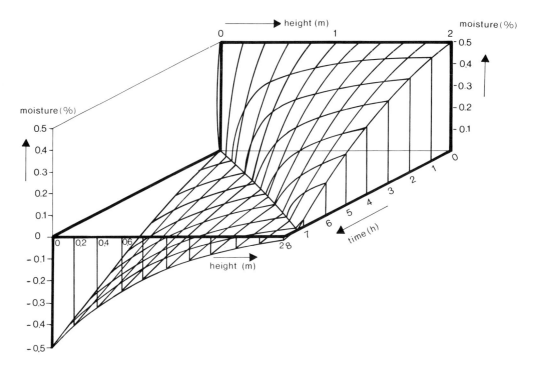

Fig. 19.3. Moisture content of potatoes during drying with air at 5 °C
and 90 % RH heated to 15 °C. The positive moisture contents indicate water on the surface and the negative values evaporation of water from the
tuber.

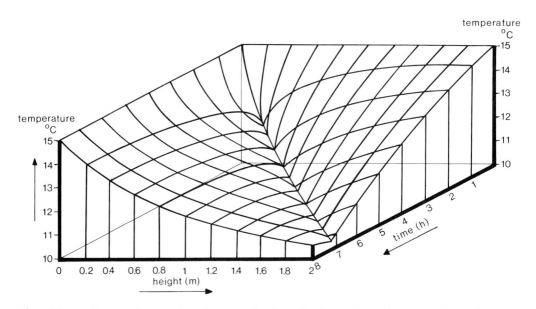

Fig. 19.4. Temperature of potatoes during drying with air at 5 °C and
90 % RH heated to 15 °C.

weight losses. In Example 1, drying is carried out with heat from the tubers.

If insufficient heat from the potatoes can be used, this technique will not be feasible. In other words, if the potatoes are cold - e.g., 5 % - drying will take a very long time, with ventilation using air at 5 °C and 90 % relative humidity. The same situation arises if a great deal of water is present on the tubers. In such case, a quantity of water will have been eliminated after a given time. All potatoes will be cold and water will still be present on them. There is no alternative to the use of heated air in such circumstances. However, it is then preferable to heat the air only slightly, and it is advisable to switch off the heating at the earliest sign of a fall in relative humidity of the discharging air, so as to limit weight losses in the bottom layers of potatoes.

The quantity of water which can be eliminated with unheated air depends on the permissible fall in temperature during the drying process. If it is possible to ventilate with air at low relative humidity and at a temperature not higher than that of the potatoes, the air need not be heated.

20   Wound healing

C.P. Meijers

20.1 Introduction

Some tubers are damaged to a greater or lesser extent during lifting
and transport and possibly also later on grading. The tuber tissue is
then exposed to external agencies through these damaged areas. Not only
are weight losses due to evaporation greatly increased; these damaged a-
reas also constitute points of entry for microorganisms such as *Fusarium*
spp. For this reason badly damaged lots are often found to keep less well
in storage.

Under favourable conditions, however, the tuber tissue is able quite
quickly to form a protective layer (wound periderm) over the damaged
area. A thin layer of suberized (corked) cells is first deposited over
the damaged area. Cork cambium (phellogen) then forms under the sealing
layer, giving rise from the inside to the outside to a dense network of
new cells without intercellular spaces, which set rapidly. This wound
periderm seems to be even more impermeable than the ordinary skin.

This curing process must obviously be promoted as much as possible to
limit weight losses and prevent the penetration of microorganisms. There
is in effect a competition between the rate of wound healing and the rate
at which microorganisms can penetrate.

A number of factors are known to influence the rate of wound healing.

20.2 Factors influencing the rate of wound healing

20.2.1   Type of damage

Smooth cuts in general heal faster and more uniformly than other types
of damage.

20.2.2   Temperature

Wound healing is appreciably faster at high than at low temperatures.
Partial wound healing is likely to take one or two weeks at temperatures
between 2.5 and 5 °C, but only four days at 10 °C and as little as one or
two days at 20 °C. Complete curing takes three to six days at 5 °C, one

or two weeks at 10 °C, but only three to six weeks at 20 °C.

[handwritten: DAYS?]

Wigginton (1974) found that the amount of wound tissue in four varieties tripled both between 5 and 10 °C and between 10 and 20 °C. The formation of wound periderm is delayed not only at low temperatures but also at very high temperatures. Artschwager (1927) found that corking was delayed at 35 °C.

20.2.3 Atmospheric humidity

The atmospheric humidity is also very important. No wound tissue appears to be formed at a relative atmospheric humidity of 30 %. The outer layers of cells then dry out to a crust, thus preventing or greatly delaying the formation of wound tissue.

On the other hand, a water-saturated atmosphere also appears to delay curing by proliferation of the cells on the surface of the wound. Fast healing is obtained at relative atmospheric humidities of 80 % or more. According to Wigginton (1974), a somewhat lower relative atmospheric humidity is offset by a higher temperature. At 20 °C he found hardly any difference at relative atmospheric humidities in the range 70 to 100 %, while a relative humidity between 80 and 100 % gave the best result at 10 °C.

20.2.4 Oxygen and carbon dioxide concentration

The work of Wigginton (1974) showed that wound healing does not occur under anaerobic conditions. Increasing the oxygen content from 0.01 to 0.21 m^3/m^3 increased both corking and periderm formation. High carbon dioxide concentrations (0.05 to 0.15 m^3/m^3) had a strongly adverse effect on wound healing even in the presence of sufficient oxygen (0.21 m^3/m^3).

20.2.5 Varietal differences

Although a number of workers have observed varietal differences in the rate of wound healing, these differences appear to be very small compared with the effects of temperature and relative atmospheric humidity.

20.2.6 Physiological age of tuber

The rate of wound healing, assuming comparable conditions, is fastest immediately after harvesting and gradually decreases during storage. In addition, differences are found to exist between individual tubers, also associated with the physiological condition of the tuber (Wigginton, 1974). This means that wounds caused after a certain period of storage - e.g., during grading - heal less quickly.

Sprout inhibitors prevent cell division and thus also slow down the process of wound healing. For this reason, (powdered) sprout inhibitors should never be applied directly after harvesting. Irritation of freshly abraded areas, in particular, gives rise to 'powder burn' after the application of these agents - i.e., the thick, tough skin which ultimately forms on these abrasions and is almost, or entirely, impossible to eliminate by steam peeling (see also Section 21.2.2.4).

20.3 Curing in practice

It is clear from the foregoing that temperature (i.e., the storage temperature) and also the relative atmospheric humidity are important determinants of the rate of curing.

A curing period of 10 to 14 d at 12 to 18 °C and a relative atmospheric humidity of 80 to 95 % are recommended for practical conditions in the Netherlands. It is essential for the lot to be and remain dry. The potatoes should be ventilated a little now and then during this curing period, to prevent the temperature and atmospheric humidity from rising too high. The storage temperature during the curing period must not be allowed to exceed 22 °C, one reason being to prevent additional respiration losses and to avoid the creation of highly favourable conditions for the spread of any fungus or bacterial diseases that may be present. This limited amount of ventilation will ensure that the condition of high relative atmospheric humidity is met.

In addition, the use of powdered sprout suppressants should be avoided in the storage of ware potatoes if rapid curing is to be promoted. It is preferable to apply liquid compounds by means of a Swingfog unit two or three weeks after the harvest (i.e., after curing).

Table 20.1 shows that a sufficient curing period is favourable in pre-

Table 20.1 Effect of curing period (days between harvest and start of ventilation) on weight loss

Ventilation		Weight losses (kg/tonne)			
Capacity	Beginning of ventilation (days	Number of days after harvest			
$(m^3/m^3/h)$	after harvest)	10	20	30	40
200	0	34	41	44	47
100	0	36	42	45	46
100	20	14	16	30	34

venting weight losses. In one of the three test situations, ventilation was begun only after 20 d; the weight losses observed in this case were much less than when ventilation commenced immediately.

When ventilation commenced after a 20-day curing period, weight losses did increase, but they remained over 1 % less than those in the other two cases; this difference remained relatively constant throughout the remainder of the storage period.

References

Artschwager, E., 1927. Wound-periderm formation in the potato as affected by temperature and humidity. J. Agric. Res. 35: 995-1000.
Wigginton, M.J., 1974. Effects of temperature, oxygen tension and relative humidity on the wound healing process in the potato tuber. Potato Res. 17: 200-214.

21 Sprout inhibition in ware potato storage

N. Buitelaar

21.1 Introduction

An important aspect of the storage of ware potatoes is sprout inhibition. Sprouted potatoes have various disadvantages both for the grower/owner and for the consumer/processor - viz., higher weight losses and softening of the potatoes. Soft potatoes are harder to peel, and difficulties are experienced in the chipping and crisping industry in cutting these potatoes into sticks and slices. Such potatoes are also more susceptible to damage and the occurrence of blue discoloration (black spot).

21.2 Sprout inhibition

There are a number of methods of preventing sprouting:
- temperature control
- chemical agents
- irradiation

21.2.1 Temperature control

A natural property of potatoes is that they do not sprout at temperatures below 4 °C. In regions where the temperature out of doors falls to 4 °C or lower, this property is utilized by cooling the potatoes with outside air. Where this is not the case, as in the tropics and subtropics, mechanical refrigeration must be used for longer-term storage.

In the Netherlands and in many other temperate-climate countries, potatoes are kept in modern stores cooled with outside air. Given correct control, the potato temperature in these stores can be kept at about 4 °C, but there must be sufficiently long periods when the outside air temperature is below 4 °C to allow a long enough period of ventilation. An examination was carried out to determine the period of the year during which the mean minimum temperature is below 4 °C in the Netherlands (Fig. 21.1). The necessary figures were obtained from the monthly weather statistics of the Royal Netherlands Meteorological Institute. This diagram shows that the mean minimum temperature in the Netherlands is below 4 °C from the beginning of November to mid-April.

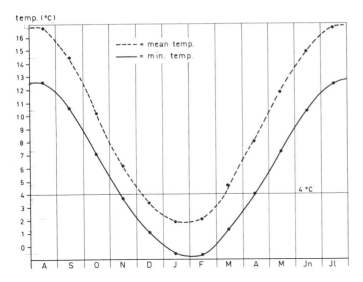

Fig. 21.1. Mean monthly temperature at five stations of the Royal Netherlands Meteorological Institute in the Netherlands (standard period 1931-
1960).

Given a correct programme of ventilation, it should therefore be possible to keep potatoes sprout-free until mid-April in well insulated air-
cooled stores in the Netherlands.

Cold storage is an attractive method from the environmental point of
view, but there are some disadvantages:
- Accumulation of reducing sugars; 'sweet' potatoes darken and then become less suitable, if not useless, for crisping and chipping.
- The required low temperature can be obtained by outside air cooling only until mid-April. Expensive mechanical refrigeration will be needed
  if the potatoes are stored for longer periods.
- Much more attention must be devoted to ventilation.
- After the potatoes have been heated prior to delivery, they will quickly sprout.

Having regard to the eventual application of the potatoes, the follo-
wing storage temperatures are now recommended:
- Ware potatoes: 4 to 7 °C.
- Potatoes for chipping and drying: 5 to 8 °C.
- Potatoes for crisping: 7 to 10 °C.
These storage temperatures necessitate the use of other sprout suppres-
sion agents or methods.

21.2.2 Chemical agents

The choice of chemical sprout inhibitors in the Netherlands is limited. The only practical and reliable agents which can be used are IPC (isopropyl N-phenylcarbamate) and CIPC (isopropyl N-(3-chlorophenyl) carbamate); IPC is also known as propham and CIPC as chlorpropham.

Other agents which inhibit sprouting or kill sprouts - e.g., maleic hydrazide (MH) and nonyl alcohol (nonanol) - are prohibited for use on potatoes in the Netherlands.

Compounds containing IPC and/or CIPC have proved to be very efficient in practice and remain active for a long period even at relatively high temperatures (e.g., 7 to 10 °C).

The use of sprout inhibitors has been controlled by law in the Netherlands since 1965. The residual content in washed, unpeeled potatoes may not exceed 5 mg/kg.

Potatoes delivered within a few months of harvesting must not be treated. Under normal conditions, potatoes must also not be marketed within a few weeks of treatment.

The propham and/or chlorpropham compounds fall into two groups: powders and liquids.

21.2.2.1 Powders

Under an agreement between the Netherlands public health authorities and the sprout suppressant manufacturers, powders intended for large-scale use may contain 10 g of active ingredient per kg of compound. To conform to the requirement as to residues, it is recommended that 1 kg of a compound, containing 10 g of active ingredient, be used per tonne of potatoes in potato stores. For ware potatoes stored in clamps, 2 kg may be used per tonne of potatoes. Lots to which powdered sprout suppressants have been applied may be treated only once with these compounds.

Small packs are available for domestic use containing a total of 5 g of propham and chlorpropham per kg of powder.

To obtain a satisfactory effect, it is essential for the compound to be applied at the correct time and to be accurately distributed.

A number of makes of powder are available on the market in the Netherlands. Powders are available in different degrees of fineness and colours to suit different applications. There are fine powders for blowing and coarser, heavier powders for dusting. Powders are available in the appropriate colours for treatment of white- and red-skinned varieties.

A Dutch manufacturer has since 1978 been marketing a crop protection agent which is a combination of a fungicide and a sprout inhibitor. This substance contains 20 g of thiabendazole (TBZ), 7.4 g of chlorpropham and 2.5 g of propham per kg of substance. Thiabendazole is used to control dry rot and silver scurf in both ware and seed potatoes. The combination of fungicide and sprout inhibitor means that the compound can be used in this form only for ware potatoes. A dose of 1.5 kg per tonne of potatoes is recommended in the instructions.

An advantage of treatment with powdered sprout suppressants is that the agent can be applied to the potatoes in a single operation which does not require excessive effort.

There are, however, the following disadvantages:

- Skin irritation may occur if insufficiently set (suberized) potatoes are treated with the powder. Although this was originally regarded as a mere surface blemish, it was later found to cause difficulty in peeling, increasing peeling and trimming losses.
- Although powders with the appropriate colours can be used for white- and red-skinned potatoes, some of the natural colour of the potatoes is nevertheless lost.
- There may be a dust nuisance when the store is emptied and during grading of the potatoes.

21.2.2.2 Liquids

Liquid sprouts suppressants can be atomized during the storage season with special equipment and distributed throughout the potatoes by means of the internal ventilation system. Compared with equal quantities of active ingredient in powdered compounds, both the effect and the residues of the liquids are smaller. For this reason more active substance may be used in the case of the liquid compounds, the maximum being 20 g of active ingredient per tonne of potatoes.

The liquid compounds are more highly concentrated, containing 250 g or more of active ingredient per liter. On the basis of the permissible amount of active ingredient, a total of 80 cm^3 of a compound with 250 g, 67 cm^3 of a compound with 300 g or 40 cm^3 of a compound with 500 g of active ingredient per liter of liquid may be applied per tonne of potatoes. This total permissible volume may be applied in one, two or three treatments as required. Good results are obtained by administering the total quantity in three treatments - e.g., 22 cm^3 per tonne of potatoes on each occasion for a compound containing 300 g a.i./l. If the sprouting potential of the potatoes is particularly high, it is recommended that the first dose can be increased somewhat and the subsequent ones reduced correspondingly.

To obtain an effective result, the first dose must be applied two or three weeks after the harvest. The potatoes have then completed their curing period and are set, so that damage (skin irritation) is unlikely. An appreciably less effective result is achieved if the first treatment is carried out later - e.g., if the eyes are already active or small sprouts are already present. Any subsequent treatments must also be carried out promptly; it is wrong to wait until sprouts are present before applying subsequent doses. Depending on the storage conditions and the sprouting potential of the potatoes, where the compound is applied in stages the second treatment should be performed in December or January and a third treatment, if required, in March or April.

A disadvantage of the liquid compounds is that they must always be applied at an early date - a point which is sometimes overlooked. Precipitation of the compound on the fan is another disadvantage; to minimize this problem, the compound should if possible be introduced into the internal ventilation system on the delivery side of the fan.

The liquid compounds have the following advantages:
- Where the compound is applied in stages, fewer treatments are necessary in the case of early delivery, so that less sprout suppressant is used.
- There is no dust nuisance as in the case of the powder.
- The potatoes retain more of their natural colour.
- Skin irritation is eliminated or greatly reduced in the potatoes, which have already set by the time of the first treatment.

21.2.2.3 Application of sprout inhibitors

Powders Accurate distribution of the powder is the fundamental requirement for an effective result. Good distribution is obtained if the powder is applied to the potatoes at the same time as the store is loaded by the conveyor belt. A perforated drum fitted above the conveyor is often used on farms to distribute the powder over the potatoes (Fig. 21.2). The drum is driven by the conveyor via an idler pulley. Powder applicators are used for larger quantities of potatoes. These units, whose powder bunkers have a capacity of 25 to 30 kg, must also be installed above the conveyor. An electric vibrator is fitted below the powder bunker to transport and apply the powder (Fig. 21.3). The drum capacity can be modified by closing off some of the perforations or increasing their number. In other types of equipment, the amount of powder to be applied can be controlled by enlarging or reducing the size of the opening of the metering slide or by changing the vibration rate.

Liquids Liquid inhibitors can best be used in air-cooled or mechanically refrigerated stores with facilities for internal ventilation. The compounds are atomized with special equipment and distributed over the potatoes through the internal ventilation system. Heavy equipment used to be used to atomize the liquids, the fog being forced between the potatoes using compressors, hoses and injectors. The equipment currently used to atomize liquid compounds - the Pulsfog and Swingfog units - is much more compact and manageable (Fig. 21.4). During the application of liquid compounds, the internal ventilation system must be in operation and must continue to operate until the fog has precipitated; this takes about a quarter of an hour after the treatment has finished. The doors and venti-

Fig. 21.2. Perforated drum driven by the conveyor belt.

Fig. 21.3. Powder applicator using an electric vibrator.

Fig. 21.4. Swingfog unit for atomization of liquid sprout inhibitors.

lation openings of the store must be properly closed during the treatment.

To allow the potatoes to absorb the compound, outside air ventilation must be avoided for two days after the treatment if possible (at least one day is essential).

To prevent precipitation of the compound on the fan, the compound should if possible be introduced to the ventilation system on the delivery side of the fan.

21.2.2.4 Skin irritation

A form of skin irritation may occur in potatoes treated with propham/ chlorpropham containing compounds, particularly if the inhibitor is applied before the skin of the potatoes has sufficiently set. In the most favourable case this form of damage gives rise to a red blister, which can still be removed by normal peeling. In badly affected tubers, grey/ brown cork tissue may be observed on the abraded skin (Fig. 21.5). Such tissue is very difficult to remove by steam, lye or mechanical peeling equipment. Final trimming of such potatoes requires a great deal of work and peeling and trimming losses are high.

Research has shown that this form of damage is most serious in potatoes treated with powders while still insufficiently suberized (Buitelaar, 1969).

Skin irritation is slight with liquid compounds applied after the skin has had time to form a cork layer, either in the ground or in the store.

The susceptibility of potatoes to this form of damage may vary as between different varieties. For example, the cv. Bintje is more susceptible than Eigenheimer. It is therefore important to allow the potatoes to set sufficiently in the ground before treatment with chlorpropham- and propham-containing powders.

350

Fig. 21.5. Tubers with severe skin irritation.

21.2.2.5   Cost of chemical sprout inhibitors

The price of these compounds varies substantially with the amount pur-
chased. On the basis of the maximum permissible dose, the cost of the
powdered and the liquid agents is about the same (approximately 1 Dutch
guilder or 0.5 US dollars per tonne of potatoes in 1978).

Since cooperatives or contract workers often treat potatoes with liquid compounds on a jobbing basis, this method is ultimately somewhat more expensive, particularly if a number of treatments are necessary.

However, compared with the price of the potatoes, the cost of treatment with sprout inhibitors - whether liquids or powders - is wholly negligible (less than 1 %).

21.2.2.6   Sprout inhibitors versus sprouting potential

The sprouting potential of seed potatoes and sowing seed can be greatly reduced and even totally eliminated by sprout inhibitors. Although
this has been pointed out repeatedly in published articles, every year
mistakes with serious consequences are still made.

To preserve the sprouting potential of seed for sowing and seed potatoes, these must not be dried, stored or kept in buildings or containers
contaminated with sprout suppressants for either long or short periods.
Fans which have come into contact with sprout suppressants must also not
be used for the ventilation, cooling or drying of this produce.

In addition to temperature control and chemical compounds, irradiation can be used to prevent the sprouting of ware potatoes during storage (Fig. 21.6). The principle of irradiation is prevention of cell division, so that the potatoes can no longer sprout.

The World Health Organization (WHO) gave its unconditional approval to the marketing of irradiated potatoes in 1976. A number of countries, including the Netherlands, have adopted this measure. The IBVL, together with the Institute for the Application of Nuclear Energy in Agriculture (ITAL), has conducted a large number of tests with potato irradiation, attention being devoted not only to sprout inhibition but also to the side-effects of irradiation. Both electron and gamma radiation was used in this research. Electron radiation penetrates only shallowly into the product, the depth of penetration depending on the energy of the electrons. For this reason, where potatoes are electron-irradiated, the tu-

Fig. 21.6. Illustration showing the sprout-inhibiting effect of different doses of gamma and electron radiation and of IPC/CIPC powder compared with untreated potatoes. A dose of 20 ppm powder was still recommended in 1967; the present recommendation is 10 ppm. Both doses have a good sprout-inhibiting effect.

bers must be fed under the radiation source in a single layer.

The produce must also be turned as it passes below the source to ensure that all sides of the tuber are exposed to the radiation.

Several years of research (Buitelaar, 1968) showed that 200 Gy (1 Gy =
1 gray = 1 J/kg) of electron radiation supplied by a source of maximum
electron energy 1.7 MeV (MeV = mega electron volt) is sufficient to keep
most varieties sprout-free over a long period of storage. This radiation
dose was found to be insufficient for the cv. Eigenheimer, also investigated in this research. The penetration of the electron radiation with a
maximum energy of 1.7 MeV was not enough to reach the deepest eyes adequately.

A lower dose of electron radiation does, however, have a temporary
sprout-inhibiting effect.

Gamma rays are extremely penetrating, so that the contents of large
boxes or cases can all be irradiated at the same time. It has been found
that the layer thickness with bilateral irradiation may be up to 80 cm,
owing to the ratio of the maximum to the minimum radiation dose D_{max}/D_{min},
which must not exceed 2. A gamma ray dose of 75 to 100 Gy is found to be
sufficient for sprout-free storage of most varieties.

The irradiation of potatoes may have a number of undesirable side-effects:
- increased *Fusarium* attack
- grey discoloration of potatoes after cooking
- increased reducing sugar content
- grey discoloration of prefried chips
- darker crisp colour.

The research carried out in the Netherlands concentrated on gamma irradiation compared with chemical sprout inhibitors and to a lesser extent on electron radiation. Except where otherwise stated, the following
discussion relates to gamma irradiation; this does not mean that it is
necessarily inapplicable to electron radiation, but insufficient is known
about this.

21.2.3.1 *Fusarium* attack

Wound healing is known to be delayed, if not entirely eliminated, by
irradiation. Damaged areas then constitute points of entry for microorganisms. Irradiated potatoes are affected substantially more by *Fusarium*
fungi than non-irradiated ones (Sparenberg & Buitelaar, 1970; Buitelaar,
1972b). In general, potatoes graded before irradiation are more susceptible to this disease than ungraded potatoes (Sparenberg & Buitelaar,
1970). With regard to the time of grading, it was not possible to show
clearly that the length of the curing period between grading and irradiation affects *Fusarium* attack. In some cases there is indeed a tendency

for the attack to be more severe the shorter the time elapsing between grading and irradiation (Sparenberg & Buitelaar, 1970).

To limit any increase in this storage disease, the number of handling operations - picking up, grading, transport, etc. - before, during and after irradiation must be kept to a minimum.

21.2.3.2 Grey discoloration after cooking

Irradiated potatoes turn grey faster and become more intensely grey after cooking than comparable potatoes treated with chemical sprout inhibitors. The appearance of cooked potatoes which have turned grey is very unattractive. The grey discoloration increases as the storage season progresses (Buitelaar, 1972a, b).

Potatoes treated with electron radiation also turn grey faster, and have a more intense grey colour, than chemically treated potatoes (Buitelaar, 1974b). The grey discoloration is less intense with electron radiation than with gamma rays, and remains at the same level throughout the storage season.

Reconditioning of gamma-irradiated potatoes for two or four weeks at 15 °C at the end of the storage period does not afford any improvement in the intensity of the grey discoloration (Sparenberg & Buitelaar, 1977).

21.2.3.3 Increase in reducing sugar content

Potato irradiation influences the content of reducing sugars (glucose and fructose). On average, this content is appreciably higher in irradiated potatoes than in potatoes treated with a chemical sprout inhibitor (Buitelaar, 1972a, 1971).

The biggest differences here are found at the beginning and end of the storage season.

High reducing sugar levels are a serious disadvantage for the crisping and chipping industry because the colour of the final product is too dark.

21.2.3.4 Grey discoloration of prefried chips

Prefried chips made from irradiated potatoes always show a moderate to intense grey discoloration (Sparenberg & Buitelaar, 1972; Buitelaar, 1974a). However, this grey discoloration is no longer evident when the produce has undergone final frying, although the final-fried product is often somewhat darker in colour than final-fried chips made from potatoes treated with a chemical sprout inhibitor.

Electron radiation appears to cause less intense grey discoloration than gamma radiation (Buitelaar, 1974b). For the section of the processing industry whose end product is prefried chips, moderate or severe grey discoloration means that the chips concerned are unsaleable.

21.2.3.5 Dark crisp colour

Potato irradiation is also found to affect the colour of crisps. The colour of crisps made from potatoes treated with both gamma and electron radiation is found to be darker until a few months after irradiation than that of crisps made from potatoes treated with a chemical sprout suppressant. Afterwards, the colour from the various sprout inhibitors become approximately equal. At the end of the storage season, the colour of crisps made from gamma-irradiated potatoes declines again to a critically low level, while that of electron-irradiated potatoes remains at the same level as that of potatoes treated with chemical sprout inhibitors.

These phenomena are in good agreement with the higher level of reducing sugars found at the beginning and end of the storage season in gamma-irradiated potatoes.

21.2.3.6 Practical possibilities for potato irradiation

The sprout-inhibiting effect of ionizing radiation is outstanding and cannot be surpassed by the chemical sprout inhibitors currently in use. Furthermore, the radiation leaves no residues. The cost of radiation treatment is much higher than that of chemical sprout control (Sparenberg & Ulmann, 1972b).

The undesirable side-effects of irradiation are unfortunate. As long as their cause is not established and eliminated, or as long as the consumers' requirements for cooked potatoes and potato products do not change, the chances for practical application of this method of sprout control seem to be slight.

References

Buitelaar, N., 1968. Kiemremming door middel van bestraling bij consumptie-aardappelen. IBVL-Publikatie 178.
Buitelaar, N., 1969. Het kiemvrij bewaren van consumptie-aardappelen. IBVL-Publikatie 204.
Buitelaar, N., 1971. Bewaarproeven met bestraalde aardappelen op semi-praktijkschaal (1969/1970). IBVL-Mededeling 371.
Buitelaar, N., 1972 (a). Bewaarproeven met bestraalde aardappelen op semi-praktijkschaal (1970/1971). IBVL-Mededeling 397.
Buitelaar, N., 1972 (b). Bewaarproeven met bestraalde aardappelen op semi-praktijkschaal (1971/1972). IBVL-Mededeling 400/ITAL-Rapport 6.

Buitelaar, N., 1974 (a). Verwerking van bestraalde aardappelen tot pommes frites en chips II. IBVL-Mededeling 422.

Buitelaar, N., 1974 (b). De kook- cn verwerkingskwaliteit van met elektronenstralen behandelde aardappelen. IBVL-Mededeling 426.

Sparenberg, H. & N. Buitelaar, 1970. Bewaarproeven met bestraalde aardappelen op semi-praktijkschaal (1968/1969). IBVL-Publikatie 229.

Sparenberg, H. & N. Buitelaar, 1972. Verwerking van bestraalde aardappelen tot pommes frites en chips. IBVL-Mededeling 394.

Sparenberg, H. & N. Buitelaar, 1977. Can reconditioning prevent the after-cooking darkening of irradiated potatoes? (1976/1977). IBVL-Publikatie 307.

Sparenberg, H. & R. Ulmann, 1972. Spruitremming van aardappelen door bestraling in Nederland; economische en commerciële aspecten. Informatiebulletin 58 van Bureau Eurisotop.

22 Protection of produce

C.P. Meijers

22.1 Introduction

In the discussion of the diseases and defects which may arise during the storage of potatoes (Chapter 6), it was pointed out that almost all microorganisms prefer a moist, warm environment for optimum growth.

Apart from avoiding damage (damaged areas constitute points of entry), it is therefore desirable to aim first of all for dry, cool storage to prevent fungal or bacterial attack.

However, weather conditions during lifting and storage in the Netherlands are sometimes such that these conditions cannot be satisfied. At the beginning of the storage period in particular, potatoes are often kept under warm and relatively moist conditions. It is then possible for certain diseases to spread.

The use of certain chemical compounds on seed and ware potatoes has been allowed in the Netherlands since 1977. These compounds, the benzimidazoles, have proved to be very helpful in combating certain fungal diseases. The compounds have no effect on bacterial diseases.

If the compounds are correctly applied, silver scurf and dry rot are very well controlled.
They also have perceptible effects on skin spot and gangrene (Logan et al., 1977; Logan & Copeland, 1976).

The benzimidazoles are also useful in preventing the spread of *Rhizoctonia* disease during storage. However, the doses recommended after lifting are quite insufficient to inactivate the sclerotic form of this fungus.

22.2 Benzimidazoles

The benzimidazoles are systemic agents, which means that they can be transported in the tissue. They do not work in the form of vapour, so that the compound has to be distributed very carefully. The active agent of Carbendazim, Benomyl and Thiophanate-methyl is BMC (benzimidazole carbamate methyl ester). Thiabendazole differs in some respects from the other benzimidazoles, in that it cannot be broken down to BMC (Schreurs, 1976). The benzimidazoles are found to affect cell division in the fungi.

357

The action of all these compounds is the same in the doses stated.

In 1980, the following benzimidazole formulations were permitted in the Netherlands in the doses stated (Table 22.1).

Table 22.1 Types of benzimidazoles, formulations and doses.

Type	Formulation	Recommended dose (g active ingredient/tonne)
Thiabendazole	Flowable paste; wettable powder, dusting powder; dusting powder with IPC/CIPC	30
Carbendazim	Wettable powder; flowable paste	30
Benomyl	Wettable powder	25
Thiophanate-methyl	Flowable paste, wettable powder	70

22.2.1 Time of application

Research both in the Netherlands and abroad has shown that the best results are obtained on application immediately after the harvest - i.e., when the store is filled. This applies particularly to silver scurf, as this disease can spread very quickly in storage conditions favourable to the fungus.

However, treatment at the time of lifting is also to be preferred to treatment on or after grading, for example to control dry rot, which usually occurs only after a few months of storage (but after only two or three weeks if the potatoes are re-stored after grading).

22.2.2 Methods of application

Various methods of application have been compared since the introduction of these compounds. Application by a Pulsfog unit and by means of smoke tablets was found to be not only expensive but also not readily feasible in practice in most cases (Meijers, 1980). The results were also found to be inferior to those of spraying. The latter method was found to be good, simple and inexpensive. Some practical experience has been recorded with the use of wettable powders. Very small quantities of liquid have also been tested. These methods are discussed below.

22.2.2.1 Spraying

Tubers are sprayed mainly with the flowable pastes and to a lesser extent with wettable powders. The product is diluted with water and 0.5 to 2 l of this suspension is applied per tonne of potatoes.

Extra attention is required in the preparation of the wettable powders. It is best to use hand-hot water and to start by adding only sufficient water to make a slurry; this can then be further diluted. The
amount of compound to be applied to obtain the recommended dose varies;
the instructions on the pack should always be consulted.

The tubers are sprayed at the end of the bin filler. Two spray nozzles
of a given type will usually be necessary for even distribution of the
liquid; where the discharge capacity is low, a single nozzle may suffice.
The nozzles must be installed 40 to 50 cm behind and a little above the
bin filler belt, in such a way that the direction of the spray cones follows the slope of the potato stack (Fig. 22.1). As a result the tubers
rolling down the slope are regularly moistened and no compound is lost.
The spray cones must not moisten the belt, as soil on the belt may otherwise cake together, possibly causing belt failure.
This is also liable to happen if the nozzles are positioned earlier on in
the discharge line. Although checking is then facilitated, in addition to
the danger of soil caking, the compound will also often not be optimally
distributed over the tubers. The tubers must roll during the treatment,
and this is always more or less the case at the end of the bin filler.

The type of spray nozzle must conform to the quantity of potatoes passing through the bin filler per unit time. It is therefore necessary to
know approximately how many tonnes of potatoes enter the store per hour
or per minute. However, a variable quantity of potatoes can be treated,
within limits, with a single nozzle by adjusting the pressure. It is also

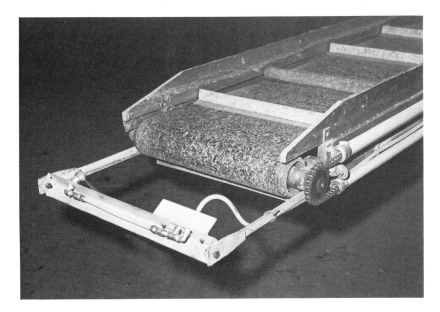

Fig. 22.1. The tubers are sprayed at the end of the bin filler (proto-
type IBVL).

essential to control the volume of liquid discharged by each nozzle per minute. This is the only way to ensure the application of the required quantity of liquid per tonne and to ascertain the relevant pressure.

The following points must be observed during and after spraying:

- Ensure that a fine mist is obtained; it is best to use a type of nozzle which requires a minimum pressure of 350 to 400 kPa to supply the necessary volume of liquid per tonne of potatoes.
- Make sure that the conveyor belt is loaded uniformly. This can be facilitated by ensuring that the feed hopper remains full. The hopper transport mechanism must therefore be stopped quickly after the tipper is empty.
- Shut down the sprayer as soon as potato transport along the conveyer stops. If this is not done, excessive wetting will occur locally in the stack, causing rot if drying is too slow. Safety systems to limit the delivery of liquid if the flow of potatoes decreases are now commercially available.
- Move the binfiller regularly from side to side while the bin is being filled. Since the supply of potatoes is often reduced when loading the top of the bin, the volume of liquid should preferably then be somewhat reduced (by lowering the pressure), or the flow should be halted altogether. Drying take place more slowly at the top of the compartment than at the bottom.
- After the bin has been filled, the lot must be blown dry immediately. If it takes several days to fill the store, forced-draught drying should preferably also be carried out in the interim. If the drying time is to be reduced for any reason, this can be done by using a larger fan. If conditions are extremely unfavourable at the time of lifting, so that the lots are very wet when loaded, and the air transport capacity of the fan is also on the low side, it is worth considering reducing the volume of liquid to 0.5 to 1 l/tonne. Of course, the dose must be varied so that 30 g of active substance is administered per tonne.
- Try to minimize the volume of liquid left in the spray tank at the end of the day, as the compound precipitates out and is sometimes difficult to put back into suspension on the following morning. The wettable powders usually settle out somewhat faster than the flowable pastes, but they can more readily be finely distributed again by vigorous stirring than the flowable compounds. In the last few years, however, considerable attention has been devoted to the stirrability of the liquid compounds. After settling and stirring, there is more chance of clogging of the spray nozzles, because the distribution obtained is usually not so fine.

Where 2 l/tonne of potatoes is used, the risk of soft rot (or more soft rot) is increased to some extent, particularly if the lot on lifting

360

already includes some tubers affected with soft rot (mother tubers), if mistakes are made in treatment or if the potatoes were not blown dry quickly enough. The application of 2 l/tonne of potatoes is perfectly in order in 'healthy' lots.

Following complaints by users that rot was increased where 2 l/tonne was applied, it was investigated whether less liquid could be used without inferior results. There were indications in Germany that less good results were obtained if the volume of liquid was reduced below 2 l/tonne (Leppack & Neumann, 1978). Research in the Netherlands, however, showed that comparable results were obtained in a test lot with little soil whether 0.5 or 2 l/tonne was used (Table 22.2). The use of four nozzles (two directly above and in front of, and two below, the soil screen of the bin filler) did not give better results than two nozzles at the end of the filler.

In practice, successful results are obtained with about 1 l/tonne.

Table 22.2 Results of test in 1979/1980; compound: Lirotect flowable, 30 g active ingredient/tonne.

Treatment	Silver scurf (% affected tuber surface)
2 l liquid/tonne - 2 nozzles	4
0.5 l liquid/tonne - 2 nozzles	3
0.5 l liquid/tonne - 4 nozzles	3
spinning-disc atomizer - small[1]	6
spinning-disc atomizer - large[1]	7
Untreated	20

1. Dose a little too small

22.2.2.2 Atomizing

It is possible to use even less than 0.5 l/tonne by atomizing the liquid compound diluted 1:1 with equipment designed for the purpose. This equipment is unsuitable for atomizing suspensions made from wettable powders, as the nozzles are clogged. In one type of equipment, a compressor is used to pressurize the liquid in a stainless steel tank, from which it is conveyed to four special atomizing nozzles. This unit is supplied with a metering system.

Another type of atomizer makes use of the paint spray principle. Compressed air entrains the aspirated liquid and distributes it extremely finely. The mist is so fine that with both types of equipment a certain area must be screened off to prevent drifting. The volume of liquid applied by this equipment is 100 to 200 ml/tonne. Provided that the units are used correctly, the distribution of the compound over the tubers is very good. The risk of more rot is negligible.

22.2.2.3 Spinning-disc atomizer

A spinning-disc atomizer enabling the liquid compounds to be applied undiluted (50 to 140 ml/tonne) has been developed in Germany. The compound is fed from a tank through a hose to a rapidly rotating disc, which distributes the compound extremely finely. The slightest breath of wind or draught blows the mist away, so that the equipment is protected by a kind of tent. To prevent drying of the undiluted liquid on the disc when the unit is not in use, a small quantity of water with washing-up liquid is pumped from a second tank to the disc to clean it after the machine is shut down. The capacity of the spinning-disc atomizer was originally insufficient for use when loading the store and was only suitable for installation on a lifting machine as is the practice in Germany. A unit suitable for Dutch conditions, with a capacity of up to 80 tonnes/h, was tested later. Reasonable results were obtained with this unit (Table 22.2), which is incidentally very expensive. As with the misters described earlier, the tubers must rotate during treatment, otherwise the compound will not be distributed uniformly. Obviously, there is no risk of rot where a spinning-disc atomizer is used.

22.2.2.4 Dusting

There is only one compound for application by this method: a dusting powder with a thiabendazole content of 20 g/kg. To obtain 30 g of active ingredient per tonne of potatoes, 1.5 kg/tonne must be applied. Even distribution of the compound is very important. Manual administration can give good results, but is in practice very difficult where large quantities are concerned. In practice, the facilities also recommended for administering powdered sprout suppressants (vibrators and rotating perforated drums) are therefore used. These are positioned above the conveyer belt, where most of the soil has already been removed. Although the powder may not be distributed optimally in this way, users have expressed satisfaction with the results. However, a serious disadvantage is that particularly large quantities of dust are observed when the store is emptied. For this reason this type of product will probably be used only where rot problems are expected.

Research has also shown that the results obtained with dusting powders are equivalent to those of spraying (Table 22.3).

A dusting powder with not only a thiabendazole content of 20 g/kg but also an IPC/CIPC content of 10 g/kg can also be used for ware potatoes.

362

Table 22.3   Results of test in 1977/1978.

Treatment	Dose of TBZ (g active ingredient/tonne)	Silver scurf (% affected tuber surface)	Dry rot (kg/tonne)
TBZ dusting powder	30	4	0.2
TBZ + IPC/CIPC	30 (+ 10)	4	1.0
Flowable' (spray)	30	4	0.4
Untreated	-	23	48.0

If it is applied directly after lifting, the points specified in connection with the use of powdered sprout suppressants must be observed: problems of skin irritation may arise when these agents are used on ware potatoes. Research is in progress to determine whether skin irritation is less probable when TBZ and IPC/CIPC are combined, as is claimed by practical users.

22.2.3   Residues

When benzimidazoles are applied, residues remain on and, to some extent, in the tuber. The permissible limit for these compounds in the Netherlands is 3 mg/kg in the washed, whole tuber. Research carried out since 1973 shows that residual levels are almost always less than 1.5 mg/kg, even shortly after treatment. A high proportion of this is in turn eliminated on peeling, so that the amount of compound in the edible part of the tuber is usually undetectable or virtually so.

22.2.4   Resistance

The repeated use of systemic agents, such as the benzimidazoles, may make the fungi resistant. This is not hitherto known to have occurred when these products are used on potatoes. Again, since only one treatment per season is carried out, the likelihood of resistance is probably not very great. However, to exclude even this small possibility it is recommended that high-grade (élite) seed potatoes should not be treated with these compounds, but only seed potatoes intended for growing ware or for export.

References

Leppack, E. & F. Neumann, 1978. Die Technik der chemischen Bekämpfung von Fusarium bei Kartoffeln. Der Kartoffelbau 7: 238-240.
Logan, C. & C.B. Copeland, 1976. Gangrene control with TBZ using the

Newforge Potato Mister. Proc. 12th Annual Conf. PCIRG.

Logan, C., C.B. Copeland & W.G. Little, 1977. Potato storage disease
control. Agr. in Northern Ireland 52 (3).

Meijers, C.P., 1980. Bestrijding van bewaarziekten bij aardappelen.
Bedrijfsontwikkeling 11 (7/8).

Schreurs, J., 1976. Control of fungal diseases of potato tubers with TBZ.
Proc. 12th Annual Conf. PCIRG.

23 Temperature control during storage

A. Rastovski

Temperature is the principal factor affecting the quality of potatoes and losses during storage. Temperature influences both the metabolic processes of the potatoes (respiration, sprouting, sweetening, etc.) and the activity (virulence) of microorganisms. Moisture loss, loss of dry matter and losses through sprouting, as well as undesirable changes in chemical composition and the spread of diseases, are greatly affected by the temperature of the potatoes.

Extremely high and extremely low temperatures - i.e., above 30 to 35 °C and below 0 °C - may even kill the potatoes.

Successful potato storage is therefore largely a question of controlling the temperature of the potatoes during storage (Chapter 14). However, the optimum storage temperature depends on the quality of the potatoes as they are loaded into the store, as well as on the eventual purpose for which the potatoes are to be used (fresh consumption, processing into potato products, seed, etc.) and the duration of storage.

Storage losses are generally greater at higher temperatures, the higher the storage temperature, the shorter the period for which potatoes can be stored.

The optimum temperature for long-term storage of potatoes is generally in the range 3 to 10 °C. In most cases the ambient temperatures differ from these optimum storage temperatures. To allow the optimum temperature of the potatoes to be maintained during the storage period, the potatoes must be kept in well insulated stores. A store must also have an efficient ventilation system for temperature control and for elimination of surplus moisture.

When potatoes are loaded into the store, their temperature is usually higher than the optimum storage temperature. This temperature ranges between 12 and 18 °C in temperate climates, but is usually much higher in warm climates, 30 °C or even higher being by no means exceptional.

The skin of freshly lifted potatoes is usually poorly corked. The potatoes also receive wounds during harvesting and transport and when the store is loaded. These potatoes are therefore highly susceptible to infection by disease and very quickly lose moisture.

To limit moisture losses and infection by microorganisms, it is desirable to stimulate corking of the skin and wound healing in the initial period after loading of the store. This is known as the curing or wound healing period. Wound healing is dealt with in Chapter 20. The optimum temperature during the curing period is 10 to 20 °C. Higher temperatures encourage rapid growth of pathogenic microorganisms, thus greatly increasing the danger of the spread of disease. For this reason the temperature of the potatoes should be reduced to less than 20 °C as quickly as possible after loading or even during loading of the store. This will always involve high moisture losses, as the freshly lifted potatoes lose moisture much faster than well corked tubers. In such a situation, however, these losses must be weighed against much higher potential losses due to rotting at high temperatures.

For this and other reasons, moisture losses from potatoes in warm climates will generally be higher than in temperate climates. To limit moisture losses, it is desirable for the humidity of the cooling air to be kept as high as possible. Storage costs in warm climates are also thereby increased, as large quantities of heat must be eliminated in a short time for rapid cooling of the warm, freshly lifted potatoes. This calls for refrigeration facilities of high installed capacity, making the equipment of the store more expensive.

If the potatoes enter the store with a great deal of surface water, this free moisture should be eliminated as quickly as possible - i.e., the potatoes must be dried. At the same time the temperature of the potatoes should not be allowed to fall below 10 °C during drying, so as to stimulate corking while drying takes place. The potatoes should preferably be dried with colder and relatively humid air to avoid high moisture losses (Chapter 19). High ventilation capacity will usually be needed for this purpose.

The potatoes must be cooled to the required temperature after drying and the curing period. Cooling of potatoes always involves evaporative moisture loss.

The moisture loss from potatoes during cooling is determined by the duration of cooling and by the vapour pressure difference between the potatoes and the air - i.e., by the relative humidity of the air. The moisture loss can thus be limited by rapidly cooling the potatoes with very humid air. If the potatoes are cooled with outside air, the cooling rate depends solely on the volume air flow through the potato heap. High cooling capacity is not expensive in this case. However, a high installed refrigeration capacity costs a great deal of money in a mechanically refrigerated store; in this situation the installed refrigeration capacity will depend on cost-benefit considerations.

Once the desired storage temperature has been attained, this need only be maintained for the rest of the storage season. During this time the potatoes need to be ventilated only in order to maintain the storage temperature and to keep the surface of the tubers dry. The temperature differences in a heap of potatoes intended for processing should not exceed 1 to 1.5 °C during this period.

Before the store is emptied, the potatoes are usually heated to 12 to 18 °C to minimize damage during unloading, grading and transport (Chapter 24).

Efficient temperature control is the main condition for preservation of the quality of the potatoes and for limiting weight losses during storage. This demands not only a well equipped store but also good management.

24 Heating of ware potatoes

C.P. Meijers

24.1 Introduction

The susceptibility of potatoes to black spot is a serious problem in some years, and both the potato trade and exporters then experience great difficulty in selling their produce. If highly susceptible tubers are incorrectly handled, they may become seriously affected with blue discoloration. When the potatoes are lifted, due account must therefore be taken of such factors as tuber and soil temperature and minimization of falling height, and weight losses during storage must also be limited as far as possible.

A very important measure to reduce tuber susceptibility to black spot is vigorous heating before the potatoes are removed from the stores. They must be heated to a temperature of 12 to 18 °C depending on how susceptible they are. As susceptibility to blue discoloration generally increases during storage, a somewhat higher temperature will be necessary later in the season.

24.2 Heating

If potatoes have to be heated, heat must be supplied to them. Potatoes produce some heat themselves through respiration, but the amount is relatively small, so that it would take too long for the required temperature increase to be achieved.

The only way of transferring heat from a given source to the potatoes is via air. The volume of air that can be used for heating is determined once and for all by the fan capacity, which is also available for cooling.

When bulk potatoes are heated, the opposite process to that occurring during cooling (Section 9.2.4) takes place.

In exactly the same way as is described in that section for cooling, Businger's (1954) method of calculation can be used to determine the theoretical temperature reached in a given position and at a given height after a specified heating period.

An example of the theoretical variation of temperature in a potato stack is set out in Table 24.1.

368

Table 24.1 Theoretical course of temperature (°C) in a potato stack. Potato temperature 5 °C; air temperature 20 °C (according to Businger's calculation).

Heating time (h)	Layer heights above ground level (m)				
	0.25	1	2	3	3.5
4	18.1	8.8	5.0	5.0	5.0
8	19.6	15.2	8.0	5.0	5.0
12	19.9	18.7	12.8	7.6	6.8
16	20.0	19.6	17.5	11.8	9.4
20	20.0	20.0	18.7	16.1	13.6
24	20.0	20.0	19.4	17.8	16.7
28	20.0	20.0	20.0	19.7	19.1

The following assumptions are made for this purpose:
- The potatoes are stored to a height of 3.5 m.
- The fan capacity is 100 m³/m³ potatoes / h (0.028 m³/m³·s).
- The temperature of the potatoes everywhere in the stack is 5 °C, the air blown in being at a constant 20 °C.

The table shows that the potatoes at the bottom of the store quickly attain the temperature of the blown air. The higher up the stack, the longer it takes before the heating has any effect. The air emerging from the top of the potato stack increases somewhat in temperature only after a heating of about 10 h. In theory, it takes over 30 h for the potatoes at the top to reach 20 °C. Since the storage compartments are never air-tight, heating will in practice take even longer. A further 50 to 100 % must be added to the theoretical time depending on the prevailing conditions.

The table also shows that it takes a long time for a uniform temperature to be attained throughout the stack. It is therefore appropriate in practice to accept a certain temperature difference in the stack. In the example above, with heating to 20 °C, it would be best to terminate the heating process when the potatoes at the top have been warmed to a temperature of about 17 °C. It might be possible to make the temperature more uniform by internal ventilation.

There is little point in heating the air to a higher temperature than that required in the potatoes, as those at the bottom of the store will then become too warm and little time will have been saved.

Substituting an air temperature of 25 °C in the example, a temperature of 19 °C will in theory have been attained at the top of the stack after 21 h instead of after 28 h. By then, however, the potatoes will have been heated to 25 °C up to a height of more than 2 m if the blown air was at a constant 25 °C.

Condensation usually forms on the surface of the cold potatoes during heating. This moisture re-evaporates as the potatoes are heated if the dew point of the air is lower than the final temperature to which the potatoes are heated.

24.3 Heating methods

A good air distribution system is essential for heating potatoes. The potatoes can be heated by the following means:
- warm outside air
- oil and gas heaters to heat the air

24.3.1 Warm outside air

The simplest, safest and cheapest method is the use of warm outside air. Very few days are warm enough in the Netherlands during the storage season, but there may be some days in autumn and spring when the outside temperature rises considerably above that of the potatoes. A perceptible effect may be expected if the outside temperature is at least 4 to 5 °C higher than that of the potatoes. Although this does not provide sufficient heating, it is nevertheless a start, and costs little.

24.3.2 Oil and gas heaters for air heating

The air will always have to be heated artificially in winter. In practice, oil and gas heaters are used for this purpose. Oil heaters are used on a large scale in agriculture, not only to heat potatoes but also for drying cereals.

There are heaters with (Fig 24.1) and without (Fig. 24.2) flues to remove the combustion gases. The latter type are most commonly used, but have the disadvantage that the carbon dioxide and water vapour formed on combustion are blown with the warm air through the potato stack. Hence, if these heaters are also used in an enclosed space, the potatoes may become wet and an oxygen deficiency may arise. The reduced oxygen concentration and increased carbon dioxide content of the air may give rise to black heart in the tubers; however, the levels at which this becomes a serious risk are not known. Black heart is observed in a few cases almost every year, often because the blown air was too hot.

Both types of heaters, of course, require sufficient fresh outside air for combustion of the oil.

Internal circulating air can be used without problems for heaters with flues, but not with non-flue heaters. A quantity of fresh outside air must always be heated in this case, and air must also be able to escape from the top of the potato stack. Hence the capacity required must be

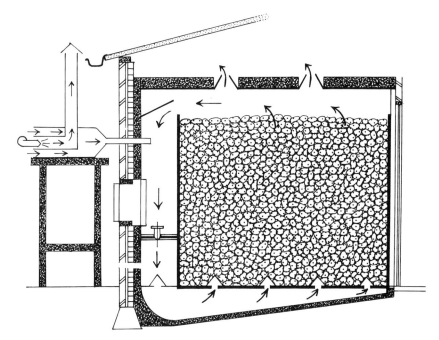

Fig. 24.1. Oil heater *with* removal of combustion gas.

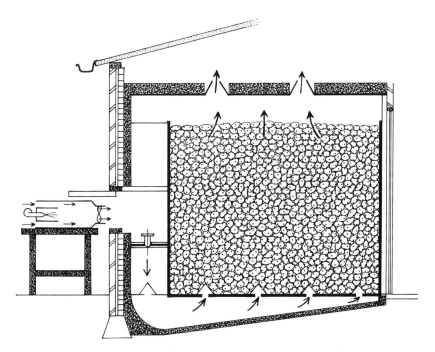

Fig. 24.2. Oil heater *without* removal of combustion gas.

rather higher with non-flue heaters than with flue-type heaters (about 1800 and about 2300 kJ/h per tonne of potatoes).

The heater capacity can be calculated as follows. To increase the temperature of 1 kg of air (0.8 m³) by 1 °C, 1 kJ is required. Hence, to heat the air from 5 to 20 °C, 1/0.8 x 15 = 18.75 kJ is required per m³ of ventilation air. If the air is to be heated by only 10 °C, the required capacity is only 1/0.8 x 10 = 12.5 kJ.

The air displacement capacity of the fan must also be known. The recommended fan capacity in the Netherlands is 100 m³ of air per m³ of potatoes per hour at 15 mm wg - i.e., 140 m³ air/tonne. If a bin contains 80 tonnes of potatoes, the heater will have to be rated at about 58.3 kW (approx. 50 000 kcal/h) on the basis of the air displacement capacity mentioned. For a temperature increase of 10 °C, the heater rating need only be about 39 kW (33 500 kcal/h), the other parameters being the same.

24.4 Heating rate

Potatoes can be heated quite rapidly without problems, provided that the temperature of the heated air does not exceed 22 °C. Black heart may occur at temperatures of just above 30 °C even in the presence of sufficient oxygen. The interior of the tuber then evidently receives insufficient oxygen. To avoid this risk, the air should preferably not be heated above 22 °C. A higher temperature is not necessary and in any case affords only a slight time saving, as shown earlier.

Slow heating (in steps of, for example, 3 to 4 °C) has some advantages over rapid heating:
- A smaller-capacity heater is sufficient (lower capital cost).
- There is less risk of mistakes (cooked potatoes or black heart).
- Blue discoloration may be less of a problem if the potatoes are kept for a somewhat longer period at a higher temperature.
- Owing to the lower temperature differences, rather less condensation may form in the potato stack.

The weight loss will be hardly, if at all, less with slow than with rapid heating, since the heating period is longer. However, there is not always enough time for slow heating. Where faster heating is required, the right approach is higher fan capacity rather than higher air temperatures.

24.5 Use of thermostats

To prevent the air from being heated excessively, a thermostat is required and must be positioned in the air duct behind or below the fan. The thermostat must be set to 20 to 22 °C. The heater capacity is adjusted to the set temperature or the heater is shut down. If internal air circulation is used (this is possible with flue-type heaters), the air will

heat up constantly after about 10 h if no thermostat is used. Let us assume that the heater raises the air temperature by precisely 15 °C, the
initial temperature of the potatoes being 5 °C. As Table 24.1 shows, the
temperature of the air emerging from the top of the stack will increase
gradually only after about 10 h. If the heater then adds a constant 15 °C·
to this internal circulation of air, the temperature of the blown air after one day will be about 30 °C, and black heart may, as stated, then be
a problem. The use of a thermostat is therefore strongly recommended, and
will also help to balance the possibly unequal capacities of the fan and
heater.

24.6 Fan and heater capacities

If a high-capacity heater is placed in front of a small fan, the air
will be heated excessively, so that the potatoes at the bottom of the
stack will be quickly brought to an excessively high temperature (Table
24.2). The values set out in Table 24.2 are based on an initial air and
potato temperature of 5 °C. The fan capacities mentioned relate to bins
for approx. 50, 70, 105 and 140 tonnes of potatoes respectively. The
small heater does not provide the required heating with large fans, but
the larger heater may only be used in bins of not less than 130 tonnes.

Table 24.2   Temperature of blown air (°C) at different
fan and heater capacities (constant outside air
temperature of 5 °C).

Heater capacity (kW)	Fan capacities (m^3/H)			
	5 000	10 000	15 000	20 000
23.26	18.3 [1]	11.7	9.3	8.3
46.52	31.7	18.3	14.0	11.7
93.04	58.3	31.7	22.7	18.3

[1]. Calculation: $23.26 \div (\frac{5000}{3600} \times 1.25 \text{ kJ}) + 5 °C = 18.3 °C$

                (heating)   (outside air temperature)

If the outside air temperature is -5 °C, the table shows that the temperature increase is 10 °C less.

24.7 Practical hints

Oil being expensive, potato heating is a costly business. Every effort must therefore be made to minimize heat losses, by, for example, blocking up chinks, etc., as far as possible.

Where potatoes are stored in a large barn, the space around the stack must be reduced, e.g., by placing plastic sheeting 1 to 2 m above and in front of the stack. This must not seal off the potatoes hermetically, as the heater must be able to obtain sufficient oxygen. The heater's air intake must always be outside the enclosed space. The fire risk must also be considered. A problem may arise if only a part of the potato stack is to be heated; this often occurs in large stores. There is usually no objection to keeping the potatoes at a temperature of 12 to 15 °C for three weeks or so provided that sprout suppressants have been applied at the appropriate time and in the correct dose. If the unloading of a large store is likely to take longer than this, it can perhaps be partially heated by installing a partition - e.g., using insulated tarpaulins - on the ceiling. The part which is not to be heated will require extra cooling, as its temperature is likely to be affected to some extent. Partial heating of a potato stack is, of course, possible only if there are separate air distribution systems.

Reference

Businger, J.A., 1954. Luchtbehandeling van produkten in gestorte toestand. Verwarming en ventilatie 11: 31-35.

25 Chitting of seed potatoes

C.P. Meijers

25.1 Effect of chitting

Chitting means the production of sprouts in various stages of development on the tubers for a short period before planting. In normal weather conditions, well developed sprouts (1.5 to 2.5 cm) will give smooth,
regular emergence, early tuberization and a plant with moderate foliage
development giving a good early crop. Such seed is said to be physiologically old (Fig. 25.1). Well chitting seed potatoes are particularly suitable for growing seed and early ware potatoes - i.e., in general, where
the growing season is short. If chitting is limited or not carried out
at all, emergence and tuberization will usually take longer than with
well chitted sets, the delay being longer the less the tubers have been
chitted. Foliage development is, however, then more vigorous, while the
yield is barely, if at all, less than in the case of good chitting provided that the plant can mature fully (Table 25.1). Such seed is said to be

Fig. 25.1. Well chitted seed potatoes.

Fig. 25.2. Limited chitting (short white sprouts).

Table 25.1 Effect of degree of chitting on total yield in 1970 and 1971
in early and late varieties.

Lifting date	Group of varieties	Chitting	Total yield (tonnes/ha) 1970	1971	Average	Average number of stems per 100 plants
		Well chitted	22.1	39.3	30.7	289
16 July	I	Rapid heating	17.3	35.3	26.3	354
		Unchitted	13.6	27.2	20.4	346
		Well chitted	16.5	33.0	24.7	354
21 July	II	Rapid heating	14.3	31.1	22.7	380
		Unheated	12.0	25.4	18.7	379
		Well chitted	61.1	57.2	59.1	-
Mature	I	Rapid heating	59.2	57.2	58.2	-
		Unchitted	58.8	51.2	55.0	-
		Well chitted	57.0	51.2	54.1	-
Mature	II	Rapid heating	55.2	49.4	52.3	-
		Unheated	54.3	45.0	49.6	-

Varieties in Group I: Bintje, Spunta, Ostara and Humalda
Varieties in Group II: Saturna, Woudster, Mentor, Prominent and Prevalent
Planting dates: 1970: 5 and 6 May; 1971: 14 and 15 April

physiologically young (Fig. 25.2). This more limited chitting is used
mainly for normal growing of ware potatoes and potatoes for the processing industry - i.e., in general, when the growing season is long. In
spring, physiological age in one and the same variety may vary in accordance with weather conditions during the growing season and the storage
temperature. Tubers of high physiological age can be obtained by warm
storage, possibly coupled with de-sprouting. If weather conditions after
planting are less favourable, however, these tubers, which are often already rather soft, may give inferior results owing to the occurrence of
little potato. Planting 'cold' straight from a refrigerated store without
any form of preliminary chitting is extremely undesirable, as the time-
lag in emergence, even if the tubers are allowed to mature fully, cannot
be made up and the yield will be less than that of seed which has had
correct preliminary treatment (Table 25.1).

This table clearly shows that good chitting is essential in the growing of seed potatoes; the shorter the growing season, the greater the
difference in yield.

Good chitting practice requires the sprouts to be properly 'greened'
so that they can withstand knocks during planting without breaking off or
being damaged. This greening is effected by exposure to daylight or artificial light. In general, sufficient daylight gives better greening than
artificial light.

25.2 Number of stems

The number of stems developing from a set largely determines the size
of the tubers. If there are many stems, there will normally also be many
tubers, although they will be smaller; and vice versa. In growing seed
potatoes, a large number of not excessively big tubers are required. The
aim will therefore be a large number of stems per m^2; the usual recommendation is at least 30 stems per m^2. Big tubers, on the other hand, are
required for table and processing potatoes, for which fewer stems are
therefore desirable; the usual objective here is 15 to 20 stems per m^2.

The number of stems per set depends very much on variety, but can be
influenced to some extent by the type of preliminary treatment (Table
25.1). To obtain a small number of stems, the storage temperature should
be moderate to high (6 to 8 °C). At first, only an apical sprout usually
develops. A few lateral sprouts will develop if the apical sprout is removed. Cold storage followed by rapid heating (18 to 20 °C) favours the
formation of a large number of sprouts, the number usually increasing the
later in the storage season the heat treatment is given (i.e., the closer
to the time of planting). This is a nuisance as regards growing, as good
chitting is essential for growing seed and heating must therefore com-

mence early on (middle or end of February). Heat treatment just before planting is now a virtually obsolete practice.

With well chitted seed, a reasonable estimate can be made of the number of primary stems to be expected. For this purpose, the well developed sprouts with root primordia must be counted. The small sprouts also present on the tuber can be disregarded. While the sprouts are still very small - e.g., after warming - it is almost impossible to predict the eventual number of primary stems.

Sprouts are often damaged on planting. If a single sprout breaks off completely, a new one will not grow in its place. If all the sprouts break off, about the same number of new sprouts will develop, but the growth of the plant will, of course, be delayed. If the tip breaks off (a common form of sprout damage), this will usually have the same effect on a small sprout as complete detachment. But if the sprout was well developed, damage to the tip will often cause it to branch. Two primary stems then arise, but their development is slower and less vigorous than that of an undamaged sprout. For the sake of completeness, it should be noted that the number of stems per m² can also be influenced by the size of set (a larger tuber gives more stems) and, of course, by planting density. In otherwise identical conditions, more stems develop in light than in heavy soils.

25.3 Chitting methods

A number of methods of chitting are commonly used in the Netherlands. It is impossible to describe them all in detail here, and instead three main groups will be discussed, the method of obtaining the required form of sprouting being specified.

25.3.1 Only a few well developed sprouts required (for very early ware crops)

The seed must be stored sprout-free from the time of lifting until November, either in bulk or in bags. The seed potatoes are then kept in planting trays at 6 to 8 °C. As soon as the sprouts are about 5 mm long, the process of chitting should be continued in daylight or artificial light.

25.3.2 Many well developed sprouts required (for growing seed and fairly early ware)

The seed potatoes (either loose or in bags) should be stored as sprout-free as possible until the middle or end of February, the optimum temperature being 3 to 5 °C. The tubers then undergo rapid heating to

18 to 20 °C. Any apical sprouts must be removed before the heat treatment, as fewer sprouts will otherwise grow from the lateral eyes owing to apical dominance.

The length of the storage period ranges from a few days to one or two weeks and depends greatly on variety as well as other factors. As soon as most tubers have one or more short, white sprouts about 5 mm long, the storage temperature must be reduced to 6 to 10 °C and the seed exposed to daylight or artificial light for hardening until the date of planting. A hardening period of at least four or five weeks is desirable, and this must be allowed for in connection with the beginning of the warming treatment and the planned planting date. Condensation must be avoided during the heat treatment, as uneven sprouting is possible if the seed potatoes and their containers become wet. A little ventilation should be provided occasionally. For details of heating, see Chapter 24.

25.3.2.1 Chitting trays

To ensure good chitting, the seed should be kept in chitting trays, which may be of wood or of plastic. The trays must not be too full - not more than 1.5 to 2 layers of tubers per tray.

Sufficient daylight or artificial light must be able to reach the tubers during chitting for the purpose of hardening and to prevent the sprouts from growing too long. For this reason the number of rows of trays standing side by side must be limited so that there are no areas which receive too little light. Where daylight is used, up to three or four rows will normally be permissible, provided that the daylight can reach them unimpeded. There should be not more than two rows beside each other with artificial light.

Fig. 25.3. Glass seed potato store.

379

Hardening can be carried out as follows:
- In a special glass seed potato store (Figs. 25.3 and 25.4).
- In a glassbarn (Fig. 25.5).
- In a barn with a large number of transparent polyester panels.
- Outside in daylight, under transparant plastic sheeting (Fig. 25.6).
- Outside on pallets or farm wagons, possibly under plastic sheeting (Fig. 25.7).
- Indoors in dark rooms with sufficient artificial light (Fig. 25.8)
  (1 fluorescent tube for every 4 to 5 m², 40-Watt rating, colour 33).

Where transparent plastic sheeting is used out of doors, the trays should be laid out in two or three rows, 40 to 50 cm apart, 10 to 12 trays high. The long sides must always remain covered with sheeting; the short sides are kept open except in inclement weather (e.g., night frost). The recommended sheeting is PVC (thick, 0.15 mm) or polyethylene (0.10 to 0.15 mm thick; liable to tear in the wind). The sheeting can be prevented from flapping by securing the stack with nets or strong ropes. This method is generally used in the Netherlands from the beginning of March (in the south west of the Netherlands and along the coast) or mid-March (in the rest of the country). If the short sides are sealed off early enough (late afternoon) a night frost of -3 to -4 °C can be withstood without

Fig. 25.4. Chitting trays in a glass seed potato store.

Fig. 25.5. Glassbarn.

problems. To prevent the tubers in the topmost trays from being 'cooked' at high daytime temperatures and from freezing in the event of severe night frost after precipitation, a roof-shaped wooden frame should preferably be placed on top of the two or three rows of trays. The plastic sheeting placed over it can then no longer touch the top layer of trays and some ventilation remains.

For artificial light chitting, the fluorescent tubes must be positioned so that there is only one row of trays on either side of each line of lights (Fig. 25.9).

It might be possible to use a smaller number of fluorescent tubes by repositioning them every day.

Outdoor chitting in planting trays on pallets or farm wagons has the

Fig. 25.6. Chitting in daylight, under transparent plastic sheeting.

Fig. 25.7. Chitting on pallets.

advantage that they can be moved back indoors in bad weather. Seed potatoes must not be allowed to remain wet for long periods, as roots may
then form; and if the weather is dry immediately after planting, emergence may then be adversely affected.

25.3.2.2 Plastic bags

Wide-mesh plastic bags can in principle also be used for chitting,
but a number of points then require close attention. It is best to place
the bags out of doors in twos, diagonally opposite each other, to maximize the access of light and air. To ensure that all sets receive sufficient light, the bags should be turned round or over a few times. If the
sprouts are insufficiently greened and grow too long, many will break off
when the bags are emptied.

25.3.2.3 Pallet boxes

In the last few years, seed potatoes have come to be chitted in the
Netherlands in wooden boxes containing 500 to 1000 kg. The seed should
preferably be graded and disinfected early on and then ventilated with
outside air on a main duct with openings corresponding with the pallets
under the boxes, the storage temperature being 5 to 8 °C. As soon as significant sprouting occurs, the boxes are turned out, the contents of one

382

Fig. 25.8. Chitting indoors in dark room with artificial light.

box being transferred to another using a forklift, hoist or fore-loader with a box tipper.

Many sprouts then break off or are damaged. Box-to-box transfer is repeated as soon as the sprouts have again grown to a length of 1 to 2 cm. If there are still no sprouts by mid-February, the tubers are subjected to rapid heating. Very few sprouts will survive this treatment, but those that do will eventually become very tough. They will also form a number

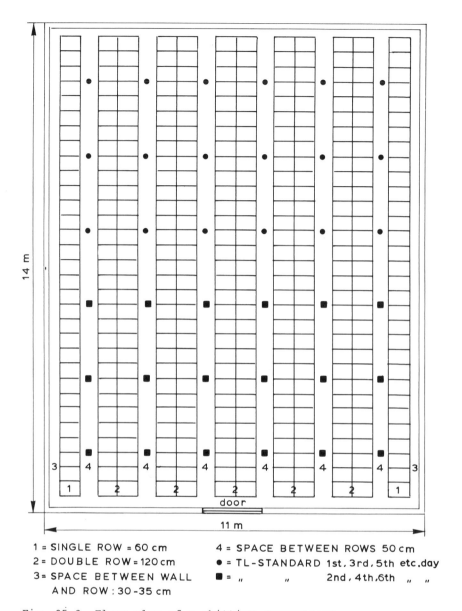

1 = SINGLE ROW = 60 cm   4 = SPACE BETWEEN ROWS 50 cm
2 = DOUBLE ROW = 120 cm   ● = TL-STANDARD 1st, 3rd, 5th etc.day
3 = SPACE BETWEEN WALL   ■ = „   „   2nd, 4th,6th   „   „
     AND ROW : 30 -35 cm

Fig. 25.9. Floor plan of a chitting compartment.

of lateral shoots, so that there are usually just as many stems as when
the seed is chitted in planting trays. Yields are very similar to those
obtained when the seed is chitted in trays.

Repeated turning-out may give rise to *Fusarium* rot, as this fungus may
infect the tubers through the broken-off sprouts. So if the lot includes
any rotten tubers, this treatment is inadvisable, as more tubers may be

384

affected. However, the risk of *Fusarium* attack can be greatly reduced by application of a benzimidazole compound.

Some experience has been gained with the Blackburn chitting box in the Netherlands. This consists of a framework of angle irons with 15 cm wide netting baskets between them. An open space about 8 cm wide is left between the baskets to admit light. The box can accommodate about 500 kg of seed potatoes.

However, light access has been found to be insufficient, so that too many white sprouts which easily break off are formed. The boxes are also expensive, and will therefore probably not become very popular.

25.3.3 *Short white sprouts only required (growing of ware and processing potatoes)*

To avoid the problems of too many sprouts and a consequently large number of smaller tubers, a chitting method without the rapid heating treatment is often used for ware and processing potatoes. The seed material for this type of produce is frequently stored in bags in refrigerated compartments. To ensure good, regular emergence, the sets must have 'started' - i.e., small, white sprouts must be present - at the time of planting (mini-chitting). Sprout breakage on planting will then be slight. To achieve this without warming, the seed is removed from the storage compartment three or four weeks before planting or the refrigeration is shut down and the temperature in the compartment allowed to rise slowly to 7 to 8 °C. This warming period may be shorter if sprouting has already commenced. If planting is delayed, sprouting will then not proceed so rapidly; if the grower has a refrigerated compartment, the seed can if necessary be returned to it, the storage temperature preferably then not being below 5 to 6 °C. If the seed is found to have long, white sprouts about a week before planting, it is usually best to remove these. Short white sprouts will again have formed by the time of planting. Sprout removal at such a late time before planting is inadvisable in weakly sprouting varieties of advanced physiological age.

If for any reason cold-stored (3 to 4 °C) seed potatoes are not removed from the storage compartment until just before planting, an attempt must be made to 'start' the sets by rapid heat treatment, which can be limited to a few days only. It is always very undesirable to plant 'cold' seed material. However, heat treatment may be somewhat risky if planting has to be postponed; sprouting is then difficult to control.

TRANSPORT AND FINISHING OPERATIONS

26 Damage to potatoes

P.H. de Haan

26.1 Introduction

One of the most important aspects of transport and handling is preservation of the quality of the produce - in particular, minimization of damage to the potatoes. Of course, efficient use of the relevant equipment is also important, and the aim will be minimization of unit costs. Clearly, it will in practice often be necessary to compromise so as to satisfy the conflicting requirements as well as possible. In the eventual decision, different degrees of importance will have to be attached to the individual requirements. The nature and function of the enterprises will also play a part in this decision.

26.2 Damage

To obtain a better impression of damage and to investigate the various agencies which cause it, it is useful to classify the different forms of damage in accordance with their nature and severity. The classification of Hesen & Kroesbergen (1959) is used for this purpose. The first distinction to be made is between external and internal damage.

26.2.1 External damage

The following types of external damage can be distinguished:
- Cuts. If a piece of the tuber has been completely cut off, this is called a cut. Damage of this kind occurs only when the tubers are lifted. It will therefore not be discussed further here.
- Skinnings. Tubers whose skin has set (suberized) insufficiently at the time of lifting may be abraded to a greater or lesser extent during lifting, transport and any subsequent handling operations. Skinnings may also occur on transport and handling after storage, but these skinnings are usually slight (Figs. 26.1 and 26.2).
- Flesh wounds. If pieces have been knocked out of the tuber, flesh wounds arise. Damage of this kind hardly ever occurs in handling and transport.
- Cracks. Cracks may occur both at the time of lifting and during trans-

Fig. 26.1. Slight skinning of the potato tuber.

port and handling. When it occurs during transport and handling, this type of damage is almost exclusively due to falls and impacts (Figs. 26.3 and 26.4).

26.2.2 Internal damage (blue discoloration or black spot)

A tuber may be bruised internally (Fig. 26.5) without any external damage being evident (both forms of damage may also be present). The cell walls of the tuber tissue are broken down, the damaged tissue almost always being discoloured owing to enzymatic processes in the presence of oxygen. Discoloration is not yet evident immediately after the damage oc-

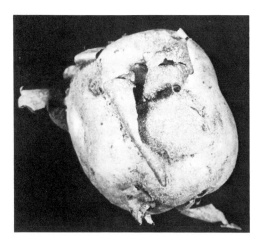

Fig. 26.2. Severe skinning of the potato tuber.

Fig. 26.3. Tuber with cracks (slight).

curs. The intensity of the discoloration increases with time, reaching a maximum after two or three days. The discoloration is not always the same. Sometimes the colour is grey and sometimes brownish, but it is usually a more or less intense blue - hence the name blue discoloration. The damage may be slight, moderate or severe.

26.2.3 Consequences of damage

- External damage. This has the following important consequences:
    Damaged tubers are more liable to attack by microorganisms (fungi and bacteria).

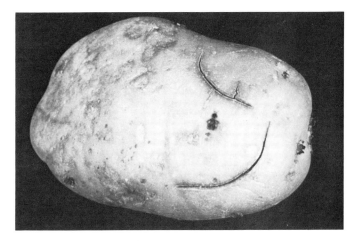

Fig. 26.4. Tuber with cracks (moderate).

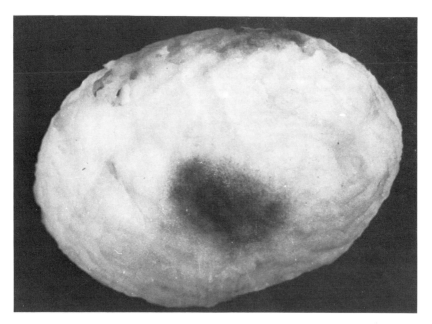

Fig. 26.5. Black spot (visible after peeling).

　　. Damaged tubers (with skinnings, cuts, flesh wounds and cracks) lose
　　　more water until the wound has suberized (higher weight losses).
　　. Additional labour is required to remove damaged tubers (sorting
　　　costs) (De Haan, 1974).
　- Blue discoloration (internal bruising). Since blue discoloration or
　　blackspot can normally be identified only after peeling, it is not pos-
　　sible to remove the affected tubers from a lot of unpeeled potatoes
　　(this can only be done if external damage has also occurred). In the
　　processing industry in particular (chipping, peeling, etc.), a lot af-
　　fected with blue discoloration gives rise to extra costs for elimina-
　　tion of the damaged tubers or parts of tubers.

26.2.4 Factors affecting the extent (degree) of damage

　　The extent of damage during transport and handling operations is determined both by the susceptibility of the tuber to damage and by the
manner of transport and handling.

26.2.4.1 Determinants of tuber susceptibility to damage

　- Varietal characteristics. Varieties are known to differ in their sus-
　　ceptibility to both external damage and blue discoloration.

392

- Growing and harvesting conditions. A number of factors - e.g., type of soil, fertilizer application and weather conditions - may play a part during growth. At harvest, the susceptibility of the crop to damage may be influenced by, for example, whether or not the skin has set sufficiently and by soil temperature.
- Conditions during storage and when the storage compartment is unloaded This is again a matter of blue discoloration; weight loss and bruising are relevant here. On removal from store, the tuber temperature is an important determinant of susceptibility to blue discoloration.

Note: It is evident from the above that potato lots may differ substantially in susceptibility to both external damage and blue discoloration. This means that the degree of damage increase may vary considerably for different potato lots on one and the same transport and handling line. This must be taken into account in assessing such lines in terms of potato damage.

External damage and blue discoloration have certain points in common as well as certain differences.

Both types of damage are caused by the effects of mechanical forces on the tuber and lots of potatoes may differ in their susceptibility to both external damage and blue discoloration.

The factors determining susceptibility to external damage are largely quite different from those determining susceptibility to blue discoloration.

- External damage. Since cuts and flesh wounds hardly ever occur in transport and handling, they will not be considered further here. Susceptibility to abrasion immediately after the harvest often depends on the setting of the skin, but varietal characteristics and other factors are also relevant. Susceptibility to cracks may be attributable to varietal differences, but factors such as tuber temperature and hardness may also be important.
- Blue discoloration (internal bruising). Since this subject has already been discussed in Chapter 6, the only factors to be dealt with here amont the many which determine susceptibility to blue discoloration are tuber temperature and weight loss.

Since the determinants of susceptibility to external damage are often quite different from those of susceptibility to blue discoloration, the following situation may arise in practice:

A lot of potatoes displaying little external damage after handling and transport may nevertheless be substantially affected by blue discoloration. Conversely, a lot with considerable external damage may have little blue discoloration.

Another important difference is that external damage can be seen on the outside immediately after it has been caused. Blue discoloration is not immediately visible after it has taken place but becomes evident only after two or three days, and even then the tubers have to be peeled or cut through to reveal it. Determination of the susceptibility to blue discoloration with a shaker apparatus before the potatoes are transported is important if unpleasant surprises are to be avoided.

26.2.4.2. Technical determinants of the extent of damage

When the tubers are transported and handled, it is impossible to prevent them from falling or sustaining impacts at certain points (e.g., on transfer from one belt to another, when filling storage compartments or boxes, etc.).

The extent to which a tuber is damaged (assuming constant susceptibility) is determined by the mechanical force exerted on the tuber; in the case of falling, it may also be said to be determined by the amount of energy which the tuber has to absorb at the end of the fall (De Haan, 1967, 1970). The following points are relevant:

- Falling height. The damage will obviously increase the greater the falling height (Figs. 26.6, 26.7 and 26.8).
- Conveyor belt speeds. The faster the tuber falls or strikes against an object, the greater the damage will be. At a given height of fall, it therefore makes a difference whether the tuber was stationary at the beginning of the fall (free fall) or already had a certain speed. In the latter case the speed at the end of the fall is higher and the damage will be greater. In practice, the tubers virtually have a certain speed at the beginning of a fall. This speed is imparted to the potatoes by the conveyor belt from which they fall. The belt speed should therefore not be too high.
- The impact surface. If the surface is hard (metal or wood), the tuber must absorb all the energy. If it is soft and springy (e.g., padding), the material can absorb part of the energy.
- Tuber weight. A large tuber must absorb more energy at the end of the fall than a small one. In otherwise identical conditions, a large tuber will therefore sustain more (and more serious) damage than a small one.
- Specific gravity of tuber. As a rule, tubers of high specific gravity (.i.e., with a high dry matter content) sustain more blue discoloration damage than tubers of a low specific gravity.
- Tuber temperature. A tuber at low temperature (e.g., 4 to 6 °C) is more susceptible to blue discoloration than one at a higher temperature (15 to 20 °C).

26.2.5 *Measures to limit damage*

- Heating of tubers. An important method of reducing blue discoloration is to heat the tubers. This is discussed in detail in Chapter 24. It may

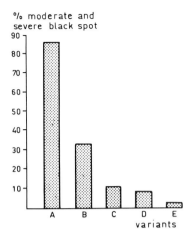

% moderate and
severe black spot

Black spot damage as a result of dropping tests

Variety	size (mm)	temperature (°C)	surface
A Woudster	55/65	4 - 6	wood
B Bintje	55/65	4 - 6	wood
C Bintje	35/45	4 - 6	wood
D Bintje	55/65	18 -20	wood
E Bintje	55/65	4 - 6	wood covered with soft material (3 cm foam)

Results: The conclusion is rather clear. A compared with B: the variety Woudster shows more black spot than Bintje (both varieties grown and stored under the same conditions) C compared with B: the smaller size (less tuber weight) is less damaged. D compared with B: the higher tempe-rature of the tuber diminishes the susceptibility to black spot. E com-pared with B: the soft material has protected the tuber.

Fig. 26.6. Some tests concerning black spot damage.
I Dropping height constant.
Variation in: variety, size, temperature of the tubers and nature of the surface.

II Tubers are the same.

Variety: Bintje; weight class: 60 to 80 g; temperature of the tubers: 20 °C. Variation in dropping height: 0.5, 1.5 and 2.5 m.

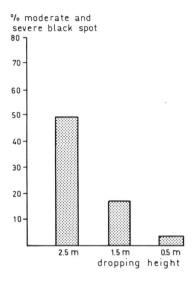

Black spot damage as a result of dropping the tubers from different heights.

Result: the effect of the dropping height is clearly shown.

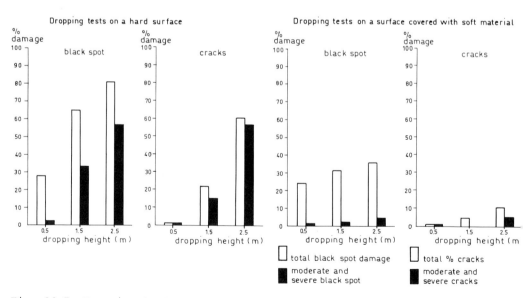

Fig. 26.7. Dropping tests on a hard surface resp. on a surface covered with soft material.

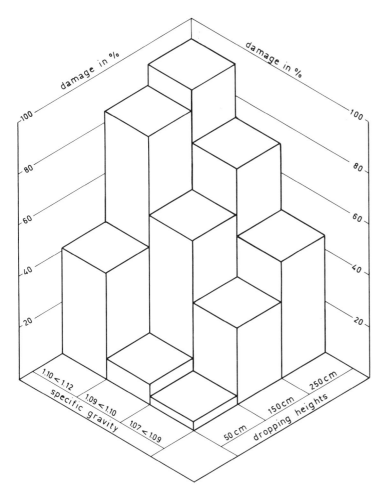

Fig. 26.8. Moderate and severe black spot damage due to dropping. Weight
class of the potatoes: 40 to 60 g; temperature of the tubers: 4 to 6 °C.

also be pointed out that the potatoes must not only be kept at a sufficient temperature while in store but that this temperature must also be
maintained throughout the transport and handling operations (loading,
unloading, grading and packing) if the full advantage of heating is to be
obtained. Again, even where all the measures discussed below are taken,
the tubers must be sufficiently warm to start with if the benefits of
the other measures are to be maximized.
- Limitation of falling height. Falling heights must be minimized; they
should never exceed 40 cm. If greater heights have to be catered for, as
when filling compartments or bunkers from the top, filling trucks, boxes,
etc., efficient and properly designed facilities should be used - e.g.,
'downward-travelling' conveyor belts (with entraining plates), chutes or
decelerating channels, box fillers, etc.

- Low belt speed. Belt speed should not exceed 30 m/min (0.5 m/s). High transport capacity (Fig. 26.9) must therefore be obtained not by a faster belt speed but by heavier loading (per unit length). This means either a wider belt or a thicker layer of potatoes on the belt.
- Use of padding. Padding materials are very effective in limiting damage. Hard surfaces on to which potatoes fall can be clad with soft padding material. Plastic or rubber foam give good results provided that the surface is protected by a layer of sheeting (loose or fixed) to minimize caking and smearing. Soil caked on the sheeting must be removed regularly.
- Limitation of number of falls. The number of times a tuber must be minimized. Particular attention must be devoted to this point in the design or enlargement of a system.
- 'Soft' transfer from belt to belt. Right-angled bends on transitions must be avoided where possible, especially on transfers from a horizontal belt to a sloping conveyor. The transition from an elevator to a horizontal belt should preferably be by way of a 'kinked' belt because the fal-

Fig. 26.9. Wide belt with high entraining plates.

Fig. 26.10. Monitoring system of a modern central sorting and grading plant.

ling height is less. Where right-angled transitions cannot be avoided, it is essential for the potatoes not to strike against a lateral structure on falling.
- Organization. Blue discoloration does not arise until one to three days after the damage is caused. Advantage can be taken of this delay, which is in fact utilized in practice. If the potatoes are processed (in the processing industry) within 24 hours of removal from store, any blue discoloration caused will as yet hardly have become evident, if at all. This, however, requires extremely efficient organization of unloading, transport, grading and despatch (De Haan, 1973a, b; De Haan & Van Zwol, 1975).

Figure 26.10 shows the monitoring system of a modern central sorting and grading plant in the Netherlands.

References

Haan, P.H. de, 1967. Oriënterende proeven over de invloed van de valhoogte en het gebruik van beschermingsmaterialen op de beschadiging van aardappelen. IBVL-Publikatie 172.
Haan, P.H. de, 1970. Beschadiging van aardappelen tengevolge van transport en bewerking. IBVL-Publikatie 217.
Haan, P.H. de, 1973. Invloed van de valhoogte, het knolgewicht, het soortelijk gewicht en de knoltemperatuur op de blauwbeschadiging en het barsten van aardappelen. IBVL-Mededeling 414.
Haan, P.H. de, 1973. Toename van blauwbeschadiging bij de verwerking van aardappelen. Bedrijfsontwikkeling 4 (2).

Haan, P.H. de, 1974. Enkele beschouwingen omtrent de invloed van het percentage uitval bij aardappelen op enige kostenfactoren bij de bewerking. IBVL-Publikatie 266.

Haan, P.H. de & B.H. van Zwol, 1975. Remgoten en chutes bij aardappeltransport. IBVL-Publikatie 278.

Hesen, J.C. & E. Kroesbergen, 1959. Mechanische beschadiging van aardappelen. IBVL-Rapport Serie A no. 29.

27 Filling of potato stores

P.H. de Haan

27.1 Transport and reception

The number of days available for lifting in the Netherlands is limited. This means that the potatoes must be transported to the store and the store must be filled in a short period. Filling must therefore take place at relatively high capacity.

In the Netherlands, with a very few exceptions, the potatoes are usually transported from the field in more or less the same way - i.e., in bulk, usually by tipper lorries (Figs. 27.1 and 27.2). Reception methods are therefore also reasonably uniform, although the design, construction, capacity and other features of the equipment used of course differ.

27.2 Loading systems

Important points to be considered when purchasing loading equipment include capacity, tendency to damage the potatoes, distribution over the storage compartment and liability to failure.

Fig. 27.1. Usual type of lorry.

Fig. 27.2. Tipping backwards.

There are three main classes of equipment:
- Mobile equipment.
- Fixed equipment.
- Partly mobile, partly fixed equipment.

27.2.1 *Mobile equipment*

This system is by far the most commonly used in the Netherlands for filling potato stores. The equipment is made up of the following parts:
- Reception and delivery hopper (Fig. 27.3).
- Elevator (Fig. 27.4).
- Bin filler (Figs. 27.5 and 27.6).
  Some variations are as follows:
- A few conveyor belts, often extendible, are installed between the hopper and the elevator.
- There is no separate elevator; the elevator and bin filler are combined in a single unit (Fig. 27.7).
- A precleaner may be installed in the supply line as a separate unit.
  Reception and delivery hopper: As the name indicates, this hopper has two functions:
- Reception of the potatoes when the rear flap of the tipper is opened.

Fig. 27.3. Reception and delivery hopper.

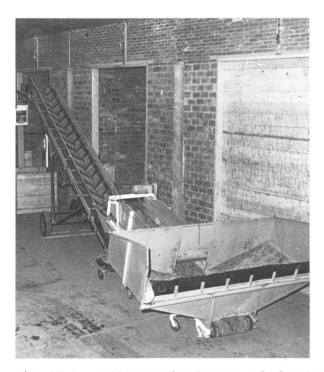

Fig. 27.4. Small reception hopper and elevator.

Fig. 27.5. Large reception hopper and elevator.

- Controlled delivery (with adjustable capacity) on to the conveyor belts
  (Fig. 27.8).
  Hopper capacity (content) may vary from a few tonnes to about eight
tonnes of potatoes; there are also special types with even larger capacities.
  The aim is to minimize truck unloading times. The unloading time is
determined partly by the capacity of the reception and delivery hopper
and partly also by the capacity of the conveyors (elevator and bin fil-

Fig. 27.6. Bin filler.

Fig. 27.7. Bin filler.

ler). Large-capacity reception and delivery hoppers involve high capital
costs and are more difficult to operate. Many farms therefore often
choose a relatively small bulk hopper but conveyors of substantial capacity. Reception and delivery hoppers have a sloping bottom, over which
entraining plates secured on either side to drive chains run. In most designs, a tarpaulin is placed over the entraining plates and linked to
them (the use of a tarpaulin over the entraining plates is preferable to
limit damage. For the same reason, the hopper should not always be completely emptied). Roller bottoms are also sometimes used. The speed of
the entraining plates is usually adjustable, and often continuously so.
On the delivery side there is often a precleaner with smooth rollers,
'star-shaped' segments or a chain conveyor.

Fig. 27.8. Bin filler with reception hopper and precleaner.

Elevator The elevator is the link between the reception and delivery hopper and the bin filler. It is important for the elevator to have sufficient capacity even when in the steepest position used. More and more elevators are built with a 'kink' at the top. This allows better alignment with the bin filler and also reduces the falling height of the potatoes on to the filler.

Bin filler The bin filler places the potatoes in the bin. The potatoes must be evenly distributed within the bin, to avoid soil coning and to obtain a consistent height of fill throughout the bin. The conveyor belt must be able to swing over the entire width. Automatic control systems with adjustable swing are becoming increasingly common. There are also safety devices to prevent accidental collisions with walls. Bin fillers must also have efficient height adjustment facilities. The falling height must not be too great when filling commences. A minimum height of 0 to 50 cm is attainable with some fillers, but other types have minimum heights of 1.25 to 1.60 m. With the latter, means of breaking the fall are required at the beginning of filling - e.g., a chute, an air cushion or if need be, a bag of straw. The maximum height is also important in terms of the height to which the potatoes are to be piled. The maximum height of the conveyor belt should be about 1 m higher than the required piling height to allow for the space required between the underside of the belt and the top of the potato stack and for the diameter of the drive pulley. The maximum height will therefore often be 5.50 m or even more. The conveyor belts of the bin fillers are almost always telescopic extensible. The filler then does not have to be moved so often during filling - provided, of course, that the required height can still be attained when the belts are retracted.

Electrical and/or hydraulic means of extending and retracting the belts are coming into increasing use, sometimes with automatic sensor control. The reach of a bin filler (i.e., the distance between the delivery point of the conveyor and the wheels) must be sufficient to ensure that the wheels do not encroach on the potatoes. A board can be placed in front of the wheels to protect tubers which roll out of the heap. Some fillers also have wheel guards. A filler with a long reach will also usually need to be moved less. 'Standard' models normally have reaches in the range 6.5 m to 9 m. A longer reach is possible in special types. Electric motors are increasingly coming to be used to move the filler.

An important safety aspect is the stability of the filler, especially where wide swings and/or long reaches are concerned. The necessary attention must be devoted to this point both in the design of the filler and when working with it in practice.

406

27.2.2 Fixed equipment

Fixed equipment is used much less commonly than mobile units to fill potato stores. It is used principally in large stores. (Fixed equipment is used almost exclusively in central grading/packing plants.)

Different types of fixed equipment are used depending on the construction of the store and the method and organization of potato reception. The general principle is that the bins are filled from above by conveyor belts from a fixed receiving system. The sequence is as follows: receiving equipment - elevator - upper longitudinal belt - shifting transverse belt - filling of bins. Depending on the situation, there may be one or more conveyors between the reception system and the elevator and/or between the elevator and the upper longitudinal belt. In these more complicated systems, ample attention must obviously be devoted to the damage aspect (belt speed, falling heights, etc.).

One of the most important differences from mobile equipment is the manner of filling. For satisfactory filling of the storage bin(s), two conveyors above the compartments (or at the top of the store) are usually used. One runs along the length of the store (upper longitudinal belt) and the other across it (transverse belt). The transverse belt is installed at a slightly lower level than the longitudinal belt, so that the po-

Fig. 27.9. Pusher plate on a conveyor.

tatoes can be transferred form the latter to the former. This part of the
system will be briefly described below.
- Fixed longitudinal belt. The longitudinal belt has a pusher plate to
transfer the potatoes to the transverse belt. This is a steel plate perpendicular to the belt and aligned at an angle of about 45 ° to the
longitudinal direction (Fig. 27.9). The tubers are thus pushed to one side of the belt and over the side. The conveyor belt must be flat and must
be supported over its entire length. This system may be liable to failure
with just-lifted potatoes with a great deal of trash, (soil, stems,
etc.). The falling height on to the transverse belt is fairly considerable, and means of breaking the fall are therefore needed (e.g., slowdown
flaps).
- Shifting longitudinal belt. To allow unloading at the end of the longitudinal belt, this belt must be able to move with the transverse belt.
There are two possible approaches here.

In one method, part of the longitudinal belt is fixed. This part is
about half the length of the storage bin or store (Fig. 27.10). A second,
shifting longitudinal belt (rather longer than half the compartment
length) can be moved along underneath the fixed belt. The second belt is
reversible. If the lower belt is moved as far as possible in the conve-
ying direction of the upper belt, it becomes in effect an extension of
the latter. If the lower belt is moved as far as possible in the other
direction and reversed, the potatoes are transported back to the other
side of the compartment. In this way the lower belt can transfer potatoes
to the transverse belt over the entire length of the compartment.

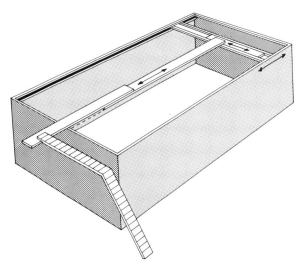

Fig. 27.10. Shifting longitudinal belt. Part of the longitudinal belt
is fixed.

408

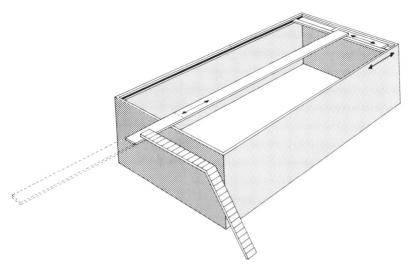

Fig. 27.11. The longitudinal belt shifts as a whole and is reversible.

In the second system, the longitudinal belt shifts as a whole and is reversible (Fig. 27.11). To discharge potatoes at one end of the store or bin, it must be possible to shift the belt almost entirely outside the store. There are often two stores of roughly the same length opposite each other, so that one longitudinal conveyor can service two stores or two storage bins.
It is also quite common for reception to take place at the side and approximately in the middle of the storage building (Fig. 27.12). An elevator then conveys the potatoes to the upper longitudinal belt in the mid-

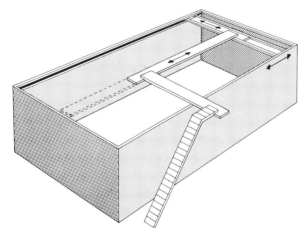

Fig. 27.12. The longitudinal belt can transfer its load over the entire length to the transverse belt.

dle of the store. If the longitudinal belt is about half the length of the building, it can transfer its load over the entire length to the transverse belt. The upper longitudinal belt can then remain inside the store building.

- Discharge from the transverse belt. The length of the transverse belt is about half the width of the store or storage compartment. Since the transverse belt can be shifted across the width of the building and also lenghtwise (and is also reversible), it can discharge at any point in the store. To discharge the potatoes from a height of 4 to 5 m into the store, chutes can be used (provided that they are efficient) (Fig. 27.13). In large stores, fixed chutes are often installed in the four corners. When filling commences (in the corners), discharge is initially via the chutes. As soon as the required falling height has been obtained, further discharge is in accordance with the angle of pile forming. Liftable chutes secured to the transverse belt may also be used in smaller stores.

Another system is the 'downward' conveyor (Figs. 27.14 and 27.15). If properly constructed (with high entraining plates, low belt speed, etc.), this system can give very good results.

Varying degrees of automatic control can be used in a fixed installation. In the most sophisticated type of control system, an entire store or storage bin is filled in accordance with a fixed plan, the movement of both the upper longitudinal belt and the transverse belt being programmed.

Fig. 27.13. Filling of bins with the aid of chutes.

Fig. 27.14. Filling with a 'downward' conveyor.

27.2.3 Partly mobile, partly fixed systems

There is a wide range of hybrid mobile-and-fixed systems, only a few of which can be examined in detail here.

One system involving only a minor departure from the mobile equipment principle is an arrangement with the reception and delivery hopper installed in a fixed position. Two telescopic belts may be interposed between the hopper and the elevator and are rotatable relative to each other in the horizontal plane (often at a considerable angle). This is a simple way of allowing all the bins to be filled without moving the re-

Fig. 27.15. The conveyor can move downwards in the bin.

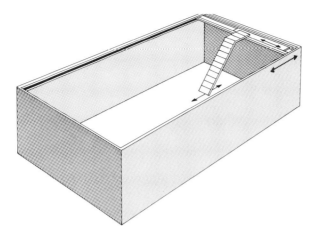

Fig. 27.16 Frame, installed over the width of the building, movable on a rail on either side along the length of the building. The frame contains a conveyor belt whose length is about half the width of the building. The belt is reversible.

ception and delivery hopper. This system is suitable mainly for stores which are not too large.

In another system, the reception and delivery hopper is installed in a fixed position. The potatoes are then conveyed by an elevator to an upper longitudinal belt which can discharge in different positions (in either shifts or has a pusher plate). A bin filler which fills the store in the usual way is situated below the discharge point of the upper longitudinal belt. The longitudinal belt is sometimes positioned in a corridor between two rows of storage bins. The bins on either side of the corridor can then be filled with the filler, which is mobile.

In wide storage buildings, it is sometimes not possible for a filler to swing over the entire width. In this case, a frame, installed over the width of the building, is movable on a rail on either side along the length of the building. The frame contains a conveyor belt whose length is about half the width of the building. The belt is reversible. (The construction is thus similar to that of the transverse belt in fixed installations described earlier (Fig. 27.16).

A reception and delivery hopper is installed in the middle of the building and is followed by an elevator which conveys the potatoes to the upper transverse belt. The elevator is secured to the frame of the upper transverse belt. If the hopper is moved (along the length of the building), the transverse belt is also moved. Filling then proceeds in the same way as in the fixed system described earlier. The hopper and conveyor can be moved from one end of the storage building to the other. Sometimes the frame and transverse belt can also be transferred to another building by forklift.

412

28   Unloading of potato stores

P.H. de Haan

According to practical experience and measurement, the risk of damage after storage (in particular, blackspot or blue discoloration) is substantially higher than at the time of filling. For this reason, every effort must be made to minimize the likelihood of damage. It is essential to remember to warm the potatoes before starting to unload the store. Falling heights must also be limited on unloading. This is particularly important when filling boxes (Figs. 28.1 and 28.2) and storage bunkers (Fig. 28.3) and loading lorries (Figs. 28.4, 28.5, 28.6 and 28.7).

A method often used in the past, which is sometimes still employed in emptying storage bins, is to introduce a conveyor belt in an underfloor (main) air duct (Fig. 28.8). If the bins are not too wide and the distances between the underfloor ducts are not excessive, most of the potatoes will fall on to the belt by themselves. The remainder must be scooped or pushed on to the belt. Although this method used to be regarded as reasonably efficient, it is now used less and less often. One objection is the substantial additional work involved (introduction of the conveyor, removal of boards, scooping and pushing). Again, the capacity is usually insufficient for loading lorries.

Fig. 28.1. Simple device at loading pallet boxes.

Fig. 28.2. Automatic pallet box filler.

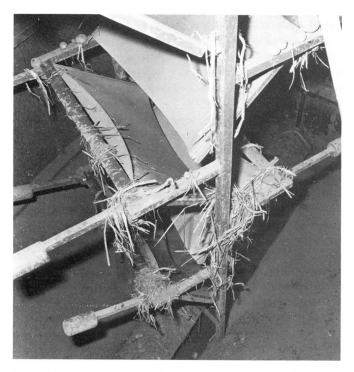

Fig. 28.3. Chutes provided with counter-weights.

414

Fig. 28.4. Vertically movable extension conveyor.

Fig. 28.5. Part of the side-board is removed.

Fig. 28.6. Loading of lorries at a central grading and sorting plant.

A very popular method of unloading potato stores is the use of spe-
cial-purpose scoop-type collecting machines (Fig. 28.9). These have been
developed over the years and can now satisfy most requirements. (These
machines are also used for other types of produce, such as onions, cele-
riac, cereals, green fodder pellets, etc.).
Self-propelled machines are the most commonly used type. The scoop-type
collecting machine consists of two parts, one for scooping and the other
for delivery or transport. The scooping unit is mounted on a chassis with
two driven wheels. The potatoes are collected by a broad steel scoop
which is pushed over the floor and under the potatoes. The scoop is followed by a smooth, flat elevator with a gentle upward slope. This is followed by the delivery device, which consists of an extendible conveyor
belt. At one end this conveyor is linked with the collector, swivelling
at the junction; the other end of the belt is usually mounted on fixed
stands on a rotating plate. The height of the conveyor (discharge point)
is adjustable by securing the belt to the stands at different heights.
Rollers allow the frame of the stands to rotate on the plate (through
about 180 °). This system allows potatoes to be collected from a large
area without the discharge point (rotary plate) having to be moved. Because of the flat, smooth belts, the elevation height of the collector is
relatively small (about 100 cm). More equipment (e.g., an elevator, a box
filler, etc.) is required to load the potatoes.

416

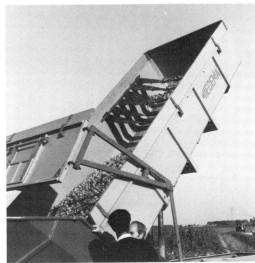

Fig. 28.7a, b and c. Use of rubber ropes, strips or soft material when loading lorries.

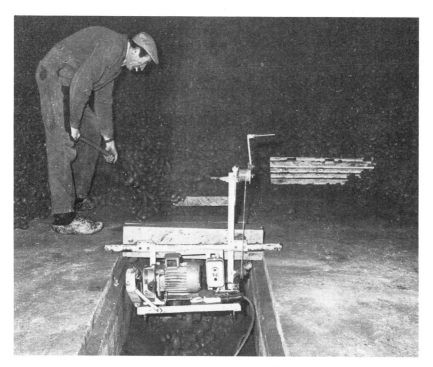

Fig. 28.8. Discharging on a conveyor in a main air duct.

The wheels and conveyor belts are driven by electric motors. Pneumatic
tyres are liable to slip, so that studded tyres are often used. For efficient use of these scoop collectors, a flat floor without obstacles such
as wall fittings, gratings, steps, etc., is necessary. Obstacles can substantially reduce the average capacity. Machines of different capacities
(i.e., nominal capacities) are available, ranging from about 15 to about

Fig. 28.9. Scoop-type collecting machine.

418

Fig. 28.10. Self-emptying storage bunker at a grading plant.

60 tonnes/h. Appreciably higher capacity is obtainable with specially
designed units.

Because lorries have to be loaded quickly, scoop collectors are generally used to unload the store. These high-capacity machines move from
farm to farm being transported on specially designed trailers.

Apart from the type described above, a much simpler unit is also available, consisting in effect of the scooping unit only. The wheels are not
driven. The belt behind the scoop is extensible. In this unit, the delivery side is fixed in position, the belt being extended into the potato
stack. The possibilities are more limited and capacity is not high; however, these units are appreciably cheaper than the other type.

Storage bins can also be unloaded with a loading bucket or fork attached to a tractor or forklift truck. Some precautions have to be taken
to prevent damage to the potatoes. The fork or bucket must be wider than
the tractor or forklift to ensure that the potatoes are not squashed by
the latter. The tips of the fork tines should also preferably be joined
together with a stick to prevent the potatoes from becoming impaled or
jammed between the tines.

Finally, there are self-unloading bins. The floors of these bins slope
towards a discharge opening so that the potatoes are automatically discharged when this is opened. Storage compartments of this kind are virtually non-existent in the Netherlands, but storage bunkers at grading/
packing plants are almost always of the self-emptying type (Fig. 28.10).

29   Grading and sorting of potatoes

P.H. de Haan and B.H. van Zwol

29.1 Grading of potatoes

   Seed potatoes, ware potatoes and potatoes for the processing industry
(chipping, crisping, etc.) are graded to size before delivery. Seed potatoes are usually graded in a larger number of sizes than others. The purpose of grading is to obtain greater uniformity in a particular size grade than in the lot as a whole and also to make the potatoes more suitable
for their intended purpose.
   A square mesh system of grading is used in the Netherlands, the potatoes being passed over riddles with a square mesh (Fig. 29.1). The size
is expressed on the basis of the side lenghts of the squares of the upper
and lower riddles. For instance, '35/45 mm' means that the largest tubers
of this grade will just pass through a square of 45 mm side length while
the smallest tubers will just not pass through a square of 35 mm side
length. Some important aspects of grading (De Haan, 1966, 1968) are as
follows:
- Uniformity in a given size grade.

Fig. 29.1. Riddles for square mesh sizing.

- Grading accuracy.
- Damage.
- Capacity.

29.1.1 Uniformity in square mesh grading

Potatoes can be graded on the basis of specific characteristics, such as weight, length, specific gravity, etc. If a particular grading criterion is chosen, how is it to be ensured that the other characteristics - e.g., weight and length - are uniform?

Measurements have been carried out at the IBVL to determine the uniformity of weight, length and other characteristics within a specific size grade. Examples are presented in Tables 29.1 and 29.2, which set out some results of measurements in a specific year in four lots of different varieties. These figures should be regarded as no more than a rough guide to the differences occuring.

The uniformity of length and weight in a given size grade depends mainly on the shape of the tubers (round, oval or elongated) and on the uniformity of shape of the tubers within a lot. Uniformity within a size grade is much less pronounced in elongated tubers (Sientje) and in less elongated tubers with less uniformity of shape within the lot (Bintje) than in a round variety (Furore). Again, the average length and weight in a given size grade differs in the four varieties depending on the tuber shape. Consequently, in one and the same size grade, the number of tubers per unit weight may differ with different tuber shapes (this is important in seed potatoes). Table 29.3 sets out the weight of 40 000 tubers of the 35/45 mm size grade on the basis of the measurements mentioned above.

Table 29.1 Percentage distribution of the number of tubers in the square mesh size grade 35/45 mm in weight and length classes for a number of varieties (F = Furore, E = Eigenheimer, B = Bintje, S = Sientje).

Weight classes (g)	Variety				Length classes (mm)	Variety			
	F	E	B	S		F	E	B	S
< 40	19	8	14	2	< 40	2	-	-	-
40 < 80	80	75	66	56	40 < 60	89	47	63	12
80 < 120	1	16	18	38	60 < 80	9	49	28	52
120 < 160	-	1	1	4	80 < 100	-	4	7	30
160 < 200	-	-	1	-	100 < 120	-	-	2	5
Total	100	100	100	100	120 < 140	-	-	-	1
					Total	100	100	100	100

Table 29.2 Percentage distribution of the number of tubers in the square mesh size grade 45/55 mm in weight and length classes for a number of varieties (F = Furore, E = Eigenheimer, B = Bintje, S = Sientje).

Weight classes (g)	Variety				Length classes (mm)	Variety			
	F	E	B	S		F	E	B	S
40 < 80	27	4	10	1	40 < 60	30	3	10	-
80 < 120	63	48	32	32	60 < 80	67	47	38	13
120 < 160	10	35	32	40	80 < 100	3	43	28	43
160 < 200	-	11	19	22	100 < 120	-	7	18	32
200 < 240	-	1	6	5	120 < 140	-	-	5	11
240 < 280	-	1	1	-	140 < 160	-	-	1	1
Total	100	100	100	100	Total	100	100	100	100

Table 29.3 Weight of 40 000 tubers of the 35/45 mm grade of a few varieties.

Variety	Weight	Relative weight
Furore	1940 kg	100
Eigenheimer	2330 kg	120
Bintje	2610 kg	135
Sientje	2820 kg	145

Table 29.3 shows that in this case 45 % more weight is required to make up the same number of tubers in the Sientje variety than in the Furore variety in the size grade 35/45 mm.

29.1.2 Grading accuracy

Hitherto, screen-type graders have predominantly been used for size grading by the square mesh method. A shaking or shock motion is imparted to the screens to move the potatoes over them and also to help them fall through the screens as they pass along.

Two points must be taken into account in assessing the grading accuracy of practical graders. Firstly, capacity must be sufficient and, secondly, damage (e.g., blue discoloration) must be minimized. These points being borne in mind, practical measurements have shown the following to be the case:
- Grading accuracy depends mainly on tuber shape; it is very high in a

round-tuber variety and inferior in varieties with more oval or elongated tubers.
- Accuracy does not usually differ very much in shaking and shock type
  screen graders. Incorrect adjustment and poor maintenance adversely affect grading accuracy. Since the requirements of correct adjustment and
  good maintenance may be taken for granted, this point will not be discussed further.

29.1.3 Damage

In screen graders, the potatoes are shaken for a short time. They may
then be damaged. If external damage occurs, this is usually limited to
slight (sometimes hardly perceptible) cracks and, in tubers whose skin
has not yet set (in particular, immediately after the harvest) to abrasions. There may sometimes also be an increase in blue discoloration in
susceptible tubers. Since grading is essential and a shaking or shock motion cannot be avoided, little can be changed in this respect. The prevention of damage must therefore be sought in limitation of falling
heights during conveyance to and removal from the grader. Rods on the
preliminary cleaner can also be padded with rubber or plastic. The wire
mesh of the screens may possible also be clad with such materials. It is
also important, in graders with screens stacked above each other, for
discharge to take place over the entire width of the screen (without guide flaps against which the tubers may strike).

29.1.4 Capacity

The capacity of a grader (at a given necessary conveyance speed over
the screens) is determined primarily by the width of the screens. Of
course, the screens must also be long enough, but once a given length is
reached (in practice, often about 2 m), lengthening the screens no longer
has any effect on capacity. Furthermore, if the screens are longer, the
tubers remain on them for a longer time and are therefore more likely to
be damaged. For high capacity, therefore, wide screens must be used. Two
graders can also be installed side by side and operated as a single unit.

Another important determinant of capacity is coverage of the screen
area with potatoes. Since capacity is expressed in weight units per hour
(e.g., tonnes per hour), capacity is less with small tubers than with
large ones. (Put differently, for a given screen coverage the potato layer is thicker with large than with small tubers.) When a screen is 100 %
covered with exclusively round tubers, the quantities (weights) of tubers
are proportional to the diameters - in other words, tubers 25 mm in diameter weigh half as much as tubers 50 mm in diameter if the screen coverage is the same. The number of size grades also affects capacity. In

graders with stacked screens, the potatoes are divided over a larger number of screens if the number of size grades is high, thus reducing coverage per screen. This 'dividing-among-screens' can also be used if a relatively large percentage of the lot falls into a single size grade. This
grade can be separated into two sizes - i.e., divided between two screens
- which are recombined on discharge. Capacity can thereby be increased
somewhat. It is clear from the foregoing that the capacity of a grader is
not easy to define accurately. A specification of capacity must therefore
be regarded more as a guide than as an exact figure. Since capacity is
influenced by so many factors and the grader must not constitute an ob-
stacle in a processing line, it is best to choose a grader with ample reserve capacity.

29.1.5 Grading systems

Screen graders have hitherto been used predominantly for grading potatoes. These may have three different types of motion; there are shaking
screen graders, shock screen graders and roller screen graders.

29.1.5.1 Shaking screen graders (Figs. 29.2 and 29.3)

A combined horizontal and vertical motion is imparted to the screens.
They also slope slightly towards the discharge side. The amplitude of the
motion of the screens is usually not adjustable.
The screens are driven from a crankshaft. The crankshaft speed can sometimes be varied over a limited range. There is also an arrangement in

Fig. 29.2. Shaking screen graders.

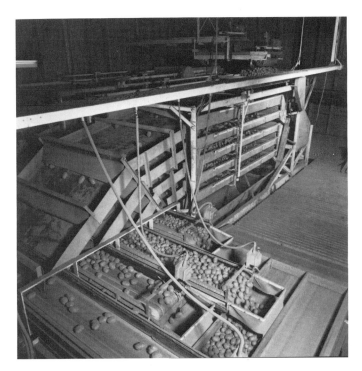

Fig. 29.3. Graders with stacked screens.

which cams on the crankshaft are used to vary the number of movements of
the screens while the crankshaft speed remains constant. This varying motion facilitates the process of grading (screening) and also prevents tubers from getting stuck in the mesh. Reciprocating ejectors are often
placed below the screens to free tubers stuck in the mesh.

29.1.5.2 Shock-type screen graders (Figs. 29.4 and 29.5)

In this type of grader, the whole screens are drawn downwards; the
downward motion tensions springs secured to the frame of the screens. The
screens are released at the lowest point and bounce back to their initial
position, giving rise to a 'shock effect'. The movement of the screens is
diagonal. Although the screens are horizontally oriented, the diagonal
motion transports the potatoes. Both the intensity of the 'shock' and the
direction of motion of the screens are usually adjustable.

29.1.5.3 Roller-type screen graders (Fig. 29.6)

In this type of grader, the screen is an endless, rotating, meshed
belt with a square mesh. The belt runs on three rollers, one of which is

Fig. 29.4. Shock-type screen grader (screens in tandem).

the drive roller. Two rollers are in the same horizontal plane. The potatoes are graded on the meshed belts between these rollers. The third roller is below the other two and equidistant from both (in cross section, a
triangle with the apex at the bottom). The potatoes fall through the rol-

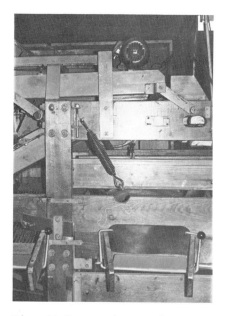

Fig. 29.5. Tension spring of the screens in Fig. 29.4.

426

Fig. 29.6. Roller-type screen grader.

ler screen and land on a transverse belt positioned in the 'triangle'. This belt may convey the tubers to a subsequent roller grader for further grading. A regular shaking motion may be imparted to the roller screen to help the tubers fall through the mesh.

In one form of this system, two graders are combined into a single u-nit, the second meshed belt being below the first; the two belts run at right angles to each other.
Graders can be distinguished by screen positioning:
- Graders with stacked screens
- Graders with screens in tandem
Both shaking and shock-type screen graders are made in both types. In practice, the screens are usually stacked in shaking graders and arranged in tandem in shock-type graders.

29.1.5.4 Roller graders (Fig. 29.7)

Potatoes are also graded with roller graders as well as screen types. Although roller graders have been available for a long time in a variety of types, they have gained little acceptance in the Netherlands.

A new type of roller grader was marketed a few years ago, and is now being used at a number of grading establishments in the Netherlands. The grading section consists of a driven roller belt (comparable with a rol-

Fig. 29.7. Roller grader.

ler-table). The rollers are not driven. Since the rollers are supported at the sides, a rolling motion is imparted to them. The rollers have rubber segments shaped so that square openings form between them. Half of the rollers (every other roller) can be lowered with respect to the other half. As they are lowered, the openings between them become larger. The grade size can be adjusted in this way. The depth of each section (e.g., a 1 m length) can be adjusted.

For instance, if a grader has six sections, the potatoes can be separated into six size grades. It is also possible to set one or more sections to the same size. If two sections are set identically, three size grades can be obtained. Of course, each section is then twice as long as when the potatoes are sorted into six size grades. Since the openings are smallest at the input end and largest at the discharge end, no tubers get stuck in the openings.

Transverse discharge belts are installed below the rollers to remove the different size grades.

29.2 Sorting of potatoes

29.2.1 Introduction

Sorting of potatoes means their separation into different qualities.

428

The potatoes can be separated in the following ways:
- Visual inspection and manual removal (hand selection; Section 29.2.2).
- Visual inspection and mechanical removal (semiautomatic sorting; Section 29.2.3).
- Automatic inspection and removal (electronic quality sorting; Section 29.2.4).

29.2.2 Hand selection

Although equipment for automatic removal of unsatisfactory tubers or impurities (soil, foliage, etc.) does exist, potatoes will usually have to be quality-sorted by hand.

Compared with the other post-lifting operations undergone by the potato - e.g., grading, transport and storage - sorting is extremely labour-intensive.

A distinction may be drawn between:
- Sorting of ware potatoes.
- Sorting of seed potatoes.

29.2.2.1 Sorting of ware potatoes

When ware potatoes are sorted, the following must be eliminated:
1. Soil, stones, foliage and similar foreign matter.
2. Rotten potatoes (*Phoma*, *Fusarium*, soft rot, *Phytophthora*).
3. Damaged potatoes (including ones with blue discoloration).
4. Green potatoes (to a limited extent).
5. Diseased potatoes (*Rhizoctonia*, common scab).
6. Potatoes with hollow hearts.
7. Potatoes of insufficient specific gravity (second growth, glassy potatoes).

The conditions mentioned in items 6 and 7 cannot be seen from the outside. To some extent they may be revealed in washed potatoes by sorting in the dark by transmitted light.

If necessary, potatoes with these defects can be removed by separation in salt baths.

29.2.2.1.1 Separation in a salt water bath
Separation in salt water baths is possible because glassy potatoes and ones with hollow hearts are less dense than healthy potatoes. If the potatoes are passed through a salt water bath with a specific gravity of 1.055, the tubers of lower specific gravity will float, while those of higher specific gravity will sink. Hence most of the potatoes which float in a bath of this composition will be 'glassy' or have hollow hearts.

Salt water baths are incidentally also used to separate lots of potatoes into two or more fractions for processing purposes.

29.2.2.1.2 *Separation of clods and stones*

Electronic clod separators (Fig. 29.8) are often used to eliminate clods and stones where there are relatively high percentages of this kind of trash.

These units detect the clods or stones by X-rays. If the equipment is correctly adjusted, it will remove about 90 % of the clods and stones.

However, about 5 % of the potatoes are eliminated with the clods and stones.

100 % separation is achieved in the 'wet clod separator', in which the clods and stones are separated from the potatoes by an upward flow of water.

29.2.2.2 Sorting of seed potatoes

The same basic 'quality standards' apply in the sorting of seed potatoes as to ware potatoes. However, the requirements as to the elimination of diseased potatoes are somewhat stricter with seed, while those concerning potatoes with blue discoloration (black spot) are rahter less severe.

29.2.2.3 Conditions to be met by the sorting process

The following ergonomic conditions must be met in the sorting of potatoes:
- Visual inspection of tubers. To facilitate visual inspection, the potatoes to be sorted must be well lit (illuminated) with two TL 65 fluorescent tubes, colour 84). The tubers must rotate in the inspector's field of view so that he can inspect their entire surface. The inspector must be able to assess both the apical and the stem end of the potato.

In quality separation, potatoes with slight defects often do not have to be removed, while more seriously defective tubers do; for this reason it must be possible to see a sufficient number of potatoes at a time to

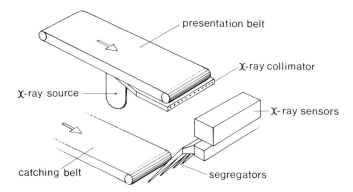

presentation belt

X-ray collimator

X-ray source

X-ray sensors

catching belt

segregators

Fig. 29.8. Electronic clod separator.

Fig. 29.9. Example of the positioning of the inspector relative to the
sorting table which satisfies most of the requirements.

allow correct separation. Hence there must be sufficient density of potatoes on the sorting table.

For correct separation, it is preferable for the potatoes to be sorted
to be of the same size (i.e., a single size grade).
- Removal of defective tubers. To facilitate removal of defective tubers,
the lighting in the sorting room must be sufficient for the defective tubers to be grasped and removed without mistakes.

The tubers must be high enough above the sorting surface to be grasped
quickly and easily.

The arrangements for disposal of rejected potatoes must not involve
additional effort on the part of the selector.

Figure 29.9 shows an example of the positioning of the inspector relative to the sorting table which satisfies most of the requirements mentioned above.

29.2.2.4 Potato sorting in practice

In the labour-intensive operation of potato sorting, it is important
for every inspector to have an optimum work load. Three points are important here, viz., the positions of the inspectors, the construction of the
sorting table and the attainable capacity.

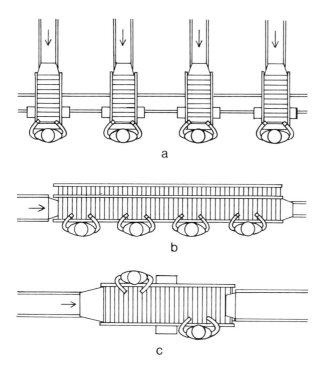

a

b

c

Fig. 29.10. Positions of the inspectors. a. Positioned in parallel (optimal); b. several inspectors working on a single stream of potatoes (duplication of work); c. positioned in parallel (practical).

29.2.2.4.1 Positions of the inspectors

To maximize the sorting capacity of each person, the inspectors must be positioned in parallel (Fig. 29.10).

This means that the potatoes to be sorted must be divided into a number of streams, each stream being sorted by one inspector. If several inspectors are working on a single stream of potatoes, each observes the stream of potatoes and removes a number of defective tubers. The next inspector again observes the same stream of potatoes and he removes a further number of defective tubers. Eventually, the good potatoes have been inspected a number of times, to the detriment of the overall selection capacity.

Again, it is evident from the attainable sorting capacity (Section 29.2.2.4.3) that capacity per inspector greatly depends on the percentage of rejects. In this configuration, the percentage of rejects is modified by the removal of defective tubers, so that it becomes impossible to achieve the optimum sorting capacity.

29.2.2.4.2 Sorting table construction

In view of the conditions stipulated as to visibility of the tubers

432

and ability to remove defective potatoes, roller tables are generally used for sorting potatoes. If they are to be suitable for both small and large potatoes, the sorting rollers must have a diameter of about 60 mm and the space between the rollers must not exceed 5 mm.

Because sorting capacity varies with the percentage of rejects, it must be possible to vary the transport rate of the sorting table from 2 to 8 m/s. Discharge trays or channels should be positioned within reach of the inspector.

The roller table must be well lit. Two TL 65 fluorescent tubes are often used, one metre above the sorting surface (colour 55 or 84). To facilitate distribution of the potatoes over the roller table and the sorting operations themselves, the roller table should be at least 1.5 m long.

The general rule should be: one inspector per sorting table, positioned either beside or at the end of the table.

It is preferable for the inspector to be positioned at the end of the table, as he can then see both the bud and the stem end of each potato (Fig. 29.9).

A roller table of this kind may be about 50 cm wide.

A roller table of the kind with the inspector standing alongside is generally 40 to 60 cm wide. With two inspectors opposite each other alongside the table, the width should be about 80 cm. The advantage of this configuration is that the potatoes furthest from the inspector, part of whose skin surface is not readily visible to one inspector, are visible to his opposite number (Fig. 29.10).

With regard to the construction of the sorting table, the machine must be matched as far as possible to the inspector (i.e., it must be ergonomically designed), so that the inspector can achieve optimum selection results through the satisfaction of the ergonomic requirements.

29.2.2.4.3 *Attainable sorting capacity*

The average capacities attainable by one inspector (input of produce) are set out in Tables 29.4 and 29.5 in kg of potatoes per hour.

Table 29.4 shows the capacities attainable when sorting entirely clean potatoes (virtually free of clinging soil) or washed potatoes. It is understood that the 'sorted produce' still contains 1.5 % substandard tubers (mistakes by the inspector).

The tables show that sorting capacity depends strongly on the percentage of rejects.

Soil, foliage, stones, etc., count as rejected material in addition to substandard tubers.

Table 29.5 sets out the attainable sorting capacities at different reject percentages if there is soil clinging to the potatoes or if sorting is difficult for other reasons, e.g., if the potatoes are affected with scab.

Table 29.4 Attainable sorting capacities (kg/h) at different
percentages tubers rejected (inspector error 1.5 %) (easily
sorted potatoes - e.g., washed potatoes).

Percentage tubers rejected	Size grades		
	28/35 mm	35/45 mm	45/55 mm
5	1200	2100	2750
10	900	1750	2275
15	700	1475	1900
20	600	1300	1700
25	500	1150	1500

Table 29.5 Attainable sorting capacity (kg/h) at different
percentages tubers rejected (inspector error 1.5 %) (potatoes
which are difficult to sort, e.g., with clinging soil).

Percentage tubers rejected	Size grades		
	28/35 mm	35/45 mm	45/55 mm
5	450	1760	1900
10	375	1400	1600
15	325	1150	1300
20	275	1000	1100
25	250	850	950

Clinging soil or serious incidence of scab is found to affect sorting
capacity susbstantially, no doubt because the defects are less readily
visible.

29.2.3 Semiautomatic sorting

With this form of sorting, the same requirements apply to the assess-
ment of the potatoes as with hand selection, except that there are no ergonomic requirements concerning removal of potatoes deemed to be substandard. Semiautomatic sorting is appropriate only if the proportion of rejects exceeds 10 %.

Up to 10 % rejects, sorting capacity is virtually unaffected by the
picking-out of defective tubers.

29.2.4 Electronic sorting

Washed potatoes can in principle be sorted by optoelectronic means. The relevant measuring system may use transmitted light, incident light or a combination of transmitted and incident light.

In each case it is essential for the potato to be free of soil - i.e., it must have been washed.

- Transmitted light. Transmitted light (Fig. 29.11a) allows the detection of internal defects such as blue or green discoloration, hollow hearts, glassiness, etc.

This method is actually not very practicable owing to differences in thickness between individual tubers.

- Incident light. The incident light measuring system (Fig. 29.11b) is in fact a technique of colour measurement. It is not possible to 'look' under the skin with this method, so that, for example, black spot, glassiness, hollow hearts or fresh damage may go undetected. On the other hand, defects which are less serious from the point of view of consump-

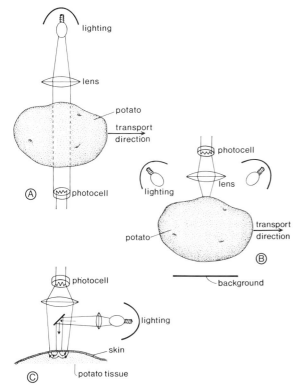

Fig. 29.11. Electronic sorting by optoelectronic means. The relevant measuring system may use a. transmitted light; b. incident light; c. a combination of transmitted and incident light.

tion, such as common scab and *Rhizoctonia*, are seen as just as serious as damage, green discolorations or rotten potatoes.

For this reason, incident-light electronic sorting is used only to separate ware potatoes into two qualities or for the utilization of small potatoes , (i.e., with materials which are very cheap relative to the labour costs of sorting).

(Incident-light electronic potato sorting is, however, used to a considerable extent for peeled potatoes and potato products in the potato-processing industry.)

- Combination of incident and transmitted light. Electronic sorting with a combination of incident and transmitted light (Fig. 29.11c) is currently under investigation at the IBVL with a view to application in the sorting of seed potatoes.

Machines for this form of electronic sorting do not yet exist.

References

Haan, P.H. de, 1966. Verslag van een aantal metingen in de praktijk betreffende de beschadiging en de nauwkeurigheid bij het sorteren van aardappelen. Intern Rapport IBVL 284.

Haan, P.H. de, 1968. Sorteerkenmerken bij aardappelen. IBVL-Jaarboek 1967/1968.

30 Packing of potatoes

P.H. de Haan

30.1 Introduction

After all the preparatory handling operations, some of the potatoes
are despatched in bulk (e.g., to the processing industry) while others
are despatched in various forms of packing. The form and size of the
packing used depends on a number of factors, such as customer requirements, the period for which the potatoes remain in the packing, destination (within the country, in Europe or outside Europe), method of transport (road, rail or sea), season, and any requirements imposed, for example, by the plant diseases authorities and official inspection bodies
(in the Netherlands, the Nederlandse Algemene Keuringsdienst (Netherlands
General Inspection Department).

In terms of the produce, the general requirement may be laid down that
quality must be maintained in the packing. Except for very short periods,
allowance must be made for the elimination of respiration products (carbon dioxide, water vapour and heat). This means that the packing must afford adequate ventilation. Some degree of permeability to air is also required. Again, the potatoes must be protected from excessive daylight, as
the tubers will otherwise turn green. If the produce is to be exposed to
daylight for long periods, the packing must be relatively opaque. Greening is more of a problem in ware than in seed potatoes.

When potatoes are transported or stored, it is important not only for
the packing itself to be sufficiently permeable to air but also for the
space in which the packed potatoes are located to be sufficiently ventilated, so that the respiration products are eliminated and fresh air
(oxygen) is supplied. Apart from the factors and requirements concerning
packing already mentioned, the possibility of mechanization is also important in practice. Since units are relatively small, it is essential to
minimize the amount of work required per unit. The suitability of the
packing material for automatic weighing, sealing and removal is very important for the relevant establishments. In some cases, this may mean
that the material chosen is not the one that would be best for the produce but instead one which is more economical. Also on grounds of cost, ef-
forts will be made to minimize the number of different kinds of packing
used.

Although there is in general a wide choice of packs in terms of type, shape and size, in fact only a limited number of types, shapes and sizes are used for potatoes for the reasons stated above; some of them are used only to a limited extent. Another possible distinction is between large and small packs, large packs being defined as units of 12.5 kg and larger and small packs as units of not more than 5 kg. Units between 5 and 12.5 kg also sometimes occur, so that a sharp boundary cannot be drawn. For the sake of simplicity, however, the above definitions will be used, particularly as they have long been accepted in practice in the Netherlands.

30.2 Types of packing

30.2.1. Large packs

Sacks containing 25 kg or 50 kg of potatoes are commonly used, but sacks of other sizes are also employed to a lesser extent.

30.2.1.1 Jute sacks

Jute is a familiar material which has been used for a very long time

Fig. 30.1. Packing in jute sacks.

438

(Fig. 30.1). It is very suitable for potatoes, in that it admits air and blocks much of the light, while the tissue can absorb moisture. Jute sacks must have a certain weight, depending on the amount of potatoes contained, for exports from the Netherlands. The weights required are lighter for destinations inside than for outside Europe.

30.2.1.2 Plastic sacks

Knitted sacks of this material are often used. They are very accessible to air, but pass more light than jute. Although they are cheaper than jute sacks, they are found to have some practical disadvantages (e.g., susceptibility to damage), and this is why they have not yet been used on a large scale. Plastic sacks of woven fabric also exist, but are used only on a limited scale. They have the same practical disadvantages as knitted plastic sacks, but to an even greater extent. Sacks made of plastic sheeting are hardly ever used for potatoes in the Netherlands. Even when perforated, they admit too little air, and there is a serious risk of condensation of moisture on the inside of the sack. These sacks may be used, if at all, only for very limited periods, preferably opened.

30.2.1.3 Paper sacks

Multi-ply, moisture-proofed paper sacks (possibly perforated) are used for potatoes (Fig. 30.2). They are not very accessible to air but admit

Fig. 30.2. Paper sacks filled with prepacked potatoes.

minimal light. They are quite vulnerable to damage. These sacks are used
to a limited extent only in the Netherlands.

30.2.1.4 Crates

Wooden crates are used in the Netherlands exclusively for exports,
mainly of seed potatoes. They usually contain 25 kg or 30 kg of potatoes,
but sometimes also 50 kg. Accessibility to air is very good (De Haan,
1969). Even when crates are closely stacked, ventilation is still good.
More light is admitted than in jute sacks. The potatoes are satisfactorily protected from damage during transport and handling. The cost of
packing in crates is high - firstly, the cost of the crates themselves
(per 100 kg of produce) is high and, secondly, the cost of filling and
closing the crates is also high, owing to the limited possibility of automation.

30.2.1.5 Cartons

Cartons made of solid or corrugated board are sometimes used in the
Netherlands for potatoes (mostly for export). The cartons have ventilation holes. Accessibility to air is often sufficient (depending on the
size and position of the holes). The cartons must be robust to withstand
the pressure arising on stacking. They must also be able to withstand
high relative atmospheric humidity. Cartons are used only to a limited
extent in the Netherlands.

30.2.1.6 Other forms of packing

Large units, such as containers, large boxes, one-tonne bags, etc.,
are sometimes used in the Netherlands in special cases. However, these
forms of packing are to be regarded more as means of transport than as
forms of packing in their own right. These methods of transport could be
described as semi-bulk conveyance.

30.2.2 Small packs (prepacking)

Polyethylene film has hitherto been used predominantly for small packs
in the Netherlands (Fig. 30.3). The bags are perforated for air renewal.
A number of bags are usually put together to form a larger unit. For instance, ten 2.5 kg bags or five 5 kg bags are sometimes combined in a
single outer, usually of paper. If the organization so allows, the bags
are often also placed in steel wire containers (roller containers) or
crates. Condensation may arise on the inside of the plastic bags, so that
the time spent by the potatoes in these bags should be minimized. Good

440

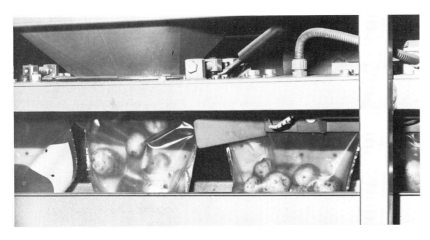

Fig. 30.3. Small packs of polyethylene.

ventilation is essential if the time cannot be kept short, as when potatoes are transported over long distances. Knitted plastic fabric or netting bags can also be used for small packs; this form of packing is su-
perior to plastic film in terms of ventilation (air accessibility). The
time spent in the bags and the packing cost determine the preferred form.

30.3 Washing and brushing of potatoes for packing in retail packs

30.3.1 Washing of potatoes for packing in retail packs

In the Netherlands potatoes for packing in retail packs are sometimes
washed usually at central preparation plants just before packing (De
Haan, 1968). Washed potatoes in small packs are more likely to rot and
sprout during transport and storage than unwashed tubers. Different lots
are found to vary substantially in their keeping properties, depending on
such factors as damage, varietal differences, differences in origin and
fertilization. Conditions during transport and storage - e.g., outside
temperature, ventilation or no ventilation, time spent in the bag - are
also important.

Early-lifted potatoes which have also been abraded to a greater or
lesser extent and may in addition have other damage, usually respire
strongly; water evaporation is also increased especially in abraded tubers. There is then a serious risk of condensation in the bags. Again,
high temperatures may arise in the period immediately after lifting. If
the potatoes are then transported over long distances (possibly with temperature fluctuations), highly unfavourable conditions - possibly exacerbated by inadequate ventilation - may arise.

Unfavourable conditions also often arise in spring at high outside temperatures, giving rise to a risk of sprouting, often coupled with rotting. The atmosphere in the bags may easily become humid and depleted in oxygen, thus favouring rotting, if the respiration products are insufficiently eliminated.

To minimize the amount of moisture entering the bag right from the time of packing, the washed potatoes should be dry before bagging. Water clinging to the tubers must first be 'sponged off' as well as possible. Most washers have 'absorbers' for this purpose. Heated air is required for further drying of the potatoes. This secondary drying is not always carried out in practice because the cost (installation and fuel) is relatively high.

30.3.2 Brushing of potatoes for packing in retail packs

Potatoes placed in retail packs without washing are brushed to eliminate easily removable particles of soil from the tubers. The tuber then has a 'cleaner' appearance, while tubers with less soil (dust) are less likely to cause fully automatic sealing machines to fail.

Solidly caked soil is virtually impossible to eliminate by brushing. Is is therefore advisable not even to attempt over-vigorous brushing, as this is likely to damage the skin of the tubers. The tubers to be brushed must be dry, otherwise the soil will simply be smeared over them.

30.4 Packing machinery and equipment

30.4.1 Large packs

Machinery and equipment are used for weighing and sealing the bags; control may be entirely manual, fully automatic, or partly manual and partly automatic.

30.4.1.1 Weighing equipment

The following types of weighing facilities may be used (discussed in increasing order of mechanization).

Balances and high-speed weighing units, with which all operations (placing on the scale, removal from the scale and actual weighing of the bags) are performed manually, are used only exceptionally for small quantities. A small step towards full mechanization comprises weighing units which weigh out the correct amount into the bag. The bags are placed in or on, and removed from, the unit by hand (Fig. 30.4).

To increase the capacity, the operations of weighing-out on the one hand and feed to and removal from the equipment on the other may be separated, as in the following examples:

442

Fig. 30.4. Weighing unit attached to a roller table.

a. There are two filling outlets (Fig. 30.5). When one sack has been
   weighed out, another is filled and weighed by resetting the flaps under the second filling outlet. The filled and weighed first sack can
   then be detached and a subsequent empty sack can be fed to the first
   filling outlet.
b. The contents of a sack are weighed out into a storage hopper. As soon
   as this hopper has reached the correct weight, it is emptied into a
   sack suspended or held below it. As soon as the hopper is empty, the
   filling and weighing operations are repeated, the full sack having
   meanwhile been removed and an empty one substituted.
c. This is an extension of system b., in which a number of storage hoppers rotate. They are filled at one point and discharged at one or two
   points. Alternatively the sacks may be attached to a revolving frame
   which passes below fixed storage hoppers. The frame stops when passing
   a hopper; the sack is filled and the frame then moves on.
   Another possibility is for the sacks to be fed in manually, discharge

Fig. 30.5. Two weighing units with one hopper (use of knitted plastic sacks).

after the stitcher being automatic (e.g., with jute sacks). There are also fully automatic packing machines, the automation covering the entire process including supply of empty sacks, suspension, filling and weighing and removal of the full sacks.

These fully automatic machines are available in different types for different types of packing materials, such as paper, plastic film and woven plastic, but not for jute (although in some machines all operations are automatic except for suspension of the empty sacks in position - see above).

30.4.1.2 Sealing of sacks

Large sacks of potatoes are usually stitch-sealed (other possibilities do exist but are seldom used - e.g., turning-over, strip-sealing and heat-sealing). Single- or double-thread chainstitch may be used for sealing (the latter is usually stipulated for exports from the Netherlands).

Stitchers may be portable (possibly suspended from a swinging arm) or permanently installed on a column (with one or two stitching heads), sack feed and discharge being automatic.

If necessary, a label may be added automatically and stitched to the sack (e.g., for seed).

30.4.2 Small packs

30.4.2.1 Washers and brushers for preparatory operations

Washers Washers are incorporated in the finishing line after the grader and roller-table and before the small-pack packer.

In one commonly used type of washer, the potatoes are fed over a number of driven rollers which have rubber cleats (Fig. 30.6). Water is sprayed on to the potatoes as they pass over the rollers, the tubers meanwhile being turned. A number of spray nozzles are positioned above the rollers, the water being sprayed on to the tubers through them. To increase the washing effect, some systems have a tank of water through which the potatoes are passed to remove clinging soil before they are fed to the washers.

A large volume of wash water is required per tonne of potatoes (about 5 m³). For this reason, a high proportion of the water is usually recir-

Fig. 30.6. Washing machine with spraying nozzles.

culated via a settling tank, a small amount of fresh water being added.
The particles of soil are sedimented out as far as possible in the tank.
When the tubers leave the water, they pass over a number of absorber rol-
lers lined with moisture-absorbent material.

Most of the water clinging to the tubers is eliminated in this way.
Pressure rollers are applied to the underside of the absorber rollers and
squeeze the water out of the absorbent material.

Another type of washer consists of a large tank filled with water and
containing a shaker screen in the lengthwise direction, just below the
surface of the water. While the potatoes are conveyed over the screen
(and through the water), a fan blows air through the water, thus creating
powerful turbulence. Drum-type washers are also used for washing potatoes. The tubers are fed through a rotating drum which has slots or holes. The potatoes pass through the water, and are sometimes also sprayed
with water. When ware potatoes are drum-washed, the inside of the drum
should be lined to minimize damage to the tubers. To 'sponge' the washed
potatoes, there are drums in which the potatoes are mixed with small pie-

Fig. 30.7. Simple brusher.

ces of a spongy material as they rotate. After discharge from the drum, the sponges are separated from the potatoes, squeezed out, dried and re-used.

Brushers Machines having a number of brush rollers are generally used for brushing (Fig. 30.7). As the potatoes are fed over the rollers, soil which does not cling too solidly is brushed off the tubers. To enhance the brushing effect, a tarpaulin or skirt is positioned above the rollers and inhibits the movement of the tubers. Stationary transverse brushes may also be positioned above the brush rollers for the same purpose. The height as well as the position of the transverse brushes is often adjustable.

30.4.2.2 Machines for packing in retail packs

Fully automatic machines are used almost exclusively for small packs in centralized establishments in the Netherlands (Fig. 30.8). These machines are suitable for 2.5 kg and 5 kg packs and sometimes also larger packs. The packing material (plastic film or woven plastic) is often wound from a roll. In the case of plastic film, some systems use 'preformed' bags while in others the bag is formed during the packing process; the plastic film is heat-sealed. With woven plastic, the bags are stitch-sealed. Net packing ('tube filling') and clip-sealing may also be used for potatoes, as well as paper bags (with or without a 'window'). However, the latter form is relatively rare in the Netherlands.

Fig. 30.8. Fully automatic machines for packing in retail packs.

References

Haan, P.H. de, 1968. Sorteerkenmerken bij aardappelen. IBVL-Jaarboek IBVL 1967/1968.

Haan, P.H. de, 1969. Verslag van een oriënterende bewaarproef met aardappelen verpakt in dozen en kratten. IBVL-Mededeling 337.

POTATO STORAGE IN THE TROPICS AND SUBTROPICS

31 Storage of potatoes at high temperatures

H. Sparenberg

31.1 Introduction

Many tropical and subtropical countries are becoming increasingly in-
terested in potato cultivation with the aim of improving food supplies.

This increasing interest is reflected in sharply rising production
(Table 31.1). This increase shows that there is a growing demand for potatoes. Although production has risen, per capita potato production in
general is still very small, particularly in African and Asian countries.
It has to be considered, however, that population has increased by 20 to
29 % in the period 1970 - 1979.

Table 31.1 Total and per capita potato production (FAO Production
Yearbook, 1979).

	total (in million tonnes)		per capita (in kg)	
Area	1970	1979	1970	1979
World	275.9	284.5	75	66
South-America	8.7	10.1	46	42
Africa	2.9	4.6	8	10
Asia	25.3	36.9	12	15

The nutritional value of the potato is not only greater but also more
varied than that of traditional foods in these developing coutries, most
of which are poor. The potato is therefore particularly suitable for com-
plementing an often one-sided diet and must be regarded as a supplement
to the main food crops of rice, maize and grain.

31.2 Aspects of increasing production

To increase potato production, the first requirement is to raise
yields per unit arae, in order to maintain or even reduce the price per
kg of product, which can vary enormously.

Secondly, losses after the harvest, during transport, handling and storage, must be minimized.

Losses due to poor handling and storage often amount to 40 to 50 %.

An increase in production involves some financial expenditure, as healthy seed of high-yielding varieties must be imported. These imports could be limited to some extent if the healthy, high-grade material could be propagated at least once. Again, the potato requires a great deal of artificial fertilizer and sometimes also pesticides and fungicides per unit area, and large quantities of water are always essential. To spread the supply and avoid price fluctuations, it must be possible to store the potatoes for a relatively long period. Costly storage facilities are often required for this purpose.

Three aspects of storage must be distinguished:
- Storage of ware potatoes for the period between two harvests, to spread the food supply evenly over the entire year and counteract (major) price fluctuations.
- Storage of part of the yield for replanting, if there are financial and/or climatological reasons why the entire seed potato requirement cannot be covered from imports.
- If necessary, temporary storage of expensive, high-quality imported seed so as to avoid losses and permit good handling (e.g., sprouting) and distribution to the growing areas at the correct time.

31.3 Conditions in tropical and subtropical countries

Temperatures in tropical regions are generally considerably above 20 °C throughout the year, often ranging between 30 and 40 °C during the day and falling to only 25 to 30 °C at night.

At such temperatures, potatoes cannot be kept in good condition for longer then four to six weeks. The optimum temperatures for many fungus- and bacteria-mediated diseases are above 20 °C, so that these diseases spread particularly fast. Many species of insects (including the tuber moth) also attack the tubers, in turn promoting the proliferation of decay bacteria.

In addition to disease and rot, the greatly increased respiration of the potato results in a high oxygen demand and before long in oxygen deficiency, giving rise to black heart. Hence mechanical refrigeration will be essential for long-term storage in the tropics. Lower temperatures often prevail in winter in subtropical regions. Here there are usually two harvests, one in spring and one in autumn, the former usually being the more important and the larger.

However, the temperature at the time of the spring harvest and in the ensuing summer months is already very high - not unusually, 40 °C or higher. The major part of the potato crop would have to be stored for

the first four or five months at high temperature. This is impossible
without substantial losses, so that mechanical refrigeration is indispen-
sable.

In winter, temperatures in subtropical countries and in the mountains
or on high plateaux in tropical regions are lower and relatively simple
stores will be sufficient.

31.4 Methods of potato storage

A number of factors are relevant to the choice of the storage method
to be used, e.g., the prevailing local climatological conditions; the a-
mount of potatoes to be stored; the storage period; and the available financial resources. In accordance with these factors, the following methods of potato storage may be appropriate: clamp storage; compartment
storage; refrigerated storage; and storage exposed to light.

31.4.1 Clamp storage

Clamp storage is when potatoes are stored in bulk heaps on the ground
or in holes in the ground. This is the simplest and cheapest method. It
can be used in areas where the temperatures are low enough, e.g., in the
mountains or on high plateaux in the tropics or in winter in the subtropics. Clamp storage was used in the past on a large scale in temperate
countries. It is still employed on a limited scale for short-term storage
(a few months).

Potatoes stored in clamps are intended to be protected from rain and
cold, as well as light (to prevent greening). The potatoes are piled in a
heap and covered with a layer of straw and soil or plastic. Since the potatoes produce heat and moisture, the heap must not be completely covered
(as long as there is no danger of freezing), to allow some ventilation
(Fig. 31.1).

Ventilation can be substantially improved if air grilles can be used
- e.g., a triangular air duct made of laths. The grille is positioned under the heap in such a way that one of the ends projects out of the heap.

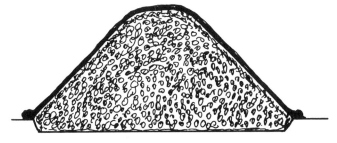

Fig. 31.1 Unventilated clamp.

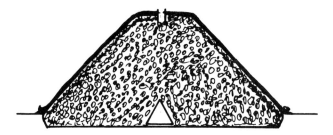

Fig. 31.2. Ventilated clamp (natural draught).

If some openings are also left at the top of the heap, natural ventilation will arise through the piled potatoes, so that moisture, heat and
carbon dioxide are eliminated and oxygen is supplied (Fig. 31.2).

If the temperatures are low enough (5 to 10 °C), the potatoes can be
piled to a height of 1.5 to 2 m. At higher temperatures, and particularly
in the case of freshly harvested potatoes, the height must not exceed 50-
100 cm.

At high altitudes, where there is also a risk of freezing, small quantities of tubers may be stored in a hole in the ground, covered with some
straw and soil (Fig. 31.3). Of course, there is virtually no ventilation
with such a method of storage, so that is is only used where a frost-free
room is unavailable.

31.4.2 Compartment storage

Small quantities of potatoes can be stored for a relatively short period (2.5 to 3 months) loose or in bags, crates, etc., in compartments
protected from light (Fig. 31.4). If these compartments are not insulated,
the mean temperature in them will be equal to the mean day and night
temperature of the outside air. Long term storage may therefore not be
possible, depending on the prevailing outside temperatures. It is essential for the heap or stack not to be too large, so that sufficient air is
admitted. The bags to be used must be of loose-weave material.

Fig. 31.3. Hole in the ground.

454

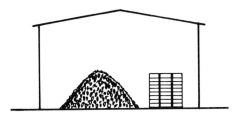

Fig. 31.4. Non-insulated storage compartment.

A great improvement in this kind of storage is afforded if the walls
and roof of the compartment are insulated to a greater or lesser extent.
Cooler air can be admitted by opening windows and/or doors at night, so
that if everything is kept closed during the day, the average night
temperature is attained in the compartment (Fig. 31.5 and 31.6). In this
way good results can be achieved in areas where the night-time temperature is about 15 °C. The potatoes can then be readily stored for three or
four months without excessive losses and without the use of sprout inhibitors.

A common feature of all the above methods is that there is virtually
no ventilation, or only natural draught ventilation. Simple methods of
this kind can therefore be used only if the heap or stack is not too big
(a few hundred kilograms).

However, as soon as the amounts of potatoes to be stored are larger,
the choice must fall upon storage in a building with forced ventilation
using fans and an air distribution system. The building must also be insulated and electricity must be available (Fig. 31.7). (Full details are
given in Parts II and III of this book).

31.4.3. Storage with mechanical refrigeration

Mechanical refrigeration will be necessary for longer periods of storage in high-temperature regions.

There are two possible systems: "space refrigeration" and forced ventilation.

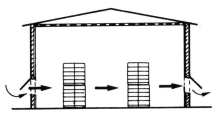

Fig. 31.5. Insulated compartment with natural ventilation.

455

Fig. 31.6. Example of an insulated store in Cameroon.

Space refrigeration In this system, the evaporator or cooler is suspended from the ceiling in the refrigerated compartment and cold air is blown freely into the compartment by fans positioned directly in front of the cooler (Fig. 31.8). The cold air flows past the produce stored in the compartment and cools it. Potatoes kept in a compartment of this kind cannot be stored in bulk heaps as it would take too long for the required temperature to be attained in the middle of the heap once it is reached elsewhere. Hence the potatoes have to be kept in sacks or in crates, which must be stacked so that even the potatoes in the middle of the stack do not take too long to reach the required temperature. Consequently, if the potatoes are kept in sacks, these must not be stacked more than two rows thick and a clearance of 30 to 40 cm must be left between the stacks. Stacks with crates must also not be too large - e.g., 2 x 2 m.

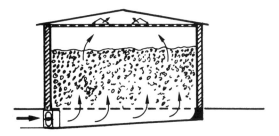

Fig. 31.7. Insulated compartment with forced ventilation.

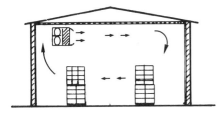

Fig. 31.8. Cold store with space refrigeration.

Cooling with forced ventilation In this system, cold air is blown
through the product by means of powerful fans and a good air distribution
system (Fig. 31.9). In this case the potatoes can be stored in bulk heaps,
up to a height of 3 to 4 m. Even with sack storage, the stack height can
be 3 m.

The difference in storage capacity is obvious. In the case of bulk potatoes, 700 kg can be stored per m² of floor area and per m of pile height;
this is about 2500 kg per m² for a pile height of 3.5 m. In the case of
sack storage, capacity per metre of stacking height is 560 kg per m²
floor area, or about 1700 kg per m² for a height of 3 m. Capacities are
substantially reduced with sack or crate storage in compartments with
space refrigeration.

With the potatoes stored in sacks, capacity will be 1000 to 1300 kg
per m² at stacking heights of 2 to 2.5 m. Much greater stacking heights
are not feasible as the stack then becomes unstable.

Capacity in crates is further reduced, to 500 to 700 kg per m² depending on the stacking height. Once again, stability considerations set limits to the permissible stacking height.

31.4.4 Seed potato storage with exposure to light

A widespread and long-established method of storing seed potatoes is
to place the tubers in crates or on racks in thin layers and to expose
them to light - either natural or artificial light (e.g., fluorescent
tubes) (Fig. 31.10).

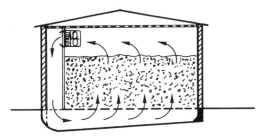

Fig. 31.9. Cold store with forced ventilation.

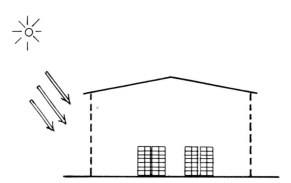

Fig. 31.10. Storage of seed in diffuse light.

    Exposure to light favourably affects the quality of the seed, espe-
cially at temperatures of 10 to 15 °C, and good results are obtained in
periods of storage exceeding three or four months.
    Light has various positive effects on the quality of seed potatoes.
Light retards the physiological aging of the tuber, thus favourably affecting the number and robustness of the sprouts. Light also inhibits the
growth of the sprout, which again enhances its vigour and robustness. Exposure to light promotes greening of the tuber, thus decreasing susceptibility to fungus diseases. However, direct sunlight must be avoided and
the potatoes must be protected from aphids (which may transmit virus diseases) and other insects such as the tuber moth. Fine cambric can be
used for this purpose.
    Krijthe (1948) investigated the effect of temperature and light on
stored seed potatoes.
    Seed potatoes of the Eersteling variety were stored for six or seven
months in the dark and exposed to light at temperatures of 2.5, 9, 13,
17, 23 and 28 °C. The results show that storage in the dark is better
than in the light at 2.5 and 9 °C. At 13 and 17 °C, the advantages of
sprouting in the light outweigh the disadvantages of storage in the dark;
the harvest of the seed potatoes stored in the light is found to be su-
perior to that of seed stored in the dark. At the high temperatures of 23
and 28 °C, the growth of the sprout is found to diminish after 3.5 to 4
months: the growing point dies, its place is taken by the lateral growing
points, and these eventually also die. There is not much development, but
large quantities of energy are consumed at these high temperatures.
    In very general terms, it can be stated that where seed potatoes are
to be stored for a relatively long period, it is best to store them in
the dark if the temperature is 2 to 10 °C, while they are best stored in
the light at 10 to 20 °C; at temperatures above 20 °C (up to 30 °C) they
should preferably also be stored in the light, but for no longer than
about 3.5 months.

31.5 Storage using chemical compounds

Hak & Vermeer (1979) and Hak (1981) investigated the possibilities of using sprout inhibitors (CIPC and IPC), alone or combined with fungicides (TBZ), at different storage temperatures. Their work included the simulation of tropical conditions, potatoes of the Bintje variety being harvested early and while still immature (after a growing time of four months) and being stored for research purposes at a temperature of 28 °C and a relative humidity of 90 %.

A combination of the sprout inhibitors CIPC and IPC with the fungistat thiabendazole seems to be promising for the purpose of limiting quantitative and qualitative losses in the storage of potatoes at temperatures of up to about 20 °C. At storage temperatures of 25 °C and above, the use of CIPC stimulates sprouting, probably owing to a reduction of apical dominance (Adlan, 1969).

In untreated potatoes, increasing storage temperature initially increases sprouting (Booth & Proctor, 1972; Krijthe, 1977), up to an optimum around 20 °C (Burton, 1966). Above this temperature, sprouting vigour declines, particularly at 25 °C and higher. After four months' storage at 28 °C, rot began to appear; this would spread rapidly at this temperature.

Hence the sprout inhibitors CIPC and IPC seem to become ineffective at storage temperatures above about 18 °C and if the storage period exceeds 3 to 3.5 months.

If the produce is mature and its skin has properly set, the sprout inhibitor can be applied immediately after the harvest, on loading into the store.

With immature, insufficiently set potatoes, a curing period of about ten days must be allowed before the sprout inhibitor is administered. If this period is not observed, the effect of the sprout inhibitor is negative. The sprout inhibitor must be applied in such a case with a Swingfog unit, and the method of storage must be appropriate for the Swingfog method (Chapter 21).

There is no objection to the application of thiabendazole in powder form immediately the potatoes are placed in store.

31.6 Practical information

31.6.1 Harvesting and transport

If potatoes are to be stored for a relatively long period (three to seven months), allowance should be made for this at the time of harvesting and transport. Before harvesting, it is important to allow the tubers to set as far as possible in the ground - e.g., by destruction of the haulm one or two weeks before the harvest, either mechanically or by chemical spray. The tuber then has a chance to form a cork layer which protects it against damage during lifting and transport.

It is also important for the harvested potatoes to be exposed as little as possible to the sun so that the tuber temperature does not rise too high (which might cause black heart). Harvesting should therefore preferably be carried out in the morning and not in the middle of the day. The potatoes must then be placed in the shade as quickly as possible and preferably protected from direct sunlight during transport.

31.6.2 Sorting and grading

Malformed, badly damaged and diseased tubers should as far as possible be removed at the time of lifting, which is often still carried out by hand.

If harvesting is mechanized and the potatoes are stored centrally in large quantities, it is preferably to sort the product and remove all substandard tubers before loading the storage compartments. If the potatoes are sufficiently corked, this may be combined with grading, small tubers and soil being removed at the same time. However, if the tubers are insufficiently mature and the skin not adequately corked, it is advisable not to sort and grade them, as this would cause too much damage, which would be detrimental to good storage results. In this case it is best for grading and sorting to be carried out after the storage period.

31.6.3 Loading and unloading

If mechanical refrigeration facilities are available, potatoes with a tuber temperature exceeding 25 °C should be cooled as quickly as possible to 15 to 20 °C. This temperature is maintained for one or two weeks to enable the potatoes to suberize.

The tubers are then further cooled to the desired storage temperature, which will usually be 3 to 5 °C for relatively long-term storage. Seed potatoes which are stored for only two or three months and are then planted, should preferably be stored at a rather higher temperature - e.g., 8 to 12 °C. This will promote sprouting.

When the compartments are unloaded, the temperature of the potatoes must first be increased sufficiently to prevent condensation. The temperature in the compartment is made to rise by switching off the refrigeration, by perhaps admitting some (warmer) outside air and also by means of the heat produced by the potatoes in respiration.

Potatoes stored in small crates can, however, usually be removed from refrigeration directly, as the condensation can evaporate quickly.

460

31.7 Factors relevant to store design

A number of parameters must be known in order to design a potato store, e.g.:
- Mean day and night temperatures (for determining the insulation value and whether or not mechanical refrigeration is required).
- How the potatoes are brought in and their condition (with or without clinging soil, dry or wet, skin set or not set, damage, diseases).
- Manner of storage (in bulk, boxes, crates, baskets or sacks).
- Must lots of potatoes be stored separately or can a number of lots be combined?
- Duration of arrival and speed of loading of compartments (important in connection with the required refrigeration capacity); also important for determination of compartment size. For satisfactory temperature control, it should not take longer than one week to load or fill a compartment.
- Period of storage.
- Are both ware and seed potatoes stored (i.e., are chemical sprout suppressants to be used)?
- Duration of unloading of store.
- Are the potatoes to be graded, what are the size grades, and is the graded produce to be removed immediately or re-stored temporarily first?

The store can be designed once these parameters have been finalized. Depending on the relevant requirements, the building can be subdivided into a large number of small storage units or a limited number of larger compartments. The air distribution system and refrigeration plant must conform to the manner of storage (in bulk, boxes, crates or sacks). Allowance must be made for any future modifications.

The capital costs depend to a great extent on the requirements to be met by the store. For example, if very small lots of potatoes are to be stored separately and have to be accessible at all times, the cost per unit of storage capacity will be high - extremely high if the lots are very small. It is therefore preferable to try to organize matters so that such stringent requirements do not arise, to enable the available space to be better used.

Other determinants of the capital cost are the local availability or non-availability of building materials and technical equipment (fans, refrigeration plant and insulation).

To improve the economic viability of the store, it will often be desirable for it to be used not only for potatoes but also for other produce, such as vegetables, fruit and onions. Allowance must, of course, be made for this in the design.

It is advisable to call in expert assistance when designing the store.

References

Adlan, A.M.B., 1970. The use of sprout inhibitors in simulated high-temperature storage of potatoes in Sudan. Publikatie 228, IBVL-Wageningen.

Booth, R.H. & F.J. Proctor, 1972. Considerations relevant to the storage of ware potatoes in the tropics. Pans 18 (4).

Burton, W.G., 1966. The potato. Second edition. H. Veenman, Wageningen, Netherlands.

Hak, P.S. & H. Vermeer, 1979. Bewaring van aardappelen bij hoge temperaturen (with English summary).

Krijthe, N., 1948. Over de invloed van temperatuur en licht tijdens de bewaring van pootaardappelen op de oogst van Eerstelingen (with English summary: Influence of temperature and light on the early potato 'Eersteling' under storage conditions). Mededeling no. 73. Laboratorium voor Plantenphysiologisch Onderzoek Wageningen.

Krijthe, N., 1977. Onderzoek over de groei van kiemen op pootaardappelen. Publikatie 295, IBVL-Wageningen.